Modern
American
Religion

Modern American Religion

Volume 1

The Irony of It All

1893-1919

Martin E. Marty

The University of Chicago Press
Chicago and London

MARTIN E. MARTY is Fairfax M. Cone Distinguished Service Professor of the History of Modern Christianity at the University of Chicago. He is the author of numerous books, including *A Nation of Behavers*, also published by the University of Chicago Press.

The University of Chicago Press, Chicago 60637
The University of Chicago Press, Ltd., London
© 1986 by the University of Chicago
All rights reserved. Published 1986
Printed in the United States of America

95 94 93 92 91 90 89 88 87 86   54321

Library of Congress Cataloging-in-Publication Data

Marty, Martin E., 1928–
    Modern American religion.

    Bibliography: v. 1, p.
    Includes index.
    Contents: v. 1. The irony of it all, 1893–1919.
    1. United States—Religion—1901–1945.
2. United States—Religion—1945–
3. United States—Church history—20th century.
I. Title.
BL2525.M37   1986   291′.0973   85-16524
ISBN 0-226-50893-5 (v. 1)

To Arthur Mann

MENTOR, COLLEAGUE, EXEMPLAR, PARTNER, FRIEND

Contents

Acknowledgments

The act of launching a four-volume historical work whose writing is to consume two decades is a lonely task. It will take up the rest of the century about which it is being written. In such an endeavor, the company of colleagues is especially welcome. Dean Franklin I. Gamwell of the University of Chicago Divinity School has given encouragement and aid from the beginning. Through a score of years, twoscore of my doctoral dissertation advisees who specialized in this period have made more contributions than they can know of or than I can directly acknowledge. Professors David Tracy, Jerald C. Brauer, Wayne C. Booth, and Myron A. Marty have read this manuscript and made valuable suggestions. William Hutchison at Harvard arranged a seminar on the main theme and followed it up with probing conversation.

Closer to home, my wife Harriet Julia Marty participated in all final stages of editing and graphic designer Micah Marty served as picture editor. Mrs. Rehova Arthur headed a team of typists through earlier drafts and Ms. Judith Lawrence was in charge through later drafts. Both have worked tirelessly and with impressive editorial competence.

Three University of Chicago research assistants played such an important role that they almost deserve to share space on the title page itself. While the chapters take shape entirely out of my own reading and teaching, they derive from sources that are not always easily accessible and that can easily turn fugitive. These co-workers help make the sources available, keep finding them when they have figuratively fled or turned obscure, and check my citations of them against the originals. The process sounds mechanical, but in practice it is intellectually creative, because these associates participate in generating and criticizing ideas. In the late 1970s James P. Wind served in this capacity. Through much of the course of teaching and writing, R. Scott Appleby continued in this task, bringing a second vantage. Both these men have now launched their own careers. In the final two drafts Stephen Graham became partner in the enterprise. I am pleased to say that he is well on his way into the materials of the second volume. My debt to these three younger scholars is immense. Kenner Swain-Harmon made many editing contributions, and I thank him.

A quirk in my academic and editorial vocation has made it possible for me to become familiar at firsthand with many of the people who carry on the legacies here portrayed. It is doubtful whether any other writer who has contributed to the American religious-history canon has ever been privileged to visit as many archives, repositories, sites, headquarters, and campuses as I. Unfailingly, the custodians of sources at these locations have been helpful and courteous. I only regret that I have not been able to mention them by name; the list would run into the hundreds. Beyond these people are the authors of monographs who wrote what are often called "secondary sources," but which are "primary" in the case of near-contemporary history. Through such writings one visits landmarks, gets a sense of terrain covered, acquires road maps, and determines means of access to sources which, especially if they are in non-English languages, would often be beyond the ken and scope of authors who write synthesizing works like this. Wherever possible I have acknowledged their writings, but acknowledgments can not do true justice to one's extensive debts. I hope I have given publicity to their work and led others to read them.

In respect to such historians I have sometimes felt like Machiavelli, who describes in his letters his nightly time in his library. He would dress up in "garments regal and courtly" as he approached the books. The authors then "lovingly received" him and, as he asked questions, they, "out of their humanity," would answer him, while he was "completely transferred into them." I know many of these authors personally but feel I know them even more through their works.

Finally, this book is dedicated to a colleague of twenty years. While researching this book I came across lines of William James that often reminded me of the way historian-critic Arthur Mann combines intelligence with tentativeness: "The wisest of critics is an altering being, subject to the better insight of the morrow, and right at any moment, only 'up to date' and 'on the whole.'" My students have often thanked Arthur Mann; now I get to. Doing so is among the rich pleasures connected with this project.

1

Modern American Religion and Irony

1:1   Four of the Aristotelian categories figure chiefly in this plot: time, space, substance, and quality. They provide the framework of a narrative and analysis of religion in the fifth American century. Three planned volumes will continue the project through the twentieth century. Each successive book will focus on a later period and each will isolate a different quality. They will also be able to stand independently of each other. Together they will make up the first history of twentieth-century American religion, the first attempt to discern its basic shapes whole.

1:2   *Modern*, first of all, will characterize the category of time. Historians necessarily style periods by discerning how people perceive and name their time. Thus one describes religion in modern as opposed to ancient or medieval times. Temporal categories are rich in personal meanings. It would be bizarre to picture turn-of-the-century Americans asking daily what it might mean to classify their time as modern. They do, however, give evidence that they tried to make sense of the moment they so regularly thus named and that they associated many events and qualities with it. They used such reflection to help endow their efforts with meaning. "Time is the central category of finitude," urged mid-century theologian Paul Tillich. "To be means to be present" in a specific time, in this case, the modern.

1:3   *American* is a nationally based reference to space. Historians

1

engage in mapping and placing. "Everything is somewhere," say theorists of mapping. Whatever else objects do not share, "they *always* share relative location, that is, spatiality." This history seeks to limn qualities of religious life that are special because they appear in America. "The present implies space," Tillich continued. "To be means to have space," a physical location including "a home, a city, a country, the world." Awareness of place both produces in people a sense of insecurity and inspires in them a need to reflect on the drama that occurs in their space. At the turn of the century, Americans were uncommonly occupied with the American question and have remained so.

1:4   *Religion* describes the substance of this book and series. The substance of some histories may be railroading, labor movements, roofing technology, or political parties. Other histories deal with the elusive but urgent spiritual experiences of a citizenry. Religion is the substance of this book and has substance in lives. Substance, Tillich resumes, "is present whenever one speaks of some*thing*," and has religious significance especially because of anxiety over the fact that this substance is temporal. "This anxiety refers to continuous change as well as to the final loss of substance." Americans in this period regularly expressed fears about a possible loss of religion in culture and in the meaning of their lives. They also expressed courage and creativity in concrete situations.

1:5   Those who observe modern American religion have reasons to be surprised over the amount of this substance they encounter. For centuries, plausible prophets had envisioned the decline of religion. Scenarios written in Europe and sometimes in America pictured an urban and industrial life inimical to faith. Instead of disappearing, however, religion prospered in selective ways. Instead of dissolving in the face of the jostling and erosion caused by American diversity, it relocated more than it declined. Instead of assuming a single nonreligious style of rationality and life, as some predicted they would, citizens kept inventing protean ways to pursue their spiritual questions.

1:6   "The conventional wisdom of the West," as British philosopher Ernest Gellner speaks of it, assumes that while "the rest of the world wishes to become rich and powerful, just like us," it can only do so by taking over "our rationality, our secularism, our liberalism." Such an outlook, he rightly observes, led many Westerners to underestimate religious power. They overlooked the ways it motivated the Islamic world and misdefined modes of rationality current in non-Western nations. Such conventional wisdom overlooks many trends in American culture itself, as this book will demonstrate.

1:7   *Irony* here characterizes the quality of situations and outcomes in modern American religion. By the category of quality Aristotle meant "that in virtue of which people [or, by extension, conditions and things] are said to be such and such." I came to the sources unprepared to discover how ironic were the outcomes of religious aspirations in this period. Since "qualities admit of variation of degree" and of scope, it seemed fitting to use a folk phrase, "the irony of it all," to characterize the intentions and consequences of actors in the religious drama of this period. The citizens and believers who are being observed did not, of course, intend ironic outcomes nor did most of them employ ironic expression at decisive moments. Yet the observer is struck by the way in which the ironic perspective so regularly describes their circumstances and the consequences of their actions.

1:8   Attention to the concept of irony in this introduction will make possible the subsequent telling of a story uncluttered by too many self-conscious references to it. The most important aspect to address at the beginning is a distinction between literary irony, which has been a constant, almost wearying theme in literary criticism since mid-century, and historical irony, the irony of a situation, which has received much less attention. The former is "a figure of speech in which the intended meaning is the opposite of that expressed by the words used," and is often employed in sarcasm or ridicule. Wayne C. Booth, for instance, has expounded *The Rhetoric of Irony*, Douglas C. Muecke has surveyed *The Compass of Irony*, and Norman Knox has chronicled *The Word Irony and Its Context*. In all these cases, it is the literary trope of irony that received notice. Muecke calls "ironologists" those who pursue and advocate this form of literary expression and a mode of life related to it.

1:9   The only version of irony which will play any part in this book, on the other hand, has to do with perceptions of historical events. The *Oxford English Dictionary* almost perfectly and with some literary elegance defines this "*irony (fig.)*" as "a condition of affairs or events as if in mockery of the promise and fitness of things." To this Gene Wise adds the necessary ingredient of human agency to separate it from "the irony of fate." Here "an ironic situation occurs when the consequences of an act are diametrically opposed to the original intention," and when "the fundamental cause of the disparity lies in the actor himself, and his original purpose."

1:10   While the bibliography on literary irony is very extensive, historical "figurative" irony receives less notice. Three important books are rare exceptions. The first, by Hayden White, deals with European history: *Metahistory: The Historical Imagination in Nineteenth-Century Europe*. The second, by Richard Reinitz, treats American history: *Irony and Consciousness: American Historiography and Reinhold Niebuhr's Vision*. His subtitle signals the third work, theologian Reinhold Niebuhr's little classic, *The Irony of American History*.

1:11   Mention of Niebuhr, perhaps the most influential American-born theologian of the century, and of his classic theme, should serve as a reminder that the employment of an ironic perspective or the discernment of ironic outcomes is not a fresh discovery awaiting breathless announcement. Just the opposite. Far from shunning a theme because it is already patented, a historian gains confidence from the fact of its familiarity. An apologia would go something like this: If a situation best admits of an ironic outcome, the conscientious historian will use it, no matter what the fashion. Historians, of all people, should not resent and should welcome the observation that what they are doing is in a continuity, for continuity is their stock-in-trade. If such a motif helps provide appropriate and meaningful continuity to a narrative, that is a help in historical writing and reading. Finally, if the ironic understanding belongs to what, in the language of hermeneuticians, relates to an author's "pre-understanding" *(Vorverständnis)*, as it does to mine, it is well to bring this forward.

1:12   Four corollary issues proceed from the choice of irony. The first has to do with what historians call "exceptionalism." That is, why employ it or discern it in this particular time, place, and issue? In one sense, all history is open to ironic construction, since "the promise and fitness of things" is so frequently a denial of human intention. Yet, since irony normally concentrates on illusions of innocence, virtue, wisdom, and power, one reserves it chiefly for well-situated agents and leaders. One would not, ordinarily, use it in connection with the oppressed or the poor, even or especially when outcomes are better than what they could have hoped for. America has seen millions of oppressed and poor people, yet this place has also been singularly rich in "the promise and fitness of things." That is why the ironic eye has been turned on events in the prehistory of this modern study. Perry Miller's grand corpus concerning American Puritans saw irony in the effects of their concepts of a covenant and chosenness. David Noble discerned something similar in the Republic-an counterpart among the national founders and the historians who attended to their story.

1:13   For all the plausibility of ironic perspectives on earlier America, as Reinitz observed it in the careers of major historians Francis Parkman, Henry Adams, Richard Hofstadter, and others, there are exceptional—which here means distinctive more than unique—reasons to use them in this turn-of-the-century "early modern" matrix of modern American religion. Religion can and—as this narrative will demonstrate—consistently did reinforce and exaggerate those illusions of innocence, virtue, wisdom, and power. It did so especially among the sets of leaders who thought they could, in the name of religion, either significantly advance the cause of modernism or, at the opposite extreme, significantly counter the whole cause of and case for modernism through reaction. Between these extremes most other American religious leaders set patterns that turn out to have been persistent in their pursuit of illusions in ways that this period sees as heightened. The extended case for exceptionalism, of course, has to be made not through promises in advance but through the telling of the story in the many scores of pages that follow.

1:14   The second issue has to do with the morality and aesthetics of the ironic choice. Most students of literary and historical irony have stressed the element of choice. Thus Douglas Muecke insists that "irony, like beauty, is in the eye of the beholder and is not a quality inherent in any remark, event, or situation." Choice here is not arbitrary, of course, yet those who perceive irony recognize in it "a view of life which recognizes that experience is open to multiple interpretations," as Samuel Hynes has put it. This means that of the interpretations, "no *one* is simply right;" instead, "the co-existence of incongruities is a part of the structure of existence." Why *this* choice, for Hayden White's supreme European ironist, Jacob Burckhardt, or for Richard Reinitz's Americans, or, in the present circumstance, for me?

1:15   Hayden White properly relates it to the fundamental outlook and character of the historian. He cites R. G. Collingwood, who "was fond of saying that the kind of history one wrote, or the way one thought about history, was ultimately a function of the kind of man one was." Then he went on to argue that "the reverse is also the case." When a reader is placed before the alternative visions that history's interpreters offer for consideration, "and without any apodictically provided theoretical grounds for preferring one over another, we are driven back to *moral* and *aesthetic* reasons for the choice of one vision over another as the more 'realistic.' "

1:16   To linger for a moment over White's own strictures is valid because he is the preeminent theoretician in the field. He wrote a 448-page work "in an Ironic mode," through a conscious choice that "represents a turning of the Ironic consciousness against Irony itself." Why? He feared that irony might tend "to dissolve all belief in the possibility of positive political actions," because of the view of "the essential folly or absurdity of the human condition" that it implies. That is the moral issue. Aesthetically, irony can feed "the skepticism and pessimism of so much contemporary historical thinking."

1:17   One who takes White's urgings seriously has the burden of proof to show that special kinds of ironic interpretation do not necessitate either passivity in the human *polis* or mere skepticism in the writing of its history. Reinhold Niebuhr's version, for which Reinitz comes up with the happy coinage "humane irony," and which the following narrative is supposed to exemplify, is a positive alternative, and it demands notice here. It alone helps the historian avoid a superciliousness, detachment, and condescension which would be the ironists' temptation even if they were validated by no other credential than that the historian was born after the outcomes of events and thus has superior hindsight.

1:18   Niebuhr contended that "the Christian faith tends to make the ironic view of human evil in history the normative one," though, as Reinitz and a number of people who facetiously referred to themselves as "atheists for Niebuhr" regularly made clear, one need not be a Christian to employ "humane irony." The theological root for Niebuhr was the view that God was "a divine judge who laughs at human pretensions without being hostile to human aspirations." The second half of that phrase is frequently overlooked, yet it is of equal weight in this form of irony and in the narrative that follows. Niebuhr's own career as a political activist and his awareness of alternative tropes like the tragic, the pathetic, and the comic, before his choice of ironic, promote a confidence in the belief that moral and aesthetic claims can be met through humane irony.

1:19   The message of such irony, and of the story to follow, and of this discernment in subsequent American religion, is not "What fools these mortals be!" Such inhumane irony would only respond to the "divine judge who laughs at human pretensions." It might also turn the historian into an illusion-filled agent who is set up for a grand ironic outcome! Niebuhr's dialectical vision is to be sustained throughout. The knowledge of irony, he urges, "depends upon an observer who is not so hostile to the victim of irony as to deny the element of virtue which must constitute a part of the ironic situation." On the other hand, the observer must not be "so sympathetic as to discount the weakness, the vanity and pretension which constitute another element." Elsewhere he adds that a situation is ironic if "virtue becomes vice through some hidden defect in the virtue," or "if wisdom becomes folly because it does not know its limits," yet one must *not* overlook the virtue and there *is* also wisdom. The historian sees creativity and human intentions in the actors and agents who acted, who had to act, in spite of some illusions and without foreknowledge of outcomes. It is my intention to see most characters in this story in such a humane light.

1:20   The agents or actors themselves are the chief subjects of this history. In a study of human agency, Frederick A. Olafson insists that, if there is to be continuity in historical narrative, "the actions in question [must] be identified under the descriptions which their agents and patients may be supposed to have used." To assure that what has come conventionally to be called "agent's description" will receive prime attention on these pages, there will be many quotations and paraphrases of their own words. A footnoting or, better, backnoting system includes numbered paragraphs, each of which refers to a note at the end. This convenient numbering system also allows for attention to the important secondary literature on which authors of works like this must and do profitably draw. As for intrusion of formal ironic interpretation, this may consequently be rather rare and understated. Muecke writes that "the accomplished ironist will use as few signals as he can," and the historian who observes irony prefers to let the story as told evoke recognitions of this theme rather than with wearying frequency pound a point home. In such an approach, "the eye of the beholder" of irony will not belong only to the latter-day historian but may just as well, indeed, may preferably, be that of contemporaries of the actors. In more rare circumstances, the actors themselves, if they lived long enough to reflect on contradictory outcomes, furnish the eyes.

1:21   Historians choose the distance for their perspective depending upon what story they have to tell. John Murray Cuddihy has argued, for instance, that the great theorists of modernization displayed an all but sovereign indifference to the high cost of change because they belonged to the Protestant core-culture. They could "theorize from within the eye of the hurricane of modernization, where all is calm and intelligible." However, he continued, "for the underclass below, as for the ethnic outside, modernization is a trauma."

1:22   The hurricane metaphor suggests four vantages, the middle two of which prevail in what follows. First, too great a distance allows for a purely sovereign indifference. Historians with cosmic shifts in mind then employ means that can be compared to vantages gained from satellites that send distant signals back to earth. Second, much closer to the activity and somewhat daring are those who compare in Cuddihy's picture to those who fly airplanes into the eye of the storm and from them release by parachute sophisticated sounding devices called *dropsondes*. Third, more daring participants who possess some expertise stay behind in disasters. They send back radio signals as most neighbors flee. The fourth vantage is that of those neighbors, the people in the huts. They have few choices: they may hunker down, close their shutters, and say their prayers—or flee. In any case, these leave behind fewer literary evidences and one must often infer their opinions.

1:23   Historians who would perceive the ironic situations issuing from religious responses to modernity use all four vantages. In the first perspective, statistical data, for instance, allow them to gather apparently neutral evidence from a great distance. Their own curiosities and empathies, however, lead them closer to documents of human opinion. These reveal to narrators something of the trauma or storm, even if from people who had the relative luxury of observing it from within the calm and quiet eye. Such people assessed forces and motions which were still at some distance from them. Third, they also rely on reactions from the courageous amateurs who stayed on the scene to track winds and storms. These lived in the midst of uncertainties and unpredictabilities. Finally, since historians share anxieties about their own time and space, about the substance and quality of their experience, they may try to find documents which will give an immediate sense of the lives people led in the huts.

1:24   There is another aspect of method in narrative history used here. Jacob Burckhardt in his cultural history promised to do what we intend, to "confine ourselves to observation, taking transverse

sections [*Querdurchschnitten*] of history in as many directions
as possible." Such sectioning across space and time does not
produce a story measured by a simple sequence of "and then's."
The mass of data from which one must select is too large. Historians who write monographs have spent decades or careers researching books on, for example, Jews in New York or Finns in
Michigan, yet their writings throw light on only a few paragraphs
in a synthetic work. The period studied in this book, hardly more
than one human generation, is so brief that the reader can use a
sense of chronological movement in the various chapters to make
connections as the writer must move on to the other parts which
make up the narrative whole.

1:25   This is the first coordinated history of twentieth-century American religion. Insofar as it succeeds, it can help change public
understandings of what is usually called secular culture. The recent past, if 1893–1919 can be considered recent, presents special difficulties for historians. The Puritans seem to lie at a safe
and graspable distance, while the earlier modern Americans remain too near, seem too much to be our kin. Let it be noted,
though, that historians of nonreligious phenomena have long
worked to chronicle and style shapes of twentieth-century life.
There are no substantive reasons for historians of religion to post-
pone their synoptic tasks. By now, as the backnotes make clear,
abundant and excellent monographic work has gone on. Using
this, one can provide some signposts, landmarks, and soundings
which can help people organize perceptions and possibly ward off
some chaos. In the present case, one principle for selection has
been to concentrate on whatever in the past helps explain conse-
quential life. Some caution, however, has been valuable, in order
to allow for surprises, because no one can reckon with the infinite
possibilities in that life.

1:26   Ernest Gellner has observed that "the ideology with which a
society has passed the hump of transition is likely to remain its
nominal doctrine, thereafter." Indeed, he adds, it is likely to become, locally, "the symbol of that overcoming of the painful
hump, of the achieved satisfactory order which is now the true
'social contract.'" Therefore, Gellner went on, "it seems as un-
likely that the West will repudiate its formal religious faiths, as
that the Russians should disavow Marxism." The effective content
of such faiths may be eroded, becoming ever more selective, symbolic, "spiritual," and the like. He compares such socially con-
tracted societies to slowly moving glaciers. They carry a heavy

moraine of that which was contemporaneous with their own birth, embedded in it. This residue increasingly demands interpreters.

1:27   America, to apply this reading of historical process, has at least twice undergone passage over such humps of transition. One occurred when the republic was formed in an eighteenth-century revolution. The second followed from the transit to modern life during the revolutionary passage to complex industrial and urban life. This second revolution, British historian Eric J. Hobsbawm has claimed, occasioned the greatest changes since the inventions of agriculture and the city, so far as the physical landscape and the psychic circumstances of people are concerned. To study the spiritual aspects of such a transit is an urgent task for understanding the subsequent national landscape.

1:28   This story begins well along into the urban-industrial era. Like all stories, it must begin once upon a time, its author and readers recognizing that that time carries the longer past with it. This narrative begins, despite occasional glances further back, in 1893, the beginning of this fifth American century. The choice of date is not arbitrary. The opening scene, the World's Parliament of Religions, provides a superior location, as soon will be clear, for the lowering of a dropsonde. The western frontier had just closed, according to the just published census of 1890. Frederick Jackson Turner at the World's Columbian Exposition in Chicago that same season, delivered an important historical paper on the significance of that epochal event. In 1893 Josiah Strong issued *The New Era*, which allows for another sounding. Henry K. Carroll's report on the government census, *The Religious Forces of the United States*, also appeared in 1893 and provides another reference point. These and other assessments and changes in the *fin de siècle* period set the scene through two decades of the new century, past the First World War to around 1919.

1:29   From the Contents page of this book it is clear that while the substance of religion and the concept of America infuse the whole work, the five parts of the book lift up variations on the word "modern." Such an investment in both conventional and coined elaborations is somewhat risky. The two italic abbreviations at the end of the first *Oxford English Dictionary* definition of the word are good reminders of transience in respect to concepts. It reads: "*Modern*. A. *adj*. 1. Being at this time; now existing. *Obs. rare*." If obsolescence comes to an old ordinary usage, it can also blight the conceptual references on these pages. In a wearied dismissal, historian Christopher Lasch has argued that terms like "modernism" and "modernity" are analytically bankrupt, yet one study after another now takes modernity or antimodernity as its theme. "'Modernity' has come to serve the same purpose for cultural historians that 'modernization' serves for social and economic historians." It serves too often, Lasch says, as a substitute for thought, and can be a banality passed off as a bold interpretive synthesis.

1:30   Cautionary words from a historian as noted as Lasch and as representative of others, including this author—we have all seen some of the misuses to which he points—deserve careful attention, and have received it. He was reviewing a book whose author could not deal fairly with those who expressed misgivings about the world of "modernity" to which that author gave allegiance. I have had to guard against the opposite problem, so easy is it to dismiss the positive values in the modernity and modernism of the acts in this book. There were other precautions. I have not imposed late twentieth-century sociological definitions on late nineteenth-century figures. Instead, they have done their own speaking, and their concerns, listened to, set the agenda. The issue is whether this work is faithful to their intentions and enterprises.

1:31   Misuse of the concept or weariness over the possible overuse of it will not make it go away or deprive it of value. As a teacher, through a long career, of "the history of modern Christianity," I am convinced that that adjective will survive and be as important and problematic an analytic tool for describing religion in the West as adjectives for periods like "ancient" and "medieval" now are. Such terms have been stamped into the psyche, and revisionist historians will not by force of argument or the desire for precision remove them without doing violence to the story of things as they were. The important question is not what is in or out of vogue; fashions in respect to this term have changed often before Lasch spoke critically and they will change often after. Following fashion or backlash to fashion, which can be its own fashion, is an unreliable way to set up inquiries and confuses the listening and representing that historians must do. Two coinages, "countermodern" and "transmodern," are explained carefully; they condense complex realities which people of the period in question did consistently address in cognate terms.

1:32   Reference to the voice and agenda of these agents of history in the past occasions a word about the genre of this work. It blends aspects of intellectual, social, and cultural history that can only with difficulty be separated or defined in any case. The ideas of all but a few of the formal thinkers in Part One are not of a nature to inspire conventional history of ideas. Even those thinkers are not thus conventionally treated here. As for social history, there is no way to deal with the scores upon scores of groups across the American religious spectrum in these decades and then give fair and extended accountings of the feel of their mundane existences. This book relies on numbers of monographs which deal with but one of these groups—and still each such monograph might run to the length of this coordinating book!

1:33   If one name would serve for it all, this is in a sense a history of rhetoric, in all the positive senses of that term applied to the public and private, the spoken, written, and symbolic efforts to represent and persuade people. If a historian cannot visit all the individual congregations, stop at all the settlement houses, attend all the revivals, go to all the philosophy classes, it is still possible to capture something of the past by different means. Here one pays attention to those people of the past who sought and gained followings, and to the words they used, whether in letters or sermons, textbooks or lectures—as they formed and held and moved those followings—or were rejected by them.

1:34   Such an approach involves its own methods and disciplines. Some of these have been formulated by Paul Crawford, a veteran scholar in this field. He speaks of the rhetorical critic as one who "must so absorb the realities of conflict and the climate of opinion and audience attitudes of the time under consideration that he can mentally place himself in the past under study, yet must not pretend to divorce himself from the advantages that recent scholarship has given to hindsight." Second, such a critic must try to identify and distinguish ideas and attitudes of rank-and-file members of a movement from the views of its leaders, "particularly as embodied in their private expressions or in remarks to relatively sophisticated hearers who may not be typical of ordinary members." Third, he or she must be alert to whether written or oral discourse or other forms of symbolic behavior were being used, and what their intention was. Some rhetoric, for example, is used with an intent to be overheard by the press as well as merely heard. Finally, such a critic must be aware that rank-and-file members and spokespersons may only have been identified with one or two phases or aspects of a movement, without a historical concern for its long range or context. Keeping those prescriptions in mind allows one to draw relatively close to movements of the past insofar as they have left artifacts and literary traces.

1:35   This concern for rhetoric demands quotations, not for forensic but empirical purposes. That is, the author does not rely on secondary sources for authority or graphic writing; after this first chapter, almost all quotations come from people in the period under discussion, not from later scholars. Their words are often nuanced and demand exact replication, but the use of too many quotation marks can grow wearying to the eye. Some paraphrasing and even some exact quotation outside such marks allow for a more even flow without sacrifice of accuracy. In any case, my authorial voice will be evident. The quotations are not there as crutches or because the material has not been viewed through the historian's lens.

1:36   One can anticipate the plot and character by reference to events and people who exemplified differing attitudes to their times. In Part One come the religious *modernists*. They were the liberal agents of the modern, progressives who actually wanted to advance the processes of change from within the Protestant core-culture. A contradictory outcome of events came along as if in mockery of the promise and fitness of their good intentions as these agents described and prescribed things. Ernest Gellner was speaking of this when he wrote that, "as the Christians have found, the modernism of one generation is doubly dated in the next." What seemed, he added, to be an elegant restatement on a par with the latest, sharpest intellectual fashions, shared all their discovered faults some decades later. The world of modernists later seemed archaic and arcane. Their descendants often saw it as in some ways more remote than the world of the colonials. It became less explicable than many competitive worldviews that looked dated already to these modernists.

1:37   Part Two deals with the ideas of gifted innovators who are usually spoken of as the *moderns*. These men and women were often seen and they thought of themselves as the developers of a distinctly modern consciousness. They were also to have been liberated from historic forms of religion. Yet many in this advance guard were forced to do what Eric Hobsbawm found "primitive rebels" and underclass industrial workers doing. They "looked backwards." They drew, he stressed, "on the only spiritual resources at their disposal, preindustrial custom and religion." For some of them this meant a reliance on medieval architectural models. Others made use of communal and even ecclesial aspects of the small-town life they had fled in late adolescence.

1:38   In Part Three, *modernity* is a neutral term. People in their figurative huts coped with it by filtering out some cultural signals or adapting to others. The first clusters of these signals combined religion with their peoplehood, which included race, ethnicity, language, and culture. They formed something like physical and spiritual cocoons, translucent shelters which kept threatening outside forces at some distance yet without wholly screening them out. Others, chiefly in the core culture, used religious denominations to erect symbolic canopies for similar purposes. Agents in these subcultures often intended to protect themselves from ideologies that came with modernity. In their eagerness to be fully American, however, they found that aspects of modernity came with national culture. The people changed decisively, often in ways that were contradictory to the promise and fitness of things as they had described these. The causes of such outcomes were partly the result of the agents' actions, these often including the stimulation of distracting and disruptive controversy within their protective shelters.

1:39   Part Four elaborates on *countermodern* efforts by reactionaries and Part Five on people who wanted to go beyond the modern as they described it. These creative people—we shall call their efforts *transmodern*—were not content with the extreme differentiation of life and feared that psychic and physical damage would result from it. Outcomes in both cases often were contradictory to the actors' intentions. The countermodernists, claiming that they were merely returning to simple and primitive forms of their faith, instead came to be regarded by all others as sects among the sects, movements among the movements, innovators and inventors of novelties. The transmodernists thought that they were selectively retrieving organic models from the past. They came, however, to be dismissed as modernist improvisers of their own. None of these people have to be regarded as fools simply because they lived earlier than the author and could not know their future, which is his past. He would neither deny the element of virtue nor oversympathetically discount the weakness in their intentions. To do so would be to contribute to a contradictory outcome, as if in mockery of the promise and fitness of this historical endeavor. This would be ironic.

Part One

The Modernists

2

A Cosmopolitan
Habit
in Theology

2:1   T he theological modernists were male members of the privileged subculture, almost all of them Protestant. Far from being reluctant adapters to changes, they wanted to work with the momentum of their faith to advance such change in an effort to be of help to other believers who welcomed the new day but for whom the old statement of faith had become a problem. Their first step in promoting modernism was to seek a universal outlook, to overcome the provincialism that they thought afflicted religion. The Reverend George Gordon of Boston's prestigious Old South Church, saw in modernity the "steady emergence of a cosmopolitan habit." It called forth, he thought, new and pragmatic approaches to religious thought. Weary of pettiness, in the mid-nineties Gordon proclaimed that a vision of a kingdom of the Spirit had risen in his day. This kingdom would appropriate the wealth of all faiths. It would be free because it would isolate itself, said the preacher, "from particular times and places."

2:2   Such a cosmopolitan habit led the modernists to cherish events that would attract people from their provincial places to confront faiths that reached back to diverse times past. Two years before Gordon wrote, there occurred the most elaborate display of religious cosmopolitanism yet seen on the continent. In Chicago, on a September morning in 1893, in the first year of the fifth American century, four thousand people jammed the Hall of Columbus

17

on the lakefront, there to greet one of the more strange processions in American history. Representatives of dozens of faiths and flags marched past cheering crowds to that hall in what was later to become the city's Art Institute. They moved to a stage for speeches and ceremonies that made up a World's Parliament of Religions. The director of the World's Columbian Exposition, Colonel George R. Davis, had opened that fair itself months earlier. He saw it as a celebration of the ceaseless, irresistible march of civilization. The times were coming to the climax when people would learn, he said, "the nearness of man to man, the Fatherhood of God and the brotherhood of the human race." While his images were all male, his exposition and the parliament also engaged a

Cosmopolitanism—and costumery—were the orders of the day at the World's Parliament of Religions in 1893. (*World's Parliament of Religions*, Chicago, Parliament Publishing Co., 1893).

larger percentage of women than such public events would involve for decades to come. A new era was unfolding.

2:3   What united the cosmopolites was a faith that they and the thousands of participants in the two-week parliament were in the vanguard of a religious triumph. Baptist George Dana Boardman of Philadelphia was to look back on the congress as an effort to array if possible all religions against irreligion. Particular religions, he and his colleagues thought, were too divided to accomplish a protest against materialism.

2:4   Reporters were dazzled by the blur of color. The ranking American Catholic prelate, scarlet-robed James Cardinal Gibbons of Baltimore, sat near Oriental delegates "whose many-colored

raiment vied with his own in brilliancy," according to one observer. They were followers of Brahma and Buddha and Mohammed. Nearby was yellow-turbaned Vivekananda in red apparel. He shared the stage with B. B. Nagarkar of the Brahmo-Somaj, a group of Hindu Theists, and Dharmapala, a Ceylonese Buddhist scholar. There were Parsee and Jain ecclesiastics, Chinese and Japanese delegates, Taoists, Confucians, and Shintoists. Each of them, said the observer, was a picturesque study in color and movement, and all were eager to explain and defend their forms of faith. The more somberly dressed American Protestants who set the stage and called most of the tunes all but blended into the woodwork. These universalizers bowed heads for recitation by Gibbons of "the Universal Prayer," the Lord's Prayer.

2:5   The need for a cosmopolitan outlook was obvious to these leaders in 1893. William R. Alger of Boston used timely references to remind conferees of the alternatives. Just before the parliament, Bombay Brahmins and Mohammedans were slaughtering each other, "hating each other more than they loved the generic humanity of God." Christians nearby in Montreal and Toronto were at the point of murdering each other. All over the world, said Alger, and who could gainsay him, hatred was made religion. The hatred of professors of religion for one another "is irreligion injected into the very core of religion." Alger optimistically called his speech "How to Achieve Religious Unity."

2:6   Aware that the provincialists and sectarians were sneering at the parliament, speaker after speaker justified it. *Monist* editor Paul Carus, a radical believer in human and religious revolution, gibed back at the throwbacks. Broad Christianity, he announced, must replace their exclusive, bigoted, narrow, and so-called orthodox Christianity. Carus then proclaimed a main modernist tenet. "The nature of religious truth is the same as that of scientific truth. There is but one truth." He could be sympathetic, he said, toward those people who must momentarily pass through all the despair of infidelity and religious emptiness. They were on the way toward modern faith. Any other kind, since it rejected science, was inevitably doomed. "It cannot survive and is destined to disappear with the progress of civilization."

2:7   Only slightly more restrained was Charles Carroll Bonney, who was a partner in promoting the parliament idea. He belonged to the Swedenborgians, or Church of the New Jerusalem, which numbered 7,095 in the 1890 census. Bonney welcomed attendees in the name of the Church of the Holy City, the Church of Reconciliation. Its creed was also modernist: "It comes to reconcile reason and faith, science and religion, miracle and law, revelation and philosophy, . . . the teachings of sacred scripture and the results of modern research." Like others at the parliament, the Swedenborgians stood by ready to present their church doctrines as the basis of a universal faith. Bonney seemed plausible as he opened the congress by announcing that it would stand in human history like a new Mount Zion, and begin "a new epoch of brotherhood and peace." He was only echoing what Oxford's Max Müller, the most notable scholar of world religion in his day, had said in his letter of regret. Müller could not attend, but he was sure that the congress would be "one of the most memorable events in the history of the world." Bonney, it should be remarked, was sophisticated in his relativism and aware of the tenacity of enduring differences. Meanwhile, he thought, each religion could immediately acquire absolute respect for the religious convictions of others. Each system now stood "in its own perfect integrity, uncompromised, in any degree, by its relation to any other," but Bonney was an essentialist who believed that there were common essentials by which everyone may be saved, in all the religions.

2:8   Bonney's partner was a much more moderate person, no modernist at all. Presbyterian Henry Barrows, wrote his daughter Mary Eleanor, was a man with a conservative love of tradition and decorum, who contributed Protestant decorousness and manners to the parliament. He was an enigma, she thought, to the less supple orthodox back home who were often "too literally logical to allow for the spirit blowing where it listeth," as he himself would allow. When Barrows later went to India to deliver lectures endowed in his honor, fellow Christians there found him orthodox. He was, however, of the new style in temper; his heart was so liberal, so world-embracing, so many-sided, it was said, that it also fit the cosmopolitan mold.

2:9   Barrows wanted to be more Christian in particular senses than Carus and Bonney. Those who found limits in his faith and who thus refused to hear its claims of universalism, were unscientific. Christianity was "the only truly redemptive and the only progressive religion." What he called the ethnic faiths were to him often curiosities or moral monstrosities, but he was civil about them and granted them a stage. The Bonney-Barrows tandem displayed some of the inner contradictions of the parliament. Both had a blueprint for universalism, yet one was more repudiative of existing Judaism, Islam, and other non-Christian faiths. Barrows was overt about the need for mild aggression. The parliament, he argued, could accomplish more than any Christian missionary society, because it was under no ecclesiastical dictation, and hence appealed in the spirit of fraternity to high-minded individuals. Barrows had to be emphatic: "The idea of evolving a cosmic or universal faith out of the Parliament was not present in the minds of its chief promoters." The elements of such a faith were already contained, he thought, in the Christian ideal and the Christian scriptures.

2:10   What Barrows lived with in ambiguity was simply denounced by Protestants who opposed the parliament. Not all were as strident as prime evangelist Billy Sunday would be years later. Sunday looked back on the parliament as one of the biggest curses that ever came to America. Already in 1892 the Presbyterian General Assembly, speaking for the church to which Barrows belonged, called the anticipated parliament uncalled for, misleading, and hurtful. Arthur Tappan Pierson, a prominent reactionary, knew that the congress gave the impression that Christianity "*may not be the only Divine religion.*" Someone, he thought, must expose the puerilities and absurdities, the contradictions and immoralities of heathen faiths. The parliament motto, he thought, should have been "laxity, apathy, and compromise."

2:11   The many hundreds of participants dispersed, to enjoy a generally good press. The proceedings of the parliament take up 1,600 pages in two volumes. Scholars were to debate for years to come the complex of parliamentarians' intentions and the frustrations of many of their goals. The swamis and other representatives from Asia packed their robes and sailed for the Orient or stayed as missionaries. Catholics began to argue over what Gibbons had said and whether they should have been there in the first place. Some Christian missionaries grumbled that the parliament had dimmed the luster of their own efforts to convert the heathen. Had unity been achieved at all? No two groups at the event began to merge. Designed to show the unity of faiths, it displayed a split within the company of conveners, a set of disparities and disputes among denominations in this world's fair of faiths. Instead of dialogue a succession of monologues had occurred. Most of the cosmopolitans showed themselves to have been covert or overt parochials. In the Hall of Washington right next door, some forty denominations were to hold their own sideshows in those weeks.

2:12   From October 8 to 15 the Evangelical Alliance, a Protestant ecumenical group, followed with a congress of its own. Josiah

Strong, whose *Our Country* back in 1885 was said to have been the American best-seller after *Uncle Tom's Cabin*, reported on that event. The alliance people, he said, found the division of Protestant Christendom lamentable, and the selfish competition of the churches scandalous. Yet alliance people thought that any organic union of Protestants would be too late, too slow. It might be generations away. Strong instead urged more faith in what speakers Lucy Rider, Grace H. Dodge, and Jane Addams told the alliance about deaconesses, working girls' clubs, and social settlements. The cosmopolitan vision, they thought, was to be practical and not speculative, sociological more than theological. "God's methods are scientific, and if we are to be intelligent helpers of God, our methods also must be scientific," Strong summarized in a case for cosmopolitanism that would overlook theoretical particularism.

2:13   What compromised Strong's own cosmopolitanism more than life in the sects was a racial outlook that marked much of Protestant modernism. His *The New Era or The Coming Kingdom*, published that year, echoes this theme found in hundreds of pages by others of the modern-minded. The old New England stock on which he had relied was dying out. What did science say next? Strong quoted a law of life by popular British sociologist Herbert Spencer. As brain power grew, said Spencer and now Strong in concurrence, its demands on the more developed nervous system necessarily diminished the reserve applicable to the setting up of new lives. This fact was evident in the disparity between large families of uncultivated immigrants and the small ones of more civilized citizens. Strong's proposal was not to lower the level of the civilized but to educate and bring the lesser breeds higher. Anglo-Saxon religious life, he was glad to note, was more vigorous, more spiritual, more Christian than any other race's. This race, however, kept things neatly in balance and was not "righteous overmuch." The Anglo-Saxons, who were the supreme missionaries, moralists, and philanthropists, outclassed even the Continental Protestants in America, who were too formalistic. Let the Germans excel in the arts, thought Strong, the Anglo-Saxons triumphed in literature, organization, and technological skill. They represented "the greatest race, the greatest civilization, the greatest numbers, the greatest wealth, the greatest physical basis for empire!"

2:14   Science, like religion, was also evolutionary and taught the survival of the fittest. The message was that the race was on.

There was henceforth to be no more West, no more frontier; "there are no more new worlds." Now as population grew, wrote Strong, the world would enter on a new stage of its history: "*the final competition of races, for which the Anglo-Saxon is being schooled.*" This kind of modernism had its cruel edge. "Can any one doubt that the result of this competition of races will be the survival of the fittest?" The Anglo-Saxon race, the fittest, had been chosen of God, to prepare the way for the full coming of his kingdom in the earth. America was to be the center of Anglo-Saxon influence in the cosmopolis; now, 1893, was the time for its leaders to make explicit moves. "Yes, this generation in America *ought* to exult in its transcendent opportunities for service." In the promise and fitness of things, the universal-minded Anglo-Saxon was poised to share the goods and thus bring people together. For the moment, he wanted his peers to exult with him: "Surely, to be a Christian and an Anglo-Saxon and an American in this generation is to stand on the very mountain-top of privilege." And, one might add, of risk. Strong and his company were ready for the hazards, so sure were they of their means and ends, of their chosenness and call under God.

3

A Religious Spirit of the Age

3:1   **M**odernism in religious thought was a more defined and serious movement than Josiah Strong's expression suggests. Congresses could not serve as its only forum. It took many shapes. By 1893 it had found a home in Felix Adler's nontheistic Ethical Culture, a humanistic Free Religious Association, the part-theistic, part-humanistic Unitarian church, and Reform Judaism. Only a few Roman Catholics at one seminary, one university, and in one journal momentarily and seriously entertained modernism. For the most part in its moderate forms it was at home in the seminaries, colleges, universities, prominent pulpits, journals, and publishing houses of some core-culture Protestants of Anglo-Saxon background. The leaders there, of course, were Christians and most of them intended to remain so. These formal modernists usually receive privileged position and mention when intellectual historians review religious thought in an age almost universally characterized as liberal, progressive, or modern. Some use the name "modernist" very precisely, applying it to a movement of the 1920s. Not content to drift with the age or live with its inertia, the broader company of these liberals would use historic symbols like God and Christ to advance the momentum of the times. They would not be denied, and they left shelves full of descriptions to show exactly what they intended.

3:2   It will be clear that the modernists in this spectrum are a more diverse camp than the ones referred to in some formal intellectual histories of the Modernist movement. When it is the subject, analysts have to take pains to compare it to European Protestant and Catholic Modernism. They are concerned to distinguish "evangelical liberalism" from "theological modernism," in which case figures like Josiah Strong would be quite premature and out of place in the company. Those are valid interests in other contexts. Here the term is generic, unless the context specifies a particular school. Often on these pages, liberalism and progressivism phase into modernism. For present purposes, the effort is to deal with the people who were called modernist, who called themselves that, or who very frankly urged profound adjustments in religious faith in the light of trends which they usually perceived not only to be fundamental and enduring but also which they welcomed.

3:3   Andover Seminary in Massachusetts was a once-orthodox school that had passed over its own hump of transition to allow for the presence of liberals. George Harris, a faculty member there, contributed to the composite called modernism. Harris contended: "There is a religious spirit of the age from which we may not separate ourselves." As if by a new determinism, one must follow this "devout Zeitgeist [spirit of the times] in faith as well as in culture, art and science, which we feel if we cannot describe." This Zeitgeist could not simply be the standard, but it was an influence not to be ignored, one that was always in the process of becoming the standard. To modernists, the symbols of God the Father, Jesus, the Brotherhood of Man, and the Kingdom of God could all remain vivid for Christians, yet it was from the history, science, and criticism of their university environments that modernists picked up their new signals.

3:4   In Chicago, radical Gerald Birney Smith at the new University of Chicago Divinity School kept stressing the need for believers to adapt: "Modern religious thinking is learning to draw its inspiration from the world in which we live." The new empirical theology, as he called it, was grounded in the human condition, testable by experience and in the laboratory. It is hard to escape noticing, however, that much of their assessment was drawn from what modernists felt in their own bones, as people who would both remain Christian and be thoroughly modern.

3:5   At Union Seminary in New York, which was also becoming host to modernism, William Adams Brown added another note: innovation would henceforth make more sense than tradition. "If we survey the chief historic definitions of Christianity, we find that it is at this point that they are most defective," said Brown. They fail to pursue the essence of what the new age requires. Brown not only did not fail to acknowledge his subjective side, he gloried in it. Perceptive people, he thought, both embodied and sensed the spirit of the times. Brown was bold in stating the principle of selectivity by which he thought one came to the essence of Christianity. It was to be "found in the interest and need of the man who defines . . . those particular qualities for which at the time we happen to have use," while the rest can then be ignored.

3:6   Harris, Smith, and Brown were professors in an age when professors were honored in new ways. They routinized the charisma that pulpiteers had been displaying before them, in the first modernist generation. The earlier princes of the pulpit, men like Brooklyn's Henry Ward Beecher and Phillips Brooks of Boston, were beginning to yield space to the systematizers. The movement's first historian, Frank Hugh Foster, admitted that no comprehensive and truly great theologian had appeared in the camp until Professor William Newton Clarke of the Colgate Theological Seminary published *An Outline of Christian Theology* in 1898. Before him, Newman Smyth had been too controversial for an Andover appointment. To Foster, however, Smyth's work had been new and epoch-making precisely because the New Haven minister spent so much time in laboratories of nearby Yale. He thereupon wrote theology with the assistance of learned professors, especially researchers in biology. He called his book of 1902 *Through Science to Faith*. It was another professor, Oberlin's Henry Churchill King, author of *Reconstruction in Theology* in 1901, whom Foster called the great theologian of the developing movement.

3:7   Women were largely excluded from these seminaries, as they had not been from the parliament or the congresses in 1893. There are, therefore, almost no descriptions by modernist women. One became a member of the modernist group by attending one of the more notable divinity schools, many of which were becoming interdenominational and university-related. At the end of this generation, a reactionary *Ministers' Monthly* polled the seminaries and, for what it was worth, published their self-descriptions. Eighteen refused to reduce their image to one character, but forty did choose to be seen as liberal while only thirty-three projected an orthodox face. This often genteel liberalism was not, of course, a simple equation to modernism, but its professors shared the interest in adapting to the spirit of the age.

3:8   Despite Foster's enthusiasm for what seemed epoch-making and what looked like greatness, not a single first-rate intellect was remembered to have been a part of the movement. An anthology of great Western religious writings might include some work by Americans such as Jonathan Edwards or John Woolman, Roger Williams or Horace Bushnell, the brothers Reinhold and H. Richard Niebuhr, or Thomas Merton. No one would think, however, of including the modernist avant garde from this generation except for period pieces, to illustrate a point. Their influence, it is true, lives on among highly chastened liberals, but they are read only by dissertation writers. Was there, one speculates, a brain drain from seminaries? Scholars decades later read Charles S. Peirce and William James, or other contemporaries of the modernists like Jane Addams and John Dewey. Was the choice by theologians to be adaptive a sign of limited genius or did it limit genius and thus drive it to other fields?

3:9   The modernists seemed aware that they stood between ages and styles. The most prominent modernist pulpiteer in the Social Gospel movement, Washington Gladden of Columbus, Ohio, found time while being a pastor to write thirty-eight books. He spoke with poignancy while the lines between times and attitudes were still fluid. "Orthodox we know that we are not," in old creedal senses, he admitted. Nor were the Christians liberal, if liberalism meant mainly criticism and denial. This was a sign that the modernists wanted to be seen in a positive light. They did not engage in defiance of what Gladden called wholesome restraints and conventions. He insisted that his group were still believers, who intended with all intelligent Christians to stand in the presence of modern thought and accept everything that had been proved by science or history or criticism, and not be frightened at all by any of it. His kind of respectfulness and diffidence often disappeared as modernists grew sure of themselves. At Oberlin Seminary, Herbert Alden Youtz closed the door on some pasts: "Surely the time has come to insist that illiberalism and conservatism are immoral and unspiritual in a world of progress."

3:10   The moods of modernist probing and expounding tell almost as much as does substance of this generally forgotten cohort. For the atmosphere, popular figures like Josiah Strong, who never rose above popularizing but who held attention of the eyes and ears of a large clientele, serve well. Science in all its forms was the key element in progress, yet, he thought, it had to be supplemented by biblical revelation. Together these two elements showed that the highest conceivable society would illustrate a then new and

voguish law of unity in diversity. Strong had to employ four "per-
fects" in one sentence to describe it. The new society, he prophesied, would be composed of persons with perfect individuality
enjoying perfect liberty, living in perfect harmony with the divine
will and perfect harmony with each other. History showed that
man had already traveled a long way in this direction. Empirical
theology could build on that foundation. Still, leftover corruption, meanness, injustice, inhumanity, tyranny, brutality, and
beastliness survived. Strong borrowed vision from evolutionary
philosopher John Fiske. Now "the modern prophet, employing the
methods of science, may again proclaim that the kingdom of
heaven is at hand." The important point to notice is this: the modernists did not want simply to reduce faith to science. They did
not want to collapse belief in the face of progress. They did not
want to be merely secular, but religious, in decisively though
never narrowly Christian ways.

3:11   Important as a representative thinker, not a seminal one, Strong
sounded almost Comtean about the passing stages of world history. The three earlier ages had stressed, in turn, theology, anthropology, and soteriology. Now the fourth age of the church used
sociology to provide the last agenda. Social science offered challenges to the doctrine of society, the relations of man to his fellows. This reality meant a necessary rescue of the science of society from unbelievers like Comte himself or from Saint-Simon,
Fourier or Mill, Proudhon or Lassalle or Marx. Christians were
also living in the sociological age of the world and they should
embrace its Zeitgeist.

3:12   Not all the serious modernists would have put it quite the same
way, but all struggled somehow with two strands of modernity
isolated by Strong, the development of the individual and the organization of society. Progress for him meant more freedom and
invention for individuals. The complexity of the new day demanded more organization and interaction in spiritual and social
life than before. The two must be balanced; they must remain
complementary in an age when centripetality was a natural force.
So sudden were the changes at this balance point that, Strong
added, "we *may* have social *revolution*, we *must* have social *evolution*." Religion should determine the choice.

3:13   This study draws definitions of modernization from the turn-
of-the-century people much more than from subsequent definers.
Here as so often Josiah Strong with all he knew about differentiation anticipated later diagnoses. "The higher the organization, the

more are its several organs with their separate functions specialized." Strong celebrated the legal differentiation of church and
state but, with all the modernists, resented the mistaken notion
that the church in consequence must be limited to an artificially
narrowed set of functions. "The sphere of the church includes that
of the state and much more." How could one blunder and sin by
limiting the sphere of conscience, he asked, excluding it from
politics, business, and what are called "secular" occupations?
The church of the new era had to have a holistic character, as must
its message.

3:14   God and Christ figured in this charter. Key to modernist doctrines of God was the notion of immanence, the idea that God was
active in the midst of the world. God was not transcendently
aloof, static, and capricious. Strong joined his more disciplined
colleagues in calling for an overcoming of that which the Latin
fathers had projected, which was a vicious dualism which runs
through life a line of cleavage, separating it into the sacred and the
secular. The heretical Manichaean world left as its legacy a conflict between soul and body, a conflict savored by monks in their
flight from the world, but one which, he and his colleagues insisted, moderns must reject.

3:15   Most problematic for people with a cosmopolitan outlook, a
universal intent, and a holistic mission was the event or symbol
named Jesus. *The New Era* included a whole chapter with an early
and mildly modernistic portrait of "The Authoritative Teacher."
On this point most of the modernists, evidently drawing on their
Sunday School memories as well as their faith and natural rever-
ence more than on a disciplined tackling of problems, remained
attached to Jesus. Most thought that they could reject the Greek
philosophy on whose basis the uniqueness of Christ as a divine
figure had long been claimed. The modernists would generally
finesse their way at this point. We live in an age of doubt, rued
Strong, and to rely on the authority of the church fathers offered
no appeal now. Science had dissipated into myth or legend much
of what once seemed to be substantial reality. Christians formerly
relied on the shifting sands of human theories, but progress of
knowledge had removed these. A firm believer in the quest for the
historical Jesus, a quest that was soon proven to be faulty on its
own nineteenth-century premises, Strong would make Jesus acceptable to all right-thinking people as "the Saviour of *man* as
well as of *men*." Yet he and his colleagues had neither empirical
means nor a theological vocabulary for showing how Jesus of

Nazareth could be the cosmic Christ who should provide coherence for programs of modernist progress. Two other issues had to be turned to advantage for their system. The evolutionary issue and biblical criticism became formal foci at the turn of the century as modernism acquired its momentum, was not yet contradicted, and seemed not to be denied.

4

Only Trying to Save the Bible

4:1 The two most familiar and urgent parts of the modernist intellectual program had to do with adaptation to evolutionary theory in science and with acceptance of biblical criticism in history. The former would blend Christian symbols with science to promote an all-embracing progressive philosophy of history. The latter would employ both scientific history and literary criticism with intent to strip away the obsolete in Christian scriptural memory. Emergent would be a God, a Jesus, and a Kingdom that exemplified the essence of the divine plan. These would match the evolutionary philosophy of history. Taken together, the two could help save the faith of the many who would otherwise lose it through ignorance and because of the challenges and lures of science. Not mere status-seekers in the age of science, most modernists were people of faith with pastoral hearts who wanted to transmit the effects of their own progressive pilgrimages to those who still were floundering. Herbert Willett, a modernist leader of the Disciples of Christ at the University of Chicago, described the critical mission: "I am only trying to save the Bible for the parents and teachers of this generation." If miracles constituted an offense against faith, evolution and criticism would help preserve it. "We believe in Jesus today rather in spite of the miracles than because of them."

4:2 The story of the struggle over evolution is sometimes told in

the framework of instant and pervasive conflict between bright
and united scientists and stupid and stupefied clerics. Novelists
have stamped on the mind the image of backcountry pietists
losing faith, with the numbers of the faithful necessarily declining. On the contrary, the scientific community was divided. It
offered to theologians sometimes attractive and often less usable
theories. For several decades Protestant, Jewish, and some Catholic thinkers found many ways to embrace the predominant forms
of evolutionary theorizing. When, among scientists, Lamarckism
lost out to a more consistent Darwinism at the turn of the century,
it was too late for the modernists to go back to old worldviews.
Only at that time did the conservatives begin to engage in massive
and organized reaction.

4:3   Until the turn of the century Jean Baptiste Lamarck no doubt
held the allegiance of the majority of American scientists who
were described as Darwinian. In 1802 Lamarck had proposed that
evolution was evident as organisms adapted to environments.
They would meet their biological needs out of resources in such
environments. Instruments that they effectively employed would
develop further, while the inefficient ones atrophied. These features, he added, were inheritable. The species were directed toward a goal, and progress seemed inevitable. No wonder progressive religionists could quickly adapt and see evolution as God's
way of doing things. Darwin, on the other hand, saw adaptation as
fortuitous, accidental, something that eluded divine design. Organisms with advantages, through natural selection, reproduced
more abundantly than did the less fortunate. The environment, it
might be said, does the selecting of just which lucky organisms
will be adapted. Not evolution itself but natural selection turned
out to be the scandal for reactionary believers. It was also a problem for thoughtful but often marooned progressives.

4:4   This history of inversions and transitions included frequent
changes of party lines. Thus, well before the 1890s many Protestant theological conservatives were more evolutionary than they
knew. They were social Darwinists, with or without the name.
They easily grafted the idea of economic competition and struggle
to some latter-day versions of Calvinist efforts to prove one's election, to show one's self worthy, to be industrious. After the 1890s
it was Protestant theological progressives who first rejected this
form of evolution. Instead they promoted cooperative models that
they thought were more congruent with Christianity. By then,

all forms of evolution had become shibboleths in conservative camps, whose members thenceforth had to find new terms to legitimate their economic competitive programs.

4:5   From the beginnings, well before 1893, those scientists and philosophers who were and would be religious, embraced evolution. These included Asa Gray, Edward L. Youmans of *Popular Science Monthly*, and philosopher John Fiske. They remained theists. John Bascom had been a Congregational minister. He was championing evolution by the time he came to be president of the University of Wisconsin in 1874. In 1897 Bascom linked the spirit and science: "By a spiritual evolution we understand one of distinct increments and of an over-ruling purpose, which in its entire process contains and expresses personal, spiritual power in the means employed, in their combination, and in their evolution." For that reason the scientist could contend that "the physical forces are, in every stage of their development, permeated and borne forward by intellectual ones." Bascom had to oppose the accidental elements in Darwinian theory in the interest of discerning a divine mind and design. "By far, then," he wrote, "the most simple and sufficient theory of life is the spiritual one."

4:6   Another Lamarckian who made things easy for other people of faith was the University of California geologist Joseph Le Conte. Science was to him a rational system of natural theology, because evolution meant "(1) continuous *progressive change*, (2) *according to certain laws*, (3) and by means of *resident forces*." There was "no real efficient force but spirit, and no real *independent* existence but God." Le Conte received praise from many clerics who credited him with helping save their faith at the time when new accountings of universal and human origins first came to dominate science. Where, they asked, was the conflict? Scientists only had to adjust their understanding of the intention of language in the biblical book of Genesis and all would come out right.

4:7   Le Conte and his followers would speak less in regret over lost old faith than with enthusiasm for a newly found one. He remembered that he had been at first "orthodox of the orthodox; later," he said, "as thought germinated and grew apace, I adopted a liberal interpretation of orthodoxy; then, gradually I became unorthodox; then, in deep sympathy with the most liberal movement of Christian thought; and finally, to some extent, a leader in that movement." Curiously, such testimony was always to impress the reactionary Protestants with the force of a gravitational pull. This meant to them, that, unless checked by very strong counterforces, the natural instinct of people would be to gravitate toward or slide into evolutionary, modernist, and eventually faithless understandings. They therefore counseled a need to resist beginnings.

4:8   The spiritual kin of the Le Contes might give the impression that they felt no trauma at all. On the contrary, diaries and letters of thoughtful people in that time witness to the way the groundwork of their universe was shifting. To move from a static worldview, which saw creation as a finished product, to a developmental view of continuing creation, even on Lamarckian terms, would not occur without a great shaking. How could the faithful see as decisive and even unique certain historical moments such as the fall of humans into sin or the unique visitation of the created order by God in the incarnation of Jesus Christ? How connect optimistic views of developing and evolving human progress with original sin and other classic Christian ways to mark finitude?

4:9   Inevitably there were clashes within religious organizations. In the 1880s James Woodrow, uncle of President Woodrow Wilson, suffered for his support of evolution at Columbia Theological Seminary in southern Presbyterianism. To the *New York Times* that three-year controversy already looked like nothing so much as an example of southern cultural lag. The more notable northern clerics seemed safe from such sniping; their churches and schools had moved on into evolutionary thinking. Such an observation was wrong, but the fact that it already seemed plausible in New York then suggests more that there was a diversity of attitudes than simple panic in the face of evolution. Even Woodrow endured and prevailed when he became moderator of his synod in his church body and later president of the University of South Carolina.

4:10   The most quoted northern evolutionist was not a notable theologian but was, like Strong, a churchly publicist. Lyman Abbott, journalist and preacher, published *The Evolution of Christianity* in 1897. The book is important for its representativeness, not its originality. Abbott was later forced to fight a rear-guard action when natural selection came to prevail. First, however, he saw evolution as the history of a process, not the explanation of a cause. Evolution, the cleric insisted, was not to be identified with Darwinism. For him it was not the doctrine of struggle for existence and survival of the fittest. Darwinism he found aesthetically repulsive: "all animate nature is wrestling, every fellow with his fellow, and . . . every life depends on the destruction of some other life, slain in the struggle by the selfishness of the victor." In Abbott's popular view God remained the creative, controlling, directing force in all phenomena. Most evolutionists still agreed with him in this view, against Darwin. Science, he argued, also perceives in nature a real thoughtfulness. Its pursuits, said Abbott, follow "along a path which pre-existing thought has marked out for it."

4:11   In 1910 the Reverend Newell Dwight Hillis, successor to Henry Ward Beecher in a Brooklyn pulpit, could still speak for his strand of modernists: "Already the time has come when almost everybody exclaims, 'Evolution—certainly; why, I always believed in theistic evolution.'" The scientific war, if that was what it had been, seemed over. When almost all evolutionary scientists were drawn to natural selection, Abbott and Hillis looked stranded, or at least their rationales were gone. It had become too late for such people to readopt static worldviews, so they worked to make evolution come out right with faith, and vice versa, without looking too closely at details.

4:12   During the fluid period, there were also many thoughtful conservatives in the evolutionary camp. George F. Wright, who taught the Harmony of Science and Revelation at Oberlin, fused Calvinist providence with evolutionary destiny. In due course Wright found that for the sake of faith he had to reject natural selection. By 1910 he was far from the main stream of science: "If anything is to be *evolved* in an orderly manner from the resident forces of primordial matter it must first have been *involved* through the creative act of the Divine Being." At the very time that naturalistic evolution was coming to dominate, Wright tried to argue that it was on the wane.

4:13   One sign that evolution as such was not yet the dividing line in religion that it would come to be in the church politics of the 1920s, which meant very late in the day, is the evidence of a set of pamphlets called *The Fundamentals*. Sent free of charge by the hundreds of thousands to church leaders after 1910, these tracts gathered both moderately and sometimes immoderately conservative Protestants who wanted to rally people against emergent modernism and to testify to the faith. Most of their authors supported science, though their science was of a Baconian inductivist sort. With their consequent love of what they thought of as facts they did not see how evolution could ever complicate their faith, even if they could not refute the theory. As for science in general, one author, A. W. Pitzer, wrote that the Christian "hails with joy each new discovery as affording additional evidence of the wisdom, power, and goodness of God." Mississippian H. M.

Sydenstricker, who contended that religious conversion was as observable to science as anything in the natural order, also naturally celebrated science. To him it was not "supposable that God is less scientific in this the very greatest of all His works than He is in the lesser things of His government." That phrase was a compliment to science in general, even though Sydenstricker was not of a generation that could any longer particularly celebrate evolution. Their Baconianism left behind the writers of *The Fundamentals* and forced them to fortify their defensive spirit.

4:14   World War I and its devastations made it more difficult for modernists to keep promoting their cheer or faith in progress based on evolution, especially when the scientists no longer gave them theories to which to attach progress. The next generation of Protestant elites would see schools of neoorthodoxy and critical realism counter the later school of modernism that defined itself in the 1920s. By 1910 a Darwinian-oriented eugenics movement was asserting its pessimism, organizing to restrict the immigration of what they saw as inferior peoples. Only thus could America preserve the white, Anglo-Saxon Protestant heritage in the face of the new lower class of immigrants. Overt racism even came to afflict the evolutionists' camp. Where the modernists were not marooned by the scientists, they came to be opposed by reactionaries in their churches. These attracted hundreds of thousands of supporters by targeting progressives' seminaries, boards, and journals. The secular intellectuals did not turn in need for support or alliance to the theologians, whose intentions they largely ignored.

4:15   Of equal extent to the evolutionary issue was the concurrent debate over the canon of the Bible. Lacking a pope, the Protestant majority of America conceived its whole faith and theology to be grounded on the Bible. Many citizens further considered the Bible to be at the basis of the national *consensus juris*, the norm for civil law and the cultural ethos. Any change in the status of the scripture would therefore represent an upheaval in the culture. A full-dress review of attitudes to the Bible in this period is not necessary here. It is only to be noted that the liberals and modernists, in adopting the imported European theories of interpretation, displayed positive intentions for saving faith. Many of the leaders lived in the somewhat sheltered and self-contained world of seminaries. They were far away from the front lines where ministers heard from laypeople who were being told that scientific criticism would take their Bible away. The liberals advertised premature ends to the controversy, before the ranks on both sides were even fully lined up. Thus in 1908 Episcopal professor Angus Crawford self-confidently summarized the case for major divinity faculties but not for constituencies: "we are all critics, I trust, and higher critics too."

4:16   At the beginning of this new period there occurred the most celebrated American heresy trial. It had to do with the methods and findings of biblical criticism. While his New York presbytery supported him, Union Theological Seminary professor Charles A. Briggs was condemned by his Presbyterian denomination. The newspapers called attention to the breach in understandings between professors. One side wanted to save the Bible for people in the age of science. The other wanted to save the Bible from professors who adopted scientific criticism. Thus *Public Opinion* magazine picked up from the Savannah, Georgia, *News*, a comment on the sense of nervousness. "The great majority of Christians regard the Bible as the inspired work of God, and, therefore, [it] cannot contain errors." This insight was exploitable by conservative church politicians. The *News* went on: "Professor Briggs's doctrines may be entirely satisfactory to those who clearly understood them, but it is about impossible to make them understood by the masses. To the average mind the whole Bible is true, or it is not the inspired work of God."

4:17   Briggs's rationale antedates but colors our period. In 1891, after a decade of forays against inherited views, this immodest pathfinder blasted: "We have undermined the breastworks of traditionalism; let us blow them to atoms. We have forced our way through the obstructions; let us remove them from the face of the earth, that no man hereafter may be kept from the Bible." Briggs then urged that higher criticism was the true friend of the Bible over against the bibliolatry, as he called it, which saw the Bible as a magical object, not the mere paper, print, and binding that it was. Behind the professor's posturing there was a serene confidence that he and the critics were making the Bible plausible as a document of faith.

4:18   The fact that biblical criticism was imported from Germany and became a kind of status symbol among some scholars was later to hurt the cause when anti-Germanism developed before and during World War I. In any case, long before that Germany had held a reputation for destructive radicalism. American scholars who identified with anything from there had little chance to show their positive intent to the mass of church people. Yet wherever one reaches for modernist writings, one finds the authors treating only the positive side. Thus Andover's George Harris spoke of a double victory in 1914. First, he gloried, "Evolution has won, and there is no more debate about it; has won us so completely that we do not think of it, as we do not think of gravitation." As for biblical criticism, the belief that the Bible is infallible and inerrant was, he said, not a religious belief at all. "It is a comparatively modern, a recent belief, making a great claim for the earthen vessel, as well as for the treasure it contains." Just as Christianity had grown as a result of its embrace of Copernicanism and Darwinism, so now biblical criticism would make Christian teaching brighter and purer. Harris now drew the line around the circle of the presumedly literate. "It would be difficult to find an intelligent person who holds to the inerrancy of all parts of the Bible, or who is disturbed by the modifications and readjustments of criticism." All of this was to him a tremendous gain, a pointer to a deeper faith.

4:19   Baptist William Newton Clarke in 1910, though aware of some growing difficulties, still promoted criticism. The Bible was safe when its methods were used; its quality as "the book of divine religion is so established," said Clarke, "that we may think of it with serene confidence." Progressive revelation, he thought, was the basis of scripture. Criticism was therefore a more interior and spiritual idea of the evidence of the present God. If God was in a book he would be found without help from theories about inerrancy. "God shines by his own light." William Adams Brown at Union Seminary was sure that the scientific view of the Bible led people more immediately to Christ, without the distractions of the old theories which had induced conflict.

4:20   George Gordon of Boston was also predictably in line. "Among intelligent people the Bible can never again be what it has been," and that meant loss, Gordon admitted. "For work," however, "the Bible is mightier than ever"; it simply could never be an idol again. While Napoleons of destructive criticism would not understand all this, those he called soldiers of faith found it providential. "The higher criticism of the Bible is simply the supreme instance of the severe but gracious process whereby believers to-day are passing from idolatry of the letter to the worship of the spirit."

4:21   Henry Churchill King at Oberlin was humane enough to regret that higher criticism had been seen as bitter, negative, antisupernaturalistic. He talked strategy to face the problem. King quoted biblical scholar George Adam Smith, who had said in warning that "if one person is likely to suffer shipwreck through the employment of higher criticism, the faith of ten will break down—is breaking down—for lack of the very help it would bring." The modernist rescue squad must come. A large-minded Christian faith would see in this wide movement of scholarship a genuine providential leading. Constructive higher criticism in King's eye was more than inevitable; it was desirable, well worth the risks of the route to its fulfillment in faith.

4:22   The best illustrator of the faith modernists put in science and in the scientific understanding of the Bible was William Rainey Harper. As founding president of the University of Chicago, partner in adult education ventures like Chautauqua and biblical correspondence courses, journal editor, restless lecturer, and tireless Baptist, Harper wanted to disseminate the critical views from Sunday School through graduate school. A less destructive critic than he one can hardly imagine. So given was Harper to apology for the Bible and so potent was he as founder of critical organizations and journals, that almost a century later some scholars blamed this pioneer for preventing truly unbiased approaches to the Bible in the academy. Harper described his mission as the act of clearing away the rubbish which traditionalists had placed between his Bible and the people.

4:23   Harper carried on an attack against dogmatic approaches which kept Jesus out of history and tried to keep the Bible uncontaminated by earthly contingency. It was, he argued, the misuse of the Bible that led people to shelve it. Biblical study, on the other hand, would help students make the painful modern passage from an unthinking to a rational faith. In 1892 at Chautauqua in New York Harper portrayed "The Rational and the Rationalistic Higher Criticism" in terms that sufficed for him through his last fifteen years. The scholar even rued the term "criticism" of the Bible, preferring the word "inquiry." Sure that the "*work* of destruction must be distinguished from the *spirit* of destruction," Harper contended that apparent destructiveness was a step toward positive understandings by the faithful of God's progressive revelation in history.

4:24   Harper connected the two vulnerable modernist intellectual planks. As part of progressive revelation, the Bible was a theistic interpretation of social evolution. Old-style prescientific theology, he thought, had never grasped the idea of law or what he named an organic development in the history of revelation. When a Missouri cleric asked whether his new theology might undercut his missionary zeal, Harper could honestly reply: "You will readily understand . . . that all my work is in a very fundamental sense missionary work." Critical views of the Bible had greatly increased his own sense of the value of Christianity for all people. That was why he organized a Hebrew language study movement and why his journal *The Biblical World* should inspire persons to work and strive for higher things, why it aided many a troubled soul which found itself in the midst of doubt and difficulty. At last, he thought, the supremacy of the historical method was helping Americans take part in a new revelation of God. His journal of biblical criticism would actually help enthrone the Bible.

4:25   Harper wrote in heady times. In 1905 he claimed that sixty thousand subscribers had already taken his outline courses. The university president even made time for local Sunday School, so he could engage in experiments. Scientific Bible study, he thought, ought to go on in public schools, colleges, and universities. Theological seminaries needed reform. He met certain kinds of discontented laypersons and spoke for them: "Many intelligent laymen in the churches have the feeling that the training provided for the students . . . does not meet the requirements of modern times." The new schools that he advanced employed the assured results of modern psychology, pedagogy, and common experience. All these matched the growth and development of those styles of thought that seminaries needed.

4:26   Harper died young, in 1906, before his almost utopian visions of how the Bible would transform America could be realized. They were soon forgotten. No successor possessed his gift or energy. Socialist critic Upton Sinclair later wrote an acid portrait of the late president Harper, one which revealed something of the popular limits of the man's dream and churchly support. During the early days of the university, wrote Sinclair, "President Harper stood for liberalism in religion, and thereby lost much Baptist money." Even most people in his own denomination would not follow the critical path.

4:27   The modernists, it might be said, won but did not win; they lost but did not simply lose. Most of the centers of scholarship did adopt and take for granted the evolutionary and critical approaches as a matter of course. The liberal laity, however, did not seem to follow the theologians in detail and the conservative laypeople seemed able to be exploited by reactionaries who could always point to the destructive sides of these scientific schools. Often quoted as typical of much lay expression, then as later, was the word of former president Grover Cleveland: "The Bible is good enough for me, just the old book under which I was brought up. I do not want notes or criticisms or explanations about authorship or origin, or even cross-references. I do not need or understand them, and they confuse me."

4:28   As an apology to the secular community the modernist intellectual program finally fell short. Many of the nonreligious chose to counter it by sounding as if they favored less plausible, less scientific, and less adaptive faiths. This response could have been a ploy, in part, because such faiths did not in any way beckon them or get in their way. More positively, such reaction may have shown respect for the spiritual power, not of religious reactionaries, but of people who stuck to their guns spiritually and were not ready to be swayed by so many turns in the mind of the age.

4:29   Harold Bolce, who toured campuses for *Cosmopolitan*, a popular magazine, in 1909, showed that he knew he had a clientele ready to be stirred up. Shocked, he cited Jacob Gould Schurman of Cornell, who remarked of the times that "history and criticism have made the Bible a new book." All the landmarks were now gone, and he reported that the "restless sea of criticism threatens to engulf religion with the records it adored."

4:30   An otherwise unremarkable Mennonite heresy-hunter named John Horsch at the end of the generation presented an interesting catalog of testimonies, including a comment from a Chicago daily newspaper. The editor was unimpressed by extreme modernist George Burman Foster at the University of Chicago. "We are struck . . . with the *hypocrisy* and *treachery* of these attacks on Christianity." Infidels wrote the infidel books; why should professors of Christian theology join their cause? "Is a theological seminary an appropriate place for a general massacre of Christian doctrine?" The paper professed not to be championing either Christianity or infidelity, but only "*condemning infidels masquerading as men of God and Christian teachers.*" Horsch could also cite new humanist Paul Elmer More, a modern thinker unimpressed by modernists, who defined "a divinity school [as] a place where they investigate poverty and spread agnosticism."

4:31   Similarly, philosopher William James in *The Varieties of Religious Experience* in 1902 showed more respect for mystics, mossbacks, and misfits than for the adaptive Protestant modernists. Horsch could also summon as witness skeptical philosopher George Santayana of Harvard. Only conservatives, said Santayana, had anything to say for refreshment to the poor or to the rich.

Only frank supernaturalism, not smooth naturalism, offered hope for the Church, and, said the philosopher, "its sole dignity also lies there." As to modernism, "it is suicide." Santayana saw modernism to be sweetening the pang of sin, stealing reality from the last judgment, removing reality from the Christ of religious tradition, leaving nothing. The Jameses and Santayanas in effect were saying, "Give me that old-time religion," if only to have something more potent to reject. That was music to reactionary Protestant ears.

4:32   After World War I the old program of modernism was fading and the leaders looked for a new rationale in the next decade. Doubts were growing as to whether it would now so simply prevail in a world of progress. Horsch pointed to Unitarian notable Charles E. Park, who saw that in his church "a predominance of gray heads and noticeable lack of young people" was a scourge. This became a common and woeful observation among people who had thought adaptive modernism would win the new generation.

4:33   The leaders themselves at times revealed some ambivalences. They had given the movement their best. Modernism had saved their own faith and provided intellectual excitement and a vocation to transform the world. Their integrity would permit them in a later day to do no more than to revise their modernism, not to turn apostasy into traditionalisms. Some kept up the show of pride. The University of Chicago's Dean Shailer Mathews drew a neat line in 1920: over against intelligence in religion, anti-intelligence, in the form of obscurant and reactionary religion was being organized.

4:34   Mathews's colleague George Burman Foster was better able to blur the line. He was condescendingly tender when he expressed hope that "our fathers and mothers might enjoy the blessed calm of the evening of life free from the spiritual bewilderment of those who have to wander in the region of doubt and to feel their feet slip just when they thought that some rock on which they stood was firm." He could not offer full and solid comfort or hope to warm hearts either. Foster was only trying "to cleave to the sunnier side of doubt." He hoped to offer enough light and warmth to keep people from freezing in the dark. The old ideal of one principle of rationality and a single direction of progress prevailing was yielding to the reality of a diversity of options. Somehow the language of doubt and dark spoke to deeper religious needs than did the exuberant vision which, once upon a time, all intelligent people on the mountain top of privilege knew was theirs.

Part Two

The Moderns

5

The Progressives
and the Past

5:1   The American historians, philosophers, and social thinkers,
the moderns who emerged around the turn of the century, were
clear about their religious intentions. In almost every case they
felt emancipated from the tradition as it had been embodied in the
small-town ethos of their childhood. Religion, especially church
religion, was not to be a communal choice for their generation.
Members of the first university-generations in America, they welcomed scientific methods and a diversity of intellectual alternatives. Nothing like intact historic faith, in this case inherited
Christianity as it was then practiced, offered much possibility to
them or their successors.

5:2   Virtually all of these shapers of new ways, however, carried in
them memories, ideals, and dreams that led them to draw on that
repository of options they thought they had rejected. All of them
repudiated the offerings of theological modernism. They did work
on a parallel track, though, and, if anything, turned out to be
more respectful of historic faith than were the modernist professors. Very few finally came back home to the traditional church
or used the old religious symbols conventionally. Almost all of
them took part in acts of formulation that gave America a distinctive passage over its hump of transition to modernity. The aggressive antireligious or assertive nonreligious outlook of comparable generations in Europe found no counterpart in America.

47

The seminar room of historian Frederick Jackson Turner typifies the new ideal of specialized progressive graduate study in universities. (The Huntington Library, San Marino, Calif.)

5:3   Sophisticated though they were, these people of talent and genius were in very few cases utopians who could repudiate all models from the past. In a way, they were immigrants into a new country of modernity. For all their sophistication they came to look somewhat like simpler, primitive people who were studied by British Marxist historian E. J. Hobsbawm. Such people, like all first-generation immigrants, "looked backwards as much as forwards." Hobsbawm's subjects were in the first generation of the modern industrial population. They were, he says, as yet far from adjusted to a way of life which was novel and revolutionary and yet they had to learn the rules of the game of modern industrial society. The American moderns, far different on the social scale, were grandchildren of New England Puritans and patriarchs, often privileged Brahmins who were seeking a new faith to support necessary new ways. More often, they were also professors in the new, avowedly secular state universities of the west, men and, sometimes, women, who had been nurtured in an evangelical Protestantism they came to reject as confining. The exceptions—

misfits like the rebellious Scandinavian Thorstein Veblen and the skeptical post-Catholic George Santayana—are interesting precisely for the characteristics even they shared with their contemporaries as well as for the light they shed on the others from their peripheral vantages.

5:4   To the historians in the first generation of these modern professionals, most of whom came to be called Progressives or supporters of the New History, historical thinking was itself a key element in modernity. People in their profession are charged with the task of locating their generation in time and space. This company did not as a class undergo a traumatic crisis of historical consciousness to match the one that shook the faith of so many intellectuals of Christian Europe in their century. With the historians across the Atlantic, however, they experienced the contingency of everything, the relativity of what had once looked stable to their parents. The most philosophically reflective of the group, Carl Becker, looked back in 1932, after the revolution in thinking had occurred, to observe: "To regard all things in their historical setting appears, indeed, to be an instructive procedure of the modern mind. We do it without thinking, because we can scarcely think at all without doing it."

5:5   Putting in brackets, for the moment, all East-Coast historians named Adams, only one of whom will stand up for his class in this chapter, it is revealing to compare the transit of major figures, who were generally of midwestern provenance. To look at traces of collective childhood biography might seem a casual enterprise in intellectual history, but it happens that their pasts are much of what concerned these particular intellects. Emancipation from them was to be a reference point for all.

5:6   First is Edward Eggleston, who because of his age and ill health had to have someone else read the address in 1900 for the American Historical Association at which he named the new history "The New History." Eggleston was a Hoosier like *The Hoosier Schoolmaster* about whom he wrote, and it was he who remained attentive longest to the ethos of his childhood. In fact, he became a Methodist preacher as a young man, then wrote for church journals, and was still a pastor when in his forties. Eggleston somewhere along the way was converted to Darwinism and evolution. These came to him first as threats and then as freedoms. He underwent what he called a "long and painful struggle for emancipation from theological dogma." The Hoosier admitted that he had kept his requisite adolescent struggle going on much longer

and later than most. It took the form of a crisis when his intellectual conscience insisted that sentiment of every sort ought to be
put aside in the search for truth. The faith of his first four decades
was thus reduced to sentiment.

5:7   Frederick Jackson Turner, the scholar who both observed and
made history in 1893 at the World's Columbian Exposition, there
noted the epic closing of the American frontier in 1890. He
pondered its significance. A son of that frontier, born in 1861 at
Portage, Wisconsin, Turner rebelled first against what he saw as
the nonsense taught in Sunday School back in that little town. By
the time he graduated from the University of Wisconsin in 1884,
he had converted his faith to a religion with twin pillars, evolution
and democracy. Turner's main scripture, he himself said, was the
whole of historical writing. As a professor he became a nominal
relaxed Unitarian, too lackadaisical in adult churchgoing fully
to please his tolerant wife. His creed, he said, was summed up in
the commandment which enjoins love of God, and of man. Yet
Turner's Unitarian creed, voiced in a letter to Woodrow Wilson in
1890, was the kind of vague expression that led to his being denied an appointment at Princeton. Such a faith was too wan and
minimal for the more orthodox trustees at Princeton, though the
embarrassing incident left Wilson, as the future president put it,
"the most chagrined fellow on the Continent."

5:8   No name is more associated with the New History than that of
James Harvey Robinson, who was born in 1863 at Bloomington,
Illinois. Robinson underwent the standard passage from Calvinism
to modernity. Like Eggleston, he claimed a liberation through
reading Darwin and he picked up from the Enlightenment an anticlerical outlook that colored many of his views of the past. With
the advance guard of his generation, he earned his doctorate in
Germany and wrote chiefly on European history, but in the end it
was the concerns of his very American New York neighbor, pragmatist John Dewey, that informed his viewpoints. He came to
moderate the repudiative spirit of his Enlightenment heroes.

5:9   Charles Beard, born in 1874, who came from maverick Quaker
stock, attended the Methodist DePauw University in his home
state of Indiana. His Quaker parents encouraged him in independence, so he underwent less of a crisis than scholars from more
confined backgrounds. Beard studied at Oxford and came back to
join New Historian James Harvey Robinson in work at Columbia.
If he did not feel such personal constrictions caused by the traditional religious ethos, he argued that the culture did, and as a

young man adopted language of the Enlightenment. In 1901 Beard wrote that the central theme of history was the human victory over "priestcraft, feudal tyrants, and warring elements." That revolution was only half completed.

5:10   Fifth in the midwestern cast was Carl Becker, whose historical writing made him a world citizen of the intellect. Born on an Iowa farm in 1873, he moved with his family eleven years later to the thriving little city of Waterloo, where the family lived next to and practiced faith with consistency at the Methodist church. The family example was a moderate one, so Becker was not an angry rebel. He did, however, part company with family, small city, and Methodist faith and practice, as he aspired to the Enlightenment outlook to which his history took him.

5:11   At Iowa's Cornell College Becker kept a "Wild Thoughts Notebook," in which he chronicled his changing opinions. The reader can already see in its jottings the waning of the childhood faith, expressed without bitterness, though at times Becker could be flip. He was this in 1928 when he wrote the Cornell librarian that "if Methodism is slowly dying in Iowa there is hope for the world." That faith died in him, but its passing did not turn into permanent hope for the world. Becker's move in 1893 from Cornell to the University of Wisconsin was more a part of his quest for something to replace the archaic Christian Evidence courses than an agony about them. He was on the way to conversion as an Enlightenment historian, under the influences of medievalist Charles Homer Haskins and frontier specialist Frederick Jackson Turner.

5:12   These five would belong on any list of the classic half dozen or so New Historians or Progressives; adding another five would no doubt lead to replication of what became a pattern of transit. In the promise and fitness of things, their mature visions should have simply continued the spirit of emancipation and progress. In some complex ways, it did. Eggleston first provided these agents' descriptions of change. He threw away the Christian classics like *The Imitation of Christ* which he had read as a circuit rider for Methodism. Now he pointed to new directions more circuitous. "The true way is to 'look upward and not downward, outward and not inward, forward and not backward.'" Eggleston would not walk again with à Kempis of old but with Darwin. As a forward-looker, he would prefer to "get one peep into the epoch-making book of the next century, whatever it may be, than to go back to the best of the crypt-worshippers." This impulse he credited to the objective life, as opposed to the subjective soundings of his youthful training. Objectivity meant faith in science and progress, along with rejection of the religious beliefs of antecedents.

5:13   Eggleston's work led him to iconoclasm in respect to the Puritans, who were being turned into bogeys by the emancipated. In 1896, in his deceptively simple yet pathbreaking book, *The Beginners of a Nation*, Eggleston professed that he had to deal "unreverently" with the Puritan age, whose government and very religion were barbarous. Even here, however, he was selective in his rejections. He did admire the Pilgrim divine John Robinson precisely because Robinson had been modern in his understanding of the progressive nature of truth. Four years later Eggleston's last book, *The Transit of Civilization*, appeared. This work with its consistent and vehement denunciation of colonial religionists found them pedantic and authoritarian. Instead of being seen as benign foreparents of America, they turned out to have been superstitious, captives of binding traditions. Emancipation was to be consistent whether from small-town Indiana or colonial America.

5:14   Turner, like Eggleston, was also a repudiator of the very colonial ethos off which intellectual America had previously lived. The frontier for him was an almost mystical reality because it had remarkably transformed European men, institutions, and ideas. The American east coast, as it developed in the course of centuries, grew, he said, to resemble the Old World in its social forms and its industry, even as it began to lose faith in the ideal of democracy. Turner placed his new faith in scientific history. From it he took a notion that historians had learned from Europeans: society grows, it is an organism. Curiously, this move led him to nostalgia for the very small-town order he had left behind, an order that modern industrialism was overwhelming. Turner began to fall into ambivalence about both old and new faiths.

5:15   Robinson's New History continued the pattern. One of its marks was also repudiative. The historians of this school, he remarked, began to spurn "supernatural, theological, and anthropocentric explanations, which had been the stock-in-trade of the philosophers of history." All this meant that historians gave up appealing to God and the devil as historical explanations. They replaced them with evolution. In the spirit of Eggleston Robinson went on: "The present has hitherto been the willing victim of the past; the time has now come when it should turn on the past and exploit it in the interests of advance." He could even sound momentarily like theological modernists when he boasted that no age had offered so much knowledge as his own. There had never been so much general good will and so much intelligent social activity as now. He counseled trust in the scientific historian to provide clues for the future.

5:16   Robinson kept looking backward in negation more consistently than the others. He would not oppose religion as such, he said, only inherited religion, which was the victim of cultural lag. "The belief on which I was reared," he remembered, "that God ordained the observance of Sunday from the clouds of Sinai, is an anachronism," one which could not have developed in the present day, yet it still enthralled millions. Similarly, public notions of what a church should do were born of ancient references, not present-day needs. Leave all to progress, he urged, for it offered unburdened people unsuspected possibilities of social readjustment and the promotion of human happiness. Robinson set forth a new icon. Progress, he said, was the greatest single idea in the whole history of mankind. He could be missionary about the conscious reformer who appeals to the future and thus is the final product of a progressive order of things. Robinson now defined the long-disputed sin against the Holy Spirit. It was the refusal to cooperate with the vital principle of betterment. Conservatism, therefore, he condemned as a hopeless and wicked anachronism.

5:17   Charles Beard, who pinned hope less on evolution and more on economics, turned out to be the most consistent secularizer of the company. This vision he preached as liberating. In his work, poor American immigrants, who once had been captive European peasants, quickly came to see that "no philosophy of innate sin, of a baffled life, no promise of transports in heaven could stem the great desire of multitudes for the delights of this life enjoyed by their superiors." Their strivings were secular in spirit and outcome. He suppressed all positive understandings of religious motivations for social change in America. The people, he said, had had to give up their battles with "ancient devils, fog giants, metaphysical dragons," and then use the material key to man's spiritual progress. Citizens had the right and power to determine their own religion and politics and thence corporately to control every form of their material environments.

5:18   In his mature work Carl Becker built on some motifs of his early "Wild Thoughts Notebook." Already standing outside what he called "the circle" in 1894, he relativized faith: "Christianity is one attempt to formulate religion." Becker was a modern in his understanding of faith's private character. Every one, he thought, had a religion. "It may be good or it may perhaps be bad, but it's no man's business but his own" and should not stand in the way of social formulation. In those early writings, religion still had its place as the secret part of the human soul which, he said, was never revealed to mortal man and which was known to himself and God alone. Yet such a retention of respect for faith was short-lived, and Becker moved on.

5:19   By 1913 he was cheering the fact that after he detected a short lapse in faith in progress, there was a revival of faith in the possibility of social regeneration. He cheered: "Out of the wreck of old creeds, there is arising a new faith, born of science and democracy, almost the only vital conviction left to us—the profound belief, namely, in progress." This encouraging faith forced the imperative command that knowledge shall serve purpose. Yet, he added, he was also drawn more and more to the question, "What light does the past throw on the present and the future?" His answer, as we shall shortly see, was more complex than that of any of his peers, each of whom began to find progress and historical science to be more ambiguous instruments than first they had imagined.

5:20   Eggleston came late to his vision of the American past, and immediately began to show some sense of nervousness about his wholesale dismissals and some foreboding about the future. He did not live long enough to enlarge upon these second thoughts. What, for instance, should he do with conscience (what he called Puritanism's one great contribution to human culture)? It had quickly become subject to authoritarianism and tradition. He was learning how to retrieve the ideal of conscience from the past, so that even Puritan pharisaism could be seen as a stage in human progress. Now, he reveled, "the successors of those who exercised their consciences on frivolous judgments . . . may put their hereditary strenuousness or their traditional preference for ethical considerations into the promotion of substantial social betterments. The ferment may not be pleasant, but the brew is good at the last." And at last, hereditary and traditional were concepts with which he could live. Was it the word of an old and gentler man, or the mature historian in him, which led Eggleston to conclude a chapter that had been full of condemnations: "But condemnation dies upon the lips when we reflect that ages to come may find many things damnable in the civilization of a more modern time." He died in 1900 and did not see the new modern-time century display itself.

5:21   A similar ambiguity developed, though on different grounds, in Turner. He saw Europe and the East Coast of America as anti-democratic, and the American West, because of the frontier, had been democratic. Now, however, corrupting industrialism encroached everywhere. Socialism, one address to the industrial problem, was a European import, so it bore no promise, but for a moment Turner thought that western Populism might give rebirth to New England's earlier, less spoiled ideals in the West. Then Turner found it flawed and failing as well, so he retreated and showed ever less faith in political forms of rescue. He thereupon transferred more of his faith to learning, to support of the new state universities. There was, he found, no secure locus for faith. The ending of the frontier and the birth of the city cut off possibility in Turner's religious vision. He became adept at speaking elegiacally in lines tinged with uncertainty as much as with progress: "The transformations through which the United States is passing in our own day are so profound, so far-reaching, that it is hardly an exaggeration to say that we are witnessing the birth of a new nation in America." The old confidence, however, was gone.

5:22   The ever more confident Robinson carried on his own faith in progress after World War I. Late in the 1920s he still beckoned attention to the new intellectual climate of the century which with a sharp and surprising alteration had promised to explain or recast "the whole estimate of religious phenomena." Robinson was not the agent of the newer changes. He did not even seem to notice that by then neoorthodox Jewish, Catholic, and Protestant ideas were beginning to replace the pre–World War I progressivism to which he as well as the modernists in theology had earlier attached themselves. Despite Robinson's prophecies, people were doing what he had seen them doing until very recently. They were looking backward for their standards and ideals.

5:23   Beard remained the secularist of greatest consistency, and never tired of promoting economic reforms as salvation. Yet he was never to be so confident again of outcomes as he was in his first book. The new cooperative society for which Beard yearned bore curious marks of the organic medieval order he otherwise dismissed. He looked back with pleasure on the ways people had freed themselves from the Roman Catholic yoke and from the Puritan regress to the shackles of superstition. He rejoiced that people had learned they should use freely their "own God-given reason." The Populist-tinged election of 1896 and World War I with what he hoped was its achievement, a world made safe for democracy, represented heights of progress for unshackled Western humans.

5:24   Whoever stayed around to see outcomes, however, would find Beard wavering not in his inclusive humanist faith but in his need to question its effects. To Carl Becker he was to write, "I wonder whether the weary world can ever get enthused again over some simple theory of history. It was grand to be alive in Queen Victoria's hopeful age when Darwins were hidden in every clump of academic bushes." That age was gone. War turned out to have been an abortion of economic planning, and it was a mistake for historians to gloss over humanity's senseless and berserk rages. On such a scale he saw medieval Catholicism and American founders as poor and unproductive foils. Beard then struck out on an eccentric career of contemporary political comment. The public came to see what he evidently felt in his bones: the limits of any angle of vision that would permanently replace the inherited religious ones.

5:25   The most nuanced revisitation of personal emancipation and an early progressivist commitment came from Carl Becker, who did look backward for some paradigms to the very Puritans the others despised. In 1910, while teaching in Kansas, Becker celebrated the fact that that state was more Puritan than the New England of the day. "Americanism," there, he added, "pure and undefiled, has a new lease on life. It is the mission of this self-selected people to see to it that it does not perish from off the earth." By 1916 he was ready to leave Kansas for Cornell, where he also left behind his agrarian crusading and the need for the Puritan model. With the crusading passion gone, he wrote European history with an ironic tinge that he had not applied to America. Like Beard, Becker momentarily recovered simple faith in progress during World War I, but the crusade for a world safe for democracy ended in early disillusionment. Becker then wrote William E. Dodd that the war was inexplicable on any ground of reason, common sense, decent aspiration, or even intelligent self-interest. What could be left of progress, he asked, since this futile, desolating, and repulsive exhibition of power and cruelty was "the result of some thousands of years of what men like to speak of as 'political, economic, intellectual and moral Progress.' If this is progress, what in Heaven's name would retardation be!" Dodd found him affirming an ancient language: "The human heart is deceitful and desperately wicked." Dispassionate historical writing would be his salvation.

5:26   Not long after the war Becker was celebrating the Midwest precisely because it was isolationist, not international—this view
being a curious twist for an Enlightenment historian. Now a bitter
tinge appeared in his view of the Enlightenment: "The eighteenth
century did not abandon the old effort to share in the mind of God;
it only went about it with greater confidence, and had at last the
presumption to think that the infinite mind of God and the finite
mind of man were one and the same thing." This sentence quite
accurately expounded the modernist faith in progress in his own
time. Becker wrote an obituary for the older agrarian faith, which
had been naive, "yet it was a humane and engaging faith" which
could not survive the harsh realities of the modern world with its
nationalism and industrialism. There was pathos in his remark
that now a more trenchant scientific criticism was "steadily dissolving its own 'universal and eternal laws' into a multiplicity of
incomplete and temporary hypotheses—these provided an atmosphere in which faith in Humanity could only gasp for breath."

5:27   Becker's best-remembered book, *The Heavenly City of the
Eighteenth-Century Philosophers*, appeared fourteen years after
the war but throws light on the limits to his faith he was recognizing by 1919. That century of Enlightenment found thinkers re-
verting to a medieval sense that there was "a cosmic drama, composed by the master dramatist according to a central theme and on
a rational plan." The Enlightenment's faith in the irreducible brute
fact of history, however, failed those who stood in its trail. Becker
was personally left with an unmarketable stoicism as the only
plausible faith for moderns. He was exposing his own gray secret:
He could neither find in history nor could he propose any grand
positive program. He even came to attack scientific history. One
enthusiastic Becker disciple remembered this attack as "sacrilege
against the deity," the history that had once been enthroned. "It
was treason against the profession. It was glorious. It was grand."
Yet the relativism undercut the faith in progress Becker had earlier
proposed as the one really vital faith of our day. His final urbane
skepticism was reflected in some lines by poet Edwin Arlington
Robinson, a poem Becker pasted on a card and cherished: "Yet we
shall have our darkness, even as they,/ And there shall be another
tale to tell."

5:28   Standing apart from this cluster but more frank in his skeptical
turn and his reversion to probably irretrievable models from the
medieval religious past was Henry Adams, who supplemented

history with the writing of enduring novels and essays. Too idiosyncratic to represent much more than only Henry Adams, his
writings do provide a kind of lever to use for prying along the fault
lines of progressivism among the moderns. To literary critics
Adams classically displayed the birth of the modern consciousness in American writing. To historians of religion and culture he
was the first antimodern, the rejecter of a modernist theology that
he found in his father, Boston Unitarian Charles Francis Adams,
against whose vision he struggled. When doubt plagued him,
Henry Adams found the adaptations of liberal Protestantism to be
the least plausible offerings for the faith he always sought but
which his ambivalence and skepticism kept at a distance. In the
1880s he could write that "man is still going fast upward," but by
1884 the novel *Esther* showed beginnings of a flight from progress. Adams invented characters who inhabited the sterile landscape of modernist Protestantism and then tantalized readers with
explorations of then unacceptable mysticism and medievalism as
alternatives.

5:29   Adams's rejection of modernity had its ugly side, for part of the
modernity he blasted was, he thought, the fabric of "money-
lenders," among them, Jews. His writings turned frankly anti-
Semitic. Where could a person of sensibility flee? To the Middle
Ages, the period his New History contemporaries and the modernist theologians found most horrific, shackling, and superstitious because of its burden of tradition. In 1900 Adams wrote
almost with envy from a safe distance, "In my view, Hell is all
there was to make life worth living. Since it was abolished, there
is no standard of value. Hell is the foundation of Heaven, and now
costs nothing and measures nothing."

5:30   *The Education of Henry Adams* has the author finding cosmic
flaws in Darwinian evolution, the synthesis designed to replace
historic faith. Natural selection, he wrote, pleased everyone except curates and bishops, but it was flawed as a basis for philosophy. True, "it was the very best substitute for religion; a safe, conservative, practical, thoroughly Common-Law deity." Adams also
did not share the faith in the New History. "In essence incoherent
and immoral, history had either to be taught as such—or falsified."

5:31   He had to carry his spiritual search for what he pointed to as
Motion, Change, Form, Law, Order, or Sequence, away from
what confronted him in the form of the Dynamo. That symbol
offered only meaningless and complex alteration. The medieval
image of the Virgin instead had offered energy that was once put

to work in the human will. Adams, using the third person, located himself: "Nature had given to the boy Henry a character that, in any previous century, would have led him into the Church; he inherited dogma and *a priori* thought from the beginning of time; and he scarcely needed a violent reaction like anti-slavery politics to sweep him back into Puritanism with a violence as great as that of a religious war." Yet that course was denied him now. It poised him only to see that the Middle Ages was a great time, and the Norman ancestors were a magnificent people. Now revolution was winning: since then, he mused, our ancestors have steadily declined and run out until we have reached pretty near bottom. His contemporaries had lost religion, art, military tastes, the meaning available in medieval art, until only an epitaph was left: "So we get Boston."

5:32   Adams ruled out a priori the possibility of transporting medieval coherence into modernity. Chartres Cathedral had seen pilgrims for seven hundred years and would welcome them for seven hundred more, but the calm and confident image of the Virgin there would never again fulfil her revolutionary purposes. She looked down "from a deserted heaven, into an empty church, on a dead faith." Thomas Aquinas, whose thirteenth-century architectonic Catholic scholasticism was perceived by others as a match for the cathedrals, represented a betrayal to Adams, because Aquinas had replaced energy with logic. The long road down to Boston and Unitarian modernism had begun with him. "From that time," wrote Adams, "the universe has steadily become more complex and less reducible to a central control." Chartres, on the other hand, suggested how "unity turned itself into complexity, multiplicity, variety, even contradiction."

5:33   *Mont-Saint-Michel and Chartres* was an antimodern summa in its celebration of organic, simple, forceful, but now unattainable forms of life. Adams rejected the individualist and competitive modern condition and wished for convergences. "Man," he wrote, "is an imperceptible atom always trying to become one with God," while "energy is the inherent effort of every multiplicity to become unity." Now Boston Unitarianism and faith in progress looked like escapes and blights which the author himself experienced as such: "From cradle to grave this problem of running order through chaos, direction through space, discipline through freedom, unity through multiplicity, has always been and must always be the task of education, as it is the moral of religion, philosophy, science, art, politics, and economy." Yet in Adams's time religious journals, he thought, offered not an act, or an expression, or an image, which showed depth of faith or hope. They revealed only an aching consciousness of religious void. Adams least of all knew how to help fill the void that he discerned so well.

5:34   The turn some of these historians took in their ambiguous affirmation of medieval energy and order found literally concrete expression in a turn that architecture for church and campus took in the progressive era. Not all historical consciousness works itself out on paper; stone is also available. Moderns who built laboratory-filled campuses with chapels on them or cathedrals near them, or modernists who wanted grand buildings to house their forward-directed pulpits, turned to medieval, notably Gothic, or colonial, notably New England meeting house, styles. Exceptions were few. Some Universalists in Oak Park, Illinois, ventured with the Unity Temple of Frank Lloyd Wright in 1906. Christian Scientists in Berkeley, California, in 1913 engaged eclectic Bernard Maybeck to blend what has been called the best modern industrial materials then available with hints of Gothic tracery, Romanesque columns, Byzantine decorations, and Japanese timberwork to produce a church that hints at the modern. Boston's Trinity Church, built by Henry Hobson Richardson in the 1880s, also anticipated the modern. Louis Sullivan and Dankmar Adler designed three contemporary-leaning synagogues in Chicago. William Drummond drew on Wright's impulse to build First Congregational Church of Austin, Illinois. Yet these were only a few mutations and, for whatever stir they created in architectural circles, they were visually overwhelmed by the multitude of buildings others erected in their drive for tradition, for Gothic.

5:35   The best-known architect of a movement that included a half-dozen people of great talent such as Bertram Grosvenor Goodhue and Charles Francis Wentworth, was their sometime partner Ralph Adams Cram. Cram was a man of modern sensibilities who deserted his father's New Hampshire Unitarian tradition for highest Anglicanism. Hosts of imitators joined Cram in building for Episcopalians and Presbyterians of wealth, or for patriotic public purpose as in 1902 with the Gothic chapel for the United States Military Academy at West Point. Promoters of Washington Cathedral, which was begun in 1907, retained Cram as a consultant, and after 1911 he redesigned the original Romanesque-Norman Cathedral Church of St. John the Divine in New York. Such buildings spoke to the religious void that Henry Adams diagnosed and boldly concretized the medieval imagery which the progressive historians had wanted to leave behind.

5:36   When international modernist styles appeared decades later in America, Cram became everyone's negative reference point, but he had served well the modernist preachers and liturgists in his time. His was to be a rejection of industrialism and spiritless modern individualism. For a time, as a Christian socialist, Cram drew motifs from medieval guild life. By 1893 he and fellow high-church Anglican converts were publishing *Knight Errant* for the company of medievalists. With some good reason, as the architectural votes were being cast by church building-committees, he felt he was on the winning side. Hunger for organicism and coherence would prevail, he thought, "until at last, when that chaos has come which is the *reductio ad absurdum* of current individualism, the restored system of idealism shall quietly take its place, to build on the wide ruins of a mistaken civilization a new life more in harmony with law and justice." The first desideratum of a church was that the worshiper should be filled with the righteous sense of awe and mystery and devotion. Cram's Gothic was a judgment on corporate and governmental mass society, where the individual was, as he put it, "a negligible point in a vast and abstract proposition where all personal relationship, personal duty, personal obligation are impossible." The parish, neighborhood, collegiate group, and other small, manageable, and personal agencies alone were redemptive.

5:37   Cram was both a popular builder and speaker. The final pages of his Lowell Lectures dating from World War I speak to his standard theme of "Decadence and the New Paganism." He romanticized personalism, classlessness, and the organicism of the Middle Ages. He invented the notion that a medieval yeoman's son commonly could become "on the one hand, page, squire, knight, baron, count; on the other, novice, monk, abbot, bishop, cardinal, and even Pope." Therefore, contra the progressives, Cram insisted that if democracy consists in abolition of privilege and equal opportunity for all, then the Middle Ages formed the only democracy of record. His readings of guild history were wildly inaccurate, but they spoke to those in a progressive era who were looking for spiritual landmarks.

5:38   The New Paganism resulted from a ceaseless flow of applied industrial invention. Explicitly Christian as none of the mature historians were, Cram celebrated the age when Christian principles dominated, and he now mourned. Christianity, he thought, had "surrendered one position after another in the vain effort to affect a compromise and maintain a working basis with the universal force that re-entered the world just five centuries ago." Haltingly restored Gothic art, he urged, may serve well as the visible protest of the church and the university against their eternal enemy, the new paganism.

5:39   While historians from Eggleston through Beard and Becker lapsed into ambiguity about progress and Adams into pathetic despair, Cram hoped that "in the end all we have known as modern civilization will have passed and a new era have come into being." Ahead were either five centuries of new Dark Ages or a new era of five centuries of a restored Christian commonwealth. The decision depended on Americans. The choice was free.

5:40   His contemporaries made their choice. Thousands of little congregations built what they thought of as churches that looked like churches, aspiring Gothic replicas. Thousands of collegians and tourists visited the Gothic buildings of modern Princeton, Cornell, Chicago, and other universities. These same people cherished the dynamo, industrial promise, technology, progress. No single principle of Enlightenment rationality or medieval or colonial synthesis brought coherence to this new generation. With many styles of consciousness they both treated the organic models with awe and the chaotic modern ones with energy. The one thing the population at large did not do is live out the early dreams based on the rejections and emancipations of the generation's historians—who, it came to be seen, had trouble living them out themselves.

6

The Right to Believe

6:1   While the progressive historians first apotheosized progress and then puzzled over its ambiguities, their contemporaries, the classic moderns in American philosophy, pondered modernity and found it spiritually wanting. While in that period European intellectuals were making many of their moves as aggressive secularizers, the American moderns left a more complex legacy. To a person, they left behind conventional church and faith, and almost to a person they went to work seeking substitutes. There were no Nietzschean "God-killers" in the group. The only recognized militant atheist of the time, Robert Ingersoll, was not to be taken seriously as an intellectual. All but George Santayana made their transit from childhood Christian nurture to a world of infinite spiritual choices. Even John Dewey found reason to use the syllable "God" and the language of religion and faith to present his supplantation. They intended to move ever further from the categories, forms, and space that historic faith once occupied. Their legacy was neither a coherent new religious academy nor a spiritual synthesis. Instead they left a set of options on which later, often lesser, intellectuals could draw to keep the blended religious-secular search and conversation going. Many decades later, therefore, scholars could write extensive books on the spirit of "American Religious Philosophy" in this decisive period.

6:2   One scholar has condensed the central search of American phi-

losophy in the modern period into an effort to provide an answer
to the question that George Santayana posed, "What will liberty
bring to the free man?" Perhaps this was too simple a summary,
but it did focus on the sense that philosophers as moderns were
free of all ecclesiastical control or collective authority. They then
had to establish new norms for human thought and conduct.
Benjamin Rand, who corrected papers for titans who clustered on
the Harvard faculty, is remembered for little except saying that
these "great philosophers" invented "modern classical philosophy." Santayana himself and Josiah Royce, Charles Sanders Peirce,
William James, and non-Harvardian John Dewey belonged to this
group, as did Alfred North Whitehead who, being British-born
and of later prime, is not presently a subject.

6:3   It is tempting simply to turn the chapter over to Harvard philosopher William James, the subject of many books and articles dealing with his religious dimensions. More and more James has come
to be seen against the background of Presbyterian grandparentage
and Swedenborgian parentage, as a member of a New York family
which was by his time religious but churchless. Without the constrictions of midwestern church piety to bind his mind and conscience or impel his emancipation, James still underwent a profound psychological and spiritual crisis and was left to do his own
formulating. Insofar as modernity means individuality and freedom of choice, James was an ideal exemplar. His definitions of
religion showed it. Insofar as modernity means resort to science,
James was at home with it, for he was trained in medicine, knew
medical materialism closeup, and pioneered as a psychologist. He
produced works in that field that matched his landmarks in philosophy. Insofar as modernity means having a problem with inherited
theism, James was also at home, though he wrestled so helpfully
with the space traditional religion had occupied that he later was
seen as a constructive figure in the religious sphere.

6:4   A personal breakdown in 1871–72 led James to recognize the
sick soul which showed up as a type in his Gifford Lectures of
1902, *The Varieties of Religious Experience*. James remained
sympathetic to soulful sufferers ever after, yet he also wanted to
build on the language of the science he had learned and taught. In
a letter to Miss Frances R. Morse he explained that the lectures
would find him defending experience against philosophy; experience was "the real backbone of the world's religious life." Of
course, he knew, his defense meant throwing philosophical *and*

psychological light on religious experience. James added: "I myself invincibly do believe, that, although all the special manifesta-
tions of religion may have been absurd (I mean its creeds and theories), yet the life of it as a whole is mankind's most important
function." Secularity would not have the last word, and aggressive
God-killers would have none at all.

6:5   James realized that the passage to modernity had been made
most aggressively in science. In 1907 he wrote, "never were as
many men of a decidedly empiricist proclivity in existence as
there are at the present day. Our children, one may say, are almost
born scientific." James, better than many of the historians, however, saw that the common person could focus consciousness on
several apparently contradictory objects: "He wants facts; he
wants science; but he also wants a religion." James could even
treat scientism as an alternative church itself. "I *can*, of course,
put myself into the sectarian scientist's attitude, and imagine viv-
idly that the world of sensations and of scientific laws and objects
may be all. But whenever I do this," he added, "I hear that inward
monitor of which W. K. Clifford once wrote, whispering the word
'bosh!'" His coda: "Humbug is humbug, even though it bear the
scientific name, and the total expression of human experience, as
I view it objectively, invincibly urges me beyond the narrow 'scientific' bounds."

6:6   Such language created problems for psychologists in the period
of clinical positivism that was to follow. It embarrassed many in
the academy who were content with purely scientific secularity.
James, however, had written the classic works—classic here
meaning works behind which one cannot get once they have been
established, because they provide the new terms—and has forced
students of American moderns to study them in their amplitude.

6:7   In 1896 James found himself standing over against both Clifford
and Thomas H. Huxley, who was the inventor of the term "agnosticism," because of what he thought was their naive faith in
conventional evidence. Clifford had claimed that "belief is dese-
crated when given to unproved and unquestioned statements, for
the solace and private pleasure of the believer." For Clifford, a belief accepted on insufficient evidence would issue in a situation in
which it was "wrong always, everywhere, and for anyone, to believe anything upon insufficient evidence." What was evidence?
James replied with a misnamed book, *The Will to Believe*. The
self-critical author later wished he had called it *Our Right to Be-*

lieve. James saw it as an "essay in justification *of* faith, a defence of our right to adopt a believing attitude in religious matters," even where our "merely logical intellect may not have been coerced."

6:8   L. T. Hobhouse attacked James, assigning to him two tenets: "The first is, that by believing a thing we make it true; the second is, that we can believe in a thing without asking ourselves seriously whether it is true or false." In his reply in 1904 against reductionism James almost lost his temper over such leading contemporaries who were "so smitten with blindness as to the meaning of printed texts." James thought that the problem of misunderstanding resulted from each person's writing out of a field of consciousness of which, he wrote, "the bogey in the background is the chief object. Your bogey is superstition; my bogey is desiccation." Each, "for his contrast-effect, clutches at any text that can be used to represent the enemy, regardless of exegetical proprieties." Here was a standoff. For James the evil shape was a vision of science in the form of "abstraction, priggishness and sawdust, lording it over all." He went on in the graphic language that purer philosophers were to find distasteful but which helped make the point: "Take the sterilest scientific prig and cad you know, compare him with the richest religious intellect you know, and you would not, any more than I would, give the former the exclusive right of way."

6:9   When it came to making a choice, James wrote as if autobiographically that "neutrality is not only inwardly difficult, it is also outwardly unrealizable, where our relations to an alternative are practical and vital." So he fused the viewpoints of agnostic and atheist alike in their notion that "our only way . . . of doubting, or refusing to believe, that a certain thing *is*, is continuing to act as if it were *not*." This meant to him that being agnostic, not-knowing, about the being of God must mean acting as if God does not exist. James did not thereby do justice to the category of doubt, which religionists themselves have seen in a creative zone between belief and nonbelief. Perhaps he tilted so easily toward belief in an age of science in order to compensate for the unbelief and then to minister to people adrift in his culture.

6:10   In 1906 in *Pragmatism* James enlarged upon the present dilemma in philosophy. People wanted a philosophy that would combine, he wrote, scientific loyalty to facts and willingness to take account of them, which we might call the modern project, with "the old confidence in human values and the resultant spontaneity, whether of the religious or of the romantic type." He spoke to and for many in his generation. "You find the two parts of your *quaesitum* hopelessly separated." James continued with personal language: "You find empiricism with inhumanism and ir-religion; or else you find a rationalistic philosophy that indeed may call itself religious, but that keeps out of all definite touch with concrete facts and joys and sorrows." This dilemma was James's own.

6:11   He spelled out the demands for decision, underlining them. An option must be *living*; it must be *forced*, so that there is no evad-ing it; it must be *momentous*, for the trivial does not belong here. Oft-quoted is his follow-up: "*Our passional nature not only law-fully may, but must, decide an option between propositions, whenever it is a genuine option that cannot by its nature be de-cided on intellectual grounds.*" To say under such circumstances "*'Do not decide but leave the question open,' is itself a passional decision—just like deciding yes or no—and is attended with the same risk of losing the truth.*" All this was very modern language, for historic faith, James knew, had usually been seen as deter-mined, as if it had passed through the genes, was enforced by law, or came with the territory. Now all was choice.

6:12   James called himself a pathfinder on this trail, seeking patterns of conduct which were consummated in religion, which was the focus of what he referred to as the genuinely strenuous life. When he had to define religion, he did so in individualist terms. These were neither institutional nor communal references, and this was another mark of the modern temper. Religion, he wrote, was "*the feelings, acts, and experiences of individual men in their solitude, so far as they apprehend themselves to stand in relation to what-ever they may consider the divine.*" Here James parted company with most of the reconstructive philosophers of his generation, people who had more problem than he with the notion of the di-vine but less than he with the notion of communalism in religion. He knew, he said, that reason's task had been to redeem religion from unwholesome privacy, and to give public status and univer-sal right-of-way to its deliverances, but such rationality had also then led to a withering of faith. Faith now had to be engendered and secured anew. The public argument, if any, could follow later.

6:13   While James had problems with prayer and personal faith in God, he kept defending the validity of religious experience. In 1895 he had declared that the "so-called order of nature, which constitutes this world's experience, is only one portion of the total universe," and "there stretches beyond this visible world an unseen world of which we now know nothing positive, but in its relation to which the true significance of our present mundane life consists." Thus a person's religious faith meant essentially one's faith in the existence "of an unseen order of some kind in which the riddles of the natural order may be found explained." Worshipers of science closed their mind to this order in the interest of flat empirical verification. He thundered: "No! our science is a drop, our ignorance a sea." It was certain that the world of present natural knowledge is enveloped in a larger world of some sort, of whose residual properties one could frame no positive idea.

6:14   For all his striving, James could no more return to orthodoxy or inherited institutions than could Henry Adams. He advised students to take a bath in religion and then to have another bout with philosophy. James wrote pioneer psychologist James H. Leuba that he himself had no "living sense of commerce with a God," while he envied those who did. But he found "*something in me* which *makes response* when I hear utterances from that quarter made by others." He recognized that deeper voice, something telling him "'*thither lies truth*'" and was sure that this was not just old theistic prejudices of infancy. He wanted a religion consistent with radical empiricism and thus consistent with his own philosophy of metaphysical pluralism.

6:15   Emphatically, despite their parallel interests, he found nothing at all to celebrate in modernist Christianity which surrounded him in Unitarian and liberal Boston and Cambridge. The modernists were attuned to the scientific spirit, he admitted, and looked better to him than the "old hell-fire theology." Yet did the modernists minister to anyone but progressives who were at ease? Could they reach anyone with sick souls? Fashionable preachers were devoted not to magnifying consciousness of sin but to making little of it. Christian salvation of souls they regarded as "something sickly and reprehensible rather than admirable." The sanguine, muscular Christian character they touted looked like the heathenness that their foreparents repudiated. "I am not asking whether or not they are right, I am only pointing out the change." Yet modernists tied destiny to evolution and in his view laid ground for a new sort of religion of Nature, which he thought, had entirely displaced Christianity from the thought of a large part of his generation. Such evolutionary meliorists could devise doctrines of progress to match the needs of only the healthy-minded. James felt more congeniality with medieval mystics, ancient saints, even modern revivalists.

6:16   The philosopher was aware that change was both threatening and promising. In religion, as in the philosophic world, he detected "a loosening of old landmarks, a softening of oppositions, a mutual borrowing from one another on the part of systems anciently closed, and an interest in new suggestions." James could be as pastoral as he was programmatic. It was still possible to pass on word to the doubter that "tragedy is only provisional and partial, and shipwreck and dissolution not the absolutely final things. This need of an eternal moral order is one of the deepest needs of our breast." If James justified theism without finding an accessible theism of his own, he passed on to others the task of recognizing religious communalism, which they desired but had difficulty finding accessible.

6:17   The case of Charles S. Peirce, now regarded as America's seminal philosopher, is instructive. He devoted less consistent attention than James to religion. Peirce, who died in 1914, held no academic posts for the last quarter-century of his life. The university, therefore, could not replace the church as his community. He could only write about a common life that lay beyond his experience. "Whether men really have anything in common, so that the *community* is to be regarded as an end in itself" was, he thought, part of the most fundamental practical question people faced in respect to public institutions. Peirce himself could not reconcile science and religion at the base of community. After the scandal of a divorce that drove him from the academic community, he demonstrated his difficulty at even getting along with peers. Peirce critically bit hands that fed him, including those of James, who kept the name of Peirce before academics when they would not recognize the eccentric.

6:18   Peirce was a sort of post-Unitarian who directed his critical powers against perversions of faith. Then he attacked American idolatry of business, or the turning of Americanism into a religion. He could not easily follow Adams, James, or Santayana in their admiration of ascetic or aesthetic sensibilities. Monks to him were sleepwalkers, too otherworldly. Nor might faith in God turn out to be more than an attractive fancy. Belief, however, seemed a fundamental ingredient of the soul, as he put it, and one dared not dismiss it as a vicious or superstitious factor.

6:19   Peirce cherished belief but he held no brief for conventional ritual. "Why observe manners toward the Heavenly Father that an earthly father would resent as priggish?" he asked. Peirce instead connected faith with the impulse toward neighborly love, something that eluded the dampening effect of dogma. Yet if ritual and dogma were beyond him, their context in medieval life still looked attractive to him insofar as it pointed to organic, whole life in contrast to the differentiated and alienating modern ways. From that medieval church his contemporaries could learn much. Some of them did bring the best of the past into churches. He personally had no use for the institutions of that sort, but he appreciated those who, as he said, were willing to get down on their knees to their work inside the church.

6:20   In his later but still never settled years Peirce turned somewhat from his earlier celebration of science and spoke well of piety. Yet formal theology seemed to him to be a corruption. He proudly announced that he did not read it. When he touched on religion it was to recall the community of experience. He noted that such a community was folly to the very dogmatists who with their definition guarded its borders. The Episcopal church evidently began to seem attractive as an option, for the same reason it looked good to Ralph Adams Cram. Some accused Peirce of idealizing the little church in which he came to worship weekly. Peirce is hard to pin down. His formal religious expressions in philosophy are relatively rare. If his God turned out to be not the classic subject of theism but was seen only as a different name for a certain Gestalt of experience, it became valuable to aging and often embittered Peirce. This man of contradictions fused medieval instincts with occasionally optimistic views of science and progress. Finding no lures in theological modernism, this founder of modern American philosophy concentrated on the virtues of religious community while continuing to have problems expressing relations, beginning with friendship. He was the perpetual outsider with, in this case, a corrective philosophy that was designed for life inside the circle of believers.

6:21   Of all the classic moderns, Josiah Royce found most congenial the inherited Christian language, symbols, and intentions. His original intentions, more than most, matched the outcomes. A Harvard faculty member from 1882 to his death in 1916, Royce crowded his book titles with such words as "Religious" or "God" or "Christianity." While orthodoxy of the sort his mother taught the child in California formally slipped away, Royce refilled its space with devotion to devotion and loyalty to loyalty. He supported his sense of community with Christian dimensions, using a terminology freighted with biblical language. A monist who apparently left little room for freedom of the personality, he saw the individual as part of the organic life of God. In the face of the atomizing tendencies of modernity, his problem was establishing the individual, the fragment of the absolute; so Royce spent much energy on the question.

6:22   This meant that, having rejected the institutional church, he also had to find an *ecclesia*, a community of ideas, belief, and conduct that merited loyalty. In *The Philosophy of Loyalty* he made the theme of loyalty to loyalty a step toward humanity's supreme good. It must be a community of interpretation, a contention Royce set against the claims of individualism. True community, he wrote, as if over against the New Historians, "is essentially a product of a time-process. . . . A community requires for its existence a history and is greatly aided in its consciousness by a memory."

6:23   Such lavish praise for loyalty, seconded by support for Christian-like theories of atonement, came, then, from still another philosopher who found a problem in inherited institutions. Royce was never an adult member of a congregation, but he did confess that some of his distaste for the church as it was was jejune. Far from moving thereupon into simple secularity, he spoke fervently about the idea of salvation, a theme in his mother's Puritan faith. In *The Sources of Religious Insight* he sounded almost like an evangelist diagnostician as he spoke of "some vast and universal burden, of imperfection, of unreasonableness, of evil, of misery, of fate, of unworthiness, or of sin" which forces the search for salvation. In *The Problem of Christianity* in 1913 Royce linked this search with loyalty to community, and matched Christ's call for the kingdom of heaven in the Sermon on the Mount with his own philosophy of loyalty.

6:24   Nowhere did Royce work harder to fight the individualizing trend of modernity than in long passages on modern man in *The Problem of Christianity*. In eloquent paragraphs he asked, "Can the modern man consistently hold a Christian creed?" and "Who is this modern man?" He found the modern man to be a convenient fiction, a creature of the day. "To-morrow some other sort of modern man must take his place." Yet he saw that the term capsuled into a word the postulate that the human race has been subject to some more or less coherent process of education. The modern man is the one who knows something of this lesson. So, Royce must respond with a defense of religion.

6:25   Religion is first of all a product of certain needs. It would be doomed were it to cease strengthening hearts or fulfilling the just

demands of the human spirit for guidance through the wilderness
of the world. Second, religion is problematic because of the workings of the law of accelerated change, which, thought Royce,
would gain ever more force. Third, modernity displaced religious
institutions from their central position in organized social life. In
medieval times, to remove them would have been to undercut society. In modern times, were such agencies suspended, commerce
and business would go on unaffected. Religion obviously has little
official support in institutionalized modernity. True, he suggested,
no reasonable man ought for a moment to underestimate the actual vitality of the religious institutions of the Christian world,
viewed simply as institutions. No one, however, could rely on
even their powerful vestiges in times of drastic change.

6:26   What, then, of the future? Royce admired those who called for
individualized mystical piety. One almost hears him responding to
William James. Tomorrow's religion could not be based on arguments about divine revelation. Instead it depended upon essential
Christian ideas and experiences so broad that they would match
every conceivable future. Again, they focused on the interaction
of community and loyalty. "Man the individual is essentially insufficient to win the goal of his own existence. Man the community is the source of salvation." So the Christian doctrine of life
was neither mere morality nor mere mysticism but "community
itself." By now Royce had worked himself into a problem comparable to Adams's. Adams advertised the integrity of medieval en-
ergetic faith in the Virgin and then found it inaccessible for moderns. Royce advertised the integrity of timeless community in the
Pauline senses but then showed how modern life did not allow for
its authentic expression. However remote these concerns were
from those of many academic contemporaries, Royce did give
further evidence that significant moderns did not accept modernity on simply secular terms.

6:27   If this portrayal of James, Peirce, and Royce finds too much
congeniality for religious faith, too little reckoning with skepticism, then George Santayana, Harvard philosopher from 1889 to
1912, provides a challenging contrast. Decisively post-Catholic,
he had seen the substance of faith disappear in the parental generation, but kept a career-long interest in religion. He looked back
with Adams and Cram and others to medieval Catholic aesthetics
and scorned accommodating modernist Protestants who were in
love with the Zeitgeist of banality. One aspect of his philosophy
can also be seen as a striving for an *ecclesia* to replace the com-

munity of Catholicism that now seemed beyond grasp. He continued to set himself down "officially as a Catholic," but, he remarked, "this is a matter of sympathy and traditional allegiance, not of philosophy." His mother had been a Deist. To his parents religion was a work of human imagination, not faith in any dogma or in the Christian epic that he admired from a distance. "I was never afraid of disillusion," he said, "and I have chosen it." Remarkably, Santayana carried this over to the field of modern science, which was another imaginative system to be mistrusted.

6:28   As a reporter on his times, Santayana was impressed by the millions of modern Americans who regarded their ancestral Catholicism sincerely and affectionately, full as it was, he said, of large disillusions about this world and minute illusions about the other. Catholicism was, in his terms, ancient, metaphysical, poetic, elaborate, ascetic, autocratic, and intolerant, and thus at the antipodes to everything in modern American life. It was also anathema, one might add, to modernist Protestants, who saw no future for anything attached to seven such adjectives. Yet it prospered, and the American Catholic was entirely at peace. "His tone in everything, even in religion, is cheerfully American." So he lives silently, amicably, and happily in a community whose spirit was profoundly hostile to that of his religion. The Catholic had no serious conflict with Protestant neighbors. Santayana grasped the modern covenant accurately. Catholic and Protestant religions, he said, "pass among them for family matters, private and sacred, with no political implications."

6:29   Santayana also carried this puzzled and ambivalent vision of religion to the rest of America. It was a country with two mentalities. One represented the hereditary spirit, the beliefs and standards of the founders in all the higher things of the mind, in religion, in literature, in the moral emotions. With England's George Bernard Shaw he found this America to be a hundred years behind the times. Yet the other mentality expressed instincts, practices, and discoveries of the younger generations. This one lived not in the colonial mansion but the skyscraper. Santayana thought that what kept the former style going, even in someone as notable as Josiah Royce, was no distinctive Christian belief but simply the agonized conscience about sin, a conscience Santayana himself never inherited.

6:30   Now this conscientious Calvinism was being transformed but not being left behind. In America, he charged, there was but one way of being saved, though it was not peculiar to any of the offi-

cial religions, which themselves must silently conform to the national orthodoxy, or else become impotent and merely ornamen-
tal. This national faith and morality, however vague in spirit, were
inexorable in fact. "They are the gospel of work and the belief in
progress." This Anglo-Saxon piety of trust and adaptability ap-
proximated in its power old speculative religious asceticisms. It
was the old Protestant ethic, though Santayana did not call it this
name. It showed Americans that they must renounce their wills
and deny themselves.

6:31   America had a philosopher, Santayana seemed on the verge of
calling him theologian, in John Dewey, who was in his eyes the
devoted spokesman of the spirit of enterprise, of experiment, of
modern industry. This man's philosophy was calculated to justify
all the assumptions of American society. Over against him was
William James, who would only psychologize the individual. This
summary judgment from 1936 still poised Santayana's citizens
classically between modern and traditional outlooks. "American
opinion is largely pre-American." This was proven even in choices
of allegiance by citizens. Americans were loyal, he thought, "not
out of rapt speculative sympathy, but because such allegiance
seems an insurance against moral dissolution, guaranteeing social
cohesion and practical success."

6:32   However much he differed from his contemporaries, Santayana
at least wistfully looked for an *ecclesia* beyond the church. While
Peirce found it personally difficult to repose in the university,
Santayana, more at home there, did see the severe limits of its current potential. The professionals there, he said, had "but cursory
and wretched notions of the inner life of the mind." These were
dead to patriotism and to religion. In medieval and New England
pasts, the "fundamental questions have been settled by the church,
the government, or the Zeitgeist," so the professor only transmitted lore across generations, adding a few original touches.
Philosophers then, at least, had a sense of responsibility, as if they
had been clergymen. Now they were lonely, isolated, necessarily
self-reliant because they were "like clergymen without a church."
They had no common philosophic doctrine to transmit. The modern university had to be representative, pluralist, even allowing atheism. Yet it left James and Royce and, he might have said,
Santayana himself in an ambiguous situation. Precisely because it
was so differentiated and pluralist, the modern university could
not be the *ecclesia* to fulfil Santayana's dream of aesthetic and
moral community.

6:33   In the end Santayana, still wistful about medieval Catholic sensibilities, remained disillusioned about finding true religion or
community in modern America. Antispiritual enterprise and the
business mentality dominated everything. Even religion was
collapsed into a matter of meetings, building-funds, schools,
charities, clubs, and picnics. When there was any sign of any
deeper understanding of religion, he noticed, it came neither from
orthodoxy nor modernism, but from the aspirations of new forms
of popular religion, not mere variations on tradition: revivalism,
spiritualism, Christian Science, the New Thought.

6:34   So Santayana joined James, Royce, and Peirce in being a modern who was uneasy about modernity. Along with others he repudiated the modernist adaptations in religion. He was an emancipated
person who never became a simple believer in science or in progress. All of these philosophers made room for spiritual experience
that defied conventionally empirical boundaries. The directions to
which they pointed were as often closed doors as open ones. The
irretrievable medieval organicism in society or a metaphysics that
could not enter modern imagination offered little promise. What
was left, they were the first to agree, was a sterile and yet busy
public religiosity, thoroughly plebeian, which made efforts toward
physiological economy and hygiene. It offered, said Santayana,
no great heights to raise people from the most vulgar and hum-
drum worldly existence. The popular religions did at least see the
possibility of physical and moral health on that common plane
and pursued it. He asked of other alternatives, "What does it
profit a man to free the whole world if his soul is not free?" The
most despised religions might address the spirit. Meanwhile, critics like Santayana were latter-day prophets come to judge the
churches of their day, but skeptical about salvation for themselves.

7

In Search of an *Ecclesia*

7:1   The word "social" acquired new social power at the turn of the century. Sociology, social settlement, social service, a Social Gospel, and social philosophy all were invented. While there had been social implications in the thought of the more standard philosophers, there rose also a less formal school of applied-philosophy pioneers: Charles Cooley, George Herbert Mead, Jane Addams, Thorstein Veblen, and philosopher John Dewey were among them. Whatever their personal religion, if any was obvious, they intended to help provide syntheses and programs that were ready for democratic and pluralist America. Thus their philosophy had to be non-Jewish and non-Christian, in no way reliant on synagogue or church. They were moderns who must find new forms of dealing with the modernity they were all somehow ready to encounter.

7:2   The first of them, Charles Cooley, remained most congenial to the inherited patterns. The others struck out on their own. Yet he too came close to devising surrogates for and corollaries to the historic social religious forms. He ministered to the hunger for wholeness that modernity had bred by its differentiation of orders in life. Charles Horton Cooley, lifelong Michigander and professor at its university in Ann Arbor throughout his career, represents the easiest case for religion. In conventional terms, he was least modern, most ready to transport inherited religious ideals and forms into actions and agencies designed to minister to the

76

needs of contemporaries. However much he must transform these he had the least difficulty wedding them to social thought. He was personally most at home in the vestigial religious institution. Cooley was the diagnostician of individualism and its limits along with the alienation he thought it was causing. So strong was this tradition, he wrote during World War I, that Americans and the British seemed hardly permitted to aspire toward an ideal society. Attempts to build such a society on the competitive market of business must fail. He would work to see society itself stand behind or shape authority. For Cooley and his colleagues, the self, which the previous generation of Social Darwinists had celebrated, dared never pose over against society. The two evolved in relation to each other.

7:3   Cooley lived out his adolescence under a very strong father, himself a professor and a judge. He made his move from constriction by diffusing the concept of authority. Cooley came to see society as "an interweaving and interworking of mental selves." For such development there must be small interpersonal groups and encounters. This meant also that he had to relativize the authoritarianism he found in Christianity just as he used cherished Christian themes to endow small social clusters with validity.

7:4   As a student at the University of Michigan in 1893, Cooley heard John Dewey lecture. He chose to take from Dewey the question of how one communicates in what was becoming a mass society. This meant to him that technology eroded face-to-face groups and jeopardized community. All the while, the growth of mass communications should have made it possible for an impersonal and remote public to share opinions more efficiently than ever before. By 1909, when Cooley wrote *Social Organization*, it was becoming ever more clear that such technology left the individual trapped. "That spiritual identification of the member with the whole" was his ideal of organization, but in modernity life, he thought, was "full of a confusion which often leaves the individual conscious only of his separateness, engaged in a struggle which, so far as he sees, has no more relation to justice and the common good than a dog-fight." Josiah Royce could hardly have said it better. Technology dared not be neglected, so it must be taken over to help engender the sense of community, the sharing in a common social or spiritual whole. Membership in this gave to all a kind of inner equality, no matter what their various roles. All this occurred through family, small group, and cell, the primary groups that had to be the norms for all disjointed society.

7:5   Two sections of *Social Organization* systematically enlarged on the religious theme. Cooley began one in a congratulatory mood. "The democratic movement, insomuch as it feels a common spirit in all men, is of the same nature as Christianity." While the world "was never so careless as now of the mechanism of religion, it was never so Christian in feeling." The teachings of Jesus provided the mind, which in its best moments was "naturally Christian," with the elements for a deeper sense of a common life. Therefore, he concluded, "Christ and modern democracy alike represent a protest against whatever is dead in institutions, and an attempt to bring life closer to the higher impulses of human nature." Both the modern democrat and Jesus are and were plain people. Was it any wonder then that the characteristic thought of the day was preponderantly Christian, even—and here was a nice turn—in the sense that when "it distrusts the Church it is on the ground that the Church is not Christian enough." Democracy, it is true, tended to secularize religious sentiment in the sense that otherworldliness now represented what was not secular. Why, he asked, dream of a world to come when there is hopeful activity in this? Social service was to him now a method of worship. God was to be found in human life as well as beyond it.

7:6   The church also belonged in his chapter on disorganization, and Cooley was realistic about this. His good cheer still often won through. Irreligion, he thought, was exaggerated. If formalism, materialism, and infidelity existed, they had flourished in all epochs. He cheered Americans by noting Lord James Bryce's comment that Christian influences were stronger on conduct in America than anywhere else. A sign of vitality was also the fact that criticism came from the prophets within, not from carpers outside the church. "We need religion, probably, as much as any age can have needed it." The church, even the church, could be a useful reinforcement for this. "We cannot hold our minds to the higher life without a form of thought." This proposition led Cooley to oppose iconoclasm on the part of intellectual anarchists who thought moderns could "dispense with institutions." Existing creeds, it was true, were incredible, but modern ones could emerge. Cooley's hopeful note remained. Systems should give way to symbols of personality. In any case, he pressed, "never was it more urgent or more difficult to justify the ways of God to men." It is easy to make Cooley sound more reposed than he was, for the reforms he called for were radical. Yet there was also a coherence in his whole endeavor to be modern and religious, to criticize the church and draw from it. He confided to his journal how his vocation and philosophy united. "Sociology is to me in so far a religion that it is a way of seeing life as an onward whole, as the manifestation of God."

7:7   Usually mentioned in the same paragraphs with Cooley is George Herbert Mead, a social philosopher of much greater social power but who underpublished and was thus less influential in his lifetime. By the time we come to Mead there is a temptation to anticipate some biographical details, so typical were they. He came from a small town, was churched, Protestant, the son of a gifted mother, who was also president of Mount Holyoke College, and a father who taught preaching. Mead later claimed to have spent twenty years unlearning the religion of his first twenty. Continue the predictable biographical comments: Mead went to church-related Oberlin College in Ohio, contemplated studying for the ministry, but with friend Henry Castle found their philosophical support for Christianity shattered.

7:8   Agnostic at graduation in 1883, both young men claimed they wanted to rebuild their faith and philosophy. While serving a stint as a high-school teacher Mead experienced a breakdown. Since he lacked faith he could not be a minister, so he and Castle went to Germany to find a grounding in metaphysics. Letters from Castle in this period suggest something of their self-emancipating mood. In 1888 he spoke of America as a place "where poor, hated un-happy Christianity, trembling for its life, claps the gag into the mouth of Free Thought and says 'Hush, hush, not a word or no-body will believe in me anymore.'" Such language typified ado-lescence and did not reach the depths both sought. Castle also spoke of "the preposterous system by which the sects in America have taken possession of the higher education," so that scien-tifically heretical facts needed what he called official method-istical or congregational pats on the back.

7:9   Castle died young. Mead worked his way back to a fabric of meaning, apart from the old supernaturalism. He was briefly em-ployed at the University of Michigan and then, in 1894, at the young University of Chicago. There he became a close friend of John Dewey and other pioneer pragmatists with whom his name was henceforth linked. Mead's original statements sound much like Dewey's, having to do, as they did, with the self and society. People communicate and connect, Mead argued, when they share symbols out of which possible shared social meanings may grow. In the modern world such meanings could not derive from any absolute origin in God, they are simply a part of social process. That said, however, Mead could recognize the validity of religious ritual as a provider of meaning that transcended workaday experience. Consistently, this provision was of an aesthetic, not transcendental, character and, equally consistently, it was important because of its social context.

7:10   So it turned out that the conflict with supernature and theology did not lead Mead to expunge roles for ritual, symbol, or religion. Over against Nietzsche's need to announce the death of God, Mead knew God as a generalized other. A kind of metareligiousness survived the end of supernature. Mead in *Mind, Self, and Society* could even speak favorably of "certain universal forms which found their expression in universal religions and also in universal economic processes." In the religious case, these were all grounded in fundamental human attitudes of helpfulness, kindliness, and assistance. The generalization of all these is behind the universal religions. Thus, he wrote, it is "out of universal cooperative activity, that the universal religions have arisen." Witness, in Christianity, the power of the Good Samaritan story.

7:11   How find the largest social context for the self? The churches could not suffice for this search. Was the nation capable of bearing the universal? Mead had the experience in World War I with which to reckon. In every war, he knew both sides emphasized the national character of the religion of the people, so deity was divided in allegiance and could not help. For socialists, the labor movement became a religion. Mead examined the tribe or the smaller communities that Cooley favored: "The religion gathered about the cult of a community becomes very concrete." It comes even to be identified with the near history and life of the community, and is then most conservative. One can almost hear Mead reflecting on his childhood congregational life. The cult, he said, tends to fix the character of the religious expression so that, in effect, the institution becomes an idol. The cosmopolitan habit or universalizing goal is thus thwarted by such institutions.

7:12   On other pages Mead could sound more sanguine about the prospect of a universalizing religious community. East and West *were* meeting, no matter what Rudyard Kipling had said. A symbol of a blessed community remained, resting on cooperative activities in the form of a kind of cosmic neighborliness. The definite field within which the religious experience appears, Mead thought, was the place which gave social stimulus to the world at large. With every one of the moderns, he found a need to attack theology. It had a bad name for having set out to narrow and confine the experience. Mead was less sure than James about the validity of mysticism, which was usually too nonsocial. On occasion, a kind of practical and transcendent teamwork led to an authentic religious expression. Mead could sound like Dewey or even Rousseau when he discerned the social order, in his case characterized by democracy, bearing a religious character.

7:13   Mead seemed to be poised with Peirce and Royce, having first pushed aside institutional religion and then established the need for a social faith. How work back to any organized community? Mead developed answers to this in two papers which, because they were not published, have to be described more as revealing than influential. Social religion must be enhoused, he argued, but not in cultic form. One must lift religious emotions above self-indulgence. He went on to say that this would exist in "keeping before consciousness ideas which cannot pass into action, in stimulating certain valuable activities which have through ritual a symbolic meaning [,] and finally in assisting to abstract from hemming and confining environment and so giving opportunity to other activities to come to expression." Those dense lines are a sophisticated translation of what people in churches often contended they were also doing. Mead seemed to be aware of this, for here he could speak favorably of even Methodist revivals, evangelist Jonathan Edwards, who opened the way for the larger politics of the revolution, and later revivalists and preachers like Charles G. Finney or Lyman Beecher and other evangelicals in antislavery movements. Few thinkers on the social side of James singled out so many representatives of church religion as did Mead in this context.

7:14   In the other paper Mead connected his psychology of emotion to John the Baptist and Jesus as universalizers of love in the symbol of the kingdom of heaven. All are welcome to the kingdom on equal terms. Jesus broke the bounds of the inherited cult, but his church formed a new one. Despite such tendencies, religion more than economics can be the life force. It takes you "into the immediate inner attitude of the other individual; you are identifying yourself with him in so far as you are assisting him, helping him, saving his soul, aiding him in this world or the world to come—your attitude is that of salvation of the individual." Mead had come a long way from where he and Henry Castle found themselves in the years in Germany. He knew the promise and the limits of the modern condition. Had he felt at home with the supernatural God of the churches, he could almost have written tracts in support of their potential social power.

7:15   While academic theology and philosophy at the time had no room for women, in no small measure because women were denied access to the places in higher education where their professions prospered, social philosophy was different. As Cooley and Mead knew and as Dewey in the public schools displayed, such thought developed best in social institutions and social work, where applied and pragmatic styles were at a premium. Here women were coming into their own. Most notable among the pioneering generation was Jane Addams, who, biographers say, was even taking on the image of secular sainthood at the time when her pacifism during World War I compromised her.

7:16   She had the same struggles of childhood and youth as her male colleagues, though she shared a Quaker upbringing as genial as Charles Beard's. From Cedarville, Illinois, she went to Rockford Female Seminary instead of the Smith College she wished to attend. There she lived a mildly rebellious life and made the most of tutoring in the classics and other boons. Given her later reputation for agnosticism, it is interesting to see that she still found a way, using British thinkers Thomas Carlyle and John Ruskin as guides, to make religion come out right. The success of a person's calling, she wrote as a collegian, depended upon her religion. She must settle the religious issue creatively to meet each new challenge. Since Addams discovered its importance on her own, she must build up her religion eclectically, from the Bible and books and people and Carlyle. "I only feel that I need religion in a practical sense, that if I could fix my relations to God & the universe, & so be in perfect harmony with nature & deity, I could use my faculties and energy so much better and could do almost anything." Such controlled striving gave religion such a generous place that Addams seems not to fit the pattern. Yet the constrictive conservatism of Rockford did keep damping her free spirit. She developed a kind of private universal Primal Cause faith. Christianity was only a branch or epiphany of that.

7:17   In Italy the medieval religious aesthetic achievements reached her as they lured so many of her tourist peers. Somewhere along the way she was baptized, but had a deeper conversion experience in 1888 in Spain. Addams had seen a bullfight and then examined her own involvement in the ritual. She then reacted negatively to it and to herself in its presence. She came up with a new vision of living. Tolstoy was then in vogue, and he also influenced her, but she suspended metaphysical and mystical searches to pursue her practical route. Soon she found her way to Chicago, where she founded Hull House, a social settlement. Women like Florence Kelley, Alice Hamilton, Julia Lathrop, and Ellen Starr only headed a list of social-work colleagues. Some of them worked with Sophonisba Breckinridge, Grace and Edith Abbott, and other University of Chicago worthies. A true sisterhood developed, with some ties to men like Mead and Dewey at the University of Chicago. With them Addams developed her own pragmatic thought, just as she applied forms of Darwinism toward social improvement. Addams had a gift for combining apparently contradictory elements and philosophies, including a passionate highly personal faith with skeptical styles, and treated the combination religiously.

7:18   Addams diagnosed the modern world in terms matching Emile Durkheim's division of labor. She saw in it the breakdown of social feelings and interdependence, with resulting anomie. With some of the historians she analyzed problems of technology and then drew on the past to humanize work. At Hull House in 1900 she founded a tool-filled Labor Museum. The worker, she thought, needed "the conception of historic continuity in order to reveal to him the purpose and utility of his work."

7:19   The culture's inherited religions seemed increasingly inaccessible and ignorable. In a journal article in 1899 Addams observed that as the college had shifted from teaching theology to teaching secular knowledge, so "the test of its successes should have shifted from the power to save men's souls to the power to adjust them in healthful relations to nature and their fellow men." This it had failed to do, and the knowledge it disseminated had no practical purpose. She sounded here like Mead in *Democracy and Social Ethics*, in respect to her desire to stimulate what she called moral connection. It would arrive only if workers grasped a sense of participation and a certain joy in its ultimate use. This seemed to be a difficult but not impossible idealization. Here as often Addams stopped short of explicit religious symbolization. She could not turn easily to formal religion and she knew it. For a time she joined a Congregational church near Hull House, but her career with it was spotty. When clergy criticized her for turning humanitarianism into a religion she wrote, "I needed religion only in a practical sense . . . to be in harmony with nature and deity." In that sense, she was still the young woman of Rockford Female Seminary, when she projected the very life she turned out to live.

7:20   If Jane Addams and her colleagues made their way alongside the academy, maverick economic thinker Thorstein Veblen, another shaper of the modern outlook, moved in and out of it. Erratic, eccentric, vagrant, womanizing, unstable, ironic, contradictory— words such as these are regularly applied to the Wisconsin-born son of Norwegian immigrants, a peasant-looking man of bad manners and lively insights. Veblen, predictably, was predestined by his immigrant parents for Lutheran ministry and shipped off one day in 1874 to the latter-day Puritan college, Carleton, at Northfield, Minnesota. This pioneer school had gifted and influential professors but never a scope wide enough for Veblen, dubbed a misfit by his most notable professor. Veblen demonstrated his marginality to the faculty with speeches on drinking and eating, "Apology for a Toper," and "Plea for Cannibalism."

7:21   It did not take Veblen long to break all restraints, declare himself an atheist, and head for graduate schools. Charles S. Peirce impressed him at Johns Hopkins, John Dewey wrote letters of recommendation for him, and he gulped drafts of Social Darwinism at Yale under the noted William Graham Sumner. Veblen emerged in 1884 with a Ph.D. Somehow he could never fit into an academic track, though the infant University of Chicago endured him for fourteen years after its founding in 1892. During this time his famed *The Theory of the Leisure Class* made him as famous as his womanizing and slovenliness made him infamous. Veblen wandered off to the edges of Stanford in California and the University of Missouri. A classic marginal person who erupted from the obscurity he usually sought with occasional literary appearances in the form of memorable books, Veblen added words to the vocabulary of American economics and social thought and left a mark at the periphery of mainline philosophy.

7:22   Many have seen Veblen as a foil for Max Weber, who connected the Protestant ethic with the spirit of capitalism. This was a voguish and urgent turn-of-the-century topic, given the fact that Americans were busy making sense of their new economic order. While Weber worried about *Rationalität*, an all-embracing principle of order that marked modern bureaucracy and threatened the life of the spirit as it was linked to technology, Veblen, a critic of capitalism, showed no fear of such rationality. When he was hopeful, he even hoped for a republic run by technologues and engineers.

7:23   As he struggled to make sense of conspicuous consumption in popular America, Veblen also criticized the kinds of patriotism

that were emerging around World War I. Patriotism was a throw-
back to primitive tribal life. It was bent on "invidious success,
which must involve as its major purpose the defeat and humilia-
tion of some competitor." Not all people displayed this tribal
mentality, he thought, yet the nation as a whole acted upon it.
Some villains, he thought, must be propagating its ideals. Veblen
found these in the captains of industry. People had to be protected
from these captains. The patriotic sentiment, he wrote, never has
been known to rise to the consummate pitch of enthusiastic abandon except when bent on some work of concentrated malev-
olence. Veblen saw no spiritual prospect in the touted patriotism
of his days. Its final appeal, he thought, was for the death, damage, discomfort, and destruction of the party of the second part.

7:24   Criticizing captains of capitalism was not sufficient. In the
libraries, basement apartments, and cubbyholes where Veblen
worked, he knew he had to come up with provocative alternatives.
His original intention was to look to a utopia of engineers and
technological managers who would somehow magically and mys-
tically help produce a democratic state, a humane society. To
make that case which all his critics have found to be wildly para-
doxical, he needed a lever. While Veblen did not convince his critics of the soundness of his approach, he remains interesting for
the way this postreligious, avowedly atheistic thinker chose to
draw his models from the Christianity he had no use for already
back in Carleton days.

7:25   Without mentioning Weber but having him in mind, as the references hint, Veblen in 1910 tried to present his alternative. He
called his essay, "Christian Morals and the Competitive System."
It fulfils the theme of Hobsbawm. Veblen was like an immigrant
into a new era, and though he sounded utopian, he looked backward as much as forward for paradigms. He had to unearth Christian evidences that went back more centuries than did those Weber
offered when he linked Protestantism with the rise of capitalism.
Veblen did reach back further, much further, to earliest Christianity. Both parts of his program were found paralleled there. For his
critique of patriotism, Veblen there discovered humble people
who practiced nonresistance. As opposed to being capitalists,
they were communalists who experienced a high degree of mutuality. The love Christians showed as a revolutionary moral principle grew out of a spiritual attitude marking their daily behavior.
This meant that primitive Christianity and its pure heirs prospered
among the oppressed and the victimized, not among the master

classes. Corrupt forms, then, linked up with modern capitalism, which he thought was born of non- and anti-Christian outlooks. Now sounding Marxist, Veblen analyzed the alienation of moderns, who lived suspended between the ideals of Christianity and capitalist greed. People and cultures could not permanently live such contradictions.

7:26   Here is where backward-looking Veblen showed a forward-looking utopian passion. He somehow hoped that this humble spirit of Christian mutuality might rise up and attack business, which, he said, had taken on the character of an impersonal, dispassionate, not to say graceless, investment for profit. Yet he had invested little in such Christianity and could have pointed to little faith of that type in the America of 1910. What is more, Veblen had already propounded beliefs in progress that were not compatible with the notion of regress to primitive Christianity. In short, he had invested more hope in the engineers than in St. Paul or the Book of Acts in the Bible. He seemed not to notice that the engineers and budding bureaucrats of technology were already defenders of the capitalist status quo, perhaps the least likely class to be moved by primitive Christianity or Thorstein Veblen's dreams. And yet, once again a most radical critic and progressive showed how difficult it was to leave behind religion in general and, in American culture, Christianity in particular.

7:27   Christianity in general, but not religion in particular, was what the half-century's dominant social philosopher left behind. John Dewey, Vermont-born, shared the kind of small-town, small-church background whose constrictions called for emancipation but whose ethos contributed to the development of genius. He shared the Calvinist and Puritan roots of the other shapers of classic American social thought. Dewey's mother, a warm and nurturing sort within a mild Congregationalism, probably wrote the document to certify his Christianity at age eleven: "I think I love Christ and want to obey him. I have thought for some time I should like to unite with the church. . . ."

7:28   Later Dewey would speak of the "inward laceration" that New England culture had effected in him because of the "divisions by way of isolation of self from the world, of soul from body, of nature from God" that it produced. Yet the burden did not seem too deep for him. He phased gradually out of the old faith, claiming but one mystical experience in his life back when he taught at Oil City, Pennsylvania, High School. There was in it no drama, no vision, no emotion, just a supremely blissful feeling that his worries were over. He added, "I've never had any doubts since then, nor any beliefs."

7:29   That retrospect was exaggerated, for Dewey remained expressive about his beliefs as a young University of Michigan professor. He did not drop out of church life until he went to teach at the University of Chicago during the 1890s. In the 1880s he spoke in rather orthodox terms to the Student Christian Association at Ann Arbor. These began to be liberalized in later addresses like one on "The Relation of the Present Philosophic Movement in Religious Thought" or, in March of 1892, on "Christianity and Democracy." The latter introduced implicitly themes that became explicit throughout Dewey's career. His Terry Lectures of 1934, *A Common Faith*, synthesized his religious views long after World War I, but they were in perfect continuity with the informal probes the philosopher had issued ever since 1892.

7:30   Already at Ann Arbor the public philosopher began to reflect on what a modern consciousness was. It represented freedom, so that one could live, he said, "free negatively, free from sin, free positively, free to live his own life, free to express himself." The little Burlington Church or even Ann Arbor Congregationalism was not the best *ecclesia* or social form for expressing this freedom. Churches were too divided and dogmatic to fill this role. Dewey therefore offered a daring leap. The new base and scope must be "the Commonwealth, the Republic, the public affair," which he always treated in such a way that it was not to be reduced to the jingoist patriotism Veblen criticized.

7:31   Deftly and boldly Dewey transferred at once the attributes of the *una sancta*, the one holy church, to the public body. Democracy, not the church, he claimed, was "the means by which the revelation of truth is carried on." The church would survive in modernity, as a place but "one among the various forces of social life." There it would cooperate with other sources "on an equal basis for the furtherance of the common end." Dewey told ministers-to-be that tomorrow's prophet would be the one who succeeded in pointing out the religious meaning of democracy, the ultimate religious value to be found in the normal flow of life itself.

7:32   Clearly, here was an alternative *ecclesia*, but a necessary one for Dewey's educational ideal. Sometimes he sounded as if the public school was to be the new established church. Clearly atheistic, he found a need to reach for language familiar to the religious. Thus in *Reconstruction in Philosophy* in 1920 Dewey could write that "when the emotional force, the mystic force one might say, of communication, of the miracle of shared life and shared experience is spontaneously felt, the hardness and crudeness of contemporary life will be bathed in the light that never was on land or sea." This quasi-mystical faith in social communication was built on what five years earlier he called a naturalistic metaphysics, one which concentrated on the community of meanings and on shared experience.

7:33   Dewey rather consistently attributed to science the virtues religion once offered, and liked to speak in terms of "faith" in science and social communication. He could chide those who lapsed, who lost faith. He recognized that every forward step in science demanded a readjustment of institutional life, and he found that this was most difficult when it came "closest to man— his social relationships"; such steps moved slowly. Ernest Renan in France had once held the faith but lost it in the face of the slowness of change. Dewey thought that eventually science could prevail ("I cannot but think that the Renan of '48 was wiser than he of '90") and all his life believed that "faith in scientific method: would be "manifest in social works," toward the end of human good.

7:34   This is not to say that overt religion was as near the center of Dewey's consciousness as it was to James's or Royce's. Not until 1934 did he write his book on the subject. He seemed to be diffident when talking about religion until then, perhaps to minimize confusion about what he meant or to prevent stigmatization by those who could consider such talk unscientific. His Chicago Ph.D. student Douglas Clyde Macintosh, later a reputed theologian, remembered Dewey seeing religion as "essentially pre-scientific." He had been eager, said the student, to eradicate from philosophy "the last vestiges of the positively religious view of the universe." If that was his intention, however, the unfolding of his life program did not permit its carrying out.

7:35   In some ways, *A Common Faith* showed Dewey moving beyond modernity, with its differentiation and specialization or, in the religious case, its denominationalism. In *Human Nature and Conduct* in 1922 he spoke of religion "as a sense of the whole," and this was consistent in his approach lifelong. It was disruptive, he thought, even in a secular society to have to choose a separating and distancing faith. So he moved beyond talking about a religion, or religions, and wanted to speak in holistic terms of religious experience. God came then to mean the "*active* relation between ideal and actual." God: why did an atheistic social philosopher

reach backward for the syllable that had come to represent the par-
ticularities? He did not mean God as first cause, ground of being,
or, certainly, God the Father of Abraham, Isaac, Jacob, and Jesus
Christ. Some called Dewey's God-concept Kantian and his religiousness, like Buddhism's, nontheistic. Yet he expressed a natural piety, as he called it, which he said was "not of necessity either
a fatalistic acquiescence in natural happenings or a romantic
idealization of the world." This natural piety Dewey turned against
supernaturalist or private faith. He called it an "essentially un-
religious attitude . . . which attributes human achievement and
purpose to man in isolation from the world of physical nature and
his fellows." Supernatural Christianity, he urged, for social purposes must yield its division between sheep and goats; the saved
and the lost; the elect and the mass. In the natural world is where
one locates the signs of faith. Once upon a time doubt dealt with
"inaccessible supernatural" lurkings, whereas now it inspires inquiry in order that we may find out natural things.

7:36   Dewey, then, was a modern who attacked the modern expression of differentiated religion. Religions as he knew them always
signified, as he said, "a special body of beliefs and practices
having some kind of institutional organization." Thus it was separated from the social and public whole. Tomorrow's common faith
was a search which would harmonize the whole "self with the
Universe (as a name for the totality of conditions with which the
self is connected)." Faith, then, was "the unification of the self
through allegiance to inclusive ideal ends."

7:37   Dewey knew he was by then on religious soil. He ended *A
Common Faith* eloquently. Things in civilization that are to be
prized "exist by grace of the doings and sufferings of the continuous human community in which we are a link." The new age
should conserve, transmit, rectify, and expand the heritage of values. Then it should make these more solid, secure, and accessible
for those who might share them in generations to come. "Here are
all the elements for a religious faith that shall not be confined to
sect, class, or race. Such a faith has always been implicitly the
common faith of mankind. It remains to make it explicit and
militant."

7:38   Decades later the United States Supreme Court was to mention
that religions could be godless. Taoism, Zen Buddhism, and Ethical Culture were this. So could Secular Humanism be. Extreme
religious conservatives connected this religion with John Dewey
as its greatest prophet. In the end, then, his enemies agreed with

him: a religious outlook, at base, had a bearing on society, the whole of society, the entire public order. Dewey did much to make the viewpoint explicit, while his enemies chose to see it as militant.

7:39   In Europe the philosophers of modernity ignored or opposed religion. The God-killers Nietzsche, Darwin, Marx, and Freud set the terms for religious reaction in the new century. In America, however, the classic philosophers and the social thinkers, to a person "emancipated" from childhood church and inherited institutions, found that in order to look forward on the modern scene in which they were figurative immigrants, they naturally did and must also look backward. They contributed to the peculiar mix of secularity and religiousness which, to some extent, survived in the intellectual communities and remained very potent in American public life through the century which followed. The promise and fitness of a merely secular modern world was contradicted in part because of what they, because they cared for society, carried over the hump of transition to the new approved social contract.

Part Three

Modernity

8

Peoplehood as a Cocoon

8:1   **M**odernity, to turn-of-the-century Americans, meant freedom for new ways of life and threats to cherished old ways. Whatever terms they used to refer to the idea of modernity, these signaled an awareness of the power and promise of science and progress as well as their assaults on tradition. Processes of change chopped and sliced away, as it were, at the wholeness people presumed they needed, or once had had, back in simpler settings. Such change exacted a price from them now when they must live with pluralism in a somewhat secular society. Modernity appealed to their hunger for novelty and then repelled because innovation could also uproot and upset them. Just as the theologians themselves were allowed on the pages of this book to describe the advance they called modernism and the academics defined the modern condition, so more precise detailings of modernity await the descriptions of agents and victims from the period between the 1890s and 1920s.

8:2   The modernists and the moderns, as theorists, used interpretive devices that allowed them to view the storms of change as if from satellite-camera distance, or in planes in the eyes of hurricanes. Of course, they too shared existence with the mass of people who lived in the path of the storms, and their writings have many autobiographical features. Yet they could also find instruments for being somewhat above the storms.

8:3   The people in the huts, to return to our original metaphor, may also have added innate gifts for interpreting. They also had talented neighborhood experts who, in this image, reported out, as if by wireless. Most of these stayed behind to face the storm. They were also given few choices but to close some shutters, pile up some sandbags, and protect themselves against the worst. To change the image, now, they needed, discovered, or developed what we might call metaphoric cocoons. These sheltered and filtered the signals and storms associated with modern change. For one set of citizens, it was their peoplehood itself, which here means ethnicity mingled with religion, that served.

8:4   The cocoon is "the envelope or case of silky threads, spun by the larvae . . . as a covering to enclose them in the chrysalis state." *To* cocoon is both "to form a cocoon" or "to swathe as in a cocoon." In the analogies to religious America in this period, the cocoon serves at least four functions for those within it: shelter or filter, providing translucence, forcing drama within, and offering duration but not permanence. The chrysalis does one day emerge.

8:5   Ironies result from the original expressed expectations or intentions of people in these enclosures. As shelter or filter, one's peoplehood was sufficiently effective in preventing the development of a single and all-embracing style of modern rationality and progress, yet not thick enough to protect those within them from selective assaults by the world of change. Second, as providers of translucence they allowed the larger culture a chance to impinge with selective symbols—for example, in the case of demands for patriotic Americanism in wartimes—and they thus did not serve to keep at a distance many forces which drastically altered the lives of those within.

8:6   Third, they were thick enough to prevent outsiders from deriving accurate knowledge of what went on within, thus limiting their cultural impact. This did mean that they were also strong enough to provoke often self-defeating conflict within, far from an outer world that counted as a more remote scene of promise or threat. Finally, they were neither shrugged off as fast as the modernists and moderns thought they would be nor did they become as permanent and stable as leaders and guardians within them thought and wanted them to be.

8:7   These extensions of an image seem a bit too condensed at this point. They will become more intelligible when illustrated with cases. American pluralism by 1893 was already so rich, that to give detailed accounting of only several of these cases would produce a shelf full of books, not part of a book. The following selection of peoples intends to be representative. It focuses also on groups whose survival informed subsequent American life. There the consequences of their original intentions, along with the often contradictory outcomes, still produce effects. In sum, these examples are neither complete nor arbitrary. As before, where possible, the actors' descriptions will be quoted in order to provide an understanding of their intentions, perceptions, and outcomes. To prevent artificial, clumsy, or embarrassing extensions of the metaphor, references to the cocoon can be as rare as, one hopes, the image will remain deep in the mind of the reader. It will be more natural to use terms from the era: reservation, ghetto, barrio, immigrant group, sect, denomination, race, or whatever to designate them in their varieties.

Reservation and the Tribal Native American

8:8   Color was the most visible mark of peoplehood. Whites stereotyped native Americans, blacks, Orientals, and Hispanics, just as they were no doubt stereotyped in return. In all cases the religious bonds of their cultures came to be seen as reinforcing agents and thus as problematic. The native American after four centuries was not only being pushed ever further from citizen consciousness and the path of inconvenience to reservations. He was not even counted. Henry K. Carroll needed only two lines in his very thorough census commentary on *The Religious Forces of the United States* in 1893: "The pagan Indians are not included in the census, and no account is made of them here." Out of sight, they seemed to be out of mind as coreligionists. Instead they remained a problem for missionaries who would convert and civilize them on reservations. The outsiders remained a problem to the Indians because it was they who had so much of the power to take land, make the rules, define the space, disrupt the rites, and impose new teachings and conduct, as they had ever since the natives were determined by whites to be expendable. The familiar story of such interactions need not be retold here; only the latest unfolding of relations and expression of intentions must.

8:9   The fourth American century, which means the fourth century after the native Americans' continents were settled by Europeans, Africans, and latter-day Asians, ended with human tragedy and a set of legislative acts. The tragedy was the massacre at Wounded Knee, South Dakota, on December 29, 1890. That event represented the end of the Indian Trail, the breaking of resistance, and the effective total control of Indian futures by whites. The legislation, chiefly the Dawes Severalty Act of 1887, determined subsequent governmental policy. The president of the United States was therewith given power and discretion to give the Indians reservation land, with the government holding title for a quarter century. Citizenship for Indians came with the allotment, as did 160 acres to each head of a family. Massachusetts Senator Henry L. Dawes had hoped that with the bill the Indians might keep some land as opposed to losing it all to rapacious interests. Dawes was no more sanguine than President Grover Cleveland about the greed of land-seizing whites. Indians had little choice but to accept an act they did not always understand and were powerless to change. Almost at once the severalty policy was seen to have been a disaster. Friends of the Indians had often left the scene, having placed too much faith in it. Imperial America treated Indian lands the way it looked at the rest of the world when this suited the march of empire. Whites found ways to gouge and criminally delude Indians and take their land. What remained was a largely unpromising landscape.

8:10   Commissioners of Indian Affairs were left with the thankless task of administering the chaos and trying to make cultural sense of it all. They were at least close enough to the scene to recognize that native Americans had rites and religions, even if they saw these as problems. One unnamed agent summarized the outsiders' view of reservation existence: As long as Indians lived in villages they would retain what he called old and injurious habits. These he connected with their religion, but in his terms they were only frequent feasts, heathen ceremonies and dances, constant visiting, all of which would keep the dense mass of Indians together—and, thus, apart.

8:11   Less than one would wish is known about the historic unfolding of these ceremonies. The Ghost Dance, a messianic movement associated with events before Wounded Knee, was prohibited and no longer meaningful. The Sun Dance came to new prominence. Myth, symbol, story, dance, and practice varied greatly from reservation to reservation, from tribe to tribe. The whites lumped and dismissed them all. After the passage of the Dawes Act, Richard Henry Pratt, who headed a commission designed to cajole Indians into acquiescence, described their attitudes as "a victory for indolence, barbarism, and degradation as against the influence of the farm, the work-shop, the schools, and the Gospel."

Why? Like people external to enclaves in this period in general, Pratt complained that "massing, inactive, herding systems" would lead to more destruction and death. At fault was the whole segregating and reservating process, as he called it. Why, he asked with some naiveté or disingenuousness, could Indians not work toward being assimilated, as European immigrants had done? Instead, they were forced to remain Indians and not become Americans because they were walled in on reservations. Missionaries, he complained, went into the Indian world but did not draw Indians out of it. Ethnologists also were a problem because ethnology, he said, "revels in war, ghost and other dances, Peyote seances and all other spectacular characteristics and encourages them."

8:12   On the eve of this period and setting many of the terms for the three decades to follow, Thomas Jefferson Morgan was commissioner. This Baptist minister and seminary professor, in Pratt's spirit, wanted to bring Indians off reservations and into the modern age, thus, he said, to "satisfy the Christian philanthropic sentiment of the country." For this, Indians needed to share in a common language and common national characteristics including, of course, a common religion. He told humanitarians that the bonus of good policy would be the displacement of Indian faith in the form of "the solace and stimulus afford by a true religion." Yes, let Indians keep their campfire stories. Then substitute to serve for models "gradually and unobtrusively the heroes of American homes and history." Morgan added, in a work on pedagogy, that schools would help them grow in loyalty to the same flag and to the acknowledgment of "the one God the maker of us all." Yet Morgan himself left his post to become a notorious Catholic-baiter, having opposed tax funds for Catholic schools on the reservations. Why, he chided, try to break the shackles of tribal provincialism and the heathenish life of the camp only to have natives then pulled back to the evils of medievalism and everything that reformer Martin Luther had opposed? Evidently it was hard for the Christians themselves to agree on "the one God the maker of us all."

8:13   William A. Jones, a successor commissioner at the turn of the century, still sought what he called "the abolishment of tribal relations." Whites must pulverize and then refine Indian culture in order to modernize it. By giving the Indian skills, whites, he said, would exterminate the Indian but develop the man. All to no effect. Indians withdrew ever more, clinging to the ceremonies and rites which helped them weave a protection so that they could keep something of the spirit to themselves where things of matter were denied. Even so they kept losing. Colorado Senator Henry M. Teller, who opposed the Dawes Act, had prophesied that one day Indians would "curse the hand that was raised professedly in their defense" with the Severalty Act. They had reason to. In 1887 they owned 140,000,000 acres. By 1909 two-thirds of that was out of their hands, and in forty-five years 90,000,000 acres were gone. Teller said that the defenders did not understand "Indian character, and Indian laws, and Indian morals, and Indian religion."

8:14   Defenders of any sort were few. The moral leadership of the nation, its heroes, provided no example. Wildly popular was Theodore Roosevelt, who would go on to be a military hero in the Spanish-American War and become president. In the 1890s he was writing *The Winning of the West*. In it he took pains to attack the defenders of Indians as unpatriotic, wafflers who were reluctant to "resort to the ultimate arbitrator—the sword." As for himself, "I suppose I should be ashamed to say that I take the Western view of the Indian." The Westerners thought "the only good Indians are the dead Indians," but, added Roosevelt, "I believe nine out of every ten are." Then, lest anyone suspect him of joining the modernizers and Americanizers like Pratt, Morgan, and Jones, he added, as if with a wink, "I shouldn't like to inquire too closely into the case of the tenth."

Segregation and the Separate, Not Equal, Blacks

8:15   Blacks and black churches provide a revealing case study of what perceptions from without did to force leaders and members to develop a complete set of institutions within the larger culture. Black churches became effective shelters, by far the most important institutions in Negro America. Their leaders helped filter signals from larger America. The warmth of fellowship within them as well as the battles among them testify to the vitality of these churches; the present point, however, is the intention of white America not to differentiate but to make victims of all.

8:16   One might have expected a different turn. Blacks had been in North America since 1619. They had shown their love for it by largely rejecting back-to-Africa movements. They served in the two wars of the period covered in this book. Their investment in land and city was growing, despite general poverty among them. Their Methodist and Baptist faith coincided with that of the more prospering Protestant white churches in the century. They were generally orthodox, not suspect. They spoke English; few were radical protesters or troublemakers. Cosmopolitan-minded modernists talked about a convergence of races around the world, and should have had room in that vision for neighbors at home.

8:17   The promise was mocked. Most southern states found ways to disenfranchise blacks in the 1890s, with churchly complicity. There were 1,100 lynchings of blacks in the decade. While northern philanthropists would help support education for southern blacks, their own churches were closed to migrating blacks in the north. In 1896 through *Plessy v. Ferguson* the United States Supreme Court, by supporting "separate but equal" policies, built figurative walls and real barriers in front of blacks. Race riots, sporadic early in the century, became epidemic after World War I. Black life remained physically insecure. Black leaders had no choice but to develop supportive, cohesive, separate black churches. They were not to find resources from which interpreters of modern theology among them would help them make adjustments. Practical adjustment was needed for survival. The increasingly secular W. E. B. Du Bois, the first black with a Harvard Ph.D., argued for a "Talented Tenth" of Negroes to emerge, but preachers in the churches had other tasks on their minds and few were poised to become nationally known on cross-cultural lines. A vacuum developed. The National Association for the Advancement of Colored People in 1910 and the National Urban League in 1911 were signs of a growing pluralist model in which religion and church played a lesser role.

8:18   All this is strange because the liberal era came to be impressively illiberal and the progressive era saw regress. The best-known advocate of Negro causes, Booker T. Washington, readily settled for little. Theodore Roosevelt might have Washington to lunch at the White House, but then retreated. Many of the worst executive acts against blacks occurred during the presidency of Woodrow Wilson, who brought southern white stereotypes with him into the White House. The leaders of the reformist Protestant Social Gospel kept a blind spot and a silent voice on the subject. They did little to see blacks as companions on the march to the kingdom of God. Modernists Lyman Abbott and Washington Gladden expected progress on this subject to wait for a century, while what they called nature's way of separateness would remain. In a moral universe, thought Abbott, whites must educate and minister to blacks, but contact stopped there. With this happening in the green tree of northern cosmopolitanism, one expects

In the spectrum of black leadership in 1906, Booker T. Washington most successfully attracted white support. Here at Tuskegee's twenty-fifth anniversary in 1906
he attracts notables like Harvard President Charles W. Eliot (3d from left),
Congregational publicist Lyman Abbott (7th), and magnate Andrew Carnegie
(10th). (Courtesy of the Library of Congress.)

little in the dry tree of the South, where a legacy of racial conflict
remained.

8:19   Washington was not the only co-conspirator in reinforcing dis-
tances and separateness. In 1900 when Massachusetts Congressman Bourke Cockran proposed repeal of the Fifteenth Amendment
and, with it, removal of the last legal rights for blacks, the black
priest at St. John's Episcopal Church in Montgomery, Alabama,
the Reverend Edgar Gardner Murphy, wrote an opinion that finds
parallels in other publications. Intelligent blacks, he said, were
ready for such a temporary limitation of rights in order to give the
white South freedom from the nightmare of black domination.
This might promote an alternative impulse, toward sympathetic
cooperation.

8:20   Instead of sympathetic cooperation, there was continued support for lynchings. The *Christian Index*, a Baptist paper in Atlanta in 1892, contended that such murders were not a sign that

southern whites lacked Christian character. Instead, they "have a high sense of honor and highest regard for female character, so they lynch the black rapist." Lynching might disappear only if through education blacks would be elevated and Christianized, given moral uplift, said the paper, above the commission of arson, assassination, rape. Some white ministers did take risks by walking to lynchings with the victims. Names are known of some who pleaded unsuccessfully with angry mobs. These mobs might well have spread the epidemic of lynching to include them. In 1899 the Presbyterian General Assembly joined, it said, "heartily with our fellow-citizens and fellow-Christians of all sections in their horror" of lynching. In 1912 the Methodist General Conference boldly asked that lynching become a federal crime.

8:21   The scale of verbal lynchings varied widely. Too much can be made of Missourian Charles Carroll's *The Negro a Beast, or in the Image of God*, which some orthodox opposed because Carroll was an evolutionist who posited a pre-Adamic race. Two blacks, he wrote, survived the Noahic flood, because they were aboard the ark with all other beasts. They survived to cohabit with non-blacks, so God sent Jesus to "redeem man from atheism, amalgamation, and idolatry." H. Paul Douglass, a trained observer, in 1909 called this book "the Scripture of tens of thousands of poor whites," but that may have been exaggerating. Texas Baptists already in 1903 asked leaders everywhere to expose and denounce the "insulting and outrageous book" which loudly professed to prove from the Bible that the Negro was not human, but a beast without a soul.

8:22   Easier to measure for power were the very popular novels by former pastor Thomas Dixon, Jr. One of these, *The Clansman* of 1905, became D. W. Griffith's film classic *The Birth of a Nation*, of 1915. "Writing history with lightning," Woodrow Wilson called it. Dixon, a Baptist preacher's child, well educated but a failed actor, bored lawyer, and ex-legislator, was a resentful son of Dixie who used his talents to keep refighting the War between the States and the battles of Reconstruction. In the first volume of his trilogy, *The Leopard's Spots*, a fictional pastor worked to maintain the racial absolutism of the Anglo-Saxon South. The preacher advised a politician: "*My boy, the future American must be an Anglo-Saxon or a Mulatto. We are now deciding which it shall be.* . . ." The politician in turn shouted by the God of the Fathers that the nation would indeed be ruled by whites until the Archangel called the end of time.

74239

8:23   One looks to church leadership for response and defense of fellow-Christian blacks. Ever after a Baptist split of 1845 northern and southern sections kept attacking each other. The Atlanta *Christian Index* spoke in terms that haunted members through the decades as it chided the not very northern *Cincinnati Journal*: "All this clatter about race-prejudice," it said, "is sheer hypocrisy; it comes from men who are just as full of the so-called race prejudice as anybody else." Then in good cosmopolitan accent the editor added a line. The paper meant *everybody* else. The feeling, he thought, was universal. Yet it was not a prejudice but an instinct. When bold clerics proposed the friendly act of exchanging pulpits across racial lines, the *Christian Index* roared: "Neither bayonets or bullets, neither human laws nor the laws of God as revealed in the Bible can change the natural instincts of either race." Each must stay in place to avoid bloodshed or extinction.

8:24   The language of spheres and separation was consistent. At the turn of the century the *Alabama Baptist* reinforced the theme. Let the black "stay absolutely in his own sphere, and let us manfully, religiously and patriotically maintain our dignity, supremacy, and social status in our own sphere." Blacks did have souls, it thought: Carroll was wrong, Dixon too radical. But a Southern Baptist Committee on Missions to the Colored People granted them little more: "Their ignorance, superstitions, and immoralities tell upon us." The black Baptists must Christianize blacks and educate them in self-defense. In 1901 the Home Mission Board of the convention seemed to sigh with relief when the National Baptist Convention was shaped in order to assure the integrity of black church life: "A race feeling among the Negroes in the South has been developed." Mention of blacks largely disappeared in white Baptist church convention proceedings.

8:25   The other dominant Protestant church, also divided on sectional lines and well poised to debate the black issue in its southern wing, was more centralized Methodism. When northerner R. S. Lovinggood in 1900 thought that race prejudice was the most stubborn problem before the Christian church in that day, the *Nashville Christian Advocate* from the front lines seconded the notion in 1906. Hatred of race, it said, "is so deep-seated and so ineradicable that the man, white or black, who looks forward to its elimination, be the progress of the negro race what it may, is simply a fool." The separate but equal notion seemed to have made its way in Methodism. In 1898 the white southern bishops congratulated themselves for this wisdom of their church through which it had eliminated "needless jealousies and irritating and damaging complications."

8:26   Black Methodists, confined in their own spheres, took responsibility for providing a complete parallel institution and looked for a better day. In 1900, 280,000 blacks remained in the Methodist Episcopal Church. Some agitated for black bishops. The general conference failed to respond. A black delegate professed loyalty and staying power: "We are at home. We are not going anywhere." His people would work and wait for a principle and, if they died without result, they would report to God that they had been faithful. They would not frustrate Methodism's purpose by running, but would hold their ground "world without end. Amen." Others put energies into the completely independent black Methodist churches, not into the world-within-a-world that the Methodist Episcopal Church offered them.

8:27   Some measure of the distance between races is clear when one hears that Mississippi Bishop Charles B. Galloway was considered a moderate. His four-point program included segregated schools and churches, no social mixing, white political control, and the end of notions that blacks should recolonize Africa. Galloway opposed lynching but supported white supremacy. Blacks, he thought, would fulfill themselves best in their own spheres. Equally ambivalent was Emory College's Professor Andrew Sledd in Georgia. "*The negro belongs to an inferior race*," he wrote, but also had "*inalienable rights*." In the course of time Sledd edged toward a more open position. When he complained that the radical difficulty did not lie with the Negro but with the white man, he had to resign from Emory. Suffragette Mrs. William Felton wrote the *Atlanta Constitution* that Sledd stood for rot. He was to her a "sniveling inkslinger" who had come up with an outrageous indictment of southern manhood.

8:28   Presbyterianism counted for less, being smaller and having far fewer black members, but its leadership was well educated, influential, worth observing. In general the leaders favored Booker T. Washington and his hopes for black education, with blacks remaining in their own corner, under a low ceiling. The *Central Presbyterian* in 1900 considered even this to be a question completely beyond the reach of human values, "one of those extreme cases that God alone can deal with." Prayer was the only hope. Race was at issue when northern Presbyterians and revivalist-minded Cumberland Presbyterians of the mid-South talked of merger. A union committee of Cumberlanders said that the northern members recognized the absolute necessity of a separation of the races in the South. Protested the *Africo-American Presbyterian*: "Can any one find any just ground for this in law, morals, or Christianity? We know not."

8:29   When drafting time came, the Special Committee on the Territorial Limits of Presbyteries used the precedent of the Dakota Indian Presbytery, which already had racial barriers based on language. Why could not the South also have them? As a race blacks were "inferior to the whites in culture, mental and moral development, and civilization," so they had a peculiar claim upon "the stronger race for help and guidance." Only six general assembly commissioners found the separate but equal theme to be "contrary to the spirit of our Church, to the Word of God" and the great Head of the church. The union-hungry assembly bought the terms and passed the overture.

8:30   This canvass has deliberately followed denominational lines in order to show that religious ties meant little so far as racial sepa-

Back-to-Africa movements, touted by leaders like Bishop Henry M. Turner, attracted few and led to frustration and even death. Here the *Laurada* prepares to sail from Savannah, Georgia, March 1, 1896.

ratenesses were concerned. So it was also in the fourth major Protestant church in the South, Episcopalianism, which had very few black members or missions and which segregated races in schools and academies. When in 1907 the general convention did allow for change in church law so that blacks could be elected as subordinates who could not vote as bishops or technically become full ones, black church paper-writer the Reverend George Bragg called these suffragan bishops "suffering bishops," and thought their post was demeaning. None were elected even as suffragans until 1916.

8:31   Episcopalianism offered the full spectrum of attitudes, ending with racist Right Reverend William Montgomery Brown, the Ohio-born bishop of Arkansas. His book of 1907 matched Dixon's and Carroll's: *The Crucial Race Question, or Where and How Shall the Color Lines Be Drawn?* Brown went on in a career as rabble-rouser and was finally defrocked as pro-Communist. Edgar Gardner Murphy was more moderate at Montgomery. Yet by 1909 he, too, was forgetting his memories of lynchings and exposed his racist hand in *The Basis of Ascendancy*. Murphy feared racial fusion and acclaimed racial antipathy as "a public good." Episcopalianism, regarding such a man as a moderate, was in no position to break down walls of separation.

8:32   For all these purposes Booker T. Washington could all too easily be quoted as an accomplice. In 1895 in the most noticed speech by a black in all these decades, Washington used the Atlanta Cotton Exposition as a forum to concur with those who felt that "the agitation of questions of social equality is the extremest folly." His more impatient and increasingly radical rival Du Bois sensed that Washington's language had a religious dimension. In *Souls of Black Folk* in 1903 Du Bois complained that all this was a religion of its own, as it were, a gospel of Work and Money, preached, he said, to such an extent as apparently almost completely to overshadow the higher aims of life. Washington, however, held the privileged place because Du Bois was right: Work and Money were the higher aims of life in much of religious America.

8:33   The black churches prospered, grew more complex and more articulate, within their own sphere, but few broke bounds. Bishop Henry McNeal Turner promoted back-to-Africa themes and supported his call both with angry dismissals of self-despising blacks and with ill-fated colonizing ventures, but his following did not match his notoriety. Turner was ahead of his times, Afro-

Americans would have said; also, excesses in his personal life limited his reliability and appeal.

8:34   The northern white churches played along with the southern mainstream. The liberal social front of Protestantism after 1908, the Federal Council of Churches, largely ignored the issue, giving only bland support to "equal rights and complete justice for all men in all stations of life." By 1913, however, a few northern voices began to criticize the separate-but-equal policy. The Chicago Methodist *Northwestern Christian Advocate* bemoaned the presence of "separate sections in our cities, separate churches, and in some instances separate schools for separate nationalities or races." These existed at the behest of racial prejudice. If, in the church, said the editor, "One cannot kneel down between a China-man and a Negro and pray the Lord's Prayer he cannot really pray it anywhere." If so, the prayer was not prayed anywhere.

8:35   One last set of steps remained. William Joseph Simmons and fifteen friends took these, as they stepped from their cars on Thanksgiving night in 1915 on Stone Mountain, Georgia. There in the face of surging blasts of wild wintry mountain winds, they burned a wooden cross, set out a flag, opened the Bible, laid bare a sword, readied some purging water, and took an oath. Simmons, an ex-minister and teacher, was a devotee of secret fraternal orders that wished to combine religion, education, and fraternal life. As if with the modernists of the day he professed to further "the great doctrine of the fatherhood of God and the brotherhood of man." His reborn organization grew slowly, naming only about two thousand members, mostly in Georgia and Alabama. Then the post–World War situation and better business heads helped the group prosper and come to a second finest hour. It followed to its end the logic of church and culture in this period. We know it as the Ku Klux Klan.

Exclusion and the Asians

8:36   Progressives in the white world spoke of "a cosmopolitan habit." They invited East to meet West at the World's Parliament of Religions in 1893. They sent missionaries from West to East out of appreciation for the souls of Asians. The whites often accepted people of the East when their labor was necessary, as in the mines or fields or along the railroads in an expanding West. Yet both civilly and religiously these cosmopolitan notions were denied by the principle of exclusion that America effected first against

Asians in the West in 1882 and finally consolidated into a law that affected all kinds of immigrants in 1924. Meanwhile in response to the exclusionary impulse, the Chinese and Japanese who were chiefly in California and elsewhere on the West Coast, developed cultural enclaves which made them seem only more remote and mysterious. Religion was a reinforcer of these enclaves and, since it was an alien religion to people with biblical heritages, it only served to increase the distance between peoples.

8:37   Late in the nineteenth century two pieces of legislation helped frame the turn-of-the-century events. The Exclusion Act of 1882, promoted by whites who feared hordes of immigrants from Asia, suspended the formal immigration but did not thus end the arrival of Chinese. The Geary Act of 1892 then raised restrictions. Around 1896 came the first climax of Yellow Peril fever. At this time the numbers of Asian arrivals remained small. In his review of the census of 1890 Henry K. Carroll mentioned only 107,475 Chinese, 72,472 of whom made up 9 percent of the California population. There Carroll could account for 178 religious shrines. Carroll knew of no Japanese shrines at all. During the sixty years before 1920 only 246,400 Japanese came, to make up but .0086 percent of the American population. In 1920 there were, counting American-born children, 111,010 Japanese in the census. Most of the immigrants were rootless young men, a caste which has always been a poor bearer of a religious tradition. Yet the Japanese, though they came later and were fewer, did effectively organize religious centers and more is known of their inner community's life than of the larger Chinese communities.

8:38   Both the Chinese and Japanese were fated to arrive precisely in the years when the frontier was closing. Coming from the west they assaulted frontier notions from a surprising direction. Whites knew more about the language of assimilation when Europeans from the East Coast made their way westward. The dispersable public lands were gone by 1890 and the race for western resources became intense. The best policy seemed to sequester the arrivals in mining camps or Chinatowns. Bewildered by their surrounding culture and snubbed by citizens, sometimes even victims of violence, the Orientals did what other recent arrivals also chose to do. They stayed together, to keep their identity, to hold some power, and to retain traditions, of which oriental religions were at least some part.

8:39   Sometimes religion was hinted at as an element for disdain in exclusion debates. Thus in 1882 a congressman pointed to differences that revealed the limits of cosmopolitanism. They do not wear our kind of clothes, he said of the Chinese; "when they die their bones are taken back to their native country." This was an allusion to the ancestor worship, as white America spoke of it, and the presumed cult of the dead which so inspired distaste among Christians. As Americans favored and supported the popular mission to China, missionaries came home exaggerating the heathenism of the religious culture they were sent to convert or displace, and only negative images developed.

8:40   Some signs that Chinese formal worship was not the main agency stimulating exclusionism was clear from serene accounts of its presence. Thus Carroll, who had dismissed the pagan Indians, reported almost benignly on the Chinese temples he could locate. Four were in New York. Maybe their principle of organization made them acceptable: he found them well supported on capitalist grounds. Carroll observed that their support came from the fact that the highest bidder won the privilege of selling articles of worship that every participant in that closed religious market had to own.

8:41   Carroll did express some suspicion. Thus the New York temples claimed 9,700 Chinese devotees but the census could find only 2,935 Chinese residents in the area. There were no familiar landmarks for Carroll and his readers, so he had to explain the peculiarities of worship in which there was no sermon preached, no priest installed, no religious instruction given: no seating accommodations were provided. Nor did worshipers meet in a congregational body, a familiar form. Carroll treated the faith as a complex of externals. Devotees, he said, took pains only to be careful to consult their gods and patron saints. Otherwise, what caught his eye were the incense and wines, offerings and genuflections, the decoration of temples, and the search for response in what he and his contemporaries knew as a religion of mere chance.

8:42   We are left with more glimpses of religious organization in the smaller Japanese communities. For the Japanese religious presence, 1893 is a precise date, for Abbot Soyen Shaku, described as the first Zen personage to make his way to the West, spoke to the World's Parliament of Religions. Since he knew no English he was eclipsed by Orientals who did, yet the presence grew and he even met President Theodore Roosevelt when he returned in 1905–6 to help organize the Rinzai sect of San Francisco Buddhists. Intellectuals began to know Zen through his *Sermons of a Buddhist Abbot* in 1906.

8:43   A Japanese yearbook from 1905 showed stirrings in a San Francisco Japanese community of 10,132. Some people, of course, were reached by Christians and belonged to a Christian Gospel Society, *Fukuin Kai*, the Methodist *Mii Kyokai* and a nuanced *Minami Mii Kyokai*, or Southern Methodist church, differentiation thus affecting even Japanese Methodists! Some of these early conversions may have helped make the Japanese more attractive than the Chinese, even though overseas China was a more romantic and appealing missionary goal.

8:44   Japanese religions began their wedge in 1899 when the Nishi Hongwanji missionaries arrived to organize the North American Buddhist Mission, today's Buddhist Churches of America. They concentrated on a denominational version of Amida Buddhism called Jodo Shinshu. These Buddhist centers remained weak and the Japanese were vulnerable to Christian evangelists. Life at the borders between communities was delicate. Thus American officials monitored activities of the first Japanese missionaries. Nisaburo Hirano had enjoyed Christian missionary aid when he arrived in San Francisco in 1891, but he refused to convert and returned to Japan. Then on July 6, 1898, two Jodo Shinshu priests arrived. One, the Reverend Eryu Honda, went to Seattle, where he consulted with the Japanese consul about his difficulties. The consul, Miki Saito, seemed annoyed. Whose side was he on, one wondered, as he thumbed through a number of documents and asked, according to a report, "whether the United States government would allow the entrance of a 'foreign religion.'" By that time his awareness of Japanese life was blurry, and Honda had to explain the basics of Japanese religion to him. Honda did walk away with the agreement that he could be an agent of this foreign religion. He also carried the conviction that missionary work would have to be intense to be even minimally successful.

8:45   The tendency to live what we have called a cocoonlike existence, a metaphor which combines protection with translucence, was clear in the stilted language and images in a request of eighty-three San Franciscans for a Nishi Hongwanji center. "In the eight directions are non-Buddhist forces surrounding the Japanese Buddhists, and we cannot be at ease." Everything was delicate. "It is as if we are sitting on the point of a pin; no matter how we move, we will be pricked." Metaphors could shift. "Our burning desire" to hear the teachings of the Buddha, they wrote, "is about to explode from every pore in our body." Perhaps fearing resistance, the leaders back in Japan did not respond to the request. Other temples took on protective coloration by calling their gatherings "churches," a more congenial term in America.

8:46   The Reverend Akira Hata of Placer, California, described the Buddhist associations or *bukkyokai* as places for immigrants to preserve "their religion which they had in Japan." They had to possess a strategic sense. Thus about five hundred Japanese sugarbeet workers who were tired of being proselytized by both Christians and Buddhists at Guadalupe, California, sent letters to Christians and Buddhists in advance to take the better support offer. The Buddhist Association, whose mail beat the Christians by one day, has held a monopoly since 1909.

However suspect a racial or immigrant group might be, when World War I came it was expected to deliver on the patriotic front—and almost always did. Here, serving and gaining credentials are Issei women at a Red Cross booth during a rally.

8:47   When the gentlemen's-agreement policy between the two governments developed in 1908, after which Japanese men could rarely enter the country, picture brides, chosen from photographs, began to arrive to form families with the men already here. Religious life developed with family life. By 1914, twenty-five Buddhist centers were connected with the one in San Francisco. In 1915 the San Francisco Panama Canal Exposition by featuring their presence and culture gave the Japanese a chance to be respectable and visible. However, as Japanese military power and presence grew, Americans began to find reason to see Shinto as a motivating political religion. Prejudice against Buddhism grew as some Americans began to blend and confuse it with Shintoism.

8:48   On such terms, as American nationalism also was growing more aggressive and defensive at once, the two nationalist faiths had to clash. In 1919 the California state controller led the attack in his work on "The Japanese Invasion." He grumbled that in their churches in California the immigrants were taught the religion of Japan with its notion that the Mikado was above evil, could do no wrong, and must be worshiped as a God. Concurrently he observed that the Japanese, whom most whites wanted to keep at a distance, stayed apart socially, industrially, politically, and religiously.

8:49   The period after World War I saw a rise of obsession with Mikado worship. California Senator James D. Phelan in 1920 told the House Committee on Immigration that the seventy-six Buddhist temples in California were "regularly attended by 'Emperor worshippers' who believe that their Emperor is the over-lord of all." The *Sacramento Bee* publisher Valentine S. McClatchy raised the issue of dual allegiance. Since Buddhism had Shintoism grafted on it, and since worship of the Mikado was part of that faith, it would apparently be subversive in America. In reply, Bishop Koyu Uchida scurried to tell the committee that the Buddhist churches had nothing at all to do with Shintoism, politics, or imperial policy. At home with the language of church and state separation, he spoke in thoroughly modern terms about the fact that Japanese faith was purely spiritual. He leaned toward accommodation, stressing "the necessity of the Americanization of our people." The clergy were directed "to educate the members in the American way of living and acting." His words counted for little. The presence of mysterious Orientals and the threat of the hordes that might follow them were major factors in the legislation of 1924, legislation to which the term "exclusion" is so properly applied. The cosmopolitan vision was denied by the very people who promoted it.

The Hispanics: "As Loyal as Any Other Americans"

8:50   The Hispanics, eventually to become America's second-largest minority group, were a small and remote presence in the Southwest at the turn of the century. Yet the forms of interaction within the barrios and of life between them and the Anglo world illustrate further the character of religious existence in enclaves we have described as cocoonlike. While many of the Mexican arrivals were rather passive or vestigial Catholics, their Catholicism, which played some part in their bonding, failed to ingratiate them any more than did the pagan faith of Indians or the heathenism of Asiatics. Prejudice was quite localized, however, and the eastern press devoted far less attention to Mexicans than to Orientals. Only after the headlines about the Mexican Revolution of 1910 were there articles about the superstitious and unmodern "wetbacks" who crossed the Rio Grande as illegal aliens, sometimes to become citizens. Like the Chinese, most of these were young men, and thus evidently almost historyless, rootless, and religionless. They also worked in mines, on railroads, or in agriculture. Social organization in such settings is weak, so leadership emerged late.

8:51   The cities had an advantage, so far as social order was concerned, and there are good glimpses of an old center like Santa Barbara, California. When the Anglo-Protestants arrived there, displacement occurred and the Spanish were crowded into the Pueblo Viejo. Even there the Chicano or Mexican-descent percentage dropped to about twenty. Protestant observers regarded events like their annual religious festival, Corpus Christi, as a confirmation of the superstitious character of Mexican Catholicism.

8:52   Life in these enclaves often stimulated as much conflict between people within them as with those around them. Since some sort of Catholicism was vaguely pervasive, the base of conflict was social more than religious. American-born *pochos* looked down on newly-arrived *cholos*, a term of derision. Adapted to America, they had forgotten the pious songs the rude newcomers sang, and they had left the folksy *jamaicas* back in Mexican churches generations earlier. Years later interviewee Walter Cordero remembered how the *cholos* segregated themselves and kept away from the "standoffish" *pochos*. Another new immigrant of 1916 remembered it most simply, "We didn't like each other."

8:53   El Paso, Texas, provides other illustrations. By World War I this was a half-Mexican Texas city of eighty thousand people, a sort of Ellis Island, a symbolic immigrant processing point. Newcomers lived in "dobe" (adobe) row huts. Though the Irish-dominated national church hardly noticed them, nine-tenths of the Hispanics were named Roman Catholic. The church structure turned out to be important. Three adobe buildings housed the congregation in sewerless Stormsville. Better-off people arrived after the Revolution and in Sunset Heights in 1914 built Holy Family Church for dispersed professionals from Mexico, now crowded into one section of this American town.

8:54   Some saw good reason to be Americanized, especially to avoid being stigmatized as revolutionaries. J. A. Escajeda, head of a patrol which people in the Chihuahuita area permitted, used the patriotic language of the day: "We are Americans; born and brought up under the Stars and Stripes and as loyal to it as any other American"; they were ready to shoulder rifles alongside Anglo-Saxons and Celts. When furies did erupt and Americans attacked Mexicans after Pancho Villa's raid of January 10, 1916, for one rare moment being taken for a black was advantageous in America. A swarthy Mexican escaped attackers shouting, "I am not a Mexican. I'm a nigger, I'm a nigger." Military loyalties did more than modernizing tendencies to make Mexicans acceptable as Americans. The cinema helped where the church could not, priest shortages being chronic. Yet the Italian and Irish arrivals who quickly learned Spanish tried to help Americanize children through Roman Catholic schools. Some nuns taught the students how to move away from old spiritual folkways that appealed to their parents. "Cleanliness and godliness" were blended, as teachers had to control the degrees of Americanization and Mexican heritage. At Sacred Heart after World War I, an Italian priest, worried that the tradition was fading too fast, taught Mexican Catholic girls to stay with the heritage of *la raza*.

8:55   The same church that taught Catholicism also promoted savings and economics, entertainment, club life, and, when war came, the draft and Liberty Bonds. Such programs were routine in oldline American religion but were novelties to Mexicans, whose homeland churches were more passive, less protean. All this while they were both fair game to Protestant evangelizers and objects of stigmatizers. Liberals S. Earl Taylor and Halford E. Luccock during World War I called for *The Christian Crusade for World Democracy*. Though they intended to express the cosmopolitan habit, their own denominational provincialism showed through. In their world, where Christian=Protestant, they stated that "the only solution of the Mexican problem is the Christian solution, an invasion of Christian preachers, teachers, and physicians, the establishment of churches, schools, and hospitals." Emphasize the word "start" in a line that canceled out the spiritual heritage of Mexican Catholicism; this would all "enable Mexico to *start* realizing her own destiny of strong and enlightened self-government and moral and spiritual progress. . . ." Nothing to date counted.

8:56   In 1906 a Reverend Dr. Ward enlivened a southern Methodist meeting by urging the Northwest Mexican Conference that a Martin Luther was needed, "and he must be a Mexican." Ward knew that "Protestant countries of the world represent the highest civilization and prosperity," and thought a Lutherized Mexico could join them. Yet in El Paso by 1916 only the Young Mens Christian Association showed much ecumenical breadth, attracting as it did a thousand members of "best families." Five Protestant denominations together, by then, had attracted only 488 women and 416 men.

8:57   These Mexican-Americans would remain Catholic for decades to come, but the Protestants were right to notice that many elements that they would call superstitious thrived among them. Records of some, of these evidences remain. Take, for instance, as a best-known case the religious blend incarnate in Sinaloan-born Teresa Urrea, "Santa Teresa." The illegitimate daughter of a Yaqui Indian and a wealthy Mexican rancher, "La Nina de Cabora" learned while young to be a *curandera*, a healer. She was also a revolutionary, and was reported to have eliminated seven hundred government soldiers on October 29, 1892, when her *tomechiteco* fighters, though outnumbered 1,500 to 65, fought with almost religious fervor. Mexicans deported her, and from Nogales, Arizona, she internationalized her movement. She came with the reputation of having recovered from apparent death, of having lived through a months-long trance. The church, spotting her heresies and resenting her criticisms, sent Porfirio Diaz to track her down in a miniature "Tomachic War," one of many outbreaks of the day. She was then to find protective coloration in El Paso, where her *teresistas* engaged in Sonoran border raids. When the

New York Times credited her with or blamed her for a thousand or more deaths, as a "humble person" she backed off, claiming she was nonviolent, decidedly a victim.

8:58   In figures like Santa Teresa, the old and the new, politics and religion, violence and cure, old superstition and adapted faith blended. The English press came to call her the Joan of Arc of the

Far from the gaze of custodians who monitored the older "core culture," Teresa Urrea attracted followings that anticipated the richer pluralism of twentieth-century America. (Collections of the Arizona Historical Society, Tucson, Arizona.)

Indians. Progressively she moved into healing and then into show business when some commercial promoters invested in her. Yet on the stage her magical powers failed her more than did her appearance, for on the road in one event she became a beauty queen. In the new century she married, retired, and died of exposure in the flood of 1905 at San Francisco. People have asked, was she user or used? Whatever the answer, her career again demonstrates how far Americans were from achieving the single style of rationality that Progressives reported on and envisioned.

8:59   Except for occasional glimpses in chronicles like the *New York Times*, most of these activities went unnoticed by Americans remote from this scene. Yet numbers grew, from 30,000 Hispanics in the first wave during the opening decade of the new century, through 498,000 in the decade following World War I. In various ways they both held to the old and they Americanized, as they were diffused across the map, yet were still largely restricted to barrios. Exclusion Acts could not do much to keep them out, as it could those who arrived by boat. The ethos of exclusivism, however, ruled them out of visible range on the approved mainstream ways of life.

The Jews Don't Want to Merge

8:60   A fifth people whose religion, when it was combined with race, served both to distance it from the core culture and to nurture the life of people within it, were the Jews. The name for their version of enclave organization of life was centuries old. The ghetto, which was both imposed from without and chosen to reinforce identity, was imported as a model and a practice from Europe. Between 1654 and 1881 the few Jewish arrivals were dispersed, adapted, and generally integrated into American life. After European pogroms the arrivals toward the end of the nineteenth century came with a density and with thick cultural backgrounds that made assimilation unattractive and at first impossible. They were a problem to cosmopolitan modernists, an embarrassment to universalizing Jewish leaders like those modernists who led the adaptive movement called Reform.

8:61   The newcomers arrived not from German university life but from shtetls, rural villages of Poland and Russia, to tenements and sweat shops, especially in New York. In 1888 there were 400,000 Jews in a population of 59,974,000. By 1907 this total grew to

1,777,185 and by 1917 to 3,388,951, a growth from 0.67 percent to 3.27 percent in a nation of 103,266,000. By European standards, anti-Semitism was not intense. At least no government policy encouraged persecution. As a biblical faith, Judaism was entangled in American religion from colonial days, even though classic theological confusions fueled some anti-Jewish movements. Many outsiders praised Judaism with one half of a sentence and condemned it with the other, allied themselves with Jews for one cause and denied them in another.

8:62   This made Jewish defense confusing, yet defense seemed somehow necessary. In 1906 the American Jewish Committee was formed to promote Jewish life, while in 1913 the Anti-Defamation League of B'nai B'rith formed to counter negative images. A year earlier, New York Jews founded the *American Citizen* as "A National Magazine of Protest against Prejudice and Injustice." A Jewish Self-Defense Association, formed in 1906, worked to "unite Jews of state without regard to political or religious opinion." A Federation of Jewish Organizations in crucial New York State wanted to unite Jews for the "principles of true and pure Americanism," but it remained small because Jews already had found less formal ways to Americanize and remain Jewish.

8:63   Political anti-Semitism was ineffective, rather rare, and strongest in the West and South where there were few Jews. Some Populists there used cultural stereotypes to oppose purported international fiscal conspiracies led by people such as the Rothschilds in Europe. In 1896 a reporter at the St. Louis convention of Populists overheard every form of anti-Jewish hatred in the hotel rooms. In 1900 when William Jennings Bryan took some Populist sympathies into the Democratic party, he offered an aside to Jewish Democrats at Chicago, one which helped diffuse and defuse anti-Semitism. His prosilver people, he stressed, were "attacking greed and avarice, which know neither race nor religion." By then colorful Populist windbag Ignatius Donnelley had done some damage. The utopian novelist and sometime representative in Congress and presidential candidate, to inspire reforms, invented the Jew combined as money-grubber and revolutionist. In 1894 Donnelley published the usual disclaimers: "We would be sorry to be understood as saying one word that would pander to prejudice against any man, because of his race, religion, nationality or color." The phrase was invoked ritually by people who did thus pander. He piously mused in a book published in 1899 that it was "inexplicable that a Christian people, worshipping a Jew, the son of a Jewess, should entertain . . . terrible bigotry against the people of his race." Yet he himself contributed to bigotry.

8:64   So did Baptist-trained Georgia politician Thomas E. "Tom" Watson, who moved from Congress to become the Populist vice-presidential candidate in 1896. He was a grand-scale, ecumenical hater who used language that forced Populists to abandon him. It was in Watson's Georgia that the most noted anti-Semitic act of the era took place. In 1913 an Atlanta Jew, Leo Frank, was almost certainly innocent, but accused of a sexual assault and murder. This head of the local B'nai B'rith was then lynched. Tom Watson contributed to the anti-Jewish fervor of the seasons, speaking of Frank's Jewish "ritual murder" of a white girl. When some Jews asked the pope for support in the cause, Watson again fused prejudices, claiming that insolent Jews now acknowledged the pope as the true and only head of the Church of Christ. His racial stereotypes also blended. "Every student of sociology knows that the black man's lust after the white woman *is not much fiercer than the lust of the licentious Jew for the Gentile.*" More urbane and tolerant newspapers countered Watson, an eccentric and extremist, who still became a United States senator after World War I.

8:65   These western and southern eruptions, whether or not ghetto Jews were much aware of them, did indicate a climate and ran counter to the democratic impulses they were advertised to serve. Similarly, only very literate Jews would be at all aware of the anti-Semitism in the elite culture of the literary moderns, yet it too indicated troubles. It is hard to picture the extent and depth of anti-Jewish language in Henry Adams and Henry James, Brooks Adams and other aristocrats of talent, moral self-exiles in America. Henry James could compliment Jews for their adaptation to ghetto life and then find them sinister; one never knew, he said, what the genius of Israel may, or may not, really be up to. James provided the urbane outsider's image of ghettoism, a Jewry that had burst all bounds, he said, and was now swarming on the Lower East Side. He diagnosed the pressures of modernity, that severer of old ties and traditions which, he said, "permits the chopping into myriads of fine-fragments," and then he disdained the failure of Jews to lose their "race-quality." He and his kind could mix sneers with awe in summary views of these "denizens of the New York Ghetto, heaped as thick as the splinters in the table of a glass-blower," who had "each, like the fine glass particle, his or her individual share of the whole hard glitter of Israel."

8:66   Far more people read now forgotten but then popular novelist Florence Kingsley, who after 1894 published a tetralogy in which Jews were killers of Jesus and the prophets. New Testament Jews were "a pack of curs," or "slippery rabbins [sic] from Jerusalem," people who moved between "malignant hatred" and "impotent rage." For her and her readers only the Christianly converted Jew could be a good Jew.

8:67   *The American Hebrew* in 1890 published responses from sixty-two non-Jews, each of whom first scrambled to say they were not anti-Semitic. Their responses were typical of the Gentile cosmopolitan culture through these decades. Thus modernist minister Robert Collyer: "Have you not held yourselves apart from the life of this New World in a nook of your own . . . looking down from your fancied eminence as the chosen race, with a certain disdain and feeling of keep your distance?" The Reverend A. H. Lewis stereotypically found Jews clannish, "a nation and yet not a nation." Similarly, naturalist John Burroughs complained that the "Jew will be a Jew; he will not fuse or amalgamate with the other races," because he was too tough to be digested or assimilated by "the modern races." *Harper's Weekly* in 1905 continued the theme. "The Jews don't want to merge. They prefer to be a part, belonging to the whole, but not merged into it." Journalist H. L. Mencken started speaking of "some of my oldest and most intimate friends," the Jews, "sticking together." This clannish feature of Jewish life most offended Progressives, who at the same time were not ready for real Jewish merger.

8:68   Conversion was another delicate topic, one that certainly reached ghetto dwellers more than did imagery from Gentile elites. Gentile ambivalence was acute here, for the Christian evangelizer evidently used motives of love to approach Jews while serving as a threat to the integrity of Jewish faith and community. They helped ghetto dwellers forget their own community bonds. Joseph Hoffman Cohn remembered how fast-reading Jews in upper floors of tenements, after reading his evangelistic tracts, would douse him with contents of pots and pans and with garbage. After World War I some Moody Bible Institute students in Chicago tried to evangelize the ghetto. A thousand angry Jews jostled their gospel wagon and, in the face of an avalanche of watermelon rinds, banana peelings, overripe tomatoes, and other edible fruit, the team of evangelist Charles Meeker had to beat a retreat.

8:69   Occasionally a reconverting Jew gave a picture of the pain evangelists caused in the ghetto. In 1894 Samuel Freuder turned Christian, to work among Boston Jews. Then, in 1908, as an Episcopal priest, the ex-rabbi surprised his audience at a Hebrew Christian Conference in Park Street Church. He tore up his speech and blurted: "You don't know what it means and costs for a Jew to be baptized—the rended soul, the disrupted family, the desertion of friends, the loss of respect." Henceforth Freuder urged Jews to stay with their faith and people and cursed himself in advance should he ever again mount a Christian pulpit.

8:70   Abrasion resulted when Jewish ghettos pushed up against crowded Gentile wards. In Brooklyn fourteen Jewish societies in 1899 complained of attacks but got no police response. They feared beatings. In 1902 New York's foremost Orthodox rabbi, Jacob Joseph, died. His followers by the thousands processed from the Lower East Side to Brooklyn, through Irish turf. Toughs there rained down not watermelon rinds but iron materials, and a riot ensued when Jews countered. Two hundred people, most of them Irish, were injured, many of them by the police.

8:71   Not all Jews were captive of the new and crowded eastern European and East Coast ghettos. For decades a modernist Reform movement had attracted Jews who were able and willing to accommodate themselves to American life and to leave behind any bewildering or scandalizing unmodern practices and beliefs. They were rationalist, progressive, respectful of selective aspects of Judaism, and as cosmopolitan as Protestant modernists. Many switched from Hebrew to English, from Sabbath to Sunday worship. Rabbi Isaac Mayer Wise of Cincinnati is best remembered as an incautious adapter who led in innovations. He would have nothing to do with ethnic Judaism coiled in its shell. A progressive, in his last year as the century ended he thought he could plausibly prophesy that "within twenty-five years, all the world will have accepted Reform Judaism." Wise was naturally stunned by the statistically predominant ghetto Judaism. Its Yiddish was jargon, its Zionism was a Russian-Polish hobby. Having housed, fed, and clothed these Russian refugees for more than a decade, he complained in 1894, why did Reform Jews have to be abused by them? "They are Jews and we are Israelites." A modernist, he saw what he named their semi-Asiatic Hassidism and medieval orthodoxy to be un-American. Wise feared that they would lower the social status of Reform, which was far above such half-civilized orthodoxy. "We are Israelites of the nineteenth century and a free country, and they gnaw the dead bones of past centuries."

8:72   Reform Jews entered with zest into the spirit of the World's Parliament of Religions in 1893. At this event Wise's colleague Kaufmann Kohler, an extreme adapter, philosophized about the limits of all religions as integrators. Religion was, at least at the outset, he said, always exclusive and isolating. Meanwhile commerce unites and broadens humanity, and trade has as large a share as religion for bringing humans together. He apologized for the ghetto: "Too long, indeed, have Chinese walls, reared by nations and sects, kept man from his brother, to render humanity asunder."

8:73   Meanwhile Rabbi Joseph Silverman from prestigious Temple Emanu-El in New York wanted to serve the cause of demystifying the Jewish world by pointing to its worlds within worlds as Orthodox, Conservative, Reform, and radical wings were taking shape. As if in a stage whisper to Jewish critics of Reform he argued that his movement, far from breaking up Judaism, had prevented Jews from going over "not to Christianity, but to Atheism." It was a modernist thing to say that all Jews agreed on certain essentials, but Silverman had to acknowledge that irreconcilable differences separated the various Jewish sects. He then defended what remained of "tribal aspirations" among Jews, for these showed not contempt for the world around but utter abandon to the charm of home.

8:74   Josephine Lazarus, whose sister Emma wrote the sonnet in the Statue of Liberty inscription, spoke up for Jewish universalism at the parliament and readied its audience for her *The Spirit of Judaism*, published two years later. Lazarus agreed that the ghetto resulted from the effects of persecution, which always strengthened solidarity. Jews, when attacked, did not counterattack: "We coil up in our shell of Judaism and entrench ourselves more strongly than before." Yet within that coil she reported on the gamut of "modern, restless thought, of shifting beliefs and unbelief." Religion was present, from "the most rigid and uncompromising formalism, or a sincere piety, to a humanitarism [sic] so broad that it has almost eliminated God, or a Deism so vast and distant that it has almost eliminated humanity," yet somehow the Jewish idea survived every contradiction.

8:75   Miss Lazarus credited the Enlightenment for having first pierced the ghetto walls. Her eloquent words deserve quotation for their aptness. "Casting off the outer shell or skeleton, which, like the bony covering of the tortoise, serves as armor, at the same time that it impedes all movement and progress, as well as inner growth," modern Judaism could still retain monotheism but must drop myth and dogma. "No religion seemed so fitted to withstand the storm and stress of modern thought, the doubt and skepticism of a critical and scientific age that has played such havoc with time-honored creeds." She did rue the fact that some Jews were

This turn-of-the-century Hester Street tenement-school picture suggests a cramped environment—but the premium on learning in places like this helped Jews move out of the older ghettos. (Jacob A. Riis Collection, Museum of the City of New York.)

drifting from their spiritual bearings, losing sight of spiritual horizons, thanks to lures of success, power, pride of life, intellect. The newcomers from Russia and Poland, coming in long black lines, crossing the frontiers or crushed within Europe's pale, could revitalize Judaism if "their narrow rites and limiting observance" did not overconfine them. If there was no compromising, might they not overreact, and be emancipated only to be "adrift on a blank sea of indifference and materialism?" This posing of dilemmas was classically stated for all kinds of American enclaves. Lazarus had to choose universalism overall: "Away then with all the Ghettos and with spiritual isolation in every form."

8:76   Away was precisely where they would not go. The Lower East Side was becoming the largest Jewish city in the world, separated from Uptown in Yorkville. Jewish philanthropists like Jacob Schiff gave money to help divert immigrants to Gulf of Mexico cities. Others unsuccessfully promoted farming; by 1909 only 3,040 Jewish farm families endured in America. The city, alien in Europe, was to be the American Jewish destiny. Jews crowded into dumbbell-shaped tenements, peopling them with up to 986 souls per acre. Mannered and civil Jews wanted to hurry their passage to modernity. In 1915 Conservative Israel Friedlaender spoke of the newcoming type as "coal—black, rugged, shapeless, yet retaining all its pristine energy which, when released, provides us with light and heat." How release it?

8:77   For a generation some Jews borrowed elements of *shtetl* life to form the *kehillah*, a kind of community. Many kept the old calendars, dietary laws, and customs. *Landsmanschaften*, secular enclaves adapted from Romanian and Galician life, were attractive to more. In one of the most drastically sudden changes in recorded spiritual history, within one generation most let the old faith slip away in neglect, sometimes in disdain. True, over three hundred congregations survived in little *shuls*, or synagogues, in 1905. Some were large enough to accommodate backsliders or disdainers, of whom a *New York Evening Post* reporter gibed in 1896 that "many of the irreligious ones relax their atheism on . . . Yom Kippur."

8:78   Modernizing and mannered Jews were embarrassed by ghetto worship, yet even they stayed to see some sense of piety break through. One *New York Evening Post* reporter decided that "this whispering, gesticulating, nodding, ecstatic crowd" could hardly be imagined doing anything but holding communion with its Maker. Then he was puzzled to see how, after it all, mundaneness came back and each worshiper wore the seal of worldly care on his face. In the midst of chaos, Jews were expected to keep *kashrut*, ritual regulations, even if there were too few rabbis to supervise kosher butchery. And the children? They resented learning under often incompetent teachers at sometimes boring *cheder* schools. Many reacted by seeking emancipation, as had the historians and philosophers in the core culture, who emerged from constrictions of small-town church culture. Socialism, Zionism, humanitarianism, union life, education, all came to compete with the old ways. Now and then a radical like Benjamin Feigenbaum, who arrived bringing vehement reactions against European Hassidic Judaism in 1891, tromped on tradition. He made fun of dietary laws and on the holiest day of the year staged Yom Kippur balls. Yet when news of worse pogroms arrived from Europe, such sacrilege was seen as a luxury, no longer in place. Jewish atheism also arrived but became ever less blatant, more respectful.

8:79   In the ghetto, Orthodoxy had the best natural base for those who remained religious. Late in the 1880s there were attempts to appoint a chief rabbi for an Association of the American Hebrew Orthodox Congregations. Amiable but ill-fated Rabbi Jacob Joseph found his leadership assignment to be impossible. Thus when he proposed that kosher meat be stamped with a seal, a *plumbe*, immigrants were in horror, because it reminded them of the Russian seal-stamping bureaucracy. The appointment in 1893 of two more chief rabbis did little to advance the cause.

8:80   In 1902 eastern European rabbis in New York made a new effort at an Agudath ha-Rabbanim, a national organization. In order to attract disaffected young Jews they invented a religious-minded Young Israel. Some young Jews used it as a passageway into American cultures of sorts that old Orthodoxy found bizarre. To Orthodox *Shul* rabbis the modern manners and decorum these cultures taught were uncongenial, but it was the rabbis who progressively lost authority. "Mushroom synagogues" survived; *Kehillah* leaders located 286 of these in 1912 at high holy days. These were in cheap dance halls, theaters, moving-picture places, factory lofts, sweatshops, and meeting rooms connected with saloons, hardly places to hold upward-bound young Jews.

8:81   Yet out of the extremes, from the adapters in Cincinnati to the resisters on the Lower East Side, grew a Judaism of broad spectrum. It generated movements to which we shall later give notice: Conservatism, Zionism, and a range of denominations in which Jewish life could be nurtured. These movements also remained translucent enough for select signals of non-Jewish American life to penetrate, to provide names and norms attractive to mobile Jews, while other Jews escaped the coils, merged or tried to pass as nondescript in the American nation of nations, people of peoples.

Orthodoxy: Primitive, Pure, and Chaste

8:82   Far from the core culture of these years was Eastern Orthodoxy, a form of Christianity whose adherents would eventually match Jews in numbers as Americans. Yet while Judaism has inspired libraries full of literature, Orthodoxy's story issued in hardly a handful of books during a century, so obscure and remote did it seem to non-Orthodox, so culturally introverted were many of its advocates. Protestant chroniclers virtually ignored it. In 1890 Daniel Dorchester gave Orthodoxy seven words on 800 pages crammed with material on American Christianity. Henry K. Carroll assigned Greek Orthodoxy five lines ("it has one chapel in this country . . . ."), but he did notice 336 Armenians and 13,004 Russian Orthodox in Alaska. In his synoptic history of American Christianity in 1898 Leonard Woolsey Bacon made no mention at all. With good reason: the Orthodox influx was tardy.

8:83   As they did arrive, who could expect English-speaking Americans to keep track of polyglot orthodoxy: Albanian, Arab, Belorussian, Bulgarian, Carpatho-Rusynian, Estonian, Finnish, Greek, Macedonian, Romanian, Russian, Serb, Syrian, Ukrainian, Cretan, Cypriot, Czechoslovak, Japanese, Polish, and more? Until 1917 many were nominally headed by the Russian Orthodox church but the Bolshevik Revolution changed that. Who would be expected to take notice of territorial Alaska, where the Russian Orthodox church had worked after 1794? How overlookable was the move of Orthodox headquarters from Sitka, Alaska, to San Francisco in 1872 and then in 1904 to New York! Citizens who ignored details of native American life would hardly become engrossed in the 1896 *Russian American Messenger* with its reckoning of twenty-one peoples served in Alaska, people named the Aleutians, Kuskokwims, Creoles, and Ingkalits and the smaller groups of Kenaians and Kvikhpakhs, Oglemuts and Kuyukans. That magazine complained that the census of 1890 minimized the size of these populations with an intent to show that these peoples, whom Orthodoxy alone served, were dying out. Bishop Nicholas of Alaska and the Aleutians in 1897 even complained to Washington that trading companies violated church holidays, engaged in island-grabbing, and left Orthodox mission properties unprotected: he had "bitter impressions."

8:84   Most important of the Orthodox were the Greeks and the Russians, both of whose groups became large enough to be noticed, inspired some local prejudices, and developed rather dense cocoons around their cultural life. The World's Parliament of Religions paid little notice, giving Orthodoxy's lonely agent ten pages in a 1,600-page report. The characteristic words of this spokesman, the Most Reverend Dionysios Latas, archbishop of Zante of the Greek church, set forth the promise and fitness of Orthodox life. It was, he claimed, organic, whole, one, the original establishment of Christianity, "pure and chaste, from which all good was to originate in this world, and on which the happiness of the nations is consequently based." Outcomes were to deny the propagation of this vision, and Orthodoxy was seen as a set of peoples and sects among the peoples and sects, no source but sidestreams or eddies in cosmopolitan America.

8:85   Latas's Greeks were at first overshadowed by the Russians, the rare Christian group that entered America from the west and worked east. Represented in California as early as 1812, it had only one congregation, in San Francisco, by 1893, and its first buildings in the next two years in Portland and Seattle. As the Greek presence grew in all three cities, they progressively went their own way, weakening the Russian hold. Some diplomats tried to promote Orthodoxy's unity among separated nationals. Archbishop Tikhon obligingly celebrated the liturgy in Greek for the first time in 1900 to oblige Chicago pioneers. Father John Nedzelnitsky looked on and dreamed: "the closer the unity among the Orthodox of various nationalities, the stronger will the Orthodox be in this land." The dream was denied. In 1904 New York Greek journals feared a Russian takeover when Tikhon led a liturgy at Holy Trinity Greek parish, and a year later Greeks militantly reincorporated as a Hellenic society. Tikhon kept proudly reporting on his services to mixed groups, but what he called the cosmopolitanism of old Seattle slipped away east of there.

8:86   When Tikhon went back to Russia, successor Archbishop Platon, who served in America from 1907 to 1914, had to complain about what he saw as the "traditional self-sufficiency of the Greeks in the questions of Religion and Faith." Archbishop Evdokim, perhaps because of a reputation for progressivism during his service from 1914 to 1917, was no more successful. His theme that Christianity "preaches eternal progress" was lost on the new Greeks, nine out of ten of whom were poor single males who were ill at ease among the Russian family parishioners. Still Evdokim boasted of American generosity back in Russia, only to find his plea for semi-independence, some kind of autocephaly, go ignored by the Holy Synod in Moscow.

8:87   The October Revolution upset plans in 1917 for an All-Russian Sobor on American models. Archbishop Alexander then surveyed the American church and saw serpentlike enemies attempting to destroy the church with "axes, hammers and sickles" while they used, he said, the language of "reformation and progressiveness." Alexander mourned, "It seems as if all the powers of hell have gathered to sink our Church in the waves of anarchy and atheism." When progressives spoke up in 1917 in New York, seven who supported rebel Father John Kedrovsky of Hartford were suspended; a Father Basil Lysenkovsky in *Golos Tserkvi* thought these rebels looked "exactly like the Bolsheviks now in Russia." The issue of communism in the homeland was to plague American Russian Orthodox organization for decades to come, and the churchly focus shifted more toward the Greeks.

8:88   In the century's last decade, only sixteen thousand Greeks arrived, but the next two decades saw ten times more. They came the usual routes, from eastern ports. While the priest was a necessary functionary, laity often kept control of more than the mere business side of the fifty-nine churches developed by 1916. They snubbed the Russian presence and were not too conscious of the ecumenical patriarchate to which they were in theory subject until 1908. In such chaos there were stories of masquerading priests with faked credentials winning legitimacy by pleasing the laity. The U.S. State Department even felt a need to intervene at one point, but Greek response was lethargic. Not until after revolts and reorganization in state and church in Greece in 1916–17 and the arrival of Metropolitan Meletios Metaxakis in 1918 was there much order. His attempt at reform was brief.

8:89   More important than these high-level twists and turns were the improvisations of club, lodge, and parish in which the Greeks, closely bonded as the Russians saw them, thrived. Single male immigrants of rural background saw the church symbolizing the old ways and the old country to which many wished to return. The parish festivals helped them keep home in mind. The coffee house, *kaffeneion*, was a gossip center and, one step more complex, the *kinotitos*, the community itself when not described in formally religious terms, bonded the life of newcomers. Schools were to promote Greek language and religion, as one urged, to "imbue our American-born children with . . . the greatness of our race" and to teach Greek character and virtue. Schools became bastions of Orthodox ways, yet elders had to urge weary children on as they adapted to "a strange language, strange customs, strange backgrounds, and strange mores," which led to their "goodbye to Hellenism!"

8:90   Eastern Orthodoxy, now a virtual program of the *kinotitos*, reinforced local life and was a window on the cosmopolitan Greek world. Members resisted an American Orthodox or, worse, Pan-Slavic church which Russians might dominate. Lacking resources, they often reduced their priests to having to grub for income and look mercenary as they charged money for holy rites. Intra-Greek partisanship troubled parishes like those in Chicago where Spartans and Tripolitans vied. As was frequent in the cocoonlike pattern, the tension occurred within, as Greek fought Greek, the conflict rarely affecting or being noticed by anyone outside. In such conflicts, Greeks were vulnerable to takeover by Russian Orthodox. Better organized as they were, the Russians could help subsidize Greek priests who then looked like traitors to Greek nationalist factions.

8:91   A class pattern developed in little Greek communities for two decades. Lay people would rent a hall, start a classical society, and bid for a priest. During the First World War alone, sixty-one such new parishes were started. How connect them? Greek seminaries did not train priests for competitive voluntary organizations, American-style. The Immigration Service interpreters investigated the immigrant clergy and found many to be monks parading as priests. They undercut the priests since they would work for half the salary that the real priests of the church demanded. The government, however, was ill-advised to patrol the churches, incompetent at credentialing clergy, and in frustration let the matter drop.

8:92   The militant Greek-language press aggravated tensions, though some papers also embarrassed priests into more responsible service. The timing was good, since it coincided with the rise of Greek Orthodoxy past the early Russian dominance. The ecumenical patriarchate to whom all Orthodox were nominally loyal took more interest. Yet here again factionalism played a part, as many priests refused to include prayers for the Greek royal family while other priests excluded liberal factions. Not until 1921 did this overseas situation stop distracting American Greek Orthodoxy, by which time many congregations had grown strong and were ready to present a more united front.

8:93   Other nationalisms were also present, and the Orthodox of each brought old-country memories and ties which led them to resist modernity and pan-Orthodoxy. In 1904 Syrians consecrated their first bishop, Archimandrite Raphael, only to find still unsettled jurisdictional disputes. In 1915 the North American bishops stepped in to help by censuring a Metropolitan Germanos who overstayed his welcome and overstepped his bounds during a fund-raising tour. He refused to return home. He founded still another complicator to the Orthodox intention to be and to appear as one, calling the tiny rival the Syrian Holy Orthodox Greek Catholic Mission in North America.

8:94   On the other hand, the Serbians, after they gathered in Jackson, California, in 1892, worked more closely with the Russians than did the Greeks. One report claimed that "each Serbian Church community made its own regulations, hiring and firing the parish priest at will," finding "no laws with which to regulate Serbian ecclesiastical life" in America. In 1913 members formed a Serbian Orthodox church independent of Russian leadership. When Belgrade ignored them, they snuggled back to the care of Russian Archbishop Evdokim who presided at their Serbian gathering in Chicago—just before the October Revolution of 1917. It forced Serbs again to go their own way.

8:95   While it is not possible to follow the course of all national groups, the Romanians demand notice for the way they illustrate localism. These rural people came, 165,000 strong, in the twenty-five years after 1895. Unskilled, most of them worked in factories and mines. Their church was also supplemented by clubs, lodges, and mutual-benefit leagues, many of which were anticlerical, as agents of communal life. Thus the constitution of the forty-four-society strong Uniunea Societăţilor Románe de Ajutor şi Cultura in 1911 banned priests from office and power. The standard plot developed: Romanian fought Romanian, attracting little notice and noticing few attractions outside the cluster. No one needed external prejudice to mold group bonds as the struggle within preoccupied many.

8:96   Orthodoxy was also tugged at in America by Roman Catholicism, which has thrived among some of the eastern nationals in Europe, and one American development demands special notice. During the 1890s numbers of Carpatho-Rusyns and other immigrants from Russian fringes, people with remote Orthodox ancestries but now members of Uniate churches, arrived. In the Austro-Hungarian empire they came under Catholic control but were allowed to keep many Orthodox practices, and these they brought, for example, to Pennsylvania coal country. At first they remained loyal to their Uniate parishes. Where they were not well served, some drifted to other Slavic-speaking churches, even if these had conventional Latin Roman Catholic rites. Feeling mistreated there, some organized a Uniate *Sojedinenije* or Union of Greek Catholic Brotherhoods in North America. Papal legate Archbishop Francesco Satolli, who arrived in 1893, encouraged their ways, but Rome acted slowly. Finally in 1902 Rome appointed apostolic visitator Andrew Hoboday, but he proved to be preening and alienating. His successor from 1907 to 1916, Bishop Soter Ortinsky, was no more successful. The *Sojedinenije* leaders found a vicar-level agent unacceptable and resisted his authority, only to be suspended. On June 14, 1907, Rome had issued the decree *Ea Semper*, which Ortinsky tried to use to draw Uniates into line. The Carpatho-Rusyns properly feared that the document would pull them away from Galician and Ruthenian European roots toward Rome, and tens of thousands of Uniates then left Catholicism for Orthodoxy. Here as so often elsewhere, the confused Orthodox cluster developed a pattern which survived beyond the 1920s. Orthodoxy kept stating cosmopolitan Christian claims but was itself fiercely divided on national lines and subjected to local control. For such reasons, with a potent and uniting voice and movement absent, the rest of American religious leadership could ignore the claims and leave inhabitants of the Orthodox enclaves alone, often to fight each other, always to try to give meaning and support to the people who made them up.

"I Am an American Catholic Citizen"

8:97   While Catholics had been in the Americas since 1492 and great numbers of Irish and then German Catholics arrived before the Civil War, what later came to be called ghetto Catholicism developed with the huge immigration surge in the half-century before 1924. A ghetto of ghettos, we might call this cluster of officially united yet practically diverse and divided set of peoples. Together they also made up, in the eyes of outsiders, something like what we have compared to a cocoonlike structure. It was spun for protection from without and nurture within, was translucent enough to permit awareness of what surrounded, opaque enough to shield from observers some of the detail of what went on inside.

8:98   Outside pressure or motivation came from proverbially anti-Catholic Protestant culture around this ghetto. While it will become clear that such prejudice has sometimes been exaggerated as an impulse to promote solidarity within, it is important to assess the character of what was present in these decades. Best known was an American Protective Association, designed to give political voice to anti-Catholicism as a revival of Nativism. The leaders of what might be called public Catholicism were quite aware of the association's attacks on the integrity of American Catholicism, but it is questionable how much power the APA had in the enclaves that made up the Catholic people. One can read whole histories of conflict within Catholic communities over a two-decade period and find not a single mention of Nativism or even of Protestantism at all. There were more reasons for Catholic Irish to fight Catholic Germans, and more satisfying ones for Catholic Poles to fight other Catholic Poles than to be distracted by buzzing, biting Protestants. If one can understand such fighting, it will become clearer why Catholicism acquired a density that made it difficult for modernisms to penetrate and how it served to protect people from some of the assaults of modernity.

8:99   Propagandists for the American Protective Association claimed 1.5 to 2.5 million supporters, but at its peak probably fewer than 100,000 people paid dues. A quirk of local politics led devout but semiparanoid Henry F. Bowers to want to protect America from popery. If Irish mill laborers in his little Clinton, Iowa, could defeat his friend, a mayoral candidate, then the pope and Jesuits could guide their national counterparts to control America. Bowers donned rites and regalia from his Masonic order and set up shop. The association aimed at lower-status groups and gathered energies from groups such as the Order of the Little Red School House, the National Order of Videttes, and the Crescents to build on unrest resulting from the depression of 1893. The organization had some Negro members, was not anti-Jewish, and included some recent non-Catholic immigrants into what its first chronicler, Humphrey Desmond, in 1911 concluded was the "envy of the growing social and industrial strength of Catholic Americans." "Whiskey Bill" William J. Traynor, a Canadian publicist "born on the Fourth of July" and now an ex-saloonkeeper, drew on panic, resentment, and a hunger for scapegoating to promote Bowers's organization.

8:100   The aims of the secret organization were not secret. In 1894 it touted thirteen principles of True Americanism, including the claim that it was tolerant of all creeds. Newcomers vowed, during their one-dollar initiation rite, never to employ a Catholic if a Protestant was available, never to engage in a labor strike alongside Catholics, and never to support a Catholic for public office. "I denounce . . . the diabolical work of the Roman-Catholic church." When conspirators cannot find conspiratorial documents they invent them. The APA's was a fake encyclical of Pope Leo XIII, dated Christmas, 1891. The Detroit *Patriotic American* printed the letter which gullible editors elsewhere picked up. It announced that in 1893 "*it will be the duty of the faithful to exterminate all heretics found within the jurisdiction of the United States.*" Burton Ames Huntington in Minneapolis claimed at book-length that the pope had 700,000 battle-ready troops in American cities. When none of the fears were fulfilled, APA apologists claimed that the Jesuits forged the document to confuse and divide true Americans.

8:101   Though the scenarios were bizarre, some people acted on them, and Toledo's mayor ordered the National Guard to alert in what the *Blade* soon called this "richest joke of the year." Still the association prospered through 1894 and in its name a few bricks were thrown through rectory windows, two people were killed in an APA-related Fourth of July saloon riot in Montana, and an APA leader was killed in Kansas City during an election riot, along with several Catholics. Meanwhile some APA documents merely appealed to prurient interests by describing "Rome's seraglios," thousands of white American female slaves who were claimed to be "victims of a lecherous priesthood," and nuns who were enthralled by thousands of stall-fed priests of Rome. Most Protestants found it easy to ignore these accusations of priestly lust and the religious mockery from the underlife beneath the planks of American culture.

8:102   A few more notable Protestant clerics did lend their names. Former Commissioner of Indian Affairs Thomas Jefferson Morgan kept opposing the use of federal funds to support Catholic Indian reservation work, and did his fighting under APA aegis. He saw in the association a well-timed renaissance of patriotism against foreign, that is Catholic, encroachments. Baptist leader Dwight Spencer in 1895 scorned armies of priests he thought paraded the streets with unblushing insolence, using rosaries and crosses. Such language was not picked up widely outside Catholicism or responded to from within. Other issues were more urgent.

8:103   The APA turns out to be a footnote, not a turning point. One can trace influence in the 1894 elections, but the association was well on the way to obscurity by 1896. Catholic periodicals had no time to get organized to oppose it. The unflappable Indianapolis *Catholic Record* editor advised, "If you want to notice them, you might give them the benefit of a smile." St. Paul's Archbishop John Ireland told defensive Catholics that they made too much of APA opposition. He trusted the American people, whom he knew from coast to coast. "Religious feeling is a foreign importation, and must soon die. It cannot live here." As for unified Catholicism, Rochester's conservative Bishop Bernard McQuaid accused Ireland of having sided with an APA candidate against a McQuaid favorite in a New York state election. Father Walter Elliott, a leader of the new Paulist order, in 1895 even argued that Catholics benefited. "For if they have turned the stupid for a moment against us, they have helped the intelligent to understand us, and have already caused many conversions to the Catholic faith." In a language too often forgotten in the heat of sectarian battle he added, "Would that it were as easy to pray for all our enemies as for the A.P.A.'s!"

8:104   For every Protestant word of support for the APA there were words of opposition. If a couple of Baptists were notable allies, others were eloquent foes. The *Examiner* editors in 1894 urged New York Baptists to set their faces as flint against the secret organization whose principles opposed the New Testament, Christ's spirit, and American law, to say nothing of the Baptist ethos, which opposed such secrecy. It was inquisitorial and devilish. Liberal Columbus, Ohio, cleric Washington Gladden edged out an assistant who was exposed as belonging to this "malicious, devilish, and perfectly asinine" organization. Americans tend to vote their interests, and if APA candidates matched these, they might get support. Soon they were dropped.

8:105   The APA ignorantly overlooked the system of overlappages and alliance in the life of the American enclaves. An appropriate example that contributed to its demise occurred in 1894. Conservative Lutherans of the Wisconsin and Missouri synods, whose doctrine taught them that the pope was the very antichrist and who had no theological reasons to be congenial to Catholics, were linked with them in Wisconsin through their common support of parochial schools. Wisconsin Democratic chairman E. C. Wall garnered support of sixty German Lutheran leaders to allege that the APA had been behind a notorious Bennett Law. This law, passed in 1889, forbade school teaching except in English, yet the parochial schools used several languages. Wall was deceptive and there was no evidence that the APA was behind the Bennett Law, but his tactic worked to keep the party together and bring victory. Similarly in Michigan, Missouri Lutherans, who opposed all secret societies, opposed this one. They were approached for anti-APA support. However, here the Democratic tactics were too obvious and backfired, proving only that the APA was too complex an issue to be of use in the politics of hatred or practical politics.

8:106   After 1896 Catholics who wanted to could not find a strong enough APA to help promote internal cohesion. Bowers could not revive it. It lives on chiefly in the memory of historians who write about the climates of intolerance. Anti-Catholicism and other anti's did not, of course, die out. In 1914 a Junior Order of the United American Mechanics, 224,000 members strong, uttered some association-type words. They only succeeded in showing that anti-Catholicism was durable and inconveniencing, not potent. Raw anti-Catholicism had to wait for the 1920s to gain its hearing, and Catholics found other bases for cohesion.

8:107   One of these was organizational and effective, especially among Irish-American laymen. Denied access to many forms of American social and convivial life, Catholics formed voluntary organizations of their own. The Knights of Columbus can represent numbers of them. Founded in 1882 as an alternative to the anti-Catholic Masonic lodge, the Knights of Columbia replicated some of its ritual instinct. It can be glimpsed in a commemorative ceremony on the village green of historically Protestant New Haven, Connecticut. Looking back four hundred years to Columbus's discovery of the New World and ahead, Father W. J. Maher orated: "We enter the wake of the modern march of American progress. . . ." Progress was not an alien concept, nor was Americanism.

8:108   A Fourth Degree was invented in 1900. The 1,100 Knights who qualified for it united in ceremony: "Proud in the olden days was the boast; 'I am a Roman Catholic'; prouder yet today is the boast, 'I am an American citizen'; but the proudest boast of all times is ours to make, 'I am an American Catholic citizen.'" A litany followed, praising Catholics for having discovered, explored, and named America, baptizing its continent and waters.

They invoked names of Lord Baltimore and Thomas Dongan and others who contributed to American toleration. Now Catholics must contribute to the virtue and permanence of the republic. Everything about the language sounded like that issuing from the Protestant core-culture.

8:109   An eloquent lay voice supporting American pluralism with a defined Catholic presence was Thomas Harrison Cummings, a Columbian and a curator at the Boston Public Library. The best Americans knew, Cummings said, that this is not a Protestant country, nor a Catholic country, nor a Hebrew country, any more than it is an Anglo-Saxon or a Latin country. Instead it is a country of "all races and all creeds, with one great, broad, unmolturable [sic] creed of fair play and equal rights for all." Cummings stressed what many non- and anti-Catholics did not know, or choose to know: "Much as their adversaries may storm and rave about the Catholic vote, and the political power of Rome in America, Catholics know that in political, material and social affairs they are really more divided than their Protestant neighbors." Had he had Protestant listeners of good faith who would have confirmed his observation, the lay sociology of religion in America would have been better informed for decades to come.

8:110   Not that no anti-Catholic prejudice worked to unite Catholics. Cummings's first line about storming and raving showed an awareness of some. The Knights' Commission on Religious Prejudices, which dates from 1914 but with more remote antecedents, paralleled the Jewish Anti-Defamation League. Yet even this commission spent much of its energies on anti-Knight Catholics. One of these was Missouri Synod Lutheran convert to Catholicism, Arthur Preuss, whose *Review* in St. Louis opposed such Americanizers. He thought the K. of C. mimicked Masonry. On the ground that it would disrupt unity he cajoled the bishop of Belleville, Illinois, John Janssen, into forbidding the formation of a council in his diocese. When Cardinal Satolli in 1904 blessed the fraternal order it was hard for seething Preuss and frustrated Janssen to prevent Bellevilleans from joining nearby councils.

8:111   The Knights suffered a bit from bogus-oath occasions. A Seattle minister nibbled once when someone invented such an oath. On September 1, 1912, he preached on the subject. Other Protestants, however, leaped on him at once for falling for this blasphemous and horrible travesty upon the real oath which they knew showed the "highest type of American citizenship." After several such incidents Washington Gladden conceived the idea of promoting interreligious work for peace and harmony, and it was this that helped inspire the Commission on Religious Prejudices. Founder Patrick Henry Callahan claimed success for it, citing the fact that from its founding in 1914 to 1917 the number of anti-Catholic publications in America dropped from sixty to two or three. Callahan may have been guilty of the *post hoc, ergo propter hoc* fallacy, attributing credit to his organization simply because something else happened after it. Anti-Catholicism was on the wane and World War I pushed the tolerance cause further. The commission was disbanded, out of work. Few anticipated the anti-Catholicism of a revived Ku Klux Klan in the 1920s.

8:112   Parochial schools helped Catholics spin their own cocoon and thus appear remote to the non-Catholic majority, which saw public schools as a kind of junior wing of the informal national religious establishment. These schools were superpatriotic, thus justifying the image of translucence for the way they filtered but still permitted signals from without. The schools allowed various ethnic groups to retain some of their language and practices just as they were agents through which dioceses and national leaders could help Americanize the children. At the beginning of this period in 1892 George D. Wolff estimated that there were 700,753 children in these schools and added 50,000 more to estimate the number of unrecorded attendees. With 25,000 more in orphan asylums, he claimed 800,000. With better records in later times, we know of 1,237,251 in 1910 and 1,701,219 in 1920. The schools took on the color of the religious orders which ran them or the national groups that made up their sponsoring parishes, and they were anything but monochromatic or uniform.

8:113   After 1904 a Catholic Educational Association helped bring some harmony of standards and outlook to them. In 1901 Father Louis S. Walsh had pleaded that for all secular subjects taught by these schools the formulated state system must dominate. The schools must teach the civic ideas that make a state or nation but use the instruments of Catholic books and with Catholic teachers to have the best of two worlds. Baltimore's Cardinal Gibbons himself followed this calculated policy, knowing that Catholic children needed teachers who spoke their own languages. This represented, he said, a much easier pathway for the foreigner to enter the American life. In no case did Gibbons picture them not entering it. Almost unconsciously they would come "into complete sympathy with American ideals, and readily adapt themselves to American manners and customs." He was just as strenuous in defending the idea that Catholic children should be kept from unwitting exposure to threatening modern ideas. In any case, the isolation benefited the church. Wolff noted properly that it was from parochial, not public, schools, that the sodalities and confraternities of the parish were chiefly recruited and received their most exemplary members. They would help spin the web enclosing young Catholics, habituating them to a subculture.

8:114   Such efforts did not always please critics of Catholic schools. In 1894 a public-school text in Massachusetts noted that 10.6 percent of the state's children who were in Catholic schools were isolated, separated from non-Catholic peers, and prevented thus from growing into the possession of those thoughts and purposes which mark interests in common and imply "one people, born and reared and molded into a sect rather than into a nation." Such textbook authors did not regard themselves as members of a sect among sects. Catholics did.

8:115   Alongside fraternal and sororal organizations and parochial schools, Catholicism even developed a literature to reinforce the combination of separateness and common Americanism. This, too, did not follow simple ethnic lines. At the turn of the century there flourished a now almost forgotten fiction with a parochial purpose. This was one among many ways encouraged to stimulate a protected outlook when modern fiction so often seemed destructive of Catholic purpose. With it came book clubs and reading programs, though not a single work of lasting literary value. While directed at the Catholic subculture, this literature was anything but suspicious of America. Nurture of such fiction matched the injunctions of Baltimore's Third Plenary Council, in 1884, calling the faithful to coherence, chiefly through schools, but knowing that schools could not do the work alone. By the time of the World's Parliament of Religions in 1893 the Catholic Educational Union could report on 250 local reading circles of Catholics. Then it was also clear that such circles could generate a cluster of Catholic writers. Novelist Katherine Conway was blunt: "the point of all this is not only to raise Catholic intellectual standards, but also to create a market for Catholic lecturers and writers." The Guild of Catholic Authors, formed in 1898, promoted without protest nothing but formula writing. In 1898 Benziger Brothers thus produced *A Catholic Speller*, *The Pictorial Game of American Catholic Authors*, and *A Game of Quotations from American Catholic Authors*. "Catholic" had become an all-purpose credentialing adjective.

8:116   Dominant through the period was Notre Dame professor and potboiler author Maurice Francis Egan, who wrote scores of novels and short stories. Secular critics like one in *The Nation* were not impressed with his work: "It does not rise to the level where serious criticism can touch it." Why should he care? He sold well as he filled his novels with debates over popular theological points or told stories of Catholics resisting the temptations of modern culture. Through such entertainments Catholics were reinforced in their pride in church and state even as they were encouraged to remain apart.

8:117   Concern for modern manners showed up in many plots. How does one transact life in both the culture and the subculture? Lelia Hardin Bugg's Catholic women characters were shown walking with folded hands, downcast eyes, and steps ahead of their husbands, into church pews. Bugg would describe in her fiction the many voluntary associations like the Society of Angel Guardians which one could join. In another novel she depicted a Catholic heroine who kept public company with a woman of ill-repute, an aspect of behavior that had serious consequences in her plot.

8:118   The major study of this fiction found it looking in two directions. Some stories inspired caution. A young opera singer in one wore a low-cut dress to her debut, suffered a chill, was ruined. In another a circus performer wore a skimpy costume, attracted an unfortunate suitor, and came to ruin. In many plots, mixed marriages were tried and found wanting. Again, ruin. Rare were instances like Mary Agnes Tincker's experiment with a utopian communal society in the plot of her *San Salvador*. Tincker broke the rules by breathing an ecumenical spirit like that of progressive Protestantism. San Salvadorans honored all Christian faiths and worked to restore primitive Christian simplicity. The author was dismissed as a maverick for her tinge of modernism and was henceforth given not even polite mention. Her restlessness points to the confining character of this fiction. In all the rest of the books, people were rescued from modernism and liberalism, the all-purpose bogeys or foes of faith to Catholic Americanism. The spun web remained secure, nurturing, constricting, and confusing at once.

8:119   Most of the spinning circled ethnic groups, most walls within walls of the ghetto followed national lines imported from Europe. To account for all this one must be illustrative, not inclusive, given the scope of research into the patterns of these many clusters of peoplehood. Yet illustration can be fair, representative, and enlivening, and should include some obvious and some less obvious but illuminating cases. No one could argue with the example of Polish Catholics, who came to resent and challenge Irish and German hegemony in some dioceses such as those in Wisconsin. They illustrate how tension within the circle distracted participants from involvement with what was outside. One can read the translated literature from two decades of a celebrated Polish church war in Wisconsin and find neither side looking past the whites of their opponents' eyes at other groups. Rare were references like one in a 1907 *Handbook for Catholic Parishioners of the Archdiocese of Milwaukee*. It warned Catholics not to borrow the "essentially Protestant principle" of lay power. Just as rare was a Polish newspaper reference to a Catholic partisan as a Martin Luther because he was embittered after not being named a bishop. For all the rest, an onlooker would never see a Protestant in the Catholic gunsights or a non-Catholic environment beyond the dust of battle. Of course, through it all, the people on both sides lived full lives as citizens in an America that they manifestly loved.

8:120   A classic study dating from this period defined the role of the Polish parish. Authors William I. Thomas and Florian Znaniecki in *The Polish Peasant in Europe and America* were writing during World War I after a great migration. They found the parish to be "simply the old primary community, reorganized and concentrated," transported to America. It was more than simply religious, for "in its concrete totality it is a substitute for both the narrower but more coherent village-group and the wider but more diffuse and vaguely outlined *okolica*." Coherence in neighborhoods followed parish lines, yet each parish could be the site of constantly expressed rivalries.

8:121   Some critics feared that even this structure brought Poles in America too close to neighbors of other styles. The Reverend Stanislaus Radziejewski urged readers of *Dziennik Chicagoski* to flee to farms and there create a new fatherland which would eventually join hands with the Old Country in close ties. He really feared the demise of Poland itself. "It is not in our power to restore Poland, but it is our duty to see that Poles continue to exist, because if a majority of Poles should become Germanized, Russianized, or Americanized, then God, even if he should desire it, would not know for whom or from what to restore Poland." The acts of crossing oceans haphazardly, intermingling with other nationalities, settling among millions of strangers, mean that

"everything about them will be strange and additional new generations will be lost to our nation." He was not to be heeded. The
Poles wanted to be Americanized, though not modernized, on
their own terms. They were loyal but not messianic, urban and not
farm-minded, and the parish was working effectively.

8:122   A visit to Wisconsin is not a diversion to backwoods and
waters. With 100,000 Polish Catholics in Milwaukee alone by
1915, this people outnumbered many nationwide Protestant
groups. By 1920 they had fourteen parishes in Milwaukee, where
even their critics saw the best in immigrant life represented. The
church steeples above the factories or, for that matter, above the
rural minorities around Green Bay, beckoned Catholics to worship, picnic, teach children, enjoy social life, have a credit union,
plan for burial. St. Josaphat's Church, for one example, became
the fifth largest basilica in the world, even if becoming so drove its
lower-income people into $70,000 debt.

8:123   Stakes were high to those who were in the circle. Four-fifths of
the members came from Polish territories in Germany. They had
suffered under Chancellor Otto von Bismarck's Kulturkampf, an
anti-Catholic "battle for civilization." Yet after migrating they
could not make common cause with Wisconsin Catholics of German descent. These instead became the enemy because so many
worked to thwart efforts to gain Polish bishops. Crowds of 40,000
or 50,000 people indicate the size and loyalty of groups rallied by
newspapers to both sides.

8:124   Two brothers led the anti-German ranks. Arriving in 1883,
tireless militant Michael Kruszka five years later founded *Kuryer
Polski* on fanatically Catholic terms. "If a Polish organization
wants to be truly Polish, it must be Catholic." His portraits show
him both dapper and fierce, with a "Don't Tread on Me" look that
went with his view that Polishness was portable. His readers, he
wrote, held in common "one blood, one faith, one Mother, and
one heart." His motto was simple: "We Demand Polish Bishops
for the Poles! We Demand That Polish Parish Property Be Assigned to the Polish Parishioners. We Demand That the Parishioners Themselves Control Parish Finances."

8:125   His half brother, the Reverend Wenceslaus Kruszka, who arrived in 1893 and was ordained in 1895, was only slightly more
restrained. He had to be careful during his years of power because
his enemies were ready with personal charges. In 1904 a rival pastor alleged that Kruszka had stayed overnight with a parishioner
family "and committed there adultery." The priest protested inno-

cence, called the accusing woman insane, but sent her money anyway. More moderating was the orthodoxy that led him to know his final devotion must be to his archbishop and a political sense that he would lose his way if he broke relations. He opposed Polish-English catechisms as compromising confusions. He also did not like any cemetery administrators, rival priests, or episcopal appointees, who he thought betrayed pure Polishness. Between 1905 and 1908 he published a thirteen-volume *Historya Polska w Ameryce* but still had time to complain of his tiny Ripon parish as oppression and exile. The psychological insight of one paragraph was impressive, perhaps because the author learned it the hard way: "Every oppressor is guilty not only of the wrong he does but of the evil to which he inclines the heart of the oppressed."

8:126   Over against such attackers stood the German hierarchy, which had just seen Milwaukee through the most threatening nationalist clash in American Catholic history, an effort to use the German base against Irish hierarchy and in support of standard national-based parishes. After 1904 its head was Sebastian G. Messmer, who would bend the rules as much as possible to win and keep Polish allegiance. An import from Green Bay, he had written Cardinal Gibbons in 1905 that Poles "are not yet American enough & keep aloof too much from the rest of us." When World War I came he still warned that Poles were "walled up against the rest of us" and would not accept a policy from non-Polish fellow citizens "merely on the plea that it was not Polish." Messmer did not account for his own ethnic sense; when the war broke out he infuriated *Kuryer* editors by petitioning God "for the just cause of Austria and Germany." To Gibbons he wrote that it would be a dangerous experiment to give the Polish people their own bishop. Such an appointed person would want to be considered "the bishop *for all the Poles* of the U.S." In conflicts with their local bishop, all would come running to him as a Pole and thus as their bishop.

8:127   Father Kruszka took hope as early as 1903 when he was given opportunity to state his case for Poles' loyalty and rights. Surely the pope would see the need to reward them lest more follow disgruntled ones into the newly formed and schismatic Polish National Catholic church. Pius X tendered him an audience but also gave evidence that he had been reached by Kruszka's American enemies. Kruszka lobbied for a half year until April 1903, and went home carrying like a talisman the pope's pledge that a decision, soon, would be "according to your wishes." When the Vatican sent Archbishop Francis Symon from Plock on a goodwill mission to Milwaukee in 1905 he stirred fifty thousand people to shouts of "Long live Poland! Long live America!" and was friendly to Kruszka, but had little to offer him.

8:128   When no satisfaction came, the *Kuryer* started a "Don't Pay" campaign that asked parishioners to withhold contributions. Little had been settled by 1921 when Messmer walked Kruszka to the door of his residence: "It would be better if you broke openly with the Church." Kruszka had gone too far and began to lose support. Polish priests greeted him at Detroit with "Shame!" and "Throw Kruszka out!" but Kruszka was not ashamed and had to be thrown out. Messmer held his ground, Kruszka yielded, and then the hierarchy acted. On February 1, 1912, the five Wisconsin bishops sent a pastoral letter to all parishes, calling the Polish agitators false prophets, like those of Jesus' time. "We hereby solemnly condemn the . . . *Kuryer-Polski*." Catholics who would read it would incur grievous sin. None dared join the Kruszka lay federations. The hard line was followed with softening gestures. In 1908 Polish-American Paul Rhode became the first bishop of Polish descent and took charge at Green Bay. Then Bishop Edward Kozlowski became an auxiliary at Milwaukee, an event that even Father Kruszka enjoyed. He announced that he would represent "the quintessence of all existing sides and parties," and that his policy was "Everything for God and Fatherland, through Love."

8:129   The *Kuryer* lost subscribers if not militancy. Power ebbed. Messmer had engineered enough compromise to buy off Polish discontent. World War I distracted and unified Poles in Wisconsin and they united with other Americans against Germany for the sake of Poland. Yet the brothers did not give up. Michael died right after the war, but in 1926 Wenceslaus was still headlining: "The Poles are entitled to their own Catholic Bishops *and they demand them*." Messmer did not have to play along; he had won. True, he lost a few malcontents to the schismatic Polish National Catholic church, whose Bishop Francis Hodur sent an able priest, Francis Bonczak. The majority of the Poles, whatever their discontents, remained firmly loyal to Catholicism and two Fatherlands. They needed no Protestant core-culture as a negative reference point for anything they wanted to achieve in their crowded enclaves in Milwaukee or on farms near Green Bay and Madison.

8:130   The second illustration, the Italians, formed another giant ethnic group thanks to immigrations in this period. They differed from the Poles because Catholicism was not such an element in their European nationalism, and, indeed, they were often indifferent toward religion or even anticlerical. Yet the complex of Italian Catholicism and parish life helped define these immigrants, hold them together, and make their passage toward American respectability. Protestants generally overestimated the hold of the formal church on Italians, perhaps because they were reflexive about identifying the Vatican with Italy and overestimating its security and influence among the people who became immigrants. Social workers had this problem even as they certified the power of parishes. Thus Edith Abbott and Sophonisba P. Breckinridge in

In an era when Catholic life was supposed to have been shaped by an antagonistic Protestant majority, Catholics could fight Catholics for years and never mention the Protestant environment. Here Milwaukee's Archbishop Sebastian Messmer fiddles for Father Boleslau Goral at a time when two of their enemies were denied Catholic burial in 1913.

Chicago spoke up in 1912 with concern lest Italian and other ethnic churches would help members hold on too long to the speech,
the ideals, and to some extent the manner of life of the mother
country. Some of those members matched the description by
W. H. Agnew, S.J., in 1913. He said they came heroically attached to their religion, well instructed in it, faithful in the use of
its sacraments, and ready to die for it. They had trouble adapting
to a church managed by non-Italians, and leaders of secular organizations warned lest Protestants and Irish usurpers would sap
their ancestral traditions.

8:131   While Italians struggled for position with each other, clerical
versus anticlerical and church leader against church leader, they
also faced disdain from other Catholic peoples. To many they
looked superstitious, their festivals and practices seemed magical. What could respectables do but distance themselves from
twentieth-century people who used physical objects to fend off
evil spirits? Non-Italians gaped in wonder as celebrators at festivals and processions pinned dollar bills on statues of the Ma-
donna, paraded, ate spicy foods, or lit the churches with candles.

8:132   Italy was still producing large supplies of nuns and priests, and
many founded missions, hospitals, and social-service agencies for
the Italian poor in America. In 1918, twenty-six such orders were
active. Loyalty was always a question, as non-Italians remained
suspicious and Italians sometimes drifted off. Thus, in Trenton,
some joined a Protestant church whose pastor spoke Italian while
they pleaded for the bishop to name one of their own as pastor.
Where they were not met with hostility they knew indifference
from a church that seemed far from their tastes and their control.

8:133   Criminal reputations also plagued the communities. In February of 1908 a Sicilian anarchist announced regret that he had not
killed all the other priests on a day when he shot but one German-
born priest at mass in Denver's St. Elizabeth's Church. Critics
traced the inspiration for attacks to the Circolo Giordano Bruno.
As far away as Chicago, priests for a time needed police protection as they carried on religious services in Italian churches. Non-
Italian Catholics faulted anarchism and "progressivism."

8:134   Meanwhile Italians had to keep their enclosures safe from
evangelistic Protestant poachers. Stefano L. Testa, who worked
for the Brooklyn City Mission and Tract Society, knew how the
Italian parishes were organized. The south Italians there, he wrote
in 1908, because they were tribal and clannish, made it "difficult
for new ideas of civilization and religion to penetrate or make any

headway among them." Nine years later Methodist worker Frederick H. Wright was still complaining about apathy in conversion efforts. When a few Italians did convert, they were segregated, and needed gradually to be "drawn into our American churches" and national life. A. Di Domenica, a Philadelphia Baptist, feared that unless Protestantism intervened, Italians would be swept into infidelity and atheism. They must convert "not only for the salvation of the Italians, but for the salvation of America as well." And in 1904, J. C. Monaghan in *The Catholic World* kept worrying lest it would, tit for tat, be Protestant evangelism instead that might lead immigrants into agnosticism, indifference to all religions, "resulting in downright atheism." If the church meant less to Italians than to Poles, it did serve as both a uniter of Italians against the larger culture and of Italian against Italian over stakes and turf within the parish and diocese.

8:135   The third illustrative case, that of Catholicism among Czechs and Slovaks, is lively because it demonstrated as nowhere else on such a scale how Catholicism was a divider within ethnic groups. In her pioneering work, Emily Balch showed how complex was the organization of the eight Slav groups so classified by the Immigration Department. Her list did not exhaust the Slav nationalities but it was, she said, enough to thoroughly bewilder most Americans. This Wellesley professor was most amazed at the intricacy of the organized life among Slavs. Consciousness of kind, she knew, always moved people who were far from home. In the vast American world the immigrant had, for the first time, a vivid sense of oneness with those who spoke the same language here as at home. Balch cited dozens of reinforcing societies which were more or less anticlerical and then pointed to Roman Catholic, Greek Catholic, and even Protestant churches that also served economic purposes, and helped in athletic, dramatic, and publishing interests.

8:136   Balch marvelled at how American patterns pleased all factions. The celebrated Bohemian freethinkers found separation of church and state a cause for relief. The religious meanwhile enjoyed the fact that the "impression that the country makes seems to be the reverse of irreligious." Father Šusteršič in his Slovenian guide, *Poduk Rojakom Slovencem* claimed that "the American nation is a believing nation," and found signs of this on coins, in Congress, everywhere. When newcomers from European state churches had to build their own structures here, that only added to their devotion.

8:137   The free-thought organizations looked much like Catholic churches, even to the point of having, Balch noted, a "profoundly pathetic little handbook of addresses,—they can hardly be called services,—for use at their funerals." Balch observed that the young Slavs did not share the negativism of their parents and would not adopt the rancor these showed "against the corrupt side of priestcraft" as it was known in Austria. A New York Bohemian doctor had noted that two Bohemians could not meet without beginning to talk of religion, but now the young showed indifference or self-indulgence. Some turned Unitarian, Protestant, socialist, or anarchist to fill the void.

8:138   In the end, Americanization was the prime issue. Balch never forgot the words of Yonkers priest Paul Tymkevich, a Ruthenian Greek-Catholic: "*My people do not live in America, they live underneath America. America goes on over their heads.*" They lived in poverty, where civilization had broken down. A man like Tymkevich, a scholarly type, lived in almost intolerable loneliness. Balch closed with a call for Americans to see that America must come to mean to them, "not a rival nationality eager to make them forget their past," but a place where they could connect their ideals with those of others. Meanwhile they would be off by themselves where they would know and show affection chiefly among and to each other.

8:139   Conflict within the Czech cocoon was more satisfying than with people around it. When Thomas Čapek looked back on *The Čechs (Bohemians) in America* at the end of the period, he saw only strife. In Bohemia, according to Austrian statistics, 960.48 of every 1,000 persons were Catholic. In America, out of every 1,000, 254 were Catholic, 110 Protestant, 16 Jewish, and 620 had no affiliation. Over half had seceded, though Čapek, the free-thinkers' friend, was ready to say that 60-70 percent were gone only from Catholicism. Some were "negativists," but others lived positively by Charles Havlicek's "harsh formula as applied to the priests: give them nothing, credit them nothing."

8:140   Čapek cited several reasons for decatholicization. The people were not, despite American scholar Edward A. Steiner's judgment, "thoroughly eaten through by infidelity." Instead, Hussitism, a pre-Reformation heresy that inspired anticlericalism, was at root. This force kept national consciousness alive in difficult circumstances. Now America provided Czechs with opportunity to live on Hussite principles. Firebrand editors blasted the church. Thus F. B. Zdrůbek, who died in 1911, was the archpropagandist of atheism. He outlasted the effects of his theological education and worked "to combat the menace of bigotry and superstition among his countrymen." Čapek saw such movements as a fight not against creeds but against the political church allied with the Hapsburgers. Where, now, could the militants find new bases for anti-Catholic slogans?

8:141   Free thought was a surprisingly strong Czech rural expression. Thus in Nebraska, where more than 55 percent of all that state's Czechs lived in five counties, three of which had a higher percentage of Czechs than any other counties in the U.S., freethinkers outnumbered Czech Catholics in four of these. They substituted women's organizations, Sokols, lodges, benevolent societies, and clubs for church. In Nebraska there were thirty-two freethinker cemeteries to twenty-two for Czech Catholics and three for Protestants. Above the Wilber, Nebraska, Czecho-Slavonic National Cemetery was a great sign speaking of the condition of the dead, "What you are, we were—what we are, you shall be." Yet hard times grew as the cemeteries did, since there were few young takers. "Believing unbelievers" were no longer in vogue. In 1926 at the seventh congress of the Freethought Union in Chicago, Jaroslav E. S. Vojan was doleful. Nebraska, he said, "has today not even the tiniest Freethought movement. All is quiet . . . Thus can one proceed from state to state." The historic furies were quieted, their day was past.

8:142   Almost every observer gaped to see the extent of Czech free thought while it prevailed. Here was a pocket of antireligion in a nation where such a voice was as rare as a Robert Ingersoll who made a lonely campaign out of it. Kenneth D. Miller, of the Board of Home Missions of the Presbyterian Church in the United States provided a Protestant view from John Hus Neighborhood House in New York. In 1922 Miller wrote of experiences during preceding decades. The immigrants, he argued, were not godless. Indeed, "the Slovaks are incurably religious, or superstitious according to the point of view. People of one faith flock together" among them. It was the Czechs who saw a 50 percent secession. The wonder was not that Catholicism had lost so many but that she had held some during the times of the virile and insidious free-thought propaganda against Rome. Catholics matched free-thought societies with their own. The odds were against Rome, but it would fight back. Still, "among no other immigrant race has there been such a break with the old-world faith as among the Czechs."

8:143   Miller had to account for change when modernity in America, in contrast to Europe, led people to religious inventiveness and not to simple secularism. The church had looked "medieval, reactionary and unnecessary" to the Czech. When one leaves the Catholic church, he leaves all churches. The moment was passed, however, for free thought, which had been crass and bigoted. It made its way only when other voices of Catholic immigrants were even less hopeful, less lacking in intellectual acumen—of which free thought itself displayed precious little. To Protestant Miller, a break with Hapsburg Roman Catholicism was a sign of intelligence and progress, and was a distinctly creditable move. At this point Miller also turned modest. "We know that we had much to learn from these newcomers to our shores." They must keep the best in their culture and then tie in with American religious ideals, which were chiefly Christian, we must add Protestant, in character. The Czech clannishness was proverbial and inhibiting, but it could be overcome. Americanization was inevitable: how assure that it come in the best ways?

8:144   The church, then, was only one of many bonding agents in Czech communities. The voices of modernity reached different elements in them at different times, with different kinds of force. In every case, however, Czechs did not measure life by response to the influence of a Protestant core-culture. They fought old imported European battles on American soil, and when the causes behind these waned, they forgot about them and forged an American identity. Their case differed vastly from that of Poles and Italians because religion helped only half of them find coherence. Formally, however, they followed the same model. Not every wind of change or altered temperature in the surrounding climate needed to threaten them. They would stay together, as Czechs and as Slovaks in America. Thus they could regulate some of the signals that reached them. They were less in control of the forces of conflict that made life within their webs and cocoonlike enclaves problematic—and exciting.

8:145   So it was that for the two major sets of agents involved, we can see that there were ironic outcomes to their described original intentions. In the core culture, including among the modernists and moderns who were progressive, a cosmopolitan vision of interactive and mutually acceptant people, and even a convergent vision of people come together, dominated. Yet the dominators placed on reservations, segregated, excluded, or ignored the nonwhite peoples in their own nation. They misrepresented or saw as irrelevant the religions and culture of the eastern and southern European peoples who were arriving in great numbers at the turn of the century. These policies and perceptions denied the very cosmopolitanism that these mainstream agents of American culture were propounding as a world ideal, even an inevitability. The peoples retained existence in their enclaves. These remained a force for their identity and a frustration to people who would integrate them on uncongenial models toward undesired ends.

8:146   The leaders of these peoples were another set of agents who also left their descriptions of what they intended. Circumstances were to deny the promise and fitness of things as they stated them. For one thing, each saw their group life in their cocoonlike shelterings as something that appeared over against the mainstream culture, something that would unite them. Yet they turned out to experience internal conflict as much as they found satisfaction in the necessity to ward off threatening outsiders. For another, the choice of virtually all of them (native Americans being the main exception) to be fully American in their own ways, even as they tried to reject the ethos of modernity, left them, in the eyes of others, at best half accepted in America. "American" and "modern" at the turn of the century came together. They were, in a sense, a package deal. Opening the portion marked America exposed these groups to much that was wrapped in its accompanying element marked Modern. More than they knew or wanted, they had become a part of a process of change which would make it impossible for them to retain or return to all the old ways from old cultures, or to the Old Country with its traditions of faith and life. In both cases, these mockeries of the promise and fitness of things deserve to be seen as ironic. They have left a legacy of intergroup life that persists in America.

9

Denomination as a Canopy

9:1   Peoplehood or ethnicity marked the identity and social location of nonwhites and southern and eastern Europeans. Outsiders
tended to perceive blacks as blacks, not as Baptists or Methodists.
Orthodox people were Greek or Armenian more than Orthodox to
alien eyes. Difference from the Anglo-Protestant norm helped
these groups keep their coherence and helped nonmembers keep
them in focus. What would serve such purposes in the case of
Anglo-Protestants, continental European people such as the Lutherans, or English-speaking Catholics such as the Irish? Few of
them took the acids or elixirs of modernity straight, undiluted, or
unfiltered. It was the denominational pattern, inherited from a
century earlier, that they transformed to shelter them, as peoplehood sheltered others.

9:2   The agents of the denominations made very clear their intentions. They would support denominational life, or factions within
it, in order to preserve the integrity of truth and traditions. At the
same time they were sufficiently exposed to the ethos of modernity to accept something of the cosmopolitan habit and ecumenical ideal. Both of these rendered the old rationales for denominations problematic. Leaders were attracted to this ecumenical spirit
and even furthered it, but they also had to dig in to preserve what
they found valuable in their denominations. In the process, what

150

they regarded as intrinsic to their own group life came to be seen as progressively more irrelevant to all those who did not share it. In the case of Lutherans and Catholics, their affirmation of Americanism and adaptation to the American ethos, particularly in World War I, showed that to the public they also were denominations among the denominations. They were moved by outside norms as much as by those doctrinal standards which each professed to find of some importance.

9:3   Several instances will help make this case, for which it is necessary to set a stage. Who made up the denominations, how many were there, were they prospering, and how were they conceived? Questions like these naturally come up when we deal with a social form undergoing transformation. Modern sociology of religion, especially as it developed in and has observed Europe, should lead historians to expect sudden decline in denominational participation as America turned urban and industrial. This turning is often associated with the decline of the sacred, insofar as the sacred had been borne by institutions of organized religion. The social analysts have observed the emptying of European churches, the lack of interest in all but nominal participation in rites of passage. Historically and macroscopically, says a scholar who has synthesized the trends and theories, "the crisis of religious practice is a product of the development of an urban life style . . . and of industrial civilization."

9:4   Certainly the promoters of denominational and interdenominational life at the turn of the century were alert to this problem in America. Josiah Strong, who deserves to be trotted out whenever representatives of the mainstream Protestants are at issue, had plenty to say on this in his best-selling *Our Country* and then again in 1893 in *The New Era*. What would be the outcome of urban life? Present tendencies of disaffection and chaos would continue, he wrote, until the cities were literally heathenized, or their arrested growth would enable the churches to regain lost ground, or the churches would awake to their duty and their opportunity. Such leaders were nervous about indifferent and apathetic masses. "It has been repeatedly said by workingmen that they do not disbelieve in Christianity but in '*Churchianity*'." At one New York meeting, he knew, they applauded the name of Christ and hissed a mention of the church. Church neglect "is indeed the cause of the alienation of the masses," but, Strong asked, "why is this effect so modern, why did it not appear many centuries ago?" His answer: "In its progress the world did not reach the sociological age until modern times." The church had grown impersonal, was beside the point to many.

9:5   Strong saw Catholicism as part of the problem of the cities, not part of the solution. Therefore he would never have admitted that Catholicism's ability to attract and hold so many workers and other urbanites prevented denominational decline in this industrializing and urbanizing period. Yet, Catholicism aside, the churches still generally held their own or even prospered during their transit to modernity. They provided both some of their old and now some new functions. The denominations served for those in the religious mainstream just as ethnicity did for those regarded as outside it. They formed what we might think of as canopies over people in social groups. The canopy has a top for protection, but open sides for free access and egress. It allowed for much nurture and protection as well as translucence for purposes of filtering. People were more free to come and go than they would be in racial or ethnic groups. This function did not square with old rationales for denominational integrity. It led to some confusion for that integrity.

9:6   It is impossible to give an accounting of all the church bodies. From 1893 to the present, social scientists have reached for hyperbole to describe the crudeness of statistics in American religion. Different bodies count membership in different ways. Some reporters brag with statistics and others have hid their local growth in those denominations which assess congregations per member. The churches have invested little in data gathering and governmental census-gathering methods were flawed, since they reached organizations, not citizens. Still, the statistics represent something and not nothing, and they permit some measures for marking contrasts and comparabilities as opposed to forcing mere guesses. Census materials from 1890 through 1906 and 1916 help cover this crucial period of change.

9:7   On the eve of this period Daniel Dorchester accounted for at least seventy denominations. Then in 1893 Henry K. Carroll, appointed by the federal government to gather, correlate, and report on religion in the United States Census of 1890, turned in one of the most extensive compilations and interpretations in American history. He found about 150 denominations in forty-two families. Since each of these has been treated in numbers of books, behind which stand many scores of archives, one cannot account for each denomination but can only select to illustrate changes in denominationalism.

9:8   Carroll could point to a thriving scene. A nation with 111,036 ministers in 165,297 reporting congregations with seating space for 43 million, two-thirds of the population, suggested scope to him. In his formula there were 3.5 times as many Protestants as there were reported communicants. Protestants, he reminded, did not include children in membership and did not list all nominal adherents. Carroll extrapolated and came to 49,630,000 in the Protestant orbit and 7,360,000 Catholics, whose more disciplined membership-standards he trusted. There remained 5,630,000 people, including Jews and other non-Christians. This left only 5 million belonging to the nonreligious and antireligious classes, including freethinkers, secularists, and infidels. There were, he added, few real atheists. Carroll's Protestant extrapolation was, to say the least, wildly generous. Yet even discounting his miscalculations and exaggerations, it was clear that this remained Protestant America.

9:9   In 1906 a Census of Religious Bodies occurred independently of the decennial census. Whereas Carroll had been wise enough to contact local leaders, not denominational offices, the government in 1906 did deal with the headquarters. Perhaps that was itself a sign of assent to bureaucracy, an institution of modernity. Local organizations, however, were cross-checked through correspondence, and response was enthusiastic and thorough, so there are reasons to compare the 1890 census with those of 1906 and 1916.

9:10   Kevin J. Christiano has helped make educated guesses about growth rates in this period. That the number of sizable cities was growing is not in dispute. In 1890 there were 58 places with 50,000 or more people, while in 1910 there were 109 of these. In 1890 fewer than 14 million people lived in cities of over 25,000, but two decades later more than twice that many, 28.5 million, did so. Contrary to expectation in this urbanizing period, church growth evidently outstripped population growth, including in the cities. Between 1890 and 1906 the population grew by 33.8 percent to 84,246,252, while church membership as reckoned by census takers grew by 59.9 percent to 32,936,445. New immigrations and efficient pastoral work meant that much of this was Roman Catholic, for this church grew by 93.5 percent, but Protestantism also outpaced the population, with its 44.8 percent growth. Thus while 32.7 percent of the people had been members in 1890, 39.1 percent were in 1906, a gain of 19.6 percent. There came to be 28.5 percent more religious organizations; the Jewish boom was evident in growth from 533 to 1,769 places, or a 231.9 percent gain in this period. The size of each local church also grew by 24 percent to 155 members, though much of this trend resulted from the much larger size of Catholic parishes. They numbered an average of 968 members each.

9:11   Carroll was also best poised to reflect on the status and meaning of the denominations at the beginning of the fifth American century. He was dazzled by the variety. We Americans, he said, like the idea of manufacturing or producing just as many articles of merchandise as possible. Then he helped define an aspect of modernity by referring to the widest range for choice and change in religion. He also had to note how meaningless much of all this was. John Milton had written of "subdichotomies of petty schisms." What would he think of the American religious scene? "No denomination has thus far proved to be too small for division," Carroll seemed to sigh as he confessed that he left out one denomination with only twenty-one members, but remained responsible for some with only twenty-five members.

9:12   Carroll was equally sure that while denominations claimed that doctrinal integrity gave them root meaning, it was not this at all that bred loyalty among the people. How keep two Reformed bodies apart? "It is not easy to remember which is sublapsarian and which supralapsarian," so how could poor laypeople know or care? They only knew that one was Dutch and the other German. One Presbyterian group has a synod and another a general synod, but who could recall which was which, or have a reason to find it important? Carroll knew: the journal of one boasted a blue cover, the other a pink one. The only remedy he could suggest for such chaos, he added, was reunion. It had not yet occurred, he wrote ruefully, because of "the prevalence of the doctrine of the perseverance of the saints. It must be that the saints of the sects think they ought to persevere in sectarian division." After that sardonic line Carroll listed several reasons: controversy over doctrine or administration or discipline; moral questions; personal character issues; race. He did believe denominations were growing a bit more liberal in spirit than before, so he could hope for the future.

9:13   From the observers in the eye of the hurricane of modernity a postdenominational prospect was emerging. From the moderate modernist sphere, the urbane and serene church historian Leonard Woolsey Bacon reviewed American church history from 1492 to

1893 and then looked into the new century. He knew that some benefits had come from separate and even competitive denominations. Yet, he wrote, "the sacred discontent of the Christian people with sectarian division continued to demand expression." The sects could not meet by accepting the distinctive tenet of every other contentious one. They were linking up with their denominational counterparts around the world, but this did not solve the American problem. Partial consolidation of sects, such as reunions of Presbyterian bodies, reduced denominational numbers but did not end denominationalism. Bacon thought it a fallacy that "the soul's best health is to be secured by sequestering it from contact with dissentient opinions." At least on local levels the beginning of change could come. "It begins to look as if in this 'strange work' God had been grinding up material for a nobler manifestation of the unity of his people," wrote Bacon, so "the sky of the declining century is red with promise." Yet that promise was to be mocked, for the period ended with more, not fewer, denominations and, despite ecumenical strivings, they were as entrenched as ever.

9:14   Explicitly modernist theologian William Adams Brown noticed a by-product that Bacon overlooked. Writing a quarter of a century later, after this transit of denominational forms inside modernity, Brown warned that "the chief danger of denominationalism is not that it leads us to attack our fellow-Christians, but that it makes us content to ignore them." Life under each canopy was demanding and effective for what it set out to do, but it did not do enough.

9:15   One strategy for making the denominations serve meaningful purposes was to encourage their breaking of ethnic and religious bounds. They must seek to convert the non-Protestant and often alien-seeming urban immigrants. Baptist church-extension agent Howard B. Grose was the most congenial evangelizer. A man of ecumenical spirit, he criticized the public for creating circumstances in which immigrants could not develop well. He insisted that, in this public, "every Christian ought to know the wrongs of our civilization, in order that he may help right them." Even Grose, however, the least anti-foreign and anti-Catholic among Protestant experts in this field, kept his reservations about Catholics who stayed Catholic. They should be converted because "the foundation principles of Protestant Americanism and Roman Catholicism are irreconcilable."

9:16   At the Federal Council of Churches meeting at which Grose spoke in 1908, Ozra S. Davis was more explicit. Like the heathen, immigrants cared not at all for denominational differences in forms of government or points of theology. Federated efforts were more reasonable in home missions and foreign missions than in regular church work. Yet here Davis either was compromising to win support or lapsing into the sectarianism he decried. To find competition reasonable and possible in regular church work would be to reinforce the problem, not to work at the solution. This is the important point: for all the strategic challenges and conciliar or federative invention, there was almost no merging. There was no merging at all across lines of denominational families. When new forces appeared on the scene, they quickly adopted denominational patterns. The councils and federations did not provide identity for lay members or for pastors. They were not able to embody the stories by which believers lived the way the canopylike structure of denominations did.

9:17   The observations of council leaders like Grose and Davis were corroborated by the distinguished foreign visitor, sociologist Max Weber. After visiting the United States in 1904, the astute analyst noted that "the kind of denomination is rather irrelevant," yet there must be a denomination, even in these changing times. "It does not matter whether one be Freemason, Christian Scientist, Adventist, Quaker, or what not." Thus he confirmed the summaries of great visitors before him, at least as far back as Alexis de Tocqueville in the 1820s. What was remarkable about the scene in 1904 is that, while erosion of denominational separateness declined, denominations themselves survived, proliferated, and often prospered when secularization was supposed to be doing its undercutting. This trend has led some later sociologists to define denominationalism as itself a secularizing trend, though it is probably better in America to see it as another part of modernizing tendencies: increased differentiation in efforts to help provide religious identities and meaning in a corrosive climate.

The Frontier Churches after the Frontier

9:18   That it mattered little to outsiders what the doctrine or polity of the denominations under their figurative canopies were is clear from a comparison of the three greatest denominational movements born on the American frontier, the Methodists, the Baptists of the south, and the Disciples of Christ. The first of these was the largest white denomination. It was quite open to conciliar and federative work on progressive lines. The southern Baptists turned out to be more militant in opposition to ecumenical ideals, more eager to preserve denominational separateness. The Disciples of Christ were to be a movement for union of all Christians, yet by the 1890s their fabric for a full-fledged and standard denomination was torn by internal conflict and schism.

9:19   The conflict between bravado and nervousness in an America it had helped shape and in the midst of modernity which was reshaping it, occurred in the Methodist Episcopal church. In a little story that has attained canonical status, promoter Joseph McCabe of the Board of Home Missions of the Methodist Episcopal Church challenged Robert Ingersoll, by far the best-known infidel antichurch leader of the day. McCabe taunted that during Ingersoll's three prime decades the Methodists had gained 1,800,000 communicants. Church property meanwhile increased in value from $29 million to $160 million, or $12,000 a day for all those years. "Colonel, you had better join the Methodist Church!" Yet only two years after the challenge, in 1899, observers sensed a decline in vitality. That year the northern Methodist church had actually lost membership while southern Methodism for the first time in a third of a century saw "an arrested movement." What would the new century see?

9:20   In 1893 the census reported 2,240,354 members in the Methodist Episcopal church; 1,209,976 in the Methodist Episcopal Church South, and 141,989 in the Methodist Protestant church that crossed sectional lines. These 3.6 million communicants made up the largest and most widespread of the largely white denominations. At the same time, almost a million blacks were in the three largest Negro Methodist denominations. The white groups, divided in 1844, had begun to work toward reunion in 1874 and stepped up efforts between 1894 and 1920. Despite strenuous meetings, much investment of energy, and exciting theological rationales, reunion proposals were voted down in 1924 and reunion waited for 1939. Methodism overall was progressive, in the North often modernist, and in every case professedly ecumenical. Yet the frustration of reunitive intentions in this period shows that separated denominations even sharing a common creed performed certain functions that theology and common sense could not replace.

9:21   Max Weber was right, in the Methodist case. Doctrinal differences played almost no part in separating the three houses—or six, if one includes the black churches. After 1904 the northern and southern churches used common orders of worship and hymnals to go along with the creeds they recited and assented to in common. Most agreed that overlappage and competition were foolish and distracting. Why, asked southerner John C. Kilgo in 1904, should his church want to pay for work where northerners were strong, in California and Oregon? Meanwhile, why should northerners invest with reckless waste in Tennessee, Texas, and Florida? Polity differences were trivial. All kinds of Methodists also were reform-minded, for example in promoting prohibition of alcohol. All groups had talented leaders, many of whom trusted each other. Yet there was resistance to the notion that the separate canopies be dismantled for the sake of weaving a new one.

9:22   Other factors had to play a part, of course, and race was one of these. There were 350,000 blacks in the northern church. In the South, some blacks were encouraging the Colored Methodist Episcopal Church to link with the largely white northern churches if they did not already belong to the large black Methodist denominations. Southerner A. J. Lamar blurted out at a union meeting in Savannah in 1918: "We all know and we have known from the beginning that the crux of the situation is the Status of the Colored Membership." Louisianan H. H. White was militant: the color line, his church knew, "must be drawn firmly and unflinchingly, in State, Church, and society, without any deviation whatever." That meant also absolute separation of social relations, even to the point of preventing contact between races every four years in general conventions. If there was to be union, there must be gradual elimination of Negro membership, with all Negro Methodists uniting in one great body under white tutorship. Other southern laymen may have been more moderate, but the northerners were adamant about inclusion of blacks, and there was stalemate.

9:23   In Louisville in January of 1920 a commission proposed the first draft of a uniting constitution. A Methodist church made up of six white and one largely Negro jurisdictional or regional conferences would meet together in general conference. Most in the North opposed the regional conference idea. Most southerners feared that 200,000 would leave their denominational house with even this mild compromise. Meanwhile in 1920 and 1922 both churches agreed in broad principle with the unification plan. Then in 1924 A. J. Lamar headed a movement that led to defeat of the plan by a vote of 297 to 74. Bishop John M. Moore reported on the motives for rejection. The cries he heard included "absorption of the South by the North," modernism in the North, and "Northern preachers will take our leading churches."

9:24   All through the period, then, divided and often prospering Methodists posed altar against altar. Southerners kept on resenting northern support of evangelizing efforts among southern blacks, and compensated by picking up displaced northerners who, not liking this policy, served as nuclei of new southern white congregations. Bishop Earl Cranston knew the whole story: "These churches cannot live side by side without ever recurring outbreaks of the denominational competitive consciousness." Formal fraternity was not a remedy but only first aid. Some day there must be organic union, not mere federation. Some day was long in the future.

9:25   The Southern Baptist Convention illustrates the same point about the denomination as shelter, filter, and contributor to irrelevance in the eyes of outsiders. It did so on grounds vastly different from the Methodist instance because, after a long tradition of separateness and independence, not to say extreme competitiveness, and then after a short flirtation with unitive impulses, it reacted and grew more obvious about its standoffishness—*and*, it prospered.

9:26   The Convention vied with Methodism for first place in the South, America's most Protestant and very strategic domain. It was much later to pass Methodism in size and never did reunite with the northern church with which it had split in 1845. Its cities had fewer Catholic and other non-Protestant immigrants to inspire Protestant cooperation for their conversion. The pace of industrial change in the South was slower. Its effects were more moderate and came later. Despite impressive internal diversities in the Convention, some of them based on idiosyncracies and localism, it was easy for Baptists to find unity over against northern Baptists, southern Methodists, and all kinds of Disciples. When in 1894–95 the Disciples of Christ responded coolly to the friendly proposal of Louisville pastor Thomas Treadwell Eaton, who talked about improving relations toward cooperation, the Disciples made their case by saying that this kind and cordial offer would not work because of Baptist "fondness for denominational peculiarities" which stood in the way.

9:27   If the Disciples of Christ detected some kindness and cordiality that might mellow the denominational fierceness, others looked on with some hope as the Baptists dipped a toe in the waters of Christian cooperation in the second decade of the century. The Baptists did acknowledge some evils in disunity. One report said they must stand behind every movement and cause in which Christians could share if this did not mean compromising conscience or loyalty to Christ. The 1912 meeting of the Convention did not dismiss out of hand the call to confer over appeals by an international Faith and Order group that was one day to help make up the World Council of Churches. The Convention said it would use all suitable means to promote this real, impressing, and growing union among all Christians. In 1913 Fort Worth professor James B. Gambrell, also editor of the *Baptist Standard*, momentarily seemed to move even more boldly. The Baptists, he wrote, must help "reunite the scattered and ofttime antagonistic forces of Christendom." Like almost all other groups, Baptists qualified this by saying that their longing was only for a Christian union on a scriptural basis, though it turned out that this basis perfectly matched existing Baptist distinctives. The document included its hedge against or its harbinger of the future when it chastised ecumenical leaders who would in any way subvert denominational loyalties.

9:28   Then in 1914 the internal tensions began to show in a Convention resolution approved as a "Pronouncement on Christian Union and Denominational Efficiency." Irenic theological master Edgar Young Mullins helped produce the Christian union half of the pronouncement, regarded as its progressive element. By now, however, the militant Baptist side of Gambrell showed. He had second thoughts or clearer intentions after his 1913 foray into friendliness. Denominational efficiency motivated him now to warn against all entangling alliances with all other Christians. Local churches and the denomination must remain autonomous. All Baptist resources and energies must go to Baptist ends. Harmony was something to be preserved in the southern house.

9:29   Gambrell's interests prevailed over Mullins's and in 1918 Gambrell aggressively chaired the Convention committee on this subject. He wanted to lay on the table what he took to be the Baptist distinctives and now scored the way church-unity themes undercut assertive foreign missions. He was finding a vocabulary: the ecumenical movement was fostering a "seducing, undoing apostasy."

9:30   Gambrell and contributors to his journal elaborated on his stand. Thus the Arkansas Baptist secretary wrote: "The colossal Union Movement is a colossal blunder, but it threatens us Baptists unmistakably." His message to Baptist preachers was, "smite, smite, hip and thigh, the 'bastard' Union Movement." Leaders should call every Baptist soul "to toe the denominational line, and then show his faith by his fruits."

9:31   In 1919 when Gambrell became the powerful Convention
president, he found new reasons for resentment. During World
War I the War Department, he thought, had favored Catholicism
and weakened denominationalism by insisting on dealing with cooperative church units. When Baptists had wanted to minister aggressively to troops, they were thwarted. His speech on the subject,
wildly applauded, was sent to all southern Baptist pastors—and
the president of the United States. That year in a book Gambrell
attacked unitive leaders for having promoted destructive policies
at Baptist expense during the war. The only unity of which he
could speak was spiritual, not organic. "To syndicate our denomination with other denominations would impair, if it did not
destroy, this message," he claimed. All efforts must go toward
unifying only Baptists, through a program "so large, so progressive, so constructive," that it would hold the imagination of Convention members and lead them to forget about unity efforts.

9:32   The Gambrell voice and forces prevailed so much that many
came to forget there had ever been any advocates like Mullins.
Toeing the denominational line became the uniform and successful policy against the bastard union movement through the twentieth century. It took root in the very period when the cosmopolitan habit and the Christian unitive call were most plausibly asserted
by conscientious leaders who, with Leonard Woolsey Bacon,
looked with hope for the unfoldings of the twentieth century,
when Christ's promise and demand for unity were progressively to
have been realized.

9:33   The most revealing case and one worth dwelling on is that of
the Disciples of Christ, which is so rich in ironies and so representative of trends. Nowhere was the power of the denominational
mold in an ecumenical age more evident than here. Founded
chiefly by Alexander Campbell early in the nineteenth century, this
was always to be a movement, never a denomination or sect. It
would use primitive New Testament models to unite all churches
into one, yet after a century it did not succeed in moving toward
union with a single church. Meanwhile, early in the twentieth
century, it subtly split into at least three movements. Henry K.
Carroll found 90,718 communicants in 1,281 organizations in
that part of the movement now called "Christians." The other, the
Disciples of Christ, numbered 641,051 people in 7,246 congregations. It was this branch that was about to divide.

9:34   Born in America, it was second to none in exuberance about
the nation in an imperial age. The Christian Standard editor in
1898 typically boasted that "the Government of the United States

is the richest gift of Protestantism to the world." The next year
George T. Smith seconded the claim: "Awe-inspiring is the mission given to the American republic, but to no portion does the
future more surely belong than to the disciples [sic] of Christ if we
be true to our ideals, faithful to the index finger of God." And in
1898 the liberal *Christian Oracle* professed that God would now
overturn all oppressive powers and "destroy the nations that are
hindering the Christianization and elevation of mankind." America was not threatened.

9:35   Nor was Anglo-Saxon racism missing from the reflexive life of
the leaders. *Christian Standard* editors urged upon the Disciples
of Christ Rudyard Kipling's noble appeal to "masterful and aggressive Anglo-Saxon" people; they should take on the White
Man's Burden. In that year of 1899, near the turn of the century,
The Christian Oracle noted that 20 million humans had been
brought under the influence of the two Anglo-Saxon nations.
Now, therefore, these subjects were open to the Gospel and Christian civilization. This meant "a very intimate relation between the
advancing influence of Christian nations and the advancement of
the Kingdom of God." It added in another article that year, "The
Anglo-Saxon race is the great missionary race and the conservator
of the great missionary religion."

9:36   Neither nation nor race by itself could do all the saving and
serving to which Christian people were called. There had to be a
distinctive movement, faithful to primitive Christianity, to accomplish God's purposes, a movement that would unite the Disciples
of Christ with all who did or might come to think of themselves as
disciples of Christ. Since it was organized on simple, New Testament grounds, where truth was clear and single and patent, there
was no need for denominations at all, and no reason for the Disciples of Christ or Christian Church movement to experience profound tension and schism. Toward the early part of the century,
however, it was clear that if the cocoonlike purposes of the movement were to be served, it would have to be partitioned or re-
produce itself as two or more protective webs.

9:37   For a movement steadfastly independent of government, it is
ironic that recognition that a schism existed came not by any denominational or convention fiat or action. It was the United States
Religious Census of 1906 that came up with the need to recognize
the separate existence of "Church*es* of Christ." It listed 159,658
members in 2,649 churches, half of the members being in Texas
and Tennessee. A leader of what became a separate movement off

to the right was David Lipscomb, among other things editor of *The Gospel Advocate*. He and his colleagues totted up the impressive statistics of the Campbell movement in the decade that the government located a split in its ranks. Between 1890 and 1906 the Disciples of Christ families had grown by 78 percent, while the Methodists and Baptists lagged behind their upstart competitor with growth rates of only 25 percent and 53 percent respectively. Lipscomb seemed a bit embarrassed at having had to turn over to the government the data which pointed to separation in such a prosperous group. In 1907 he looked back and asserted that "there is a distinct people taking the word of God as their only and sufficient rule of faith, calling their churches 'church of Christ,' or 'churches of God,' distinct and separate in name, work, and rule of faith from all other bodies or peoples." Lipscomb claimed never to have done anything to make the division of this people manifest. When civil authorities, who had been monitoring his paper, wrote him and asked for statistics of the churches walking in the old paths, he could not refuse. Well, one could hardly overlook 2,649 "disgressive" churches in a denomination turning "progressive."

9:38   Lipscomb was not as innocent as he wanted to sound. He liked to print calls like one by T. R. Burnett in 1895: "Brethren, proceed to re-establish the ancient order of things. . . ." This meant they should gather all the brethren together, as Burnett said, "who love Bible order better than modern fads and foolishness." He warmed up to the subject. "It is better to have one dozen true disciples in a cheap house than a thousand apostate pretenders in a palace who love modern innovations better than Bible truth."

9:39   Modernism and modernity were at issue, here as so often, and at least two groups chose opposing ways to relate to both. There were a few extreme modernists, like the philosophy chairman at the University of Chicago, Edward Scribner Ames, who also headed the University Christian Church. Ames would look forward, not backward. "Today it is not obvious that union is best stated in terms of a return to apostolic conditions, or, that such a return, if it were possible, would bring union," he argued. At the end of the period, after World War I, Edgar F. Daugherty, siding with the Amesian flank, chose a colorful metaphor to describe the movement: "The folk in our household of faith are not craw-fish, lobsters or crabs, but most of us have not seen anything else going forward by looking backward." He compounded the heresy as he repudiated the idea of a primitive Golden Age: "There has been more bunk, piffle, persiflage, futilely foisted on the world of faith and comment *in re* the 'New Testament faith' than Barnum ever loosed in the morning time of American humbuggery."

9:40   Such language indicates that in those decades modernists were quite heady. In 1907 a young Chicago minister, Charles Clayton Morrison, bought a defunct magazine started as the *Christian Oracle* but at the turn of the century optimistically renamed *The Christian Century*. Morrison fought denominational battles in it for a time, but in 1919 added the subtitle "An Undenominational Journal of Religion" to promote the progressive version of ecumenism, not the crawfish approach, as he saw it. Morrison wanted to pick a fight. Why confine truth to those denominationalists who claimed they alone could restore primitive Christianity? Truth could come from anywhere, argued *Oracle* editors. Even if sanctification, faith healing, Christian Science, or Christian Socialism offered truth, he wrote, "we are free to accept it."

9:41   Given the conflicting attitudes over primitive past and golden future, restoration or progress, the old ways and modernism, it was clear that a single shelter could no longer serve for all. With no difficulty one can point to nine or ten elements leading to the forming of two or three denominations where there was to have been only one movement. To do so is instructive for the way it illumines similar battles elsewhere. For example, there was a rural and urban tension. Chicago, Indianapolis, Lexington, and other centers became open to modernism. In 1906 only 10 percent of the membership lived in places with 25,000 inhabitants or more. Rural folk sulked as complex organizations and the appeals of journals promoted urban missions. One complained: "The modern rendering of the great commission appears to be, Go into the large cities and preach the Gospel, or go where the people will pay a good salary and entertain the preacher in good style." Another "anti" believed that "opera, the theater, and the sängerfest [sic]" educated city church people to "gape for flutes, horns and organs," instruments uncalled for by the Bible. In 1897 Daniel Sommers summarized the case well. The town and city churches, he thought, became proud and sufficiently worldly-minded to desire popularity. With unscriptural ends, they used "the hired pastor, the church choir, instrumental music, [and] man-made societies to advance the gospel, and human devices to raise money." In so doing they divided the brotherhood of Disciples.

9:42   As in the Methodist and Baptist cases, sectionalism played its part in causing strains. In the 1906 census, 101,734 of the

156,658 Church of Christ members lived in what had been the Confederacy while another 30,206 lived in border states. North of the Ohio only Indiana had over 5,000 members. Meanwhile only 138,703 of the Disciples of Christ membership of almost a million were in southern states. Here is another decisive example showing how much culture has to do in styling the shelters called denominations. Journals of northern and southern Disciples were the main instruments of warfare, yet only rarely did church leaders admit, as one put it, that a Mason and Dixon line was drawn through the Bible and the Church of Christ. Doctrinal differences were more respectable and worth fighting for than were elusives like sectionalism.

9:43   With these two differences there were also signs of class consciousness. Defenders of the old ways attacked expensive churches, the renting of pews, wearing of finery to church, college diplomas, and hireling pastors. They resented announcements of the sort that mentioned East Des Moines Christian Church's new building as "an ornament to the city" and the "finest church building" in town. The editor of the *Christian Standard* mourned the appearance of the "old leaven of worldliness that destroyed so many churches in the olden times." Church members now gained a measure of worldly property and lost their heads over silly allurements of society. How does one carry on disputes over class? By disguising them as doctrinal arguments, when it was ways of life that were really at stake.

9:44   Some battles were distinctive to these Campbellites. They had gathered on the principle that "where the scriptures are silent, we are silent." Scriptures were silent about organs in supporting music at worship, so Disciples of Christ dared not use them. At Lexington, Kentucky, and then elsewhere they came into service. In Newbern, Tennessee, the anti-faction went to court in 1902, complaining "they have corrupted the faith, principles and practices of said church . . . by the introduction of innovations which are unscriptural, sacrilegious and objectionable." After three years the court decided that the issue was "not of sufficient importance to justify the intervention of the Court." What was civilly irrelevant was central to the faith and style of an antimodern faction.

9:45   How deal next with the symbols of modernity in the cases of finance, the magnates, and philanthropists? Prominent Disciples of Christ member T. W. Phillips of the T. W. Phillips Gas and Oil Company despised Baptist John D. Rockefeller, who had once forced him into bankruptcy. Now Rockefeller was helping float a heretical school, the University of Chicago, with the complicity of subversive Disciples. Phillips would help subsidize the university that bears his name at Enid, Oklahoma, but wanted his church body to refuse Rockefeller's "tainted money." Some such money did reach some Disciples agencies, so the issue came close to home. Phillips charged immorality when the Disciples Foreign Society accepted $25,000 from Rockefeller. The society kept the gift, but sought no more from such a tainted source. By then the damage had been done in journalistic warfare. The wry question of one contributor to the controversy was unable to help with the light touch: "Possibly giving is the only thing that can save Mr. Rockefeller and others greatly in danger. Why should we not help him give by receiving?"

9:46   Another symbolic issue of moment to Disciples and of no concern beyond their orbit was debate over the policy of open membership. Churches in Cleveland and Indianapolis began it at the turn of the century. Disciples contended that New Testament baptism was by immersion. No one could enter the church without such baptism, but now some Disciples of Christ were not complying. Contenders could monitor such practices best on the foreign mission front. Would not open membership blur the boundaries of the movement? Liberals near the University of Chicago and graduates of moderate seminaries spread the practice of open membership, and those of the "closed" mind could not tolerate it.

9:47   To modernism and urbanism and sectionalism, to organs and magnates and open members, add the three major issues of education, higher criticism, and ecumenism. This primitive Christian movement did praise education, but modern learning seemed to challenge the foundations of New Testament authority and literalism. Butler University in Indianapolis, Drake University in Iowa, the Divinity House in Chicago, and some smaller colleges did the opening. John W. McGarvey rose to rally the conservatives from his base at the College of the Bible in Lexington, Kentucky, and the issue of higher education almost at once was transformed into the problem of higher criticism. The anti-forces in 1906 forced the resignation of modern critic Hugh C. Garvin at Butler. Herbert L. Willett at Chicago drew more fire, and on the terms of those forces deserved to. In one *Christian Standard* cartoon, Willett was shown as a blind, hairless critic in clerical garb who was snipping away with the scissors of unbelief at the Book of Revelation. The caption interpreted the fallen debris: "The Spirit of Higher Criticism: 'And what remains of the Bible, beloved, is divinely inspired.'"

9:48   The College of the Bible itself came to be the battleground, despite McGarvey's pioneering defenses from there. In 1917 McGarvey's outlook was championed by Dean Hall L. Calhoun. The *Christian Standard* supported him when it gave publicity to a student who reported that destructive critics were denying basic biblical teachings. When 87 percent of the student bodies at the college and at sister Transylvania College supported the embattled professor, the journal was well stocked with responses. Despite this, in May of 1917 the trustees acquitted the charged liberals. Dean Calhoun, who resigned, moved over to the Churches of Christ.

9:49   The outcome at Lexington pointed to a denomination-wide battle over interdenominational education. Benjamin C. Deweese at Eureka College posed the issue: "Will our people be content to have what its promoters consider the best training school for our ministry established in connection with a Baptist University?" He knew all about erosion. "Is that the environment to generate enthusiasm for our plea, and the place to train men to proclaim the gospel as we think it should be proclaimed?" To McGarvey, Chicago was "the greatest organized enemy of evangelical Christianity on the earth today." Since it was not easy to handle lampblack without smutting one's fingers, it was better for Disciples of Christ to keep their people close to home. Yet James Garrison, a moderate, sided with the Chicago group against denominational introversion: "A cause that can only flourish in isolation from the rest of the world's life and thought, deserves to perish."

9:50   Finally, the unity-minded group foundered over the modern meanings of unity. During the era of simple frontier competition its vision was not tested. Now in a cosmopolitan age everything seemed bewildering. One revealing phrase summarized the charge against the innovators. When the Reverend Guy Sarvis, an advocate of open membership in Chicago, was assigned to China to teach at the cooperative Nanking University, enemies charged him with "consorting with the denominations." The implication was that the Disciples movement was never one of them. When the general convention in 1907 voted to help form the Federal Council of Churches of Christ in America, the "anti's" had new ammunition. Could founder Campbell ever have had in mind consorting with anything conceived of as a denomination?

9:51   Many of the tensions came to focus at the centennial convention of 1909, which Phillips as chairman promoted heavily. The railroads prospered: 30,000 exuberant members came to overflow halls in Pittsburgh, where 20,000 lined up at Forbes Field for the Lord's Supper. They rejoiced in progress reports of 167 overseas missionaries, 75,000 women active in auxiliaries, 256 women missionaries. For a moment it looked as if the battles of 1906–7 might be forgotten, and even modernist Herbert Willett was allowed to speak. Some "anti's" wanted him off the stage, and missionary executives feared loss of funds. Doughty James Garrison however, wrote to a representative: "It is time we had determined whether or not we are a free people." Better to go to Pittsburgh with diminished offerings than to go there "with the shackles on our minds and hearts." For a time Willett withdrew, but on terms unacceptable to the "anti's," and in the end he did speak to thousands at this best-attended of all the lecture events.

9:52   After the convention the push for unity further divided the movement. Peter Ainslee, a new "Apostle of Goodwill and Unity," took the limelight at the Topeka convention of 1910. A student of McGarvey at Lexington, he looked back on this college of a denomination, where what he called a denominational atmosphere was inevitable. He learned to become a thorough denominationalist for fifteen years. Then during a Baltimore pastorate it dawned on him that the Disciples of Christ terms of union had been unrealistic with their "everybody come over and join us" appeal. In Topeka he broke a new plan. "Unless we turn our course in conformity to [Thomas, Alexander's father] Campbell's clarion call for unity, we are destined to become one of the most sectarian bodies." Negative reaction was palpable. Ainslee left the platform in gloom: "Are these my people?"

9:53   Progressives did follow up Topeka with a Commission on Unity, later named an Association for the Promotion of Christian Unity. It failed to fulfil Ainslee's purposes, but he himself went on to become a major figure at international ecumenical gatherings. Ainslee accepted Lutherans and other infant-baptizers and wanted Anglicans to open the Lord's Table to Disciples of Christ. Garrison wrote his son a few lines which showed the personal dimension of efforts to stretch the web of shelter. Ainslee, he said, was "better known among various religious bodies than any other Disciple." Denominational lines meant too little to him, and he seemed to be showing "one of the unfortunate results of becoming too well acquainted with other religious bodies." Those who stayed under the canopy had great power and name-recognition among their own but seemed irrelevant to Christians and others in the republic; those who used the home base found public ties hard to come by. For the vast majority, the denominational form prevailed.

The Lutherans and Their Languages

9:54   To these three frontier denominations add a fourth cluster, the slightly anomalous case of the new-immigrant Lutherans who settled in the upper Midwest farms and cities. They added to the ranks of but did not join with those Lutherans who had been in America since colonial times. The late nineteenth-century new-comers came for the usual causes of economic betterment and opportunity. The church leadership among them, lay and clerical, had other burdens. Some came for religious freedom in resistance to imposed forms of state church life in Europe. Others were pietists who were not at home with the formalism back home. Often unwelcome for their strange ways and foreign languages but half-welcome as heirs of the great Reformer, Luther, they expressed clear intentions.

9:55   They all wanted to show their at-homeness in America and their love for it. Most came with practices of loyalty, indeed, subservience to the state, practices bred into European Lutheran peoples for centuries. They also wanted to retain the language of faith from the Old Country. Most were convinced that their own piety was superior or their doctrinal integrity was profound and unique. They alone had a hold on full truth. These Lutherans formed scores of small denominations whose plural presence helped defeat the purpose of each. How could the larger American citizenry take seriously the witness of these independent, isolated, often mutually condemning groups? When acceptance did come after pain to the largest group among them, the Germans, it turned out that nothing in their programs or teaching so commended them to society as the evidence of their loyalty in World War I.

9:56   Lutheranism, in short, was an enclave of enclaves marked by the disparate European heritages and languages, the times and places of arrival, the charisms of the leaders, and just plain accident. As for language, in 1914 prominent pastor and professor George H. Gerberding made the claim that Lutheranism was "the most polyglot Protestant church in America." He stressed, "We like to boast that the Gospel is preached in Lutheran pulpits in more languages than some heard on the day of Pentecost." The boast had its underside for realist Gerberding: the many tongues, he said, that "are on one hand our glory . . . on the other hand our heavy cross."

9:57   By then there were almost 2 million Lutherans, in aggregate a challenge to Methodists and Baptists in some parts of the country. In the Midwest stronghold their 13 percent of the population in the 1890s was third only to Catholics, who had 17 percent, and Methodists with 15 percent. Henry K. Carroll and his census of 1890 showed that 460,000 were exclusively German-language members. There were also 190,000 such Norwegian members, 88,000 Swedes, and 14,000 Danes—plus a few Icelandic and Finnish Lutherans who would later be joined by some Baltic and Slovak Lutherans. The pattern of their differentiation is made clear when one instinctively revisits them following ethnic, not strictly denominational, lines, even though the two had very much to do with each other.

9:58   Each of the national groups was self-contained in the valleys and wards of this new Lutherandom. For example, the Norwegians, whose immigrants made up the second-largest group, were part of a loss to their old country second only to that experienced in Catholic Ireland. In 1910, 404,000 of the 1,000,000 American Norwegians were foreign-born. Many were churchless in America, having shrugged off the nominal ties that came with baptism into the Norwegian state church. Others of them caught the fever of American religion. Great numbers had been pietist rebels against the state church. They formed several competitive groups in Minnesota, Wisconsin, the Dakotas, and surrounding states. The principles of division were hard to explain. Thus when the largest Norwegian body, impeccably conservative in its credentials, showed friendliness with the Germans of a synod bearing a name condensable to "Missouri," forty ministers broke off to found a new church body, named the Anti-Missourian Brotherhood. This fraternal assembly announced its intention to unite all the Norwegian Lutherans, but it only led to more schism. Not until 1917 did many of the Norwegians come together to form the then third-largest Lutheran group. Numerous contentions remained and at least seven small sects survived. Some of the Norwegians were victims and quickly introduced the English language when that became advisable in wartime. They were well on their way to being Americanized; modernism held no lures at all.

9:59   The Swedes adapted more readily. Most of those who came before 1890 remained farmers, but after that date many had no choice but to go urban. Still, at the end of World War I more American than Swedish acres of farmland were tilled by Swedes. There were enough immigrants to go around. By 1910, two-thirds lived in cities. Chicago alone had 145,000 first- and second-generation Swedes, who made up 9 percent of its population at the turn of the century, while 30 percent of Minneapolis was then Swedish. Some of the old European pietist-versus-establishment tensions remained, and this ethnic group saw the Swedish Mission Covenant church develop and prosper. The Swedes differed from the Norwegians in that they assimilated easily and became one of the least visible ethnic groups in America. Still, in church life a separate Swedish legacy was to endure, a distinctive pattern of church life was preserved in congregations, colleges, and other places where a cultural shell could help filter out some of the unwelcome American ways, though it was no defense against others.

9:60   The smaller and more dispersed Danish groups broke the mold. Only the church helped preserve identity as the Danes married non-Danes and took to English. They did preserve Leonard Woolsey Bacon's dictum, however, that no groups were too small to divide. In 1894 two factions split over cultural issues. Frederick Lange Grundtvig, the son of a great Danish bishop, led the faction devoted, as was his father's movement, to Danish peoplehood and religious folkways. His Danish Folk Society, however, was worldly, offensive to the pietists who formed a larger United Evangelical Lutheran Church in America, still on ethnic lines. The church must have meant less to the Danish diaspora than to the more congealed people from elsewhere in Scandinavia, for only one in five had joined the two synods by 1910 and only one-third of the Danes were believed ever to have joined any American church.

9:61   Even this relaxed Lutheran body for a time found it necessary to wrestle with the issue of language as a boundary setter. From a lonely outpost in Portland, Maine, Hans P. Blom argued in *Ungdom*, the Danish-American Young People's League paper, for Danish: "It would be to idolize the English if the Danish Church should change her church language, as it may be proved that she has no responsibility towards those who do not understand Danish." In the heartland, at Trinity Seminary in Des Moines, Iowa, in 1918, President P. S. Vig, the group's most notable historian, also warned against rapid Englishing: "within a few months we have moved on at least fifty years. . . . It is now doubly important not to go too far, either to one or the other side." Yet things had moved far enough that the political Dr. Vig promoted survival through adaptation, not in spite of it. "If we wish to continue as a church group, we must give up our tendency toward self-sufficient independence and isolated individualism," the natural tendencies of a scattered people. The immigrants must bond together and listen to preachers use both languages. Vig showed disdain for students who went to unapproved theological schools, where they ended up, he said, "neither fish, flesh nor fowl, nor good red herring; but what is perhaps even worse: they come home wise in their own conceit." In such a group it was clear that everything was a matter of modulating and fine tuning. Vig was on the way to recognizing that modern America would have its way, by force if resisted, and with controlled subtlety if properly regulated.

9:62   The most revealing intragroup conflict occurred among the Finnish immigrants, who most resembled in Protestantism the Czechs among the Catholics. That is, they carried to frontier country a radical division between clerical and anticlerical, churched and unchurched, believer and unbeliever. Finns came late; there were only eleven congregations when Carroll counted in 1890. At the time the Suomi clerics organized, the Finnish anticlericals, usually Marxist, counterorganized. In 1890 at Calumet, Michigan, Pastor J. W. Eloheimo asked for armed policemen to defend himself against the freethinkers. Outshouted by them at a rally, he excommunicated five hundred people on the spot. He had to flee to Ironwood, Michigan, where his travails led to emotional instability. Now he became "William Elohim," a man possessed of theocratic ideas. He formed a momentary Fenno-American Evangelical Lutheran Church, which was neither theocratic nor utopian nor built to survive.

9:63   The Marxist-Lutheran confrontation was more serious, a sign that ethnicity did not always bind groups and that religious issues could divide them in the public sphere. In many towns, churches vied with labor temples, preachers with atheists, hours of worship with hours of meeting, religious newspapers with labor newspapers, verbal violence from the pulpit with stormy rhetoric from the platform. The Communists exploited the depression and panic of 1893–96 to the churches' disadvantage. Thus on a typically tense evening in 1900, Ishpeming, Michigan, agitator Martin Hendrickson was confronted by shouting middle-class Finns, who called his crowd, "atheists, anti-church and horned devils." While this was going on, a radical Dr. Sorsen countered from the audience: "Jesus was the first socialist, and if you oppose socialism, you are also opposing Jesus." Religious symbols worked for both sides. In 1904 the Marxists chose to produce a labor paper, *Worker*, in Hancock, Michigan. One called this the "walls of Holy Jericho" near Suomi Synod headquarters; confrontations had to be frequent.

9:64   Violence came on Christmas Eve in 1913. A women's group of the Western Federation of Miners planned a churchless, Christless Christmas party in the Italian Hall at Calumet. Big Annie Clemenc and her colleagues gathered some gifts for children who lacked any, and crowded hundreds into a second-floor room. At the height of festivities a man who allegedly wore one of the "Citizens Alliance" buttons, designating opposition to strikers, induced panic by shouting "Fire!" The fleeing crowd converged on a narrow passageway. In the stampede, fifty children were among the victims. Word of this tragedy spread through the mining country and the nation. When Citizens Alliance people tried to help by collecting relief funds, they had doors slammed in their faces. The WFM president would have nothing of any words that asked, in the midst of the great sorrow, that all should forget their differences. He said that it was the radicals who wanted to live by the teaching of him who said, "These are of the children of heaven."

9:65   No concord followed the rites at three Lutheran churches, where thirty-five of seventy-four victims received burial rites. A congressional committee later did establish that the Citizens Alliance was a vigilante group for management. On the management side were many members of the Suomi Synod, who furnished support for an Anti-Socialist League. It would fight socialism, because socialism, its leaders said, disdained "Christianity, culture, patriotism and national laws." Such tensions meant lost morale, lost church membership, continuing bitterness between groups. These were more evidences that the meaningful battles went on more within the protective canopies of religion than between people in them and the outside world. Being Finnish did not unite people; it was the context for the most intense and even lethal divisions. The church was seen as being on one side and in any case was not an effective reconciler. Its members pursued their religious life through it, and welcomed the ways it protected them from some winds of change, but it had become for the immigrant groups as such a mere force among the forces, often powerless in their whole lives.

9:66   It is the German Lutherans who hold the most interest, because of the weight of numbers, the articulateness of their leaders, and the drama that occurred when this foreign-language group was suspected of disloyalty when America fought Germany in World War I. These later-coming Germans found some allies in the eastern states with latter-day celebrators of sixteenth-century Lutheran confessions. They disdained the other long-term American Lutherans who had taken on the protective coloration of the generally Protestant environment.

9:67   The later German arrivals were also, of course, divided among themselves. Some were radicals who brought free thought after the revolution of 1848 to cities like St. Louis, Cincinnati, Milwaukee, and Chicago. Almost all of them opposed the church. Hundreds of thousands of Germans were Catholic. The Lutherans came, in some cases, for economic reasons. They simply reexpressed their church life on the model of a governmentally imposed Lutheran-Reformed mix from Prussia and elsewhere. The most expressive groups were those who arrived feeling that they were martyrs and exiles because they opposed rationalism or this religion "unionism." They came to America to be apart. However much they loved America, they would massively resist modernity and its lures and have no alliances with any who did not agree completely with them.

9:68   Some gathered in a Wisconsin synod, more moderates in Iowa and Buffalo and Ohio synods, but most provocative were those in the Missouri synod. They might have been *Gemütlich* and beery in their own culture, but they looked fierce to most other Lutherans. They would pray with no others, lest they dilute the prayer or diffuse their boundaries. They attached Orthodoxy to the German language. Heinrich C. Schwan, a synodical president in the 1890s, said that the English language as such was not the danger to faith. What threatened was what he named the American spirit which would come with it—a spirit not of patriotism but of innovation, modernity, secularity.

9:69   These Lutherans, like the Catholics, used parochial schools, in which German was the norm, in order to keep children from the corrosive influences of the public schools and to instill biblical ways and Lutheran doctrines. Support for these schools even led many of them to oppose the common American Protestant institution that was prevalent in other Lutheranism, the Sunday School. In a formal conference paper a Pastor J. Wefel argued that the two school systems could not coexist, because, he quoted, "a house divided against itself will not stand." In 1899 President Franz Pieper attacked an eastern Lutheran who was praising the Sunday School as a progressive agency, "God's infantry." Pieper retorted, "it is absolutely wrong to speak of the Sunday school as progress." It was a great step backward, one which owed its origins to the laziness and ignorance of Christian parents. Only day schools would keep children together, loyal, indoctrinated, pure.

9:70   Language plus parochial school plus cause helped promote group cohesion. Back in 1889 the Missouri and Wisconsin synods linked momentarily, as we have seen, with Catholics against Wisconsin's Bennett Law in order to remain free to teach in German. During that battle Missouri's president looked on presciently from St. Louis: "We know that our offspring will become Americanized, but we ought not to be blamed when we try to make this change a gradual one." Gradualism worked and these Lutherans were ignorable from 1889 until at least 1914, when Wilson's policies began to make an enemy out of Germany and an ally out of England. The Missourians were no friends of German church life, but they had some relatives and memories, and cherished things German. So they broke their taboo against political involvement. When challenged about their newfound political sense, the synodical president stressed that "anything that touches moral issues is within the sphere of the church." Keeping America neutral, definitely not anti-German, was such a moral case. When in 1915 the St. Louis Concordia Seminary professor Friedrich Bente testified before the Senate Foreign Relations Committee in defense of neutrality or at least against anti-Germanism, the prejudice of the established English-speaking type was evident. Senator Henry Cabot Lodge wrote Theodore Roosevelt deriding Bente for his "lecture" on Washington and patriotism. Lodge showed his true hand when he made fun of an accent so strong that, he sneered, "you could stumble over it." Lodge defined the world against German Lutherans: "Some of us are not hyphenates—we are just plain Americans—and the wrath of the members of the Committee, Democrats and Republicans, was pleasing to witness. I think they [German Lutherans] have overdone it."

9:71   Never ready to underdo loyalty or patriotism, these generally passive but never pacifist Lutherans used their interpretation of a Pauline teaching about subservience to rulers. They showed their loyalty after declaration of war. They could not all learn English or borrow their neighbors' customs at once, and many suffered. Zealots torched one of their Lutheran schools at Lincoln, Missouri, and dynamited one at Schumm, Ohio. At Steeleville, Illinois, congregants armed themselves on the way to church in the face of mob threats. A wealthy Fort Wayne, Indiana, Lutheran farmer had to be rescued with guns when a mob converged on him as a putative German sympathizer. Another mob pummeled a Bremen, Illinois, pastor and wife, and when a young Lutheran used German to say good-bye in public to his father at Campbell Hill, Illinois, he was fined fifty dollars for his choice of language.

9:72   The Reverend J. W. Miller of Fort Wayne was accurate about what followed declaration of war. The German Lutherans vied with others to promote Liberty Bonds, wave flags, send sons to fight in Germany. "There is no group of citizens as loyal to the Republic, there is no body of citizens as vitally necessary to the success of this land as are the Lutheran people." They may have resented Wilson's breaking of his promise not to lead the nation to war. They did remain sullen about how policies of neutrality had been broken. The snideness of people like Henry Cabot Lodge brought distrust. None of that counted, however, when it came to the issue of being obedient to the call of America.

9:73   After the war the issue of Germanism began to die, to be revived and used only by Lutherans or Protestants who were competing with this growing group in the Midwest. The tar of the Germanism charge did not stick long, however, because Germans assimilated well and joined mainstream ethnic groups in sharing American privilege. Through it all, such groups had other elements to reinforce the web around them. There was a selective moral strictness which was expressed in opposition to social dancing and birth control. It rarely extended to liquor, and these Lutherans opposed Prohibition because they liked their beer and despised the liberal Protestants who would resort to legislation to promote the dry kingdom of God. So at home with the bottle were they that they scandalized neighbors around their St. Louis seminary. In 1899 its Board of Control passed formal resolutions to curtail seminary beer parties, but enforcement was casual. When some students protested excesses by their fellows, the faculty allowed them to register their names in order to clear their consciences, but not to stop the flow of beer. Old-line English Protestantism in America rejected such practices as well as the observance by Lutherans of the "Continental Sabbath," Sundays which they kept quite casually, with play and work if they wanted.

9:74   None of these elements, including language, common experience, or moral outlook, did so much to promote internal unity as a cause which colored Wisconsin and Missouri Lutheranism even if it converted or attracted no one beyond that group. This was the claim by those Lutherans of their solid hold on absolute truth, the notion that their movement was the True Visible Church on earth. All denominations made and meant truth claims, but few in the modern period's beginnings used these so uncritically and with such eagerness to see them as definers. In 1922 a Wisconsin synod editor could compliment the seventy-five-year-old Missouri synod: "Never has the pure doctrine of God's Word been in uninterrupted control of one and the same church body for so long a time" as it had been in that of Missouri. Franz Pieper, chief custodian of doctrine as seminary and synodical president, in 1905 argued that "as certainly as Holy Scripture is God's Word—which it is—so certain is it that our doctrinal position is correct." Therefore, he threatened, "whoever contests our doctrinal position contends against the divine truth." There was no talk of progress. How could there be, asked Bente, for that meant change and "that would be to accuse God Himself indeed, to mock God, who has commanded that these very doctrines be taught."

9:75   Such a group could commune with no other Lutherans, pray with no one else, Protestant or not, nor make anything but civil common cause with other Christians. Living in America, however, they could not help but feel sympathy or common cause when others resisted modernism. When reactive Protestants after 1910 began publishing antimodernist tracts called *The Fundamentals*, their leaders took positive notice. However, the people of this party promoted what to Missouri were heretical views of the second coming of Christ for a thousand-year-rule, what was called premillennialism, but to the Missourians was chiliasm. When that motif became clear, the promoters of *The Fundamentals* were written off as "false prophets" and kept at a distance. Missouri was safe from modernism, evolution was unheard of. As for "popularized Higher Criticism," as he called it, Professor Theodore Graebner was cavalier. It was a fad to which some would take as "boys in kneepants take to swearing and cigarettes, because it makes them feel big, while they are only bad boys."

9:76   Not for decades was the canopy over Missouri to begin to open. Everything named modernism and much that went with modernity were to be resisted. Yet the synod took no pains to withdraw as the Amish or Jehovah's Witnesses did. The ceiling was thick but porous, the boundaries wide but penetrable. In its desire to be American in World War I and to accept many of the benefits of civil life, as Lutherans were always expected to do, they began to undergo vast processes of change. Meanwhile, what they held to as their rationale for existence was uncompelling to other truth-claimants down the block, each of whom had another view of truth. Missouri and Wisconsin were not known for peculiar Lutheran teachings about justification by faith but for their refusal to pray with others, their readiness to fight against the Old Country, and other factors they would not have ranked as central. Thus the American process worked its effects on selective resisters against its normative ways.

Mainstream Catholic Programs

9:77   Finally, the denominational canopy stretched over the largest single church, the Roman Catholic. On all sides it was visible to non-Catholics. Believers under its canopy were increasingly aware of modern American trends. Yet its membership in an international church—until 1908 it was considered a missionary field by Rome—whose enemies saw it controlled by aliens, assured that it would have a distinctive character. Its elaborate ritual and path of salvation, its cultivated patterns of conduct, the use of Latin in its worship, all helped make it mysterious to those who observed it overall. And the members, for all their diversity, experienced its shelter. They also found themselves as often in meaningful conflict with each other as they were with suspicious fellow citizens beyond its protective arc.

9:78   To treat Catholics as only ethnic groups is not to do justice to the way the mainstream Catholic church was coming to be seen in this period as a denomination among the denominations. This was an ironic development, for orthodox and imperial Catholics, like other high-church ecclesiastics, wanted to be only a church, or, better, *The Church*, not one of the organizations among many. This intention, however meaningful it may have been to those who professed it, was always to be denied and contradicted by American circumstances. The more the Catholic church edged into American public life in order to serve its people and achieve its ends, the less mysterious and set-aside it became. When World

War I helped occasion the invention of a set of national agencies, one could say that for the first time there was the *American* Catholic church. Its enemies who previously saw it as a monolith overlooked the internal ethnic and stylistic differences and seemed unaware of its organizational chaos. Adaptation to modernity in America minimized the chaos, even if the instruments for generating order and ecclesial coherence had almost nothing to do with historic definitions of Catholicism.

9:79   America entered its fifth century celebrating the triumphs of the Catholic discoverer Columbus. By then his church had a membership far larger than that of the largest Protestant churches. If America was turning urban and industrial, Catholicism, with its huge immigrant influx, had most at stake. Estimates put half the entire labor force in the United States at the time in the Catholic camp. The lay and clerical leadership was largely middle class. It tended instinctively to champion a laissez-faire economic order and was developing an informal theology that supported competitive individualism as much as did the Social Darwinist Protestants who thought they themselves were Calvinist in making that choice.

9:80   Change was coming. On the eve of this period, in 1889, the most noted hierarch of all, Baltimore's James Cardinal Gibbons, had helped prevent Vatican condemnation of the Knights of Labor, a fledgling union. Acts like that helped hold worker loyalty. To prevent condemnation, however, was not the same thing as having a positive policy. Too much had depended on Gibbons's person or on political intrigues between American factions and Rome, and too little on reflection and American organization. As the period began, in the midst of economic uncertainty, recession, class tension, and the Panic of 1893, the Catholic church, with most at stake, had to have high on its agenda a way to minister to and help represent this bulk of its members. Its leadership was, of course, largely ethnic. The generally Irish, sometimes Germanic bishops, priests, and nuns, long-time victims of ethnic snubs, came to be seen increasingly for programmatic reasons as people who had responsibility for a denomination, not as a cluster of self-enclosed and newly arrived European peoples.

9:81   According to the census of 1916, this muscular and flexing body numbered 16 million people. This figure represented 37.5 percent of a national church membership that was then dispersed among over 150 denominations. Two-thirds of all church members who lived in cities of over 300,000 were Roman Catholics, and 56.5 percent of the Catholics lived in cities with more than

25,000 people. The fate of cities, as Anglo-Saxon Protestant jeremiads never wearied of pointing out in alarm, depended in no small measure on Catholicism.

9:82   As to the official theology, such as it was, and the image of formal Catholicism, these were entirely conservative, but change was coming in respect to the image and many practices. St. Paul's assertive Archbishop John Ireland, accused of being an Americanizer, could sound like the Protestants and the pagans, and his enemies never tired of charging him with betrayal. "Progress," Ireland could say, "is the law of God's creation," and the church must go with it. The words "modernist" and "liberal" were more dangerous than "progress," given Rome's suspicion and, indeed, condemnation of phenomena bearing those names. A glimpse of the landscape where these terms were applied came when in 1893 a man named Merwin-Marie Snell, who had been the secretary to another Americanizer, Archbishop John Keane, used his time of apostasy to do some classifying for non-Catholics. Snell was fair enough to say that there were no Protestant-style liberals in Catholicism. Only Bishop John Spalding and Monsignor Denis O'Connell came close, especially because of O'Connell's alertness to the issues that he said were connected with scientific and scriptural problems—evolution and the destructive criticism. Keane himself was "very much in touch with Evangelical Protestantism," said Snell, and Keane, along with Ireland and Gibbons, was at home with Protestantizing motifs he picked up from his contacts. If that was the best a sometime apostate could point to, there had to be little for nervous and orthodox Rome to worry about in its American daughter.

9:83   Despite the absence of modernism and the presence of only mild progressivism, the turns Catholicism took during this period assured that intra-Catholic conflict would be more important than the reaction of Catholicism to nativisms like those of the new American Protective Association ever could be.

9:84   One center of resistance was the conservative nest at St. Louis, typified by Condé B. Pallen. His *Church Progress* already resisted progress as it was typified by work on an agenda for the Columbian Catholic Congress back in 1893. American pluralism as an attraction dared not be an issue: "The question to [be] resolute about is our conviction, as Catholics, of the necessity of the Temporal Power of the Holy Father." Congress notions that "the national welfare and the highest material prosperity are compatible with the widest propagation of the Catholic Religion and the fullest freedom of its adherents" were also repulsive.

9:85   Pallen expected the apostolic delegate, Francesco Satolli, to crack the whip. Instead Satolli, in a brief if uncharacteristic moment of affirmation, told the Columbians, "Go forward! in one hand bearing the Book of Christian truth and in the other the Constitution of the United States." Pallen wanted to sound more secure in opposition. The overardent Americanism then being expressed came, he thought, not from people "born on the native soil with native generations back of them," but from nervous newcomers. He was thereby noticing something that is standard in observation of American immigrants, but he was merely a sniper at the edges. Important opposition also came from conservative bishops who feared loss of power to the new agencies and congresses that were being used for Catholic adaptation to American denominationalism.

9:86   Still, even snipers bear watching, and Pallen significantly aimed high, not only at Satolli but also at Gibbons himself. Let Pallen represent sharp and literate conservative reaction to Gibbons for his appearance at the World's Parliament of Religions. There Gibbons had said that while religions differed in faith, "thank God there is one platform on which we stand united, and that is the platform of charity and benevolence." Pallen could snort: "Comedy of convocations! Think of putting a creed upon exhibition as at a Fair, as one might bring cattle to a show!" Such an appearance put Catholicism on a plane level with heresy and paganism. In classic antimodernist language the St. Louisan went on, then "it is presumed that everybody is right and nobody wrong, that man is not fallen and perverse, but rather struggling upwards from lower conditions (the evolutionary hypothesis) needing no redemption or regeneration from on high."

9:87   Pallen and his kind found attacking easy. They protected the church that had been, while the new leadership was anticipating the needs of the faithful. These were aware that a new kind of church was needed. Many were alert to the ways modernity chopped up life and left the church with one of its pieces. Catholic University's William Kerby voiced this concern in 1907, the very year in which the pope condemned Modernism. Kerby knew that there was an American cultural tendency to indifference concerning a person's religion, because state, church, labor union and party presented "but partial views of human interests." What happened to religion, he asked, when "the interests and sympathies which men have in common monopolize conversation, attention," while "religion and its particular interests silently recede from our social intercourse"? Later sociologists of religion have not improved on his analysis of the way religion had become a private affair, "a matter of mere personal concern," without social effect. Progressives wanted to repeal this tendency, or address its victims.

9:88   John Burke, a Paulist priest who was important in developing a Catholic national consciousness, also added to this diagnosis of differentiation. Burke's goal was wholeness, in the face of national problems that forced national thinking. Burke editorialized: "The individual, the parish, the society, the diocese, must emphasize and sacrifice itself to that larger Catholic unity of which each is a reflection." Therefore Catholics must be "all in one, one in Christ, every part of the Church and country in touch with the whole." Like the Protestant denominationalists, of course, he equated his church's particularity with the universal. "The Catholic Faith is the only key to the right principles of that national life." Burke echoed them when he argued that "our democracy of America cannot guarantee its free and continued existence unless the life of its people is sustained by Catholic truth." Only the second-last word would have been changed by a Protestant.

9:89   In his *Catholic World*, Father Burke agreed with Kerby: laypeople, now increasingly educated in world affairs, needed more of a voice. The two cheered the formation of many associations in this period. They were aware of Pope Leo XIII's nervousness about such associations, since these brought Catholics into close contact with non-Catholics. In *Longinqua oceani* the pope was explicit: "Therefore, shun not only openly condemned groups but those judged by intelligent men, especially the Bishops, to be suspicious and dangerous." Burke and Kerby would not transgress, but they thought bishops must share power and permit more lay exposure.

9:90   The Third Plenary Council at Baltimore in 1884 did help somewhat in forming a national Catholic church. Momentum came, however, after Americans adapted Leo XIII's encyclical of 1891, *Rerum Novarum*, to domestic purposes. From then, through the removal of the American church from the Society for the Propagation of the Faith and mission status in 1908, through World War I, with its nationalist effects, to the enactment of a bishops' program in 1919, this impulse moved. Monsignor John Augustine Ryan, the major agent of social Catholicism in the period, for reasons of strategy and perfect agreement with the document, always credited *Rerum Novarum* for providing the consistent thread. American workers did not leave the church; their loyalty, he said, was due mainly, if not entirely, to the encyclical. That may have been true, but it took the ingenuity of the Ryans and the Burkes to help it along.

9:91   A papal document had more force in 1891 or 1919 than it would decades later. Therefore, Pope Leo's tilt toward cooperative economic activity even while he would protect private property was helpful to the progressives in American Catholicism. Leo's openness toward interests temporal or earthly pleased those who, with him, would not have the church deal only with spiritual concerns. They joined him in opposing both ideological socialism and unrestrained free-enterprise capitalism, and in urging that the nation-state must defend the natural rights of all, that unions could represent the rights of workers in such a system.

9:92   Alarmed as they were over the shocking conditions of workers and the anomie that individualism was creating, some progressives had extravagant hopes. Down the street from Washington Gladden in Columbus, Ohio, Catholic Bishop John A. Watterson dreamed that all religious groups, including non-Catholics, would see the new labor encyclical as a basis for unitive expression. A bit more realistically, John J. Keane at least hoped it would help secure a unity of view and action among Catholics themselves. Keane would use the Catholic University of America, a papally chartered new intellectual stronghold and soon a battleground, to propagate the papal teaching.

9:93   A papal document on such a sensitive topic had to be both diplomatic and capable of many interpretations. The Americanizers pulled it both ways. During the Pullman strike of 1894 John Ireland told Gibbons he opposed strikers and feared agents of anarchy, because it was urgent to hold the church "before the American people as the great prop of social order and law." Bishop William Stang of Fall River, Massachusetts, claimed he had met a socialist and, hence, again presumably a person of anarchic bent, and asked him "Is there nothing in your way?" The answer: "Yes, sir, there is one thing in our way, and that one obstacle is the Catholic church." Yet if Ireland generally opposed unions, Stang did not, thinking that in due course they could even become a conservative force in the land.

9:94   Clearly, the spectre of socialism was haunting America and its Catholic church. Victor L. Berger, Eugene V. Debs, and other leaders of the Socialist party of America, had to run parallel to or in conflict with Catholic leadership, because half the worker force was Catholic. The papal document, translated into American terms, must have worked some effects in buying off discontent. Only a few Catholics helped form groups like Catholic Socialists of Chicago, chartered in 1909. The only two priests who were active in the Socialist movement, Thomas J. Hagerty and Thomas McGrady, quickly lost power in the church. Foes of socialism could too easily pose it as an enemy of marriage and other stable institutions that were supported by Catholicism, and thus stigmatize it.

9:95   Those who were near the workers, however, also knew that it was not enough to warn against socialism. Labor had to be listened to. Ohioan Roderick A. McEachen, who worked in mining country with Slovaks and Hungarians, kept telling their story to the middle-class church. When workers were disappointed, he said, their minds were prepared for "socialism and its most dangerous principles." Most laborers, he said, were "honest, virtuous, stronghearted, industrious and religious," yet they were too often dismissed as Dago or Bohunk and scored as the "scum of society and a curse to the land." Such workers had to be strangers in the House of God because they were never called there by their mother tongues. That was why each could so easily become "a castaway to the faith, infidel, anarchist, atheist, or Protestant." The good priest must choose to be despised with the worker, must share his sorrow, in order to win such immigrants.

9:96   The antisocialist aspect of the encyclical was attractive even to many Protestants. When Unitarian William Howard Taft was accused of friendliness to Catholicism Taft agreed; since the church was "one of the bulwarks against socialism and anarchy in this country," he welcomed its presence. Protestant tycoon James J. Hill knew that the Catholic church was the only authority that the millions of foreigners pouring into this country would fear and respect. Uneasily the *Catholic World* recognized that many generous non-Catholic donations to Catholicism came because "practical, hard-headed business men are beginning to realize that for the money invested the output of religion as a manufactured article is of higher quality and better grade" and there is "more of it to the yard from the Catholic loom than from any other source." Whatever other ends it served, this helped Catholicism make its passage toward denominational conventionality in America. Its ever-increasing practical purposes obscured its theological confession.

9:97   The papal document revealed its other side as well, and a minority voice rose to challenge the conservative individualist use of
it. Agents of this voice feared the hold of great wealth by the few,
worried about the ways industrial poverty led to misery and radicalism. They wanted to see government help distribute economic
boons, regulate excesses, and hear the voice of workers. In short,
they could link up with aspects of the Progressive movement, even
if other aspects of it were anti-Catholic. Still others did not need
that movement to work for similar ends, especially when Progressives kept their guard up against "anti-democratic" Catholicism.
This led to some organization of networks of their own, away
from the taint of anti-Catholic associations. To Father William J.
Kerby this looked like the forming of cocoons, separatenesses. In
1910 he attacked the provincialism of Catholic Charities for its
"spirit of offishness," its "defensive attitude."

9:98   Onto this scene stepped young Minnesotan John A. Ryan.
A trained moralist whose great energies and skills outpaced his
more limited rhetorical gifts, he was at home with non-Catholic
economists like path-breaker Richard Ely. After Ireland exposed
Ryan to the papal encyclical during the latter's seminary years in
St. Paul, Ryan was sent to the Catholic University of America. He
taught at St. Paul after 1902 and then back in Washington from
1915, where he also came to head the Social Action Department
of the National Catholic Welfare Conference. It is not likely that
any bishop did as much as this monsignor to give Catholicism the
workings and image of a purposive denomination in America.

9:99   Ryan well remembered that day in 1894 when a professor assigned his class an essay on the then three-year-old encyclical.
The seminarian had a conversion experience. "The doctrine of
state intervention which I had come to accept and which was
sometimes denounced as 'socialistic' in those benighted days, I
now read in a Papal encyclical." From it Ryan learned that the
social question was not merely economic; it was first of all a
moral and religious matter. He also cherished the way "the great
Pontiff of the Workingman hurled his thunderbolts of authoritative
doctrine." The church, he learned and professed, must go back
and find models from the more organic ways in the Middle Ages.
He would apply natural-law models from Thomas Aquinas to help
change the modern world. His course was set for fifty strenuous
years.

9:100   Ryan deftly and stridently turned the neglected side of the encyclical against the individualist capitalists, accusing them of

being the departers from tradition, from medieval and scholastic natural-law teaching. He gave every evidence of genuinely believing that this tradition would help Catholicism move beyond the alienation caused by modernity. It would promote a new churchly and national unity and provide a cooperative order, a spiritual wholeness now being lost from view. No substitute existed for the natural law as a basis for a rational ethical system. In natural-rights teaching "the purpose of government is to promote the common good, which means in the concrete, the welfare of all individuals." Ryan had positioned himself well. When the papacy condemned Modernism and Americanism he could show that his work was grounded in traditional teaching and a new papal encyclical. He was a loyalist who would never have entertained the idea of going beyond such Catholicism for his resource.

9:101   Whatever Ryan wrote in the decades after World War I was entirely consistent with his turn-of-the-century positions. The system, he argued, treated labor like a commodity, as if it were corn or cotton, subject to laws of supply and demand. Few paid attention to the human dimensions, to ethics. Ryan devoted his energies to the concept of a living wage. Since unions could not yet fully protect labor interest, the state must do so, with class legislation. True, the church was not a social-reform organization, nor was social betterment her main function, he agreed, but, since economic actions are either right or wrong, an ethical church interested in Christian discipline and in preaching the Gospel could not stand by uninvolved.

9:102   For all the agitation by professors, journalists, and venturesome bishops, not much could happen in the dispersed Catholic church. Despite the Protestant views of Catholicism as an articulated organization if not a monopolistic conspiracy, the church was a collection of dioceses out of touch with each other, religious orders working independently, busy priests and nuns who lacked means of acquiring national interests or a national voice. In 1916 the Reverend Peter Dietz spoke for many. There was still, he said, no American Catholic social movement in any national sense of the term. In Omaha the *True Voice* fingered villains: "Our leaders have not been over anxious to point the way for us to go." The hierarchy was cautious, since papal condemnations of Americanism in 1899 and Modernism in 1907 pointed to the dangerous boundaries of expression, yet they were finding a safer middle zone. While the void was being filled by professional and voluntary societies to promote hospitals, education, the press, and charities, Catholicism could draw on talent from these. Yet it was to be World War I that was the pressuring agent or magnet which helped give unity to unorganized Catholicism.

9:103   When war did come, the bishops sounded fanatically national-istic, and genuinely were. It seems incredible to latter-day readers to hear that they were ever suspect as alien forces. They drew on a constant tradition of superpatriotism. Thus Archbishop Ireland celebrated the centenary of the American hierarchy back in 1905 with language that almost sounded Protestant nativist. God wit-nessed, Ireland agreed, that the "large accessions of Catholics from foreign countries" were welcome, but he cautioned: they dared not bring "a foreign aspect," since "exotics have but sickly forms." Ireland wanted Catholics to be the "first patriots in the land." Josiah Strong could have written his script. Providence in the course of history, Ireland argued, selects "now one nation, now another, to be the guide and the exemplar of humanity's prog-ress." America was "the chosen nation of the future." Ireland was only a more exuberant trumpeter of a message to be found in in-numerable Catholic addresses of the age: "The Church triumph-ing in America, Catholic truth will travel on the wings of Ameri-can influence, and encircle the universe." Such language both replicated and competed with the intentions of Anglo-Saxon progressivism in its similarly imperial moods.

9:104   It fell to bishops like John Lancaster Spalding to be more guarded. Before Ireland waxed exuberant, Spalding had entered into the record his own thoughts on "The Patriot." When patrio-tism is most intense, he said in 1899, "it is most narrow and intol-erant." There was, after all, "a higher love than love of country— the love of truth, the love of justice, the love of righteousness." So the national life was at fault when it was not in harmony with what Spalding called "the eternal principles on which all right hu-man life rests." At the Anti-Imperial meeting in Chicago on that April 30 he criticized those who believed in "Destiny, the divinity of fatalists and materialists." He even took on Americans who as victims of commercialism "have caught the contagion of the in-sanity that the richest nations are the worthiest and most endur-ing." Spalding was a check on unrestrained chauvinism, an un-questioned patriot himself, a lonely prophet on such subjects, and more a revisionist in the Americanizers' house than someone who should inspire suspicion.

9:105   The era in which Spalding spoke was the pre–World War I time of testing. Since America was opposed to a Catholic power in the

Spanish-American War, many felt that the American church as part of the international papal domain would be at best neutral. Yet most leadership supported this not very morally creditable or justifiable war. Ireland had no doubts at all as to why God gave victory and greatness. At war's end he averred that this occurred not because we "take pride in our power." No, it is that "Almighty God has assigned to this republic the mission of putting before the world the ideal of popular liberty, the ideal of the high elevation of all humanity."

9:106   Now that time has given revisionists their chance to put World War I into perspective, it is hard to see why Catholic leadership should join Protestant voices in obsessive and uncritical support of its central moral claims. The bishops plunged into propaganda work. They competed with Protestants in contests to prove loyalty, promoted Liberty Bonds, engaged in relief and chaplaincy work, and supported the military. Because many Catholics, like the Lutherans, were of German background, they had to overcome a double handicap, and did. Bishops supported Wilsonian idealism and praised the president for having turned the battle against the Boche into a Christian crusade for a new world order. Leaders were obsequious over the attention they received when the government needed them. After the war a lapsed and then reconverted Catholic, journalist Michael Williams, remembered how the clergy had been forward in patriotic zeal. They crystallized the conscience and fired the spirit because, he wrote, they "interpreted the war rightly as a holy crusade."

9:107   Williams was minor compared to the great Cardinal Gibbons, who in a letter of June 18, 1918, condensed what he also said often in public: "The mission of our country, so ably expressed by our President, is above all else a spiritual one." The American course was sacred, universal, unselfish, most noble. It set, he noted, "the soul of the nation above the meanness and pettiness of selfish conquest or unchristian hate." In a formal redraft of the letter Gibbons added that "in the world today the strongest response to new internationalism must come from the church of the ages." It dared not be sheltered, self-isolated. "Today, as never before, the Catholic Church in the United States has an opportunity for doing nation-wide work." The Catholic people, now as ever, would rise as one person to serve the nation.

9:108   Little skill would be needed to prepare an anthology of such language from the 133 bishops, and then to second it with comment from journalists, theologians, and other Catholics. Bishop

Thomas Cusack of Albany summarized it all in the summer of
1918: "We are better Americans because we are Catholics," because for Catholics, loyalty was "not merely a patriotic duty, but
a religious one." Catholic leaders, meanwhile, were, he said,
"fortified by a knowledge of facts not known by the individual
citizens," so they outdid ordinary citizens in their sense of
responsibility.

9:109   When the war first came, the Knights of Columbus and other
associations immediately were of service. Yet Father William J.
Kerby, Monsignor John A. Ryan, and others promoted national
organization to quicken foot-dragging bishops. In August of 1917
delegates of many organizations came to Catholic University of
America. Williams found them overcoming a climate of what he
called "misunderstanding, of contending corporate ambitions, of
cross-purposes, and, in particular, a confused and in some instances an erroneous consciousness of the purposes of the convention and of the necessities of the situation." They came up with
the National Catholic War Council. Slow, inept, at first, it did not
succeed as an accredited war agency until August of 1918, only
three months before the war's end.

9:110   After the war, national Catholics, now owning their council,
were burdened with a leftover "W" for a finished War. They translated it into "W" for the Welfare in the NCWC-acronym: The
Catholic World sensed the moment: "The hour of destiny has
struck for Catholic work in this and every country," it editorialized
in February of 1919. "The War has thrown open vast tracts of opportunity, devastated or untilled." The war turned out to be the
chief impulse for Catholic coherence and a public relations boost
for a still-defensive, supposedly alien papal church becoming an
American denomination.

9:111   John A. Ryan found himself in the employ of this revised National Catholic Welfare Conference. He had to help sustain morale and idealism in the less glamorous postwar days of steel
strikes, labor unrest, and middle-class complacency. In 1919 the
progressives raised a new theme, "Reconstruction." Critics called
it utopian, a dream. Yet Ryan was a pragmatist, a realist, a fixer
for whom the reconstruction moment was an opportunity. During
the war, he remembered that government had exercised many and
great new industrial functions, on which progressives might build.
This was the time for industrial devices of cooperation and co-
partnership. Workers could become owners, which he termed
"the ultimate goal of our industrial system, and the only enduring

remedy for our social unrest." This did not mean Ryan was for
socialism, since that would mean "bureaucracy, political tyranny,
the helplessness of the individual as a factor in the ordering of his
own life, and in general social inefficiency and decadence."

9:112   Pleased to see the roots of Ryan's idealism in *Rerum Novarum*
overcome mistrust, the majority of bishops supported his approach. Tensions remained, however, after their chartering vote of
December 10, 1918. Some felt that the NCWC undercut their own
authority. Others, like Boston's William Cardinal O'Connell, considered its favored child-labor amendment to be socialistic and attacked a supporter (Ryan) and also the "sly methods in which he
seems to be an expert." O'Connell was to make a crusade of his
opposition to Ryan and the NCWC. That was to be expected. It
only certified the contention that under the canopy of Catholicism
as a denomination the interesting struggles were between factions, not with outsiders.

9:113   Those outsiders came to have a new perception of this newly
organized denomination. In Hearst's *Metropolitan Magazine*
William Hard discerned the meanings: "We see the oldest and
largest of churches brought by its human social situation to a new
refreshment of its ancient gift of prophecy for the poor." Some
labor leaders, like John Fitzpatrick of the Chicago Federation of
Labor, were cheered. Fitzpatrick exulted that the new bishops'
program was undoubtedly the greatest pronouncement ever put
forth by any religious body on this subject. High-church Catholics
were free to make unique claims for their church as The Church.
Henceforth, however, it looked and acted like a denomination
among the denominations. Orthodox it remained, fearful of Vatican suspicion. Protected by its interpretations of papal documents,
however, it was able to take part in the public life of America and
the private lives of Americans. In becoming a denomination and
huddling under its canopy, Catholicism provided its members
with means of being protected from the worst storms of modernity
while giving them freedom to transact in the midst of them. As in
the case of Methodists, Baptists, Disciples, Lutherans, or others
whose story is told elsewhere, Catholics had invented, which
means both "discovered" and "made up," a form appropriate for
their religious needs and interest in modern America.

Part Four

Countermodernism

10

Conservative Catholicism and Judaism

10:1   T‌he turn of the century more than any other period in American history attracts descriptions as the Liberal, Modernist, or Progressive era. Agents in culture, theology, or politics made such names the focus of their intentions. Now, if ever this adverb is in place it is here: ironically, this was also the era in which virtually every enduring and vital American religious conservatism was born. Thus a contradictory outcome of events mocked the promise and fitness of people who thought cosmopolitan habits were to prevail, that progress would dominate, that modernist rationality could serve as a universal interpreter.

10:2   Who are the agents or actors whose original intentions come to disparate and frustrating consequences? Historians, some literary figures, and philosophers drifted with the Zeitgeist and described an age in terms that did not anticipate or include reactions against it. They thought that emancipated, modernist, and progressive outcomes were inevitable. They did not foresee the reactions they were helping instigate. They did not grant sufficient potency to the cocoons or canopies which sheltered so many Americans nor did they realize that in the eyes of others they occupied particularized compartments themselves. These, the modernists and the moderns, remain at least backstage to provide a vantage for ironic observation.

10:3   To dwell further only on such an outcome, however, could turn

193

this into an obvious or repetitive story. Instead, it will also be important to read the actors' descriptions of the reactionaries themselves, to learn their original intentions, and to see how they were partly the cause of consequences that occurred in disparity with their own purposes. These take on varied forms and help set the terms for reaction ever after. The conservatisms off which late twentieth-century American religionists lived were never the simple continuities and traditions with a settled longer past that these conservatives professed them to be. They were, in large part, very modern inventions of these countermodernists.

10:4   One could illustrate this thesis obliquely by reference to virtually all groups noted so far. If before the Dawes Act of 1887 and Wounded Knee in 1890, native Americans now and then envisioned themselves or were envisioned to be subject to massive Christian conversion or civilizing, which meant disruption of tribal ways, it was in this period that change came. What they had taken for granted before, namely, their adherence to old ways, became something that they articulated on the reservations. They did so as a form of protest and a means of preserving something valuable to them in the midst of chaos and under domination. The native American church, the Ghost Dance, the survivals and rebirths of Indian rite and ceremony were never what had been envisioned by Commissioners of Indian Affairs or the Christian missionaries of the nineteenth century.

10:5   Similarly, whether liberal-minded integrators or racist-minded segregationists were envisioning the future for American blacks, they tended to unite in the notion that the passage of time would lead to adaptation of inferior blacks to the white majority ways in religion. Blacks already had a good start with the denominational structures, theological affirmations, and behavioral expressions of revivalist Methodism and Baptist churches. Their more secular NAACPs and Urban Leagues replicated white self-help and representational agencies. Who could have foreseen in such a period that reaction would occur, beginning with Bishop Henry McNeal Turner and his Black God and Back to Africa movements? These were to be followed later by militant particularisms from Marcus Garveyism to the Black Muslims in the next century. Let whites call these radical, their advocates would retrieve and conserve African or slave-era traditions over against the cosmopolitanism of modernist white integrators or the domination of white segregationists.

10:6   The story is better followed, however, in those parts of the culture where the agents involved had readier access to the instruments of public opinion, to denominational presses, theological schools, and core-culture media. Twentieth-century Roman Catholic traditionalism, of the sort that revived after the changes occasioned by the Second Vatican Council (1962–65), took its structure and some of its normative character from turn-of-the-century responses to modernism. The Catholic story merits first place, in order to be a counterpoise to the story of Catholic denominational progressivism in the preceding chapter.

10:7   Throughout the decades after 1893 cautious Rome had reason to monitor American Catholic progressivism, to help Romanize what it feared would become Americanized or modernized. The arrival in 1893 of Cardinal Francesco Satolli as the first apostolic delegate to America was part of the effort. In some ways, Satolli at first looked like someone compatible with the vision of the more liberal element. The Congregation Propaganda de Fide instructed him to help blend the ethnic components of the American church so that they could be politically and socially homogeneous with the nation, a notion progressives were propagating themselves. At the same time, his orders said, there must be "the most intimate union of the bishops among themselves and with the Apostolic See," a direction that on the face of things did not look complicating to the Americanizers' picture.

10:8   At the Catholic Congress in Chicago in that September of 1893 newcomer Satolli did cheer the liberals with his famous charge, which we have already read, and a blessing: "Christian truth and American liberty will make you free, happy and prosperous." The romance with Satolli ended very quickly, however. When Cardinal Gibbons argued that the World's Parliament of Religions in which he participated offered "a solemn affirmation of religious principles against the great evil of our days, materialism, agnosticism, atheism," Satolli came to disagree. He smelled a greater evil, indifferentism, the code name for the notion that religious distinctions made little difference, a notion that could sap Catholic vitality. For a year or so Satolli and the liberal element papered over their conflicts while they made mutual defense against more trivial enemies like the American Protective Association. Then as the apostolic delegate turned on Gibbons and his colleagues again, Catholics got down to the more serious battle of acting and reacting upon each other. Satolli began to stimulate Vatican decrees against soft practices in America, fearing, for instance, that some prelates were not sufficiently hard on secret societies such as the Masons.

10:9   Satolli was backed by big guns, aimed not always accurately. Thus on January 5, 1895, Leo XIII issued the apostolic letter to the American church, *Longinqua oceani*. It condemned the societies but also touched on that delicate subject which gave aid and comfort to APA types and other Nativists. The letter said that "it would be erroneous to draw the conclusion that in America is to be sought the type of the most desirable status of the Church, or that it would be lawful or expedient for State and Church to be as in America, dissevered and divorced." The letter continued, in condescending tone, by saying that the pope wished to "certify that, in Our Judgment and affection, America occupies the same place and rights as other States, be they ever so mighty and imperial." Rome would "draw more closely the bonds of duty and friendship which connect you and so many thousands of Catholics with the Apostolic See." In other words: Watch out. Don't stray. Don't get the impression that you can patent a new formula for Catholic life. Satolli was obviously pleased with what he considered to be his new charter, and reactionaries entered the period with a new rallying document and charge.

10:10   Gibbons sensed trouble and booked ship for Rome, but was largely rebuffed there. In fact, Roman officials were at the time busy taking aim at the moderately liberal leadership of the American College at Rome under William O'Connell. This was as nothing, however, compared to the suspicion Satolli was able to generate two years later in reaction to the liberals who had been at the World's Parliament of Religions. French Modernists, on the verge of being named heretics, were citing the parliament as a precedent. Leo XIII helped the Satolli cause when he demanded that in the future Catholics should not come to general meetings but should hold only "assemblies apart," where non-Catholics would be guests. This note the American conservatives publicized widely. One year later more pressure came when the Vatican forced the resignation of John J. Keane as head of the Catholic University of America, the period's other symbol of progressivism.

10:11   In the next controversy, modernity and Americanism came into a strange conjunction. American liberals were gradually connecting with counterparts in Europe, while European Catholic parties right and left took notice of and sides in American political campaigns, such as that between William McKinley and William Jennings Bryan in 1896. They praised or blamed American bishops, depending upon their political outlooks. It was necessary for people like William O'Connell to try to build some bridges in

Rome. In 1897 he wrote John Ireland about his strategy of enlarging the idea of openness. Notions had to be planted, including, he explained, the assumption "that the Pope is laboring for the advancement of civilization & science, to put the Church at the head of the age," where the modern-minded prelates always thought it should be.

10:12   On March 28 of that year, Ireland still sounded as exuberant as could Josiah Strong about "The New Age." It was time to break the growing alliance between French and American rightists, and this Ireland thought he could do by claiming the mantle of Pope Leo. It was time in the American church for "but one tendency, one movement, one mode of adaptation—those indicated by Leo." The cloud was growing, however, and he took note of it. "The specious titles of conservatism and traditional Catholicity, a religious fear of novelties is nothing but rebellion" against Leo. The papal name became an incantation: "Loyal Catholics have but one name—Catholics. They have but one rule of action, Leo's will and example." Such a vision meant transcending Catholic ethnicity, for "there is for me no race, no language, no color," for these were accidentals among loyal Catholics. For the moment liberals seemed safe in the ultramontane and papal camps.

10:13   During the decade, however, the European events confused the Vatican image of America and undercut the strategy of O'Connell, Ireland, and others. It happened that in 1891 an Abbé Felix Klein wrote a too modernist-minded preface to a French translation of *The Life of Father Hecker*. Hecker, a celebrated convert, had founded the Paulist Fathers in order to help commend Catholicism to America and to stimulate conversions to Catholicism. Thoroughly orthodox himself, he was misrepresented as a kind of modernist by Klein. O'Connell in 1897 did not notice the new vulnerability, thinking that Klein's was a "masterly preface that is a tour de force of itself," and he observed that it received a stupendous welcome. He said so in Germany, and liberals on both sides of the Atlantic, as they rallied behind O'Connell's statements, tried to see to it that the spirit of the book would be seen to be in harmony with Leonine directions. When an arch-conservative German professor was forced to resign, Ireland prematurely announced victory. "The greatest & last battle of the war has been fought and won." The war was hardly beginning.

10:14   Jesuits in Rome sought revenge for the action against the German professor, but O'Connell did not always appear to catch the early signs. He wrote Ireland that "the whole atmosphere of Eu-

rope is now redolent of Americanism," which meant "no longer
provincialism but modern society, modern law in contrast with the
ancient law." O'Connell also underestimated the rage of French
reactionaries. Nor could he have foreseen the way America's
shooting war with Spain would lead European conservatives to fear
that American Catholicism was becoming too potent. O'Connell
himself shared imperial tastes. Spain's impending defeat would
mean, he wrote in a letter, the decline of "the meanness & nar-
rowness of old Europe" and the coming of "the freedom & openness of America. This is God's way of developing the world." His
letter almost raved. The war was the "question of all that is old &
vile & mean & rotten & cruel & false in Europe against all this
[sic] is free & noble & open & true & humane in America." As
God "passes the banner to the hands of America," O'Connell did
begin to discern that "all continental Europe feels the war is
against itself, and that is why they are all against us, and Rome
more than all. . . ." So he was becoming aware of the threats.

10:15   Through several seasons parties in both Europe and America
scurried in contention for and claimed the pope's favor, and on
such a momentous theme Leo had to act. On January 22, 1899, he
issued *Testem Benevolentiae*, the charter for Catholic reaction for
decades to come. The pope made no secret of the side he took.
Religious Americanism "involves a greater danger and is more
hostile to Catholic doctrine and discipline" than were the over-
stated conservative contentions against the Hecker book. The reason was simple: Americanism introduced novelties in respect to
liberty. Ireland and the American liberals tried to put the best face
on things. They redefined the letter and their positions to escape
censure. Reactionaries seized the moment with efforts to have
papal strictures applied pointedly against their Americanist foes.
These suffered from Vatican ignorance of the American scene and
were vulnerable to the misrepresentations of conservatives who
were more adept at Vatican intrigue than were the moderates.
American pluralism, a boon to bishops in the United States, was
to many in Rome a befuddlement.

10:16   The second impulse for twentieth-century conservatism came
several years later when the Vatican in 1908 condemned formal
Modernism. There was not much of such a movement in America, but one should note its small traces in order to see domestic
reaction in a domestic light. It was papal response to European
movements with tiny American counterparts that gave weaponry
to reactionaries in the United States. Few Catholics in America

were poised to test Modernist waters, especially since circumstances had allowed the nineteenth-century American church to develop little theological potential. True, at Notre Dame Father John Zahm in *Evolution and Dogma* of 1896 was spreading notions of a synthesis between Catholic concepts of creation and emergent theories of evolution in terms mildly redolent of Protestant modernism. At Dunwoodie Seminary with its *New York Review* Father Francis Driscoll, in charge from 1902 to 1909, made some modernist noises, and this bears more notice.

10:17   Driscoll's Sulpician order, which had pioneered in American seminary education since 1642, had always been a most intransigent force. Change had come. The Sulpician leadership in Paris wanted Driscoll to rein in his colleague, Francis Gigot, for his revisionist views of Scripture. Driscoll and Gigot chafed against the scholasticism which they refused to see as exhaustive of orthodoxy. It prevented Catholics from coming to terms with the world-views and modes of modern science. To a friend Driscoll wrote that "it would be impossible for me to teach the old rubbish—the word may be strong but it is the only one that fits my appreciation." Abbé Félix Klein, who embarrassed the Americanists with his translation of the Hecker biography, visited and found the Dunwoodie school up-to-date. Courses on "Periodic Evolution," "Is Evolution Admissible?" and "Origin of the Universe" were matches, he thought, for courses in Paris.

10:18   Driscoll ventured further. He permitted his students to take courses at secular universities and invited non-Catholic, sometimes liberal Protestant scholars, to speak to the students. His *New York Review* would enhance such exposures and show Catholics a more excellent way for modern times. The first issue announced a program in which scientific and historical research of the past half century would elicit the restatement of many theological problems. The more dangerous articles dealt with biblical criticism. Gigot announced that "the time is gone when questions involved in the higher criticism might be simply identified with rationalistic attacks upon the revealed word." Instead he sounded like Chicago's William Rainey Harper in praising the necessary and positive Christian potential of scientific biblical criticism.

10:19   There was also Father William L. Sullivan, who moved in modernist directions in his published attempts to update theories of what it was to be human. Sullivan wanted to relate these to Catholicism, just as he would provide rationales for Catholicism to fuse with democratic life. He borrowed evolving and organismic views of the church from British and German contemporaries, and posed these dangerously over against the static and classic views of the church as a finished product.

10:20   Modernism was less safe than Americanism, and this little flowering was soon to wither. In 1906 five professors left Dunwoodie to become diocesan priests, an outcome attractive to the local archbishop, who was by then intervening in seminary life. Driscoll tried to sound increasingly safe. Forced to abandon the journal in 1908, he pleaded financial exigency to keep up appearances and because he did lack funds. For almost a half century thereafter, nothing remotely as free as it appeared in American Catholicism.

10:21   In 1908 Pius X, Leo's successor, blended the very different issues of Americanism and Modernism and condemned the combination in *Pascendi Dominici gregis*. He thought that Modernists wanted to "adopt the principle of the Americanists," stressing a complicated issue that is beside the point here, a claim "that the active virtues are more important than the passive." It need only be noted that the Americanists had never held the positions Pius X there attributed to them and he was inaccurately describing the bit of modernism that was present in America. The pope was too powerful to be challenged, however, on such points of inaccuracy. Stigmatized and defensive liberals were better advised to take on the protective coloration of the environment and busy themselves in other ways.

10:22   Father Driscoll was assigned by Archbishop John Farley to a parish. The new and unscholarly head of the seminary cut off modernist influences. The few true modernists were dispersed and silenced. They had not been able to leave a deposit of creative resources in the American church. They only succeeded in giving a trace of plausibility to reactionaries who with confusing papal support helped give shape to the conservative anti-intellectualism that ruled Catholic life for a half century to come. Progressives put their energies into social programs and service activities, and the church prospered, but with little attempt to anticipate the kind of formulations that necessitated and issued from the Second Vatican Council of 1962–65.

10:23   Movements in various religious bodies not only have internal diversity, as Catholic reactionaryism did, but are at best only analogous to the Catholic turn. To move to Conservative Judaism, then, as a response to and reaction against Reform Judaism's modernism, is not to find parallels in every respect with Catholic conservatism. The two had different traditions behind them, vastly diverse patterns of authority, and independent positive programs. Yet their parallel efforts at expressing countermodernism make them candidates for common treatment as non-Protestant inventions at the turn of the century.

10:24   For decades what was called the Historical School in Judaism had vied with Reform, but it was slower to organize and find a center. There was considerable fluidity between factions in the late nineteenth century, and there were many shadings within Reform as it came to formulation. In the course of time, however, it became clear to many rabbis and congregations that they must more aggressively resist the universalizing style that seemed—no, that stated—it wanted to forget much of historic Judaism. The result would be a cosmopolitan Judaism that would be at home among all peoples. It took on forms, sometimes like Sunday worship, that were congenial to liberal American Protestants. Diffusion and dilution were going far.

10:25   One catalyst for Conservatism was the fact that Reform was ill poised for serving and was unattractive to the hundreds of thousands of new immigrants, chiefly in New York, in the 1880s and after. Conservative Judaism more than Catholic traditionalism did find much to celebrate in the modern world, but leaders were also eager to keep what they could from the past. The pioneers formed a center in 1887 with the birth of a struggling Jewish Theological Seminary in New York. They were disappointed to find that Orthodoxy snubbed it as being too compromising.

10:26   Conservatism was modern-minded in that its founders declared that, when it came to determining Jewish life, the practices of the "living body" of Israel, or the "conscience of Catholic Israel," took precedence over Orthodoxy's medieval leftovers. There could be some practical compromise with modernity. Conservatives gave women a greater role in religious life, though they did not follow Reform in allowing women to read from the Torah. With a bow to Orthodoxy, the leaders decreed that worshipers' heads must be covered and, more substantially, that the Torah was to remain the great determiner of Jewish life. At the same time, they bowed toward Reform and stressed a decorum and manners in worship where Orthodoxy remained boisterous and noisy.

10:27   Half-way houses have always had problems with identity, and the Jewish Theological Seminary at first suffered from a confusion of purpose and image. Halfway been Uptown and Downtown seemed no place at all. By 1900 over half the eleven original Conservative congregations had tilted into Reform. In its first fifteen years only twenty-one students ever showed up and four of these dropped out. Then a Johns Hopkins professor who helped plan the World's Columbian Exposition, Cyrus Adler, spotted an opening. Some restless young Orthodox prospects indicated that they might make use of the seminary if this meant that, while being Orthodox graduates, they might fill Conservative pulpits. Yes, said Adler and some men of means that he gathered for support, including Jacob Schiff, Daniel and Simon Guggenheim, and Mayer Sulzberger. They were all in their own ways vigorous Americanizers but they were also people who were more eager than many in Reform to help new immigrants make their own transit. Old and new, traditional Judaism and modern America, might meet in this venture and locale.

10:28   The stroke that perhaps saved and certainly solidified Conservatism was the arrival of a rabbi of genius, England's Jewish scholar, Solomon Schechter, who came at the strategic moment in 1902. He had rejected the radical biblical criticism then in vogue in Reform Jewish and Christian modernist circles. He was not, however, a stranger to the modern issues, to the university and intellectuality. A Zionist who would appeal to supporters of that new movement, he would later help take part in forming the United Synagogue of American Hebrew Congregations and left his stamp on Conservatism. By 1918 he would even have helped Reform become the minority voice and have made some inroads on Orthodoxy.

10:29   Being poised so delicately, the Conservatism he addressed was always vulnerable to tension and schism between its own right and left. Yet this set of enclaves within an enclave remarkably survived and became attractive to many. Schechter sensed a need and hunger for some Jews to be able to affirm more of the Jewish past than Reform encouraged and to grasp more of American modernity than Orthodox ways allowed. New York gave him a chance to wear his British academic honors but to leave a carping British spirit behind.

10:30   Eight years later Schechter spelled this all out. Recent Judaism had gone wrong. "We always spoke of the superiority of universal religion to national religion." Was it not time to learn from the new Zionist parties "about the necessity of pepetuating the Jewish nation, if Judaism is at all to survive the crisis"? Perhaps Jews should learn less from enlightened and rationalist compromisers and more from the Ba'al Shem Tov, founder of mystical and exotic Hassidism, or from Theodor Herzl, the Zionist founder. A return to the Bible and to "Catholic Israel" would contribute to this quest. Schechter was not a scholastic about the Bible, but saw "the Bible as it repeats itself in history, in other words, as it is interpreted by Tradition," and as cherished in twenty-three centuries of synagogue life. Schechter would listen to biblical criticism, but guardedly: "if tradition is not infallible neither are any of its critics." The synagogue "must retain its authority as the sole true guide for the present and the future." This synagogue had grown weak in the immigrant world and attracted small minorities. It must be rebuilt.

10:31   America demanded leaders who would bridge Western and Eastern Judaism. For Eastern Jewry, universality meant "what it meant with the prophets and their *Jewish* successors—that the whole world should become Jews, not that Judaism should fade out into the world." As for the West, he said, we have the method and the East has the madness; "only if we combine can the victory be ours." To invent a Judaism half way between Orthodoxy and Reform seemed futile. "No, my friends, there are laws of gravitation in the spiritual as there are in the physical world; we cannot create halting places at will. We must either remain faithful to history or go the way of all flesh and join the great majority."

10:32   Such a theme had been behind the founding of Jewish Theological Seminary. There, "in spite of all our 'modernity,'" as he called it, Schechter would propagate the historical notions that "most of our sentiments are 'nothing else but organized traditions; our thoughts nothing else but reminiscences, conscious and unconscious,' while in our actions we are largely executive officers, carrying out the ordinances passed by a wise legislation of many years ago." Still he would conciliate Reform, not wanting to be a sectarian and wanting to make peace.

10:33   Reform, however, must look at the immigrant world, each train of which brought what he called "its own idiosyncracies and peculiarities, its own ritual and ceremonies, and its own dogmas and dogmatisms, all of which are struggling for existence and perpetuation, thus converting the New World into a multitude of petty Old Worlds." New York, this pluralist knew, was an epitome of all the Judaisms of the world, from precisionism and mysticism of the East to the advanced radicalism of the far West. There were even "shadowy no-Judaisms hovering on the borderland." The Yiddish language was not to survive. This "mere accident in our history, doomed to die" was dying before his very eyes. Let it go from Orthodoxy, Schechter advised, but do not let Reform kill the Hebrew language by neglect.

10:34   In 1913, when Schechter helped convene the first gathering of Conservative congregations, he proposed among the binding procedures a sermon in English and "Order and decorum in the synagogue." He hoped this combination would attract and hold the young men who now passed through the seminary and then moved on to Reform, repelled as they were by what they saw as grossness of synagogue worship in Orthodoxy and some Conservatism.

10:35   Schechter's inaugural address at Jewish Theological Seminary in 1903, coming so early in the century as it did, serves as a description of the Conservative Jewish placement in its milieu. Contra Reform and Protestant modernism, he stressed, "if there is a feature in American religious life more prominent than any other, it is its conservative tendency." This country was, after all, "a creation of the Bible, particularly the Old Testament, and the Bible is still holding its own, exercising enormous influence as a real spiritual power, in spite of all the destructive tendencies, mostly of foreign make." Against the trend of the modernizers, then, but convinced he spoke not only for all Jews but for all people who cherished life in their own enclaves and traditions, he concluded: "The large bulk of the real American people have, in matters of religion, retained their sobriety and loyal adherence to the Scriptures, as their Puritan forefathers did." In sum, "America thus stands both for wideness of scope and for conservatism."

10:36   Orthodox congregations lacked wideness of scope. Their antiquarianism belied the development sense of *K'lal Yisrael*. And Reform replaced conservatism with chaos. Conservatism was on its course, holding its place as a Jewish option for the century to come, though it had to settle for being only a part of "Catholic Israel," not the move toward universalism that Schechter and his supporters and colleagues hoped for. They needed help, and got it from a parallel movement with its own intentions.

10:37   This movement, Zionism, has not always been regarded as conservative and to some has even looked politically radical and innovative. Yet both because of its appeal to long traditions and because it was more supported by and useful to Conservatism as another means of thwarting Reform's universalizing, it remains to be seen as countermodernism. In Europe many Jews were giving up on Enlightenment reasonableness and their own assimilation into cultural mainstreams since these did not effectively reduce anti-Semitism or make Jews world citizens. Indeed the modern world saw an increase of such anti-Judaism. Not only the pogroms in eastern Europe after 1881 but the fashionable political and philosophical anti-Semitisms of Germany and France led more and more to question the dreams of integration. Meanwhile the other peoples of Central Europe were expressing a nationalism whose map in Europe denied Jews a place. Little wonder then that the old dream, even prayer, of a return to Israel would draw fresh impulses. Theodor Herzl issued his cry for a *Judenstaat* for Israel in 1896. Reform and many Conservative assimilators in America were ill prepared for such calls, and feared an actual rise of anti-Semitism if American Jews even hinted at dual loyalties.

10:38   Rabbi Isaac Mayer Wise in Cincinnati quite naturally represented the modernists against early Zionism, and Reform followed him, with a few exceptions, until the late 1930s. We have heard how Wise insisted that the adapted Jews were Israelites who did not even have a name in common with the new immigrants, who gnawed the dead bones of past centuries and should be called Jews. At times Wise and colleagues could see both religious and practical reasons for some return to Palestine. For example, Jews might be missionaries of civilization to Arabs. With the passing of time however, his opposition to what he saw as a "momentary furore," a reaction to Europe's "present anti-Semitic craze," which would soon be over, became firm. Wise could not even get the name right when he criticized "Thomas Hirzl with his novel scheme of the 'Jewish state'" in 1896. In 1897 Zionism was only a "bubble" which had already "burst and dissolved into nothingness." That September Wise editorialized: "Go to the fantasts and the fanatics with your Basle-Herzl projects. We, dwelling in the heart of civilization, who have practical understanding, have no use for such hallucinations." Wise had scant patience, he said, for any one who wanted something better for Jews than what the United States offered.

10:39   The Pittsburgh Platform that helped organize Reform in 1885 spoke in cosmopolitan terms congenial to all but two or three rabbis who broke Reform ranks on this subject by 1917. "We recognize, in the modern era of universal culture of heart and intellect, the approaching of the realization of Israel's great Messianic hope for the establishment of the kingdom of truth, justice, and peace among all men." However, the platform went on, Jews considered themselves no longer a nation but a religious community, and expected no return to Palestine.

10:40   In 1899 Rabbi Samuel Sale called Zionists prophets of evil, for undercutting universalism. In a rabbinical conference sermon of 1906 Rabbi Samuel Schulman also scorched Zionism along with other nationalisms in language uncharacteristically harsh for that imperial age. Ancient Jewish nationalism itself had not smacked of "that boasting and jealous Chauvinism" which modern nations were adopting. Schulman appreciated the way Orthodoxy also had no secular national aspirations. Then in 1908 President David Philipson told the annual conference of rabbis that what he termed "ghettoism and reactionism" were merely phases in the Americanization of the most recently arrived brethren. No one should fear, American Judaism would not be ghettoized or Russianized. Instead the heirs of the immigrants would some day look back in gratitude on "that union of progressive modernity and sane conservatism which this Conference symbolizes." In Philipson's perspective, "every age is the modern age compared with the foregoing," so Judaism had to change along with this progressive modernism.

10:41   Even though many Jews had come from Germany and might have sided with that nation, their loyalty during World War I was so strong that it became clear to many doubters: America was the Zion for most Jews. Yet after the war new anti-Semitisms broke out and in 1920, at the conference, Detroit Rabbi Leo Franklin, its president, spoke of the scapegoating that went on in his city. Henry Ford was there engaging in bizarre promotions against Jews. Franklin reacted against some Christian misuses of the concept of Americanization in this period. During the war the term had become one with which to conjure. It was natural that Christian churches would try to identify it with Christianization, he said, but this linkage should outrage Jews. Jews paid their dues in the war through the normal sacrifices of battle. These were sufficient to fill the Jewish cup of suffering, but then came the new anti-Semitism. Despite this uneasiness, Franklin was still not ready to follow up on the Balfour Declaration of 1918 and begin to work toward a new Israel, a home for Jews in Palestine. Only Hillel Silver and Stephen S. Wise, no relative to Isaac Mayer Wise, were long prominent in Reform support of Israel as a nation.

10:42   A man identified with neither rabbinate, indeed, no rabbi himself but a Boston reformer, distinguished jurist, and after 1916 an associate justice of the United States Supreme Court, Louis Brandeis, appeared on the scene at the crucial moment to support Zionism. In 1916 Brandeis wrote that "in the opinion of the President there is no conflict between Zionism and loyalty to America," so visible had his support become. He did more than any other prominent figure to overcome the dual loyalties theme. *"To be good Americans, we must be better Jews, and to be better Jews, we must become Zionists,"* became his theme. Multiple loyalties were objectionable only if they were inconsistent, and these were not. Assimilation, on the other hand, he called *"national suicide."* Cultural pluralism became his model. Brandeis was leader of the non-Conservative flank of Zionists, one which saw Zionism to be a component in universalism. As such, he did not use Zionism quite the way Schechter and others did to slow or render complex the other processes of modernization among Jews.

10:43   Schechter helped turn the seminary into a citadel of Zionist defenders, to see Zionism itself as a necessary component in Conservatism. He had a strong base, since the Historical School, Conservatism's antecedent, had favored return of Israel to political statehood before Herzl. In 1898 the little seminary saw the birth of the first Jewish fraternity to go by the letters ZBT, a translation of the Hebrew phrase that meant "Zion shall be redeemed with Justice." The ZBT wanted to gather educated people to help add respect to the Zionist movement. A mentor from the Historical School, H. P. Mendes, did not think that this return to tradition meant any retreat from universalism. Mendes contended: "By the restoration of Palestine to the Hebrews, we mean the establishment of a spiritual center for the world, and ultimately the establishment of the Kingdom of God on earth." This, indeed, was "Prophetic Zionism," "Bible-Zionism," or "Spiritual Zionism," and was in no sense a compromise on the part of Conservative Judaism. Reform and the moderns would not have their unchallenged way. Conservative Judaism as an organized element or a motif took its place as the third strong pillar of American Jewish religious life in the twentieth century.

11

The Carapaces of Reactive Protestantism

The religious ethnic groups, eager to be American but selective about modernity, inhabited firm but translucent cocoons of peoplehood. This "cocoon" became a first metaphor for early twentieth-century American religious movements. More exposed Protestants and Catholics could be seen as being under the canopies of denominationalism. There vision, access, and breezes were present, yet the canopies provided some shelter. In this third instance, many Protestants who had confronted overt progressivism and modernism and found both to be a threat to their traditions selected some elements from them with which to erect what we might think of as carapaces. In this case these would mean spiritually opaque and resistant coverings. Hard, like tortoise shells, these are, in the dictionary, "figures" for shelters. Outside influences are unable to penetrate and people within have made their aggressive choice to keep only each other's spiritual company. The countermodernist reactionaries made up companies under such figurative carapaces.

To recall the thesis about ironic outcomes: in the period wherein bearers of the dominant culture, the modernists and the moderns, pictured and intended a single main line of rational development and progress; in the time called liberal and modern and progressive; in *that* period of time the new century's durable and even thriving conservative movements in religion got their start. One

208

can add nuance to the names and distinctions between these movements in many ways, but the heart of the story can be told by reference to a turn in evangelistic movements, new millennial visions, fresh rationales for biblical inerrancy as the base for authority, and the rise of Pentecostalism. Proponents pictured each of these as simple repristinations or replications of timeless Christian and, hence, evangelically Protestant movements. Yet to all but those inventors, indeed to other conservative Protestants who did not follow these in all details, they were each complex innovations or inventions that refashioned elements taken from longer pasts.

The Hard Line in the New Evangelism

11:3   The countermodern reaction at the turn of the century in the field of Protestant evangelism and soul-winning was so complete that latter-day readers may have to be reminded: what later connoted "The Old Time Religion" had, in earlier eras, been seen variously as New Light, New Side, New School, or New Measures. Thus the greatest eighteenth-century evangelist, Jonathan Edwards, was capable of expressing doom. Yet his vision was postmillennial, and hence progressive. Edwards would be an agent in helping make the world attractive for Christ's return. The major evangelistic figure in the early half of the nineteenth century, Charles Grandison Finney, also used revivalist rhetoric to portray portending doom to an unrepentant world. Then he worked to reform the world with a kind of progressive social vision. As late as the Great Prayer Meeting Revival of 1857–58, a lay movement with a perfectionist tinge, much of the impulse went into an almost optimistic effort to change society. It has since even been seen as an impetus for the later Social Gospel. This image was soon to change, however, in the newer evangelism at the turn of the century.

11:4   What some historians have called the Great Reversal began to occur during the 1870s and 1880s, when Dwight L. Moody, who had been active already as a very young man in the revival of 1857–58, set the norms. A complex layperson, he attracted enormous middle-class crowds in urban America and England. With his expansive personality Moody could embrace moderate Christian evolutionists while despising evolution. He could reject negative biblical criticism but accept moderate and believing biblical critics. The battle lines were not yet hardened. Moody still dominated the scene in 1893 when his revivals outdrew and closed down the Sunday events at the World's Columbian Exposition. That year he retired from the circuit in order to spend his last six years consolidating his movement in educational institutions. It was under Moody or in his time that what had once been the New now became the Old-Time religion and, though effervescent and tolerant himself, Moody began to reject progressivist trends. Able to exploit modern technology, he was ambivalent about its ethos and context.

11:5   Under Moody and his colleagues evangelism began to take turns toward what was called premillennialism and, with it, new kinds of culture-negation. He saw to a narrowing of the zones in which the church was to be at home. While professors and publicists kept detailing premillennialism, Moody in mild ways popularized it before large crowds who did not recognize its novelty. An outgoing man reflexively at home in the business culture where he started out as an entrepreneur, Moody came to see the world as something from which to rescue souls in travail before the second coming of Christ. It was no longer a milieu to change in preparation for that coming. Not an inhumane or unconcerned man, Moody was distracted from or he despaired of social efforts to reform institutions and produce a more just and humane world. From England he imported prophetic visions of cultural desolation and spread these from city to city. His vast tabernacles were beginning to represent the spiritual carapaces which walled out other signals and built a world within the world for those under them. He uttered his negations before winding down in 1893 and before the Panic of that year. Because Moody did not have a depressive personality and since his turn occurred before a major economic depression, it can have had little to do with shifts which had begun before 1893–94.

11:6   Premillennialists kept refining their position in order to enroll in retrospect as orthodox and as their own many saints and sages from the Christian past who had not held quite their view of the world and its future. During that period they were able to enlist most of the new evangelists. One historian's roll call included names that have not become household words but that did dominate at the turn of the century: George Needham, W. J. Erdman, Major D. W. Whittle, J. Wilbur Chapman, Leander Munhall, Reuben A. Torrey, and most notably, soon after, Billy Sunday. All were of the antiprogressive school.

11:7   Moody spread the teachings at his Moody Bible Institute in Chicago and in notable summer conferences which combined evangelism and premillennialism as technique and theme. Moody's faculty taught the many students—137 graduates in 1900 alone went from Chicago—to reject biblical criticism. It was, they were told, "ruining revival work and emptying churches." Naturally the Moodyites also rejected the "later is better" notion of progressive Christianity and evolution. In 1914 institute leader Howard Pope told how he had converted from older postmillennial liberalism to premillennial evangelism while at Yale. His former position did not help motivate him to rescue souls, and he was, he remembered, "converted to the premillennial view as quickly as Saul was converted to Christ." Pope was not alone in such a desertion of progressivism in its peak period.

11:8   Premillennialists did not predict the date of the Second Coming, though they were sure it was imminent. An evangelist could mount a platform and use the threat of the end soon, perhaps that year, perhaps that night, to inspire a conversion from the doomed world, and then in the same sermon ask listeners to write Moody Bible Institute into their wills so the message could be preached for generations to come. Moody successor Reuben A. Torrey called himself an optimist because he was "absolutely sure that a golden age is swiftly coming to this earth," during Christ's promised thousand-year rule. Unlike the modernists, however, Torrey would not be a "blind optimist" who would shut his eyes to unpleasant facts. A storm was coming. Christians faced "the wildest, fiercest, most appalling storm this old world ever passed through." Then would come the Second Coming and the new age, "the only solution of the political and social and commercial problems that now vex us," he added. Such common preaching themes meant a natural stifling of the impulses to work for long-term reform.

11:9   Those in Torrey's train soon acquired a belligerent style and a hard psychic shell. Moody's son Paul early in the 1920s pictured how his own father would then have been more in sympathy with loving modernists than, as he put it, "with those who are attempting to persecute them because they will not subscribe to certain shibboleths." A new language was developing; code words and passwords and jargon measured who was under the carapace and who was not. The blurred lines were passing. Already back in 1900, soon after Moody's death, his friend at Glasgow, moderate biblical critic George Adam Smith, mourned that Christians had lost a man who, he said, was more able than any other to act as a reconciler of present divisions. Both were probably wrong about where Moody would have stood and right about how he would have treated both sides. After 1900 it was too late. No-man's-land is no place for reconcilers, and a new warfare split Protestant ranks.

11:10   Moody's followers rendered scholastic what he had kept fluid. In 1895, against modernist biblical attacks on the verbal inspiration of the Bible, Moody merely surmised that "someone was inspired to write it, and so all was given by inspiration and is profitable. Inspiration must have been verbal in many, if not in all cases." Moody defended literal readings of the often challenged Jonah and Samson miracle stories, fearing that when one "begins to doubt portions of the Word of God he soon doubts it all." In 1894 Moody had written that "verbal infallibility of the scriptures as originally given in Hebrew, Aramaic, and Greek" was a basic understanding. No, the new militants were not substantively wrong about Moody.

11:11   The evangelist always attacked modernism as the preaching of negation: "People are tired of negation. They will listen to a man who can get up with something definite to tell them." The year before he died he was using the language of separation. When a minister begins to pick the Bible to pieces, he advised, "get up and go out." Such a minister was doing the devil's business. No German infidel would be allowed to cut up his Bible. Yet Moody still feared distracting debates. Smith even claimed that Moody wanted a truce for ten years so that evangelists could "get on with the practical work of the Kingdom."

11:12   Ever since Moody, it has seemed anomalous to find a major evangelist in social gospel or liberal camps. Whenever one strays into them, he is either cut off from the evangelistic community or becomes an individual entrepreneur of limited prospects. In the twilight years, however, the crowd-pleasing evangelist did not always win everything. Thus in 1899 Samuel P. Jones, a flamboyant revivalist, took on Samuel M. "Golden Rule" Jones, the Toledo mayor who was seeking reelection. Samuel P. Jones was an anti-intellectual who said he favored southern revivals because "they haven't got the intellectual difficulties that curse the other portions of the country." He went his undenominational way in cities promoting a Social Darwinist ethic to go with evangelism: "God projected this world on the root-hog-or-die-poor principle. If the hog, or man either, don't root, let him die." Jones said that in the face of Moody's Gospelism, he would be a "Sinai" legalist who would reform America by laying down the law against the vices of drink, prostitution, and the like. His disdain for modernists was obvious. "We have been clamoring for forty years for a learned ministry, and we have got it today and the church is deader than it ever has been in history. Half of the literary preachers in this town are A.B.'s, Ph.D.'s, D.D.'s, LL.D.'s and A.S.S.'s."

11:13   In contrast, Golden Rule Jones wanted to help bring in the Kingdom by converting his Acme Sucker Rod Factory to a Golden Rule approach between employers and employees. Although he was a teetotaler, the temperance-minded clergy thought he catered to the foreign-born workers in the city of 100,000. He refused to placate clergy by shutting down the saloons, on Golden Rule principles. Many of Toledo's workers were ethnic Catholics who never had shared a temperance ethic. Samuel P. Jones came to town to take him on at the invitation of sixty ministers. Against the "white-washed Dutchman or an anarchistic Irishman" who would like to drink on Sunday, Jones railed: "Let us have an American sabbath and be decent." His act was not "fooling with politics," because he named no names. Mayor Jones found all this to be neither Christian nor scientific in method. The revivalist announced that he was also for the Golden Rule, but only "up to a certain point," after which he would then lift shotgun or club. Jones versus Jones it was, then. The mayor won and the preachers lost, as Golden Rule Jones won the mayoral election by 17,782 to 4,472 and 3,293 for his evangelist-backed opponents. Sam P. Jones went his prosperous way, avoiding Toledo.

11:14   Slowly it became evident that the overreaching Sam P. Jones was not an exception. In toe-to-toe encounters evangelists with hard lines were winning out over the gentler modern preachers. In Columbus, Ohio, the nation's best-known Social Gospel liberal minister, Washington Gladden, evidently had the backing of much of the clergy. They deserted him in 1912 when evangelist Billy Sunday came to town with a message and mode that undercut the modernist. More and more clergy were caught between.

11:15   Early in the new century Amzi Clarence Dixon, a congregationally based evangelist who headed Chicago's Moody church, drew the battle lines. He wrote *Evangelism Old and New* to attack religion which "depends upon change of environment to produce change of character." This included all academic evangelism that promoted intellectual training, moral culture, and humanitarian activity in what to Dixon were "hot-beds of infidelity or refrigerators of indifference." At the root of them all, he was sure, was support of naturalistic evolution.

11:16   Dixon, who advocated tabernacle evangelism, was a militant sort who could take on an infidel like Robert Ingersoll or a liberal like William Rainey Harper with equal zest. Union Oil president Lyman Stewart in California welcomed the chance to help him promote publication after 1910 of booklets called *The Fundamentals*. These lived later in the name of a movement designed to fuse reactive evangelism and theological countermodernism. By the time these booklets appeared, the old fluidity and suppleness of Moody were seen to be progressively disappearing in the hands of his successor.

11:17   Reuben A. Torrey could equally claim the Moody lineage, and he even more than Dixon made a bête noire of modernism. Torrey attracted wealthy laypeople to support Moody Bible Institute and Church. Heads of the Quaker Oats Company and Wanamaker department stores encouraged other people of wealth to support his reaction. He made a last half-hearted reach across the schism and wanted to identify with the scientific and intellectual camp, but it was getting late. "I claim," he said, "to be a scholarly preacher . . . and yet I believe the old fashioned Bible doctrine regarding hell," when that was no longer acceptable among intellectuals. Torrey found his own crowd-pleasing ways to disprove evolution and prove the existence of God, to the delight of sometimes gullible and in any case sensational press followings. Thus a Philadelphia headline bannered: DARWINIAN THEORY TORN TO SHREDS BY TORREY AT REVIVAL.

11:18   If every rule has its exception, this countermodern principle in the new evangelism seemed to have one too, but it was brief and, in the end, incomplete. One major revivalist, B. Fay Mills, did embrace social progressivism in the 1890s. He led revivals and remained a friend of Golden Rule Jones and Gladden and other reformers. Mills was a genius at organizing revivals, but then found his own patterns to be mechanical and unpleasantly obtrusive. They did work, however, so for some time he stayed on the trail. Already in 1893 and 1894 he converted to social Christianity and a form of millennialism that announced a utopian kingdom of heaven on earth. An anti-individualist, Mills had to part company with other evangelists. He alone among them came to believe that the world was growing better. None had room for his claim that "God intended the establishment of a terrestrial, spiritual, universal, everlasting kingdom upon the earth through human agency." When the old company of evangelists challenged such novel language, Mills had to admit that he had been led to accept "most of the conclusions and hypotheses of what might be called modern thought concerning the unity of the universe, the development of the world, and the progressive character of revelation."

11:19   By 1899 the evangelists had shut out their former colleague. He demonstrated the correctness of all their hunches when he defected to the Unitarian ministry. When he returned to Presbyterianism but not to the revivalist trail, Mills gave personal testimony to the strengths of faith he thought modernism lacked. The Gospel was still social, but if it was to be Gospel it must take account, as modernism did not, of the depravity or helplessness of ordinary human nature. All traces of progressivism left his mind when World War I convinced Mills, as he summed it up, that "this is not an earth whose regeneration may be expected day after tomorrow according to my optimistic prophecies." Instead it was a lost world, "helpless and hopeless save through some demonstration in history of an essential redemption and salvation." Moody and company could not have said it better.

11:20   Between Moody and Sunday the prime evangelist was John Wilbur Chapman, who after years in Moody's shadow set out in 1905 to promote the Chapman Simultaneous Evangelistic Campaign. This method sectored cities so evangelists could target them efficiently. In 1909 at Boston the Chapman brigade, as he called it, led 990 services between January 26 and February 17. The new evangelism was not afraid of modern techniques. It was as bureaucratized and rationalized as anything Max Weber was portraying in business and government. Chapman knew that. A moderate, like Moody, he tried to keep differing camps together, but he too had to decide among them—and did. He chose an individualistic ethic and rejected all missionaries who would not sign the dotted line in support of scriptural inerrancy. Chapman blamed the moral collapse of the German people in the war on the bitter fruits of destructive criticism of the Bible. In a way, he later became a victim of the free-enterprise competition he advocated in economics. In revivalism, where one was now only as good as his last act, he lost favor as the more sensational Billy Sunday rose to prime after 1909.

11:21   His successor used the modern techniques of organizing and publicity while rejecting modernism of all hues. William A. "Billy" Sunday was an ex-baseball player and showman who already in 1902 was charging that infidelity was rampant and rank unbelief was preached from many a pulpit. He went on to tell

Evangelist Billy Sunday attracted thousands of admirers and some critics as well.
Melting Pot claimed he was a stooge of Big Business. Sunday sued, then settled
out of court.

Iowans that "walking theological mummies with isms, schism,
and ologies" stood over against his work as "an old-fashioned
preacher of the old-time religion."

11:22   Old-fashionedness was limited and could go only so far. At
times Sunday also spoke of his as "progressive orthodoxy." As
did his predecessors, he attracted financial support from magnates with names like Dodge, Morgan, McCormick, Swift, Ar-

mour, Drexel, and Wanamaker, who seemed undisturbed by what the evangelist meant by progressiveness and unrepelled by his orthodoxy. He did not claim to be able to take on evolution or modernism in scholarly terms and even exulted: "I don't know any more about theology than a jack-rabbit knows about ping-pong, but I'm on my way to glory." He rejected the biblical criticism of those who, he said, pondered two Isaiahs "over a pipe of tobacco and a mug of beer at Leipzig or Heidelberg." When the word of God says one thing and scholarship says another, "scholarship can go to hell!"

11:23   The modernist social program also drew fire. In 1915 he attacked it as "godless social service nonsense." Some political leaders billed as progressive, however, were attracted and Theodore Roosevelt spoke from his platform to support this "most wide-awake, militant preacher of Christianity" that Roosevelt knew. As war in Europe approached, Sunday was a 100 percent American, unready to pray for war's end in 1915. "Never will I try to rearrange God's plan. How do I know that he isn't using the Allies to punish Germany for the higher criticism and heresies?"

11:24   After the war Sunday had lost novelty and some prominence. His campaigns settled for smaller cities where his celebrity lingered. Though because of an anti-Confederate heritage he had previously neglected the South, now he was welcomed chiefly there. The press made less of his celebrity and the eastern reporters were hardest on him. By then he had made his contributions to entertainment, revivalism, and prohibition. He also had formulated evangelism on lines which allowed it to be turned over almost intact when the later Fundamentalist movement was born. All traces of social Christianity and modern affirmation were gone. The Great Reversal had taken place and would remain unchallenged among revivalists for decades to come.

11:25   The evangelical tradition, while seeing antimodern evangelism develop, also saw the frustration of some of its original intentions. The rise of the urban professional campaigner whose operations necessarily took on the aspects of sensationalism and, by the time of Billy Sunday, often of mere show business, saw a decline of interest in evangelizing by Christians of other cultural outlooks and tastes who might otherwise share the same faith. The increasing tie to one view of the future, premillennialism, left out those with historically stated views of the future that had been proposed in the great tradition of earlier American evangelicalism. The constant prophesying of the imminent end came with a cocksureness that had little to do with broader biblical notions of readiness for God's actions in history.

11:26   For a generation some scions of moneyed families in Protestantism helped pay for urban revivalism, but its impulses and imagery soon tied it to one solid class. The alienated immigrant was unreached, and people of education often found evangelism to be anti-intellectual, anticultural, and antisocial in ways that did not square with their ideas of biblical wholeness or fulfil their notions of biblical mission. In the fight with modernism and the adoption of premillennialism it often also turned toward a kind of Manichaean worldview. The saved agreed perfectly with the evangelists and everyone else was unsaved or irrelevant to Kingdom purposes. In choosing to be specialists at one aspect of church work, the evangelists and their followers themselves contributed to the kind of chopping up of life, the specialization that was itself an aspect of modernization. It created problems for many kinds of thoughtful people in the culture, many Christians of evangelically catholic temper and outlook. Not all of these outcomes can have been intended by those who prayed for a great work of God in the form of organized evangelism at the turn of the century.

A Competitive Philosophy of History: Premillennialism

11:27   Countermodernity necessarily competed with other philosophies of history. The promise and fitness of things when America began to confront modern thought assured that a progressive philosophy would prevail, and the modernists allowed for no other. To oppose them meant to discern that they promoted such a view and to oppose them effectively meant to come up with an alternative. By philosophy of history I mean what Arthur Danto describes as looking "for the significance of events before the later events, in connection with which the former *acquire* significance, have happened." The philosopher has observed that such visions must deal as if with the whole of history. This implies a sort of theological commitment. On logical, rational, and historical grounds alone one cannot know the meaning of the present in the light of the future which has not yet occurred, and thus from whose vantage one can see nothing.

11:28   The Western world was in conflict over which view of the future would prevail. Evolutionary theories offered progressive, devolutionary, or random outcomes. Marxism, which had some minor representatives at the edges of contemporary American socialism, was as much a matter of faith as of empirics. Its proponents claimed to know outcomes of economic and class development in somehow inevitable futures. In the American cultural mainstream simpler progressivisms were also attractive in political, social and religious circles. To theological modernists, progressivism belonged to the Zeitgeist. It came with the air one breathed. All thoughtful people, they believed, would make something or other of it. Not to share in it was to miss out on the main course of history and was to fail the Kingdom of God in its unfolding and forward march.

11:29   Millions of Americans of Protestant loyalties did choose to miss out on evolutionary, socialistic, and progressive worldviews. The countermodernists, in fact, chose the progressive moment to develop novel antiprogressive eschatologies, or views of the end. Instead of helping plan and build a world that was here to stay, they were apocalyptic about a world that would pass away in fire, to be replaced by an emphatically better, indeed perfect, one. Instead of seeing biblical prophecy of the end in the mythic terms that the new higher criticism used to explain it, they rejected such criticism. They chose to literalize some of the very biblical language that earlier orthodoxy had treated as allegory, metaphor, or as too obscure for precise application to the world of the day's newspapers. To classify these inventions as conservative is imprecise, since many of them were fresh statements, not retentions. A radical inventive power was here at work which discovered or created a future whose threat and promise motivated people to strenuous activity. The leaders developed a carapace under which participants developed an arcane vocabulary. They communicated to each other with the peculiar language of insiders. They developed organizations to propagate their views during forays to outsiders, and found means to interpret their newspapers and the signs of the times independently of the generally approved constructions of reality.

11:30   In this period when old worldviews were breaking up and new ones were competing with each other, many rivals with many nuances survived. To concentrate on a representative view that has held allegiance for almost a century and has power in world events after that period will illustrate the process. No *Origin of Species* or *Das Kapital* classically stated it, yet one book published in 1909 impressively shaped much of the movement. The

Scofield Reference Bible, which sold two million copies in its first generation alone, plunges readers into the middle of the story whose prepublication history is informative.

11:31   Most Americans have never heard of this document and would not know whence those citizens who hold them derived their special views of the future. Oxford University Press nicely bound its closely printed editions, cramming it typographically with the standard-looking partitions of columns and the marginal notes that Bible readers favored. What was different in the notes was the word "dispensation." Annotator C. I. Scofield defined this as "a period of time during which man is tested in respect of obedience to some specific revelation of the will of God." That sounded innocent. Then: "These periods are marked off in Scripture by some change in God's method of dealing with mankind . . . and each ends in judgment—marking [human] utter failure in every dispensation." *Each ends in judgment* was a stark and summary note that denied all progress and development in history lived under God.

11:32   Cyrus Ingerson Scofield, announcer of doom and of subsequent millennial bliss, began his career as a Kansas lawyer and politician. He was raised in the Episcopal church, an orthodox Christian body that never heard of dispensations. After a YMCA agent converted him to dispensationalism, St. Louis pastor J. H. Brookes, also a devotee of it, tutored him. Scofield became a Congregational minister and a popular teacher at the Niagara Bible Conferences, where the followers of Dwight L. Moody and other evangelists met annually to share the new privileged views of Jesus Christ's second coming. As Scofield gained a following he found generous backers and by 1902 could state a sense of destiny: "The clear perception of this doctrine of the Ages makes a most important step in the progress of the student of the divine oracles. It has the same relation to the right understanding of the Scriptures that correct outline work has to map making."

11:33   Scofield's approach seems to the uninitiated to be a maze of mazes, a boxful of Chinese boxes, but its very arcane and complex character added to its appeal for laity. He had a numerologist's passion and saw significance in sequences; there were seven dispensations, seven types of resurrections, eleven mysteries, eight covenants. All students of his reference Bible could stay busy learning meanings that believers in eighteen Christian centuries had overlooked and yet read that "the editor disclaims originality." He had better, for his camp convinced itself that this was the constant and true interpretation of Christian scripture. God rules by utterly different but clear principles in different stages of history, several of which occurred within biblical times. What mattered now was Number Seven, called the "Fullness of Times or the Kingdom." God was then to "restore the Davidic monarchy in His own person, re-gather dispersed Israel, establish His power over all the earth, and reign one thousand years." The Kingdom of heaven when thus established would have "for its object the restoration of the divine authority in the earth. . . ."

11:34   Dispensationalism gave readers the excitement of sensing that they knew about the newspaper stories and, about the future, what their neighbors could not know. It was also based on another attraction, a peculiar understanding of the very act of reading the Bible. Theologians speak of a hermeneutical circle, referring to the fact that a preunderstanding that one brings to a text helps promote and confirm understandings then drawn from it. Dispensationalists thought of themselves as literalists. To them this preunderstanding meant that they must deal with the visionary and prophetic portions of the Bible as they would with newspaper accounts, adding some awe for the fact that these were God's words. Classic Protestant orthodoxy, for instance, brought preunderstandings that would never have allowed it to share the new understandings. Among these new ones was the contention that the "figures" found in the prophets always had a literal corollary or fulfillment such as "Jerusalem is always Jerusalem, Israel is always Israel, Zion is always Zion."

11:35   All students of hermeneutics would notice that this special literalism was based on a special history. Most readers of a *Scofield Reference Bible* would not know it, but as if by osmosis they built on a Baconian foundation. Premillennialist teacher Arthur T. Pierson did know, and spelled it out in 1895 at a conference. He rejected all biblical theology that starts "with the superficial Aristotelian method of reason" since it fit facts to the crook of a philosophical hypothesis. Instead, "a Baconian system, which first gathers the teachings of the word of God, and then seeks to deduce some general law upon which those facts can be arranged," did not seem to Baconians, as it did to all others, to be a hypothesis, but only a plain fact. As such, who could argue with it?

11:36   This Baconianism was channeled to America through an earlier dominant philosophy in the academy, Scottish common-sense realism. By 1895 it lingered chiefly at Princeton Seminary, there to give one sort of Protestants the conviction that their view was fact-filled, antispeculative, indeed, scientific. Through sense experience a person knew facts at first hand. A God who cared for people would not leave them without the necessary facts of the sort he put into the Bible. Humans need only organize and study these, and the reader then had to take them literally. In this spirit a pioneer premillennialist, Nathaniel West, thus argued that the number "483 years" in a prophetic vision had to mean exactly 483 years. The fact was fixed. "Science, the boast of modern times, has nothing more fixed, nothing more exact," to compel all unbiased persons.

11:37   Scofield gave new meaning to a King James Bible translation phrase and ran with the clue in his book title, *Rightly Dividing the Word of Truth*. Divide, for him, meant to chop the Bible and its ages and prophecies into neat divisions. He proposed: "The Word of Truth, then, has right division . . . *so any study* of that Word which ignores those divisions must be in large measure profitless and confusing." There could be no ambiguity or mystery, no basis for disagreement among sincere fact-minded Christians. These divisions in Scripture, given by God, were necessarily absolute. What applied to one age did not apply to another. Those who were to take prophecies thus literally favored one that spoke of a thousand-year reign of Christ in the near future.

11:38   Millennial ideas were as old as Christianity, but this very particular set of them may be traced back to the cottage of Margaret Macdonald of Scotland, who just before 1830 claimed visions of the end time. John Nelson Darby, who may have covered up tracks to that cottage-revivalist's influence or who may on his own have patented a coincidental view of "pretribulationist rapture" was more successful at spreading the view. The reader who wanders into a chapter with a term like the one just quoted may be bewildered by the verbal landscape, the absence of landmarks. One must plead here for the same sort of patience that one might need for learning the vocabularies of Darwin or Marx.

11:39   Rapture referred to nothing erotic but to the "catching away" of the church before Christ's second coming, as 1 Thessalonians 4:16–17 foretold it. Many thought this rapture would come at the end of a foretold "tribulation," during which event Antichrist would rule at the end time. Darbyites read this rapture as occurring before the tribulation, hence the "pre-," when Christ would come *for* his saints. Later he would come back to earth *with* his saints. The Antichrist would come to deceive after the rapture. He would attack Jewish worship and want to be God, but God would counterattack with plagues. Armies were then prophesied to converge from four directions on Israel, making efforts to kill the people of God at Armageddon. Then Christ and his people would return to destroy these forces and Antichrist, to bind Satan, to judge nations, and to see Messiah restore and sit on the throne of David for a thousand years. The world would then see a restored Jewish temple and kingdom. After the millennium an unbound Satan would make a brief but futile attempt to regain power. The saints would rise and God would judge between those who should go to heaven or hell, but in any case he would claim a permanent place for his own on earth.

11:40   Darby brought this arcane and dazzling interpretation to America, but Moody was its more effective carrier. Moody had no formal interest in contributing to—one pauses to breathe before writing—pretribulationist dispensational premillennialism, but he informally absorbed its spirit and detail. After his death the Moody Bible Institute refined and promoted Darby and Scofield inventions as traditions. They found these effective to support Moody's way of converting: "I look on this world as a wrecked vessel. God has given me a lifeboat, and said to me, 'Moody, save all you can.'" One would have expected gloom to result since, as Moody preached, "this world is getting darker." Instead the insiders were privileged and happy under their carapace. "I have felt like working three times as hard ever since I came to understand that my Lord was coming back again," said the often buoyant preacher who was wise enough not to date the Lord's return. Hearers of such evangelists were to be at the same time edgy, watchful, busy, *and* secure in each other's company under God.

11:41   The Moody people profited, for a full generation, from the development of this tradition in America. The Niagara conference had begun in 1875. Premillennialists promoted it at similar conferences in Allegheny, Pennsylvania, in 1895, Boston in 1901, Chicago in 1914, and in New York and Philadelphia after that. Other kinds of millennialists, even other sorts of premillennialists and styles of dispensationalists, began to be pushed aside at these events. While major seminaries resisted the novelties of evangelists like Billy Sunday, others joined in—pastors like Brookes and Pierson, a few merchants like the Wanamakers. Paradoxically, for people who expected Christ's imminent return, they invested and

engaged in long-range planning. James M. Gray at the Moody
Bible Institute was wise enough to teach followers to live as if
Christ would not return, and then build permanent institutions.

11:42   Most of those attracted had already reacted against modernity
and the influence of immigrants, the pleasures of dancing and
drinking and theater. Duty became the watchword: do what you
want to be found doing when Jesus suddenly comes. Unlike
Millerites in the 1840s they did not sell their property while awaiting the end; they acquired more. Their personal conduct differed
little from that of the rest of the staid middle class. The norms
were not novel, but their view of the church was; indeed, this view
was radical. To what denomination did Moody belong? Down-
playing denomination was not at all accidental, not the mere result
of the fact that many forces penetrated denominational canopies
while the carapace of this movement was more protective.

11:43   Instead, the choice of lowering the status of church was conscious. The prophet Daniel had talked of a future period of "seventy weeks" or "seventy sevens," said a literalist of this camp.
The number referred to the rebuilding of Jerusalem. These figures
added up to 490 years, 483 of which referred to the time from
Jerusalem's rebuilding in Old Testament days to the time of Christ.
What should one do with the seven leftover "weeks" which got
translated not too literally into "years"? Here came the great dispensationalist inventive leap of fact or faith. The seventieth
"week" did not immediately follow the first sixty-nine. Everything was in suspense. The entire period of Christian history
therefore existed in a no-count or no-account period of truly inde-
terminate length. For his own reasons God had "turned off the
time-clock" and left the church in a parenthesis in time. At his
chosen moment, God would start the ticking again toward the
end-time events. In the end time would come Antichrist and Armageddon, after God had fulfilled other mysterious purposes, including having given evangelists time to rescue more souls.

11:44   In the most astonishingly novel interpretation, the Sermon on
the Mount and the Lord's Prayer and all Gospel stories then belonged to the old Jewish dispensation. Only with the resurrection
and the epistles of Paul did newness and grace arrive. *The* church,
which had little to do with the organizations called churches, belonged to the end time. The institutional churches must exist for
functional reasons but they were in a way irrelevant, often materi-
alistic and apostate. God dealt with remnants, and dispensationalists knew they were one. The history of Israel, literal Israel, not the

figure of the church, was what mattered. C. H. Mackintosh, a dispensationalist, was emphatic: "It is vain to look into the prophetic page in order to find the church's position, her calling, her hope," as Christians had done. No, "they are not there. It is entirely out of place for the church to be occupied with dates and historic events." The Christian belongs only to and in heaven. Scofield argued that the church did not exist even during the earthly life of Christ. There is no "church history." Israel is "of and for the earth" and history, but the church is "of and for heaven."

11:45   No other Christians believed what the minority who gathered under this carapace did. Catholics and most Protestants had no idea of what was going on there. Secular progressives would have found it bizarre. Not even all evangelists and premillennialists followed Darby and Scofield scripts and many offered their own plots. Yet dispensationalists fortified each other with their privileged spectacles for reading the Bible and contemporary signs. An elite was forming, and Torrey used the sad and taunting language of an insider to mark it as he looked back at those "who are out of Christ, unbelievers." They would, he warned, be "left behind, left behind when God takes away the restraining power that holds back the manifestation of the anti-Christ." Torrey named some names of outsider's camps: Christian Science, Millennial Dawnism (Jehovah's Witnesses), Occultism, Theosophy, or Baha'i were most remote. German theology was devilish. Boston's Courtland Myers, during the wartime prophetic conference at Philadelphia, thundered that "the abomination of abominations in the modern religious world is that ripe, rank, rampant, rotten new theology made in Germany." Theologians had replaced the Gospel with "the law of the survival of the fittest, with the result now manifest in our world-tidal wave of barbarism, savagery, and immorality." Americans ought to fight this war-producing theology to the finish; "no foreigner can transact this unholy business with me," said Myers in the spirit of an ever more nationalistic theology.

11:46   This countermodernism successfully roused liberals to equally unlovely response. Some University of Chicago modernists stooped as low as Myers and painted themselves as the superpatriots who could fit the war into their own long-term views of progress. Divinity School Dean Shailer Mathews in *Will Christ Come Again?* attacked the dispensationalists as treasonous. His colleague and successor as dean, Shirley Jackson Case, published a work in 1918 that saw all millennialism as opposed to the progress of democratic ideals. The empirical theologian had no empirical grounds for claiming, but he claimed anyhow, that $2,000 a week was spent by dispensationalist propagandists: "Where the money comes from is unknown, but there is a strong suspicion *that it emanates from German sources. In my belief the fund would be a profitable field for government investigation.*"

11:47   Both sides could find and misapply compromising words in the prewar writing of their foes. Thus in 1915, safely before the war enforced conformity and orthodoxy, the premillennialist *Christian Workers Magazine* argued that the notion that governments receive their just powers from the consent of the governed, the root of American democracy, was a nonbiblical idea. It was, said the writer, "the antithesis of autocracy—God's ideal of government," under Christ as absolute monarch. Such talk was politically harmless in its day, still merely the word of passive citizens who were loyal in wartime.

11:48   Reform was essential to the progressives' program and no part at all of the premillennial one. Arno Gaebelein, a major figure, said "the world, to which we do not belong, can do its own reforming without our help." Indeed, reform itself belonged to a world under Satan, not under God. Departing from a long evangelical tradition of reform, Gaebelein wrote, "Satan, I doubt not, wants to reform his world a little, to help on the deception that men do not need to be born again." Some premillennialists on instinct joined to work for prohibition of alcohol, since all of them did favor temperance and vigilance before the end time. Some, however, went as far as Charles Reihl, who opposed prohibitionism as much as he did drunkenness. The latter, after all, was an obvious evil, while prohibition was subtle, dreamed up by the Devil, who, said Reihl, thought it would "hinder Christ's return and extend his own probation." Reform delayed the Second Coming and deluded those who would be converted.

11:49   Such extreme positions misdescribe ordinary, middle-class, safe, predictable premillennialists. James Gray in wartime acknowledged that his party could never absolutely separate themselves from American society, its literature, its politics, its commerce, but it could lead believers to separate themselves from "its methods, its spirit, and its aims." Modernist Protestantism was satanic to him because it did not do such separating. On Gray's grounds, some premillennialists engaged in moderate reform. Billy Sunday wanted to be known as a cleaner-up where vice prevailed. On similar terms, many of them invested heavily in the

worldly things of a capitalist society, believing they could enjoy
it until Christ came, if only they would rescue others from the
world's sin and stay vigilant.

11:50   The great dispensationalist achievement was to devise the carapace which offered dawn-to-dark, cradle-to-grave means of finding coherence during the period of the church's parenthesis.
Leaders built churchlike networks and organizations. They were
fated to be contentious and soon found that some of their more
exciting battles occurred with each other under the hard covering.
Moody had tried to keep the parties fluid. At Boston's Tremont
Temple he cautioned, "Don't criticize if our watches don't agree
about the time that we know [Christ] is coming." He resisted precise dispensationalist programs: "I differ. I don't know! I don't
think any one knows what is going to happen."

11:51   Others "knew," and more drew sharp lines. As early as 1896
premillennialist Robert Cameron attacked Darbyist twists as "a
revolution . . . a theory absolutely without a single advocate in all
the history of the Church, from Polycarp down." When Cameron
lost out in influence to the Darby and Plymouth Brethren forces,
he complained that they "have moulded the teachings of nearly all
the recent writers on prophetic subjects." He knew he was losing
out. Early in the new century J. H. Brookes foresaw the "sad fact
that pre-millennialists, notwithstanding their knowledge of the
truth are going to pieces." He reflected awareness of the positions
of Cameron and before him of Nathaniel West, who in 1893
charged that the Darby doctrine had "nothing new in it that is true
and nothing true in it that is new." West and Cameron settled in for
a long pull before the Second Coming, while Brookes expected
and wanted it to occur soon. Cameron provided a clue as to why.
On a conference verandah in 1895 Brookes revealed an inordinate
fear of death and pleaded, "Can't you leave me the hope, after
all these years have passed away, that I may live to see my Lord
come, and escape the clutches of that awful enemy, death?"
Brookes died two years later.

11:52   With Brookes off the scene in the new century, James Gray and
C. I. Scofield led the "any moment" faction, while Cameron and
the "post-tribulationists" opposed them. Arno Gaebelein would
not even allow the latter camp to contribute to his magazine *Our
Hope*. This fact led Cameron to charge that Gaebelein and others
were actually revolutionary, only apparent conservatives who
were, in their own way, like the modernist innovators. Who said
that this heretical pretribulationism dared become a test of Chris-

tian truth? "Do you think it wise to exalt into a 'test of fellowship'
a doctrine so recently enunciated, that does not have a single passage of Scripture beyond the question of a doubt upon which to
rest its feet?" Here was no modernist talking, but a conservative
evangelical who believed in the millennium. Cameron continued
that the doctrine had "such a questionable origin, from the lips of
a heretic, and supported by the testimony of demons."

11:53   Marxists and Darwinians fought as vehemently in their own
houses, without being able to claim supernatural and absolute
support for their sides. The faction that became Scofieldian had
a more satisfying view for those who would interpret perplexing
times and would motivate evangelism. Why hasten, if the Second
Coming was distant? Conferences headed by Gaebelein therefore
stressed the immediacy of the Second Coming. It was at such a
conference at Sea Cliff, Long Island, during a shore stroll, that
Scofield mentioned his idea of producing a reference Bible, which
he later referred to as "the new beginning and this new testimony
in Sea Cliff" in the name of what later came to be thought of as a
conservative accent.

11:54   It is possible to follow such evangelicals under their shell and
see them as curiosities standing apart, and then to dismiss them as
irrelevant. Just when such a moment might near, a feature of their
worldview comes to light which has, decades later, produced
enormous consequences in international affairs. The premillennialists were major contributors to what might be called Protestant
Zionism, which was more articulate and active early in the twentieth century than was even the international Jewish movement.
Since these were biblical literalists in the tradition which tended
to see Jews as "Christ-killers," and since they came from sections
and classes where anti-Semitism was believed to be high, Jews
could well have expected them to be anti-Zionist. How they came
to be the foremost Christian Zionists in America is clear from an
understanding of their intricate and certain readings of prophecy.

11:55   The root notion was that in the dispensationalist view the word
"Israel" was not figurative, like "carapace" is; it really and literally meant Israel, the nation of Israel. The true pioneer of this
application was William E. Blackstone, an Oak Park, Illinois,
layman after whom a forest in modern Israel, with good reason,
came to be named. In 1891 he addressed a petition to President
Benjamin Harrison. Wealthy and prominent Protestants signed
and supported it. Blackstone, acting on behalf of some perse-

cuted Russian Jews, urged that the United States take part in helping found a new political state of Israel as a refuge. Palestine
was, according to God's distribution of nations, the home of
Jews as "an inalienable possession." It is not likely that John D.
Rockefeller, J. Pierpont Morgan, the speaker of the House of Representatives, the chief justice of the United States Supreme Court,
and metropolitan mayors who signed the petition bothered to back
its biblical judgments with research. They merely wanted to express sympathy for suffering Jews. Blackstone was to follow this
with a second memorial in 1916, again signed by wealthy people
and even some liberal Protestants who were far from premillennialism, yet his memorial of 1891 is significant for having plowed
the new political ground first. Theodor Herzl gained publicity for
his *Judenstaat* only five years later. In 1918 Blackstone could
look back in satisfaction on his advocacy of Zionism through
these decades because it was "founded on the plan, purpose, and
fiat of the everlasting and omnipotent God, as prophetically recorded in His Holy Word, the Bible."

11:56   As for the Jews, in Blackstone's reading, they had three choices.
Few would become true Christians. More, he thought, would be
assimilants, neither Christians nor Zionists, who would barnacle
themselves on the social, political, and commercial ships around
them. Or, third, they could be Zionists, holding fast to the ancient
hopes of the fathers, the assured deliverance of Israel, through the
coming of their Messiah, and then "complete national restoration
and permanent settlement in the land which God has given them."

11:57   Dispensationalists enlarged upon this. An *Our Hope* editor,
Ernst F. Stroeter, told conferees at Allegheny in 1895 that Jews
would be "*re-established forever in their own city and in the
promised land.*" Jews would one day welcome such sectarian
Christian support, though they would be less happy with the next
line, which said that "*the Lord Himself (Jehovah-Jesus) will be in
the midst of His redeemed people.*" In this reading, Jews were
all to regroup in Palestine. Those who already regarded Jesus as
Messiah would suffer briefly. Gentile armies would invade. Jesus
would come to rescue, destroying Antichrist's troops and restoring
the Kingdom of Israel at the site of the Temple. Those Jews not yet
converted would then acknowledge Christ as their Messiah.

11:58   Six years later at a Boston conference it was Protestant premillennialists who talked more boldly than almost any American Jews about the return to and rebuilding of Israel. Professor

William G. Moorehead, president of a Presbyterian seminary in Xenia, Ohio, typically argued that "the Jewish state and the Jewish national life shall once more be established" and would become "the world's hope." In 1914 at the next conference at Chicago's Moody Bible Institute the rising leader William Bell Riley took note of the not yet significant secular Zionism. He claimed that "it may shortly prove to be more significant than all the other movements" of the day.

11:59   Some speakers in 1914 were even ready to help American Jews who were beginning to suffer from charges of possible dual loyalties. Robert McWatty Russell, moderator of the United Presbyterian Church's General Assembly and president of Westminister College elaborated: "As members of the great American republic we need feel no sense of jealousy toward Israel," which was to lead the nations of the world. It is hard to conceive of any position further from Reform Judaism or liberal Protestantism, both of which promoted Jewish spiritual universalism abroad and assimilation of sorts at home. The events of the World War and the Balfour Declaration confirmed the premillennialist side.

11:60   Two weeks after Armistice Day, at Carnegie Hall in New York, Gaebelein exulted, "What rejoicing when it became known that the unspeakably wicked Turk, with his equally wicked German master had been defeated, that the crescent was downed and the flag of the British Lion wafted over David's City!" He urged political Zionism as a cause because, as he said, "divine providence has used this horrible war to take away Palestine from the Turk and make it possible for the Jewish people to return." Gaebelein cautioned, however, that with Armageddon ahead, "this war is not the last war which the holy land has seen." And Riley added his conclusion: "America shall not rule; but a nation that is now weak, that is now scattered to the ends of the earth, without a land in which to dwell, a city to become her capitol, or even a flag floating for her protection, that nation will be the people of God."

11:61   Aware of their image as pessimists, dispensationalists used the issue of Israel and the war years to counter it. WHO ARE THE PESSIMISTS NOW? ran a headline in a 1914 *Christian Worker's Magazine*. "Premillennialists are charged with pessimism. They resent the charge." With "unshaked optimism" they watched God work out his purposes. By 1917 Protestant Zionism was becoming such a fashion that various editors had to vie for prominence in the movement. Had the old-time dispensationalists, asked one, not "earned their right to be heard by the grace of God through hard work"? At the same time, the moderates and modernists were still out of step. So-called church leaders and those "sitting in the high places of theological seminaries and editorial sanctums" were still unbelieving, complained the writer. The dispensationalists under their hard protective cover took consolation when their religious best-sellers and authors were overlooked by outsiders. For long they were "despised and rejected of men. Men have turned their faces from them." But now, at last, "things are coming their way." Reform Jews, in Scofield's world, were in an even worse position, since God has "decreed the reconstitution of the nation of Israel upon the sacred soil of Palestine," but they stood on the sidelines with the "spiritualizing school" of liberal Christians. "Ah, I do not wonder that Russian Jews are orthodox! Suppose we were to go to the sorrowful victims of the persecution in the land, and tell them that 'the nineteenth century is the Messiah!'" as modernist Jews and Christians did?

11:62   Jews never got gifts from Christians without strings attached, and the dispensationalists offered entangling and befuddling ones. Most of them wanted to evangelize the Jews. People like Gaebelein insisted that conversion would not disrupt Jewish family life or tradition, but would only make for better Hebrews, when Jews accepted Jesus as the Messiah.

11:63   We have come a long way from the cottage of Margaret Macdonald in Scotland past Atlantic commuters like John Darby and Dwight L. Moody through the world of the Balfour Declaration to a foretaste of the Israel born in 1948. The transit mocked the promise and fitness of things. It contradicted the old image that modernist Protestants and Reform Jews were in the vanguard of world history and that self-proclaimed biblical literalists were in the rearguard. The premillennial vision was the one that began to be enacted politically. Here, too, was a confusion of the picture in which mainstream Protestants were agents of all interfaith connections and those called conservative and orthodox tended to be anti-Semitic. When Jews included the support of Zionism as the key to philo-Semitism, a reversal of parties in favor with Jews suddenly occurred. Yet if Jews looked for alliance with people who respected the integrity of the Judaism that existed, not the Judaism to be converted or transformed by the Messiah "Jehovah-Jesus," they found their best support among the friendly modernists who respected their universalism, not among premillennialists

who relished their particularity. Finally, the nineteenth-century innovators who set forth a novel view of the millennium, acquired the
image of being conservative supporters of the old-time religion.

The Protective Weapon of Biblical Inerrancy

11:64   If evangelism was a foray out from under, and premillennialism
an interpretation beneath the carapace of Protestant countermodernism, it remains to ask: what was the structure and substance of the hard covering itself? Since the modernists were relativists about authority, their critics had to be absolutists. Because
the liberals favored dynamic and fluid views of history, the anti-
progressives needed a stable and rigid superstructure. They found
this in an assertion of the infallibility or, more scrupulously, the
inerrancy of the canonical Bible, which was made up of the Hebrew Scriptures and the New Testament. Of course, Protestants
from the beginning, lacking a papal authority for infallibilism,
had always held very high their highly diverse views of the authority of biblical words. Now, in reaction to the erosions they felt
precisely when modern biblical criticism reached American foundations, they fabricated a more articulated view of inerrancy than
before. Indeed, the word itself became both a weapon against
heretics and, as Moody would have called it, a shibboleth for
making distinctions between parties.

11:65   Princeton Seminary became the intellectual center of the inerrancy party, though it was by no means lonely. Reformed and
Lutheran conservatives who arrived in reaction to German rationalism in the nineteenth century often repristinated the dogmatic orthodoxy of the seventeenth century. They insisted on verbal inspiration and the errorlessness of the Bible. Let the critics
urge that no clear word of scripture claimed such kinds of absence
of error or of the possibility of error in historical, scientific, or
other natural matters. These midwestern scholastics often re-
sorted to syllogisms to defend the obviousness, to them, of their
view that the Bible as the word of a perfect God had to be scien-
tifically accurate and, hence, perfect or errorless as well. The
Princetonians used the admittedly waning academic philosophy of
the early part of their century, Scottish common-sense realism, to
provide their own rationale. Some southern Baptists and northern
evangelicals who did not even know such Princetonian names as
Alexander, Hodge, or Warfield, informally and unwittingly put

their more sophisticated arguments to work in defense of the be-
sieged Bible.

11:66   While the Enlightenment in Europe undercut biblical authority,
one aspect of its Scottish version was used to support inerrancy.
Scottish forebears of Princeton divines had trained their sons to be
controversialists. They had memorized catechisms as children and
learned systems of John Calvin as adults. What religious experience could do for Methodists or liturgy did for Episcopalians,
doctrine could do for Presbyterians: it provided the structure,
boundaries, a reason for being, something to export to non-
Presbyterians who wanted the same. So skillfully was all this
grafted on to common sense that advocates had trouble seeing
how anyone in good faith would fail to see that all this was simply
congruent with the structure of the universe and the mind.

11:67   A layperson, it was argued, could trust common sense and
sense-experience, and on these terms could have direct access to
the universe of meanings, including to an apparently complex and
difficult book about them, the Bible. Truths do not vary depending upon environment, genes, perspective, or historical development. Propositions deal with facts available to experience, and a
person of good faith will assent to such propositions. The word
"facts" adds the one special twist to this American application,
recalling as it does the figure of Francis Bacon. The Baconians
argued that if all facts were organized by induction, truth incon-
trovertible must emerge. The biblical scholar was something like
the botanist, geologist, or museum-keeper. We have already seen
the dispensationalist lining up and classifying all the specimen
texts from Daniel, Ezekiel, and Revelation, treating them literally,
showing them manifestly being what they seemed to be.

11:68   On such terms the case-study group, the Princetonians, faced
modern science. They snatched claims for science away from the
moderns, insisting only that they themselves be permitted to define science, hence, in Baconian terms. Charles Hodge's *Systematic Theology* in 1874 was a classic, though not unique or original, statement. As natural science was, he wrote, "concerned
with the facts and laws of nature," so "theology is concerned with
the facts and the principles of the Bible." Therefore, "if the object
of the one be to arrange and systematize the facts of the external
world, and to ascertain the laws by which they are determined,"
so "the object of the other is to systematize the facts of the Bible,
and ascertain the principles or general truths which those facts in-

volve." Those who accepted Hodge's "if . . . so" connection, or his leap—depending upon how one saw the move—gained a psychological advantage. They had it all over those who would appeal to lay minds that were burdened by ambiguity, awareness of context, perspective, and relativity in the forming and interpreting of texts. Those who could not make a leap from what they saw to be a metaphysically condemned base found his reasoning inaccessible. His approach was not to be privileged as the only way to assert biblical authority. Indeed, it was likely to be seen by others as the most wrong way.

11:69   Hodge and his successor, Benjamin Breckinridge Warfield, for all they talked of sense experience, concentrated more on what the mind did with the sense data. They did not see themselves as anti-intellectual. They were indeed rationalists of a sort. In relation to biblical propositions and hence, for faith, they argued, the mind came first. For Hodge, "intellectual apprehension produces feelings, and not feeling intellectual apprehension." Feelings were unreliable. This contention caused some strain when the Princeton scholars had to make an uneasy alliance with the more emotional revivalists who were forming countermodernist coalitions with their own kind. Yet the Princeton view could later be grafted on to and merged with revivalist appeals to the heart. Such acts of grafting and merging were tours de force that created the coalitions. Hodge and Warfield went even further: the mind needed firm bases for its ideas and conclusions. Neither feelings nor thoughts but words, words as hard data, as objects and facts standing behind processes of induction, such words mattered. Hence, verbal inspiration.

11:70   All these views congealed before the turn of the century. Archibald Alexander Hodge and Warfield already in 1881 wrote on "Inspiration" for *The Princeton Review*. Protestants who never heard their names have been influenced by the argument. Bible words did not merely contain, no, they "ARE THE WORD OF GOD, and hence . . . all their elements and all their affirmations are absolutely errorless." This conclusion assured "the truth to fact of every statement in the Scripture." The Bible was, then, the theologian's "store-house of fact." This claim gave the inerrancy party a reason for militancy and a motive for charging bad faith against all outsiders or any deviants within their camp. If there was disagreement over a biblical teaching, this had to be because the opponent was thoughtless, lazy, evil, willfully blind, intentionally ignorant, or a prejudiced denier of obvious facts. While secular philosophy had long before abandoned the root argument behind this defense of scriptures, tougher minded church leaders who could see no alternatives to it welcomed the assets it provided for the insecure in a time of radical change.

11:71   When this inerrancy party met its academic foes, Warfield claimed for it the mantle of true science and reason. "It is the distinction of Christianity," he wrote in 1903, "that it has come into the world clothed with the mission to *reason* its way to its dominion." The heirs of revivalists at last found simple intellectual props for their positions, the authority they needed but could not argue on their own. Let other religions appeal to emotion or sword, "Christianity makes its appeal to right reason, and stands out among all religions, therefore, as distinctively 'the Apologetic religion.'" Everything hinged on that adjective "right" before reason.

11:72   The pathos of this situation lay in the fact that most Christians before, then, and since, could not believe in reason on these Baconian and common-sense realist grounds. By 1903 the philosophers at Princeton University, only yards away from the seminary, no longer understood how the Warfields could take these grounds for granted. Yet there was enormous attraction in the combination for educated conservative Protestants who wanted to live in the world of science and reason. In their coup, the inerrancy party could make all other Christians, including the classically catholic and orthodox, look ignorant or unfaithful to some degree or other.

11:73   In 1912 Francis L. Patton, the last Princeton University president to serve as an apologist, spoke at the seminary centennial. Against all who found the school's views odd and arcane, he urged that it had "no oddities of manner, no shibboleths, no pet phrases, no theological labels, no trademark." While the whole rest of the informed world thought Princeton philosophy to be peculiar, Patton felt privileged to say that "there has been a New Haven Theology and an Andover Theology," but "there never was a distinctively Princeton Theology," since Princeton simply taught universal, biblical, Reformation truth.

11:74   In the early days of his *Systematic Theology* Hodge could still allow for an as yet inexplicable tinge of error in the Bible, but, he insisted, "the errors in matters of fact which skeptics search out bear no proportion to the whole." "No sane man," he said, "would deny that the Parthenon was built of marble even if here and there a speck of sandstone should be detected in its structure." In his early period there was still some luxury for such qualified lapses: "Not less unreasonable is it to deny the inspiration of such a book as the Bible, because one sacred writer says that on a given occasion twenty-four thousand, and another says that twenty-three thousand, men were slain." When the party lines and the carapace cover had hardened by 1912 no sandstone was left to be acknowledged in the marble of biblical inerrancy. His successor, Warfield, tidied matters. True, he acknowledged, Hodge had once admitted "alleged errors," but they were "for the most part trivial," "only apparent," never having "any real importance." Instead of admitting that such an approach had to be a fundamental problem for the Baconian and common-sense realist dogmatics, Warfield simply reminded that Hodge also frequently spoke of the Bible's "freedom from error."

11:75   At the turn of the century some inerrancy advocates began to contend that Hodge's "apparent" errors had to come from copying of manuscripts; that the originals, if available, must be without error. This might have struck terror in the hearts of laypeople who could not feel secure about whether the only Bible they could have was errorless, but at this point the inerrancy theorists began to minister to fears by reference to an old theme, the analogy of faith. It assured the Bible's central point. Facts in the Bible proved that a self-revealing God would not have allowed for transmission of a document that would violate the whole divine intent. Christians at least since Augustine had argued that way, but when Warfield reclaimed this analogy, rival Protestant theologians claimed he was changing the rules of his own game at mid-course. Warfield could afford to appear smug. If "one proved error" would demolish inerrancy, no one could ever find that error of fact, because it could not be proven that this was not a mere error of transmission.

11:76   The inerrancy party now had a weapon against heresy, a banner under which to rally bewildered believers, a cement for the structure covering their camp. Simple people of faith did not need to follow all the premises. They could profit from the conclusion, just as Communists who could make no sense of Marxian texts depended upon the assurances of elites that they had worked out difficulties. In the pre–Civil War South it was important that high views of biblical authority prevail because the Bible included some texts that could support slavery. Now no party had a heavier investment in inerrancy than the premillennialist. Only with an inerrant set of facts in the Bible could it hold together with abso-

lute assurance. At the end of the Bible-conference era Boston's
Reverend Cortland Myers set the epochal question of authority in
context for the premillennialists. He wrote, "We will have no
Pope infallible or otherwise, for our authority. . . . We will have
only the Christ of the Book for our authority." Inerrancy clauses
for the first time began to be treated like creeds or confessions in
some conservative Protestant denominations.

11:77   At the end of World War I some militant countermodernists
took a name left over from the set of tracts called *The Fundamentals* that had appeared ten years earlier. No other theme appeared
more than four times in these tracts, yet twenty-seven of ninety-
four topics opposed the higher criticism of the Bible as proposed
by modernists. The organizers in this lineage formed a World's
Christian Fundamentals Association. In parts of their nine-point
statement of faith they combined premillennialism and inerrancy
as creedal linchpins or new definers of boundaries. By the mid-
twenties the informal coalescence of such groups led to the development of a party called Fundamentalist that became locked with
a party called Modernist for control of several denominations.
Not all fundamentalists by any means were to be pretribulationist
or dispensationalist or premillennialist, but all were inerrantist.
Let the universities, the interdenominational seminaries, the theologians and journalists waver, and let them in their privileged
aeries be biblical critics and relativists. The evangelists and fundamentalists, with their firm views of inerrancy, could hold the
loyalties of millions through the decades to come.

Pentecostalism: "Almost Incomprehensible at This Day"

11:78   It was in the May 20, 1920, issue of the Baptist *Watchman-
Examiner*, that Curtis Lee Laws and 154 others called for a "General Conference on Fundamentals" to be held before the annual
meeting of northern Baptists. When he asked for "fundamentalists" to do "battle royal for the Fundamentals," Laws was
patenting a new term for a party which was being shaped through
two decades and more. A relentless logic lay behind the development of fundamentalism, which was chiefly doctrinal. While the
155 signers protested "a widespread and growing worldliness" in
their church body, as doctrinaires they focused less on practice
than on ideology. Their document expressed alarm, therefore,
over "the havoc which rationalism" was working. In this case as
others, the ideological side of what they opposed came to be

called not only modernism but rationalism. On June 15, 1922, the same magazine defined the enemy: "Rationalism fully developed denies that there is any authority over a man external to his own mind or any revelation of truth except through science." Since the structure of fundamentalism was based on Baconian and Scottish common-sense realist views of reason, however, one can see the new battle as a contest over rationalisms. The reactionaries did not have a "fully developed" but rather an "otherwisely developed" rationalism.

11:79   To concentrate only on philosophy and dogma, however, no matter how important were the trickled-down versions of these to many laypeople and pastors, would be to miss much of the heart of turn-of-the-century reaction to modernism in theology and modernity in general. Americans of this period were not only debating dispensations at Niagara or induction and facts at Princeton and their counterparts. Just as there were people who stressed the affective side in this revanchist Protestant party, so a new and quite independent response was also taking shape at the borders of Protestant respectability. Rising from the soil of evangelism and seeded by movements which had roots in Methodism and its "holiness" offsprings, this new growth spread chiefly across the American South after 1900. Before the close of the next century it was at home throughout the United States and had become the fastest-growing non-Catholic force around the Christian world. Even Catholics were to develop a counterpart charismatic movement as decades went by.

11:80   Whoever would anticipate the story of Pentecostalism has to be ready for many contradictions of the promise and fitness of things as secular and mainstream Protestant intellectuals of 1900 foresaw them. Whoever expected one mode of rationality to characterize modern religion must be surprised to observe Pentecostalism's emergent "irrationalism." In the eyes of progressives, it retrogressively reached back for long-buried models of primitive Christian ecstasy and enthusiasm. While spontaneous and fluid at first, it became dogmatically sure that it had the truth direct from the Holy Spirit. Its rise befuddled liberals who looked for tolerance to be a sign of the new century's religion. Prophets of science were shocked to see that many of its people rejected even medical science. If socialists expected peasants and workers to unite in class-based revolution, here now were lower and lower-middle class "holy rollers," "hillbillies," and marginal urbanites forming a movement that looked and was socially unrevolutionary. Efficient ecumenical people anticipated church cooperation and union, but the Pentecostal people advocated "come-outism" and propagated new sects. Modernity meant bureaucratic rationality while Pentecostals followed charismatic emotionalism. Modernism adapted, using theological naturalism, but the Pentecostalists were raging supernaturalists. Modernity demanded manners and decorum, as in the staid churches; the Pentecostalists were often unmannered and indecorous in their eruptive worship. Where was vaunted cosmopolitanism in the urban wards and the rural hollows as Pentecostal leaders cultivated local color and a provincial feel? If some of these descriptions are stereotypes that overlook some Pentecostal varieties, they appeared as constants among those agents of modernity who first tried to ignore and later often had to watch the new movements take shape.

11:81   The women and men who responded to Pentecostal evangelists unquestionably had their own souls' interests at stake, apart from any ideology. Their leaders, however, were finding a place in a crowded landscape and they consistently defended themselves as alternatives to modernist compromisers or eroders of faith. Latter-day historians can and do collect virtual anthologies of such expressions. For example, to writers in the *Pentecostal Evangel* through the twenties, liberal ecumenism was "Religious Babylonianism." W. T. Gaston put it in militant terms: "The religious battle of the last days is clearly drawn before this generation. It is between natural and supernatural religion." After the parties had lined up, an editor warned that "the modernist pulpit today is preparing the audience, the constituency, for the Antichrist." Modernism was an import from atheist Germans and Bolshevik Russians: "The triangle of Satan is atheism, evolution and modern theology."

11:82   Decades before these partisan writings, people began to report on a positive movement of the Spirit. Cyrus I. Scofield kept score on the Holy Spirit and in 1899 contended that more books, booklets, and tracts on that subject were issued during the previous eighty years than in all previous time since the invention of printing. Reuben A. Torrey wrote at book length about *The Baptism with the Holy Spirit.* He was puzzled because in biblical times Spirit-filled people spoke in tongues, in unrepressed speech, yet no one did now. They soon would, some of them claiming not mere *glossolalia*, ordinarily unintelligible syllables that demanded interpretation, but even *xenoglossia* wherein people claimed to speak in foreign tongues that they did not know apart from the

Spirit. Speaking in tongues, as the Pentecostal people insisted, was but one of many signs of the Spirit.

11:83   Revivalists looked for such signs everywhere as the new century began, and reported on stirrings in Wales, Australia, and elsewhere. The missionary movement, now at its peak, reported back to conservative churches about growth on remote islands. Yet the new eruption occurred in America, among blacks and whites, often under female leadership. Many pointed to Miss Agnes N. Ozman, as significantly a Methodist as she was a woman. Methodism was the grandparent of the movement that was developing as a restless Miss Ozman searched for an intense experience at Bible schools. In late 1900 she found herself in the sphere of controversial holiness preacher Charles Fox Parham, who was calling for "baptism with the Holy Spirit."

11:84   At Topeka, Kansas, Parham imposed virtually monastic discipline on his followers, including the hypochondriac and ailing Miss Ozman. When he commanded study, she studied; when he ordered students to make converts, she proselytized. She longed for the Holy Spirit, she said, more than for her food. When Parham commanded her and others to seek signs of the Holy Spirit, she and her cohorts approached New Year's Day, 1901, testifying to the power of tongue-speaking of the sort they read about in the Book of Acts, "when the Pentecostal blessing fell." If disciples then "spake with other tongues," why not now?

11:85   Why not? New Year's Eve was prayer-service time. On the first morning of the new century, Ozman later remembered it: "I asked Bro. Parham to pray and to lay hands on me that I might receive the Baptism in the Holy Ghost. . . ." While he did so, "Bless HIM! I talked several languages for it was manifested when a dilect [sic] was spoken." Ozman claimed to be using Chinese and other foreign languages. Here was the new Book of Acts being written in Kansas. Two days later at a nearby Free Methodist church others spoke in tongues. When normal boundaries break, participants look for signals. Parham spoke in "Sweedish tongue, which later changed to other languages. . . ." Howard D. Stanley testified: "I saw the clovend [sic] tongues as of fire came down into the room and my vocal cords and tongue changed and I was speaking with another language and so was most of the others."

11:86   Like all such mythically cast stories, these had certain features that remain open to question. In an earlier stratum of testimony Miss Ozman referred to having spoken in tongues three weeks before New Year's Day, a less neat date, but one which others corroborated. She also claimed that she realized the significance of her speaking only later, but it is known that Parham had instructed her in advance to look for precisely that sign. The Pentecostals were generating group-behavior patterns that resulted at least in some measure from their participating within a highly conducive atmosphere. These people together generated a common cherishable experience. No Pentecostal would have listened to any explanation that took away the supernatural role of the Spirit.

11:87   Language was only part of the issue, but it was most colorful. Years later Sarah Parham wrote a fabulous life of Charles Fox Parham. By now she claimed that linguistics professors, foreigners, and government interpreters soon listened in at "Stone's Folly," the temporary abode of the Parham school. They heard twenty distinct unstuttered and clear Chinese dialects. She averred that even a rabbi was astounded when a student read in Hebrew from an English Bible. "No not that one," he said when offered the text. "I want to see the Hebrew Bible. That man read in the Hebrew tongue." *The Topeka Capitol* called it all fakery, as it reported: "Queer Faith, Strange Acts . . . Believers Speak in Strange Languages." The *Kansas City World* saw the events as misfit in modernity: "These people have a faith almost incomprehensible at this day." Yet not all remained well. Parham soon abandoned Stone's Mansion, calling it a "pleasure resort," and in fulfillment of a dream he'd had, it burned. Parham cherished charred woodwork from the mansion's "Upper Room," a symbol which self-consciously tied this scene to Pentecost. He headed west to spread his gospel.

11:88   Pentecostalists found it important to claim roots in primitive Christianity, ties to the Reformation, and precedents in nineteenth-century evangelical life. Margaret Macdonald in her Scottish cottage combined dispensational prophecy with tongues-speaking. From such circles came not only Darby and the Darbyites but also Edward Irving and his Irvingites. Expelled from the Presbyterian church, they spread ecstatic experience. To spotty, random, brief, and rare pages in Christian history Pentecostals added precedents found in Methodism.

11:89   These referred to "come-out" Methodists who after 1894 experienced "crush-out" by Methodist bishops. The come-outers claimed that they best kept alive John Wesley's perfectionist drive for entire sanctification. The bishops of the Methodist Episcopal church noted an ominous trend: "There has sprung up among us a party with holiness as a watchword; they have holiness associations, holiness meetings, holiness preachers, holiness evangelists, and holiness property." The bishops resented the monopolistic claims of holiness, but would not stand in judgment on the zeal.

11:90   In 1894 there were founded, without glossolalia, the Pentecostal Churches of America, the Metropolitan Church Association, the United Holy Church of America, and the New Testament Church of Christ, and in 1895 a Fire-Baptized Holiness Church. Also in 1895 up to 100,000 Methodists split off to form, at Los Angeles, a soon-to-prosper Church of the Nazarene. A score more of new denominations developed in five years. They both later fed into and were threatened by the twentieth-century Pentecostalisms.

11:91   For a movement of the Spirit and of spontaneous joy, Pentecostalism could be belligerent. Hulking Ambrose Blackmon Crumpler of North Carolina induced trances as he preached up holiness against what he called "no-hellite" churches. George Floyd Taylor observed, "Many said that it was the best side show they ever attended." Modern people were not supposed to revert to "jerks," "fits," and "holy dances" of the sort that revivalists tolerated a century earlier, yet here they were, under Carolina tents. Crumpler was even so daring as to attack the North Carolina staple, tobacco, but he smoke-screened that blast by criticizing the theater, alcohol, and modern dress. New movements often attack their ancestors. Crumpler excoriated the Methodist women with their bobbed hair, feathers, flowers, and rings. Methodism was the "church of the holy refrigerator," and had, he said, become a collection of "old theater-going, whiskey-drinking, card-playing, tobacco-using, secret lodge-loving, oyster-frying, ice cream supper, dancing church" backsliders. He called his the "Pentecostal Holiness Church."

11:92   When Crumpler's back was turned, tongues-speaking split his church in 1901. In 1907 the glossolalia faction began to win out, so he turned on it with his own tongue long trained to attack Methodists. He accused rival G. B. Cashwell of attracting "jabbering followers." In 1908 Crumpler saw no more hope for the two halves of his movement getting along than there could be for harmony between Holiness and Hard-Shell Baptists. When his element lost out at a convention he and two of his fifteen churches stomped out and he lapsed back into Methodism, where he put his energy into Prohibition. Cashwell soon after also left the Pentecostal scene, after first having nudged another pioneer Holiness church onto it.

11:93   The Pentecostal torch was passed. Midwesterner Benjamin Harden Irwin conceived the idea of a "third blessing" which, added to water baptism and the Spirit's "baptism of fire," warmed his "Fire-Baptized Holiness" movement. It was George F. Taylor again who looked on as "some said they felt the fire burning in their souls, but others claimed it as burning in their bodies also." Tongues, faces, fingers, palms, feet, arms, and eventually Bibles felt warm to the touch. "The church would seem to be lighted with fire," he said. When the believers traveled, "the noise of the engine seemed to sound notes of praise to God, and the clatter of the wheels beneath the cars seemed to be saying, 'Glory to God, hallelujah!' while the wheels testified, 'Fire! Fire!! Holy Fire!!!'"

11:94   Able to inspire use of multiple exclamation points, Irwin had to form his own extremist church. In this "no hog-meat, no neck-tie" denomination, some preachers were reported as saying they would rather have rattlesnakes than the neckties as symbols of worldliness around their necks. Taylor developed a hierarchy of fire experiences described by one woman as first *Dynamite*, then *Lyddite*, and finally *Oxidite*. Then came the fall. Irwin slunk away after exposure as living in the "open and gross sin" of adultery. Joseph Hillery King, a man of "theologue appearance," brought respectability but not reunion to the church, though in 1911 the group did merge into the Pentecostal Holiness Church. When Parham crossed Irwin's path in the west, he was repulsed by the latter's excesses. On a clear night, he said, he could hear revival for three miles, until "the blood vessels stood out like whipcords." Yet he also liked that idea of a third experience, a baptism with the Holy Spirit *and* with fire.

11:95   Parham also traveled to Zion, Illinois, to learn from Scottish-born Australian Alexander Dowie, whose healing services attracted notice even at the Chicago World's Columbian Exposition in 1893. Dowie attacked "Drugs, Doctors, and Devils," and, in return, was attacked in 1895 by the *Chicago Tribune* for unlicensed practice of medicine. Whenever he was arrested for this, Dowie cited the experience of Jesus for inspiration. Celebrities helped the cause. Buffalo Bill's niece praised this healer for adding three inches to her shortened leg. On New Year's Eve in 1899 Dowie announced that his new Christian Catholic Church would build Zion City on the lakeshore north of Chicago. Within two years almost ten thousand followers took leases in his theocratic empire. Parham had little to learn, however, from the man who in 1901 announced himself as Elijah the Restorer but then was ejected by his own people. They took over his $6 million debt, considering him a paranoiac swindler. Parham also listened in for lessons on A. B. Simpson, who was founding the Christian and Missionary Alliance in New York. All these served him well in California.

11:96   Still another influence on the search for tongues-speaking was Mrs. Mary B. Woodworth-Etter, who claimed it for her followers as early as 1890. This revivalist toured everything from Universalist to Lutheran churches at Springfield, Illinois, but alienated them all, so she worked in tents and halls. She endured through a controversial ministry that lasted through the World War and wrote an autobiography whose fantastic claims had wide influence.

11:97   Parham acquired a partner in 1905 in the form of a one-eyed black Holiness minister, William Joseph Seymour. This unlettered ex-slave and ex-waiter, an apparently passive and unkempt person, could erupt on stage with such uncanny power that his enemies called it diabolical. While Parham was nervous about having a Negro follower, as Crumpler had understandably been back in North Carolina, he could not deny Seymour. Pentecostalism had so little to lose that the revival might as well be racially integrated. Parham permitted Seymour to answer a call to a Los Angeles storefront church. En route, Seymour was urged by another black, Neely Turner, to pick up lessons at Denver from one Alma White where he learned a "holy dance" at her Pillar of Fire church. White disdained him: "I had met all kinds of religious fakirs and tramps, but I felt he excelled them all."

11:98   Nazarenes in Los Angeles locked Seymour out as a sensationalist and a heretic, so he and his group moved to 812 Azusa Street, where a Los Angeles livery stable awaited demolition. Los Angeles historians generally neglect mention of this stable, and so do most church historians. To Pentecostalists, however, it became a second Jerusalem and Seymour a new apostle. In 1906 the *Los Angeles Times* had to reach for colorful language to describe this "majordomo" of his company, an "old colored exhorter" with a "stony optic" eye who led "colored mammys" to issue in a "gurgle" of "wordless talk." On April 18 that year Seymour predicted destruction and, in an apparent divine near-miss, with his followers felt tremors a bit north; these destroyed San Francisco one day after his prophecy. For three more years earthquake served as a metaphor for the Azusa Street events.

11:99   By late summer large groups flocked to a new Upper Room. Eyewitness Frank Bartleman was awed by the informality and chaos when unadvertised and unorganized Pentecostals experienced eruptions and quaking. Seymour did not need the stage to himself and sometimes covered his head with a shoe box, to sit passively as he turned the pulpit over to others. Sometimes he could erupt in anger against rivals, or in fever as he urged on the tongue-speakers. Bartleman, who soon broke with Seymour but still credited him, summarized it all: "Pentecost has come to Los Angeles, the American Jerusalem."

11:100   Seymour looked on as the revivals attracted black and white men and women who hugged and kissed each other with "looseness." Alma White's follower, Hettie Harwood, sensed winds of perdition as she saw a black woman praying with her arms around a white man. Since Seymour's "hypnotists" went beyond even his relaxed bounds, Parham tried to cool extremes and fanaticism which, he said, violated bounds of common sense and reason. Parham worried: with all this chattering, jabbering and sputtering, would Pentecostalism outdo and undo itself? He could not compete with all this, and he grumbled about how spiritual power was being prostituted by these "holy rollers." His competitive church at the nearby Women's Christian Temperance Union soon failed. Parham later had to deny rumors that he was a homosexual. No longer able to lead, he found more and more reasons to recede, and did.

11:101   Azusa influenced the Holiness leaders who kept coming to observe and learn, but eventually its fires died. A Pentecostal church some years later, not interested in relics, its leaders said, passed up the chance to keep the building as a shrine. Pentecostalism cherished not relics but present experience. A network of evangelists, publishing firms, storefronts, tents, Bible schools, and camps nurtured it. Many followers were poor and wanted leaders to replicate what they thought was primitive Christian style. Bartleman spoke for many as an enemy of organization: "I made my choice between a popular, paying pulpit, and a humble walk of poverty and suffering. . . . I chose the streets and slums for my pulpit."

11:102   Blacks did come from streets and slums to integrate the pulpits and pews, but as Pentecostalism turned respectable it also became increasingly segregated. In 1895 Elder C. H. Mason and his colleague C. P. Jones, Mississippi Baptists, formed the Church of God in Christ. Mason made much of the fact that this church, chartered in 1897, antedated the others. He was glad to see that his gaining of credentials helped white Holiness preachers get railroad discounts and perform marriages. Mason lived to be almost a hundred years old, long enough to see his church become the second-largest Pentecostal body in America. In 1907 he and Jones engaged in the characteristic activity within the new movement. They fought and parted, with Jones and the anti-Pentecostalists winning and Mason successfully starting over in a movement that came to be almost exclusively black.

11:103   Tempting as it is to follow the picaresque trails to picturesque gatherings, one must be content with reference to the beginnings, not the development, of Pentecostalism. On those terms, still waiting for notice are A. J. and Homer Tomlinson, a father-and-son team, who show how quickly populist movements could turn authoritarian. A. J. Tomlinson, a Hoosier Quaker, after 1901 was a member of "The Church of the Living God for the Evangelization of the World, Gathering of Israel, New Order of Things at the Close of the Gentile Age." He called his own split-off the "True Church of God" and then "Church of God." His was, Tomlinson said, the only true Christian communion this side of the Dark Ages, which was the time the true original church had been lost. He was frank: "The Church of God is theocratic in principle," and "God's people must be taught submission. They must be trained to bow to authority. They must learn obedience." Against modern individualism Tomlinson argued that the church dared not be democratic. "I will only vote for Jesus."

11:104   Institutionalized Pentecostalism had to compete under the canopy of denominationalism but remained the most consistent populist wing. Before the second coming of Christ, Parham argued, "the government, the rich and the churches will be on one side," and the masses, which presumably included Pentecostals, would be on the other. In rare political language but with characteristic sentiment, he prophesied that "capital must exterminate and enslave the masses or be exterminated." In the mood of Armageddon, he added, then "the rich will be killed like dogs." Yet the Tomlinsons and he opposed labor unions. They did not organize their resentments against modern styles and wealth but were more interested in erecting a protective carapace over the people who would join them.

11:105   While the Pentecostalists fought each other under their carapace, they also roused the hostility that they sought from outside. Robert P. Richardson antagonized in song as he led his Seattle group, "Out of the rubbish heap the Lord lifted me!" The rubbish heap was the old Seattle Baptist church they had left. Of course, all Pentecostals opposed Catholicism as "the great whore." In

1914 the *Christian Evangel* saw Jesuits and capitalists forming a class, a Monarchial party to run Congress while it encouraged armed mobs of immigrants from Europe, Asia, and Africa.

11:106   Pentecostals also made allies. While the claim of direct Spirit inspiration made by many was repulsive to the inerrancy party, the Pentecostalists generally favored literalist views of an inerrant scripture. Many were at home with dispensationalism. They coalesced more than they united with the growing Fundamentalist party, though from a distance it was easy to lump them together. At least in negation they were as one in rejecting much of modernity and all of modernism. By 1920 they had made their essential points against naturalism, rationalism, and modernism. No single style of spirituality or organization could contain all the furies or charter all the experiments while Americans were on soul searches in a confusing time. As actors and reactors, Pentecostals insisted that theirs was the movement of the Spirit for the new age. They were, of course, to be denied the monopoly they dreamed of. They did settle, however, for a larger and growing share of the religious economy than any that modernist nightmares would have assigned them.

Part Five

Transmodernism

12

Restitutio ad Integrum The Schism in the Soul

12:1   The story of early twentieth-century American religion includes responses that are properly seen as transmodern in intent. The prefix *trans* here picks up the dictionary sense of "beyond, surpassing, transcending, . . . on the other side of," as in transhuman, transmaterial, or transrational. The agents of these causes inherited the mixed benefits of modernity, in the forms of its technology and its individualism, and more. They then diagnosed its negative aspects. Finally they took initiatives to pass through whatever modernity meant to them and proposed ways beyond it. When they reached for historic models and impulses, they then projected these so that they could help others find means to move beyond the modern.

12:2   One aspect of modernity upon which they all seized was its differentiation, the way it chopped up aspects of life which once they thought had been held together. Lovers of freedom, they believed they saw in extreme individualism real threats to full humanity, so they stressed communal forms. With a psychological insight shared with Karl Marx in Europe they diagnosed alienation. They also found that the world of specialization sundered bonds that they considered integral to health. Appreciating science and at home with technology, they still feared that these would contribute to the loss of the human. With what someone called a hunger for wholeness, they reached for organic forms.

251

12:3   Four impulses illustrate their discontents and responses. First and most personally, the turn of the century saw the rise of new therapies and a fresh religious accent on healing and wholeness. Second, the extremely divided churches wanted to project primitive organic models into a future and seek reunion; these are the years in which the modern ecumenical movement was born. Third, innovators also reached back to premodern times when, they thought, the faith had a more direct bearing on all of life, the entire social and economic order included. Out of this came the social gospel and its analogues outside Protestantism. In these middle two cases, in contradiction to the intentions of the proponents, they came to be regarded by the reactionaries as mere modernists themselves. Finally, the innovators promoted a sense of the whole in respect to the race and the nation in an imperial age unprecedented in American history. These four were signs of initiative and invention by critics of the drift of the time. The responses of these therapeutic-minded people produced major religious agencies that lasted through the twentieth century. Since these agencies were themselves diverse and divided, and since they occasioned schisms and awakened conflict, they produced ironic outcomes—still more differentiation of forms and the perception that the pioneers were only modernists themselves.

Restitutio ad integrum: *The Accent on Therapy*

12:4   "The ideas of Christian churches are not efficacious in the therapeutic direction to-day, whatever they may have been in earlier centuries." If true, this diagnosis by William James, America's pioneer and premier psychologist, had to be seen as devastating. Judaism and Christianity had always regarded themselves as agents of therapy. They saw healing, wholeness, and unity to be goals in their program for salvation. As a physician and a citizen, distanced from churches and himself a victim of a "dividedness" that took the form of a mental breakdown, James in one phrase condensed his own positive ideal. He spoke of the kind of person who had such a divided soul that he despaired of coming to the point of a *restitutio ad integrum*. The phrase is rare, perhaps unique to one passage in James, but it summarizes much of his and his generation's search for something like what he called the primal "happiness of Eden." In law, the *restitutio in integrum* restores parties to the condition in which they were before entering into an agreement. In personal or social therapy it figuratively restores a primal wholeness. Here it becomes a metaphor for the whole attempt to move mind, soul, and body beyond the sundering that came, people then believed, as a result of modernity. In an obscure scientific reference from the sixteenth century the *Oxford English Dictionary* finds Thomas Blundevil defining *integrum* as "Anything that is whole, and not broken, or divided into parts," and so it will be in this story.

12:5   James traced modern work-sickness back to Puritan roots that were now twined with what he called the Gospel of Efficiency. People were compulsive even when they were not overworked. A melancholic depression or self-hatred often resulted. America, through following a succession of pattern-setters whom it was now impossible to trace, he noted, had at last settled down into a collective and characteristic national type that did not result from climate. Americans should therefore assign to psychology or sociology, not to their climate, their "overtension and jerkiness and breathlessness and intensity and agony of expression" (his sentence structure partook of all of these), which were bad social habits: "Bottled lightning!" From Brother Lawrence and others who long ago had practiced the presence of God James drew a model of "letting-go" and a "Gospel of Relaxation." He thought that girls especially did not need more exacerbation or responsibility but, by the grace of God, the "toning-down of their moral tensions."

12:6   While James may have gone unread in the Baptist towns of Tennessee, unnoticed among Norwegian Lutheran women in the Dakotas, and have had little to say to the new migrants to Los Angeles, he had the genius to give classic terms to modern human needs. He did think that "the advance of liberalism, so-called," in Christianity, during the previous fifty years was itself some kind of victory for healthy-mindedness aimed to overcome the old schism in salvation-hungry souls. This liberalism, however, seemed glib and superficial and was tied to an unpromising evolutionary optimism. James was therefore ready to grant some favor to the many mind-cure and New Thought movements, whose practical unifying results were measurable, even if they gave fits to medical professionals. Witness the mainstream reactions to then-expanding Christian Science. New Thought and mind-cure were post-Christian movements that blended traces of Christianity with pantheism, mysticism, transcendental idealism, Vedantism, the modern psychology of the subliminal self, and, one might add, old-fashioned American optimism. "Its doctrine of the oneness of our life with God's life," said James, formed a link with Christian teaching, but then it went its own way. Mind-cure with its gospel of healthy-mindedness had come as a revelation, he observed, to many whose hearts the church and Christianity had left hardened. "It has let loose their springs of higher life."

12:7   The main themes of Christian Science had been set before the World's Parliament of Religions. There the new healing movement had its best opportunity to date to present its case, and the speech by Judge Septimius Hanna drew one of the largest responses of anything at the event. The years spent after 1893 by Mrs. Mary Baker Eddy, the founder, in consolidating her vision of healing into a solid and complex church body make a story that is not here germane. The continued accent on healing is. James was involved momentarily in 1894 when orthodox medical practice was seeking legal ways to suppress such healing in Massachusetts. James wrote the *Boston Transcript*: "I assuredly hold no brief for any of these healers, and must confess that my intellect has been unable to assimilate their theories, so far as I have heard them given." He could not leave matters there, however. "But their *facts* are patent and startling"; anything that interfered with the multiplication of such facts or of free opportunity to observe and study them would be a public calamity.

12:8   Christian Science competition helped give birth to the Emmanuel movement, one of a number in which mainstream Protestants began to recapture attention for interest in therapy. Dismissed by most of them as neither Christian nor scientist, it did win at least some grudging attention for the way it pressed the healing agenda at an opportune movement. One George F. Greene, in 1902 said that while its theology was "eclectic, fragmentary, and now and then, flagrantly absurd," it did give adherents a sense of divine power close at hand. The Reverend A. J. Gordon, who wrote *The Ministry of Healing*, developed this kind of theme. He insisted that Christians who did not heal were not faithful to the apostolic witness. Mrs. Eddy took these stirrings as signs that she was making her point. If the lives of Christian Scientists attest their fidelity to Truth, she predicted that in the twentieth century every Christian church in America and some far away would "approximate the understanding of Christian Science sufficiently to heal the sick in his [Christ's] name."

12:9   The census of 1906 turned up 85,000 Christian Scientists. It is likely that about the same number of Americans were by then drawn to the cluster of New Thought movements that drew just as ambiguously on the impulses James was noticing and gently criticizing. Ralph Waldo Trine's *In Tune with the Infinite* sold a million copies, and it was but the best-known of scores of efforts. Most chapters of such books accented the theme of wholeness, of oneness with the universe. In Trine were revealed Edenic myths, the drawing on "All-Supply" as a reservoir of power that appealed to a hunger for wholeness. Orison Swett Marden, who advocated this accent in the world of business, spoke for many when he wrote, "Everything in Nature seemed to speak to me to try to make up to me for my homelessness." New Thought and mind-cure represented paths toward home. The very name "Unity" for a "School of Christianity" that was being organized during the 1890s summed up the appeal and spoke to widespread needs: tens of thousands subscribed to its periodicals and bought the books issued by Charles and Myrtle Fillmore from near Kansas City, Missouri.

12:10   As a philosopher who had a high tolerance for experiment, James now and then said he was disgusted and allowed that he would like the chill northwest winds of science to blow into the suffocating rooms of some of these sects. His was the view of a watcher from the eye of the hurricane though his own breakdown made it possible for him to be empathic with people in the figurative huts in its path. From his distance the new movements looked more respectable than they would have up close. Yet people who also worked for the restoration of physical health came in many forms and styles, sometimes unrespectably at what the historic churches considered to be the margins of what was proper.

12:11   The prime example of folk diagnosis and religious invention, one that James did not notice, was the Seventh-Day Adventist movement. Its parentage under William Miller was among the most derided and despised in American religion. In 1843 and 1844 Miller made mistakes that no modern dispensationalists would repeat: he set the date for Christ's second coming. After two failures, many followers dispersed while others reinterpreted the events of those years. In 1887 Daniel Dorchester's chronicle considered Adventism already to have made its exit. In 1847, he summarized, "finally the excitement ended. Some returned to their vocations, some to the churches, some became infidels, and others passed over into the belief of materialism, annihilationism, etc." Henry K. Carroll, however, could spot in the census of 1890 six kinds of Adventist groups, the most notable of these being Seventh-Day Adventism with its 28,991 communicants in 995 organizations. Carroll listed the two most visible features of Adventism, Sabbath worship and belief in a second coming soon. He entirely overlooked one of its main appeals to its followers, the healing of the body.

12:12 The main agent for shaping Adventism in its second phase was Ellen G. White, herself a lifelong battler for her own health and then a promoter of vegetarianism, hydrotherapy, restraint in sex, and abstinence from beverages with alcohol or caffeine. She spent the 1890s in New Zealand, building the American-born movement. It is true that before her return in 1900 there were signs that Adventism was spent. Church historian Leonard Woolsey Bacon in 1898 was glad for such progress of scriptural knowledge that henceforth no one "except among the ignorant and unintelligent" would ever follow anything like the Millerite craze.

12:13 Ellen White gave them reason to. Less well known than Christian Science's Mary Baker Eddy, she belonged to the company of evangelical health-seekers of the second half of the nineteenth century. Through the years she transmitted thousands of pages transcribed from what she regarded as direct visions of the divine. As early as June 5, 1863, in Otsego, Michigan, she was set on her course when a vision told her to stop dwelling on "the dark, gloomy side" of life. Weeks later she told her vision to a self-trained Adventist doctor, Horatio S. Lay. Claiming little medical knowledge, she revealed that "pain and sickness were not ordinarily, as was commonly supposed, due to a foreign influence, attacking the body." Instead, and this became her fundamental diagnosis, in most cases it resulted from "an effort of nature to overcome unnatural conditions resulting from the transgression of some of nature's laws." White would help restore those laws which, she believed, were both natural and biblical. Her *restitutio ad integrum* and preparation for the Advent included application of the gospel and following disciplines of self-care. For this she drew on her own visions, her imagination, and more than she or many followers would have admitted, on writings which some modern scholars consider sources for her plagiarism.

12:14 For thirty years she and her followers, who included the celebrated Kelloggs of Battle Creek, Michigan, with a clear goal but without perfect consistency, promoted the health campaign. Though her Bible commanded avoidance of unclean animals and she advised vegetarianism, not until 1894 in Australia did she become consistent, thanks to the plea by a Catholic woman for compassion to animals. In 1908 she promoted a pledge of total abstinence from "flesh meats, tea and coffee, and all injurious foods," though White found she had to make some compromises on that diet. If new rationales differed from old ones, she credited visions. She also borrowed theories about germs from Louis Pasteur and Robert Koch. She by no means disparaged, indeed she strongly encouraged, modern medicine.

12:15   When Ellen White died at age eighty-seven in 1915, she had addressed innumerable diseases and promoted numerable cures. Best remembered for prophecies of a world soon to end and her attack on Sunday worship, she would be recognized decades later for a health rule that led her fellow-believers in Adventism to significantly longer lives, on the median, than the rest of the population. If the old churches were deficient in therapy, her new one would not be. By the time of her death there were 136,000 followers and a legacy of thirty-three sanitaria and hundreds of treatment rooms all over the world. The memorial her followers erected was, quite naturally, an Ellen G. White Memorial Hospital in Los Angeles. From this College of Medical Evangelists would come forth people whose doctrines were reactionary but whose therapies moved them beyond the modern distinctions between sacred and secular, soul and body, scientific medicine and spiritual care.

12:16   With so much at stake, Protestant clergy were not going to turn over all therapy of mind to mind-cure, mind and body to Christian Science, or body to Adventism. They also could recover wholeness. Washington Gladden in 1895 insisted that "Christianity is no longer anti-natural; it is in the deepest sense natural." Thus it could help bring people into unity with nature and their own bodies. Of course, such talk put the modernists at odds with those conservatives who offered wholeness on opposite terms. They argued, in turn, that after the human fall into sin it was division and brokenness that were natural. Supernature, through prayer and miracle of the body, through conversion of the mind, alone restored wholeness in Christ. They, too, did not want to be seen as unscientific. The Reverend H. M. Sydenstricker in one of *The Fundamentals* was typically clear. Even conversion itself was now to be subject to scientific investigation. "The penetration of scientific investigation into the erstwhile unknown regions of things is one of the wonders of the age." He was sure most of the reactionaries were wholehearted supporters of modern medicine, so long as it left the soul as Christianity's preserve and allowed believers to hope for miracles and to recognize them.

12:17   In the mainstream Protestant churches the seminaries took note of the needs and opportunities. During the professional revolution, and while differentiating in their curricula, they included new understandings and techniques for pastoral care. Still, it was not until 1916 that Boston University's School of Theology included a course on psychotherapy to follow up on the psychology of religion courses which that school, Hartford, Chicago, and other theological schools offered after the turn of the century. Many alumni found even these to be behind the times and not in step with parishioners' needs. Some turned to William James and

Under Ellen Gould White, Adventism became a millennial, sabbatarian, *and* health movement. The Battle Creek Sanitarium in Michigan promoted water treatments, as this collage demonstrates.

after 1909 even to Sigmund Freud for the language of therapy, which challenged Christian anthropology at basic points. The language referring to the unconscious and the subconscious entered the Christian vocabulary as pastoral counselors probed the divided self and offered the unified one.

12:18 Conservatives and liberals alike welcomed athletic metaphors and images. They touted a muscular Christianity that found natural homes in the then-prospering Boy Scouts and Young Men's Christian Association. At the turn of the century 450 YMCAs were making their contribution. While Young Women's Christian Associations, Girl Scouts, and women's athletic interests were also beginning to be pursued, a male-dominated public religious world translated James's call for "the strenuous life" into a search for virility. Little of their imagery or intention was helpful to women.

12:19 Modernists like William Newton Clarke saw little difficulty in bridging from faith to therapy, because, as he said, "the theology of any age is largely an expression of the Christian experience of that age." The current experience was natural, developmental, holistic. The most ambitious experiment at using such insights was the Emmanuel Movement, founded in 1905 at Boston's Emmanuel Church and after 1908 spread through the journal *Psychotherapy*. For Emmanuel the warfare between the new sciences and religion was over. Where once dogma was preached and people came up sawdust aisles to announce their conversions, now Emmanuel-trained ministers encouraged patients to consult psychologists and physicians and thus to seek development. Its leaders claimed that their form of science would counter those irrational healing cults that James thought were outdoing churches as healing agents. They could hardly overlook Christian Science, which was headquartered, as it were, right down the street.

12:20 Elwood Worcester, Emmanuel's founder, credited the praise by James of strenuousness and energy for his own healing. Worcester also promoted strong character. Emmanuel in a few years almost collapsed into its own form of reduction. It made less and less of Christian symbols and came to look like an amateur branch of the medical profession. Physicians began to shy away from it. In 1909 psychologist Richard Cabot saw the physicians chafe, he said, at "anything done by clergymen for anyone who is, or has been, or ever will be, the patient of any doctor." Because Emmanuel was hurting Cabot's scientific reputation, he backed off from it. Those who would do bridging were safe at neither bank. Emmanuel waned around 1920. The clergy found diverse other forms, depending upon their denominations, doctrinal stands, and choice of scientific prescriptions.

12:21   Philosopher Josiah Royce, no match for James in medicine and psychology, has often been overlooked as a telling diagnostician. He knew what was wrong with some of these therapies. They were too individualistic and isolated; narcissistic, some would call them. Royce focused: "Whoever, in his own mind, makes the whole great world center about the fact that he, just this private individual, once was ill and now is well, is still a patient." Like James, Royce had undergone a breakdown in the 1880s and out of it also found some raw material for a social therapy. In grandiose terms, he wrote James about that vastation. As its consequence he announced he had "largely straightened out the big metaphysical tangle about continuity, freedom, and the world-formula, which, as you remember, I had aboard with me when I started." Too sanguinely Royce said of his depression, "*That* experience is done for and over forever." He was to spend his remaining years to 1916 working on philosophically satisfying addresses to the need for a *restitutio ad integrum* to match his philosophy of loyalty.

12:22   How, he asked, does one keep and improve the fragile self, which often seemed to be a mere accident and child of circumstance, no more than "a chaos of bodily products"? With James, Royce drew on classic Puritan themes and faced up to the work ethic that produced convulsion and neurosis. He came close to Karl Marx's appraisal of alienation in the face of modernity. From Hegel he drew the ideas of the self-estranged social mind and alienation itself. These malaises resulted from the imperial grasping activity of "high civilization." Now the patriarchal family was disappearing, government had become distant and impersonal, organizations imposed "mechanical bondage" of estranged and arbitrary sorts on the nation. Royce cherished terms like "restlessness," "unsettlement," and referred to the way the alienated were like mere spokes in the wheel. The machine as such was not at fault, but modern civilization made dealing with it difficult.

12:23   With psychological and theological sophistication Royce watched a war develop between the individual and the collective. Modern Americans surprised some prophets by avoiding social revolution but warped themselves through "revolt inwardly," where they found spiritual enemies in their own souls. Terms from St. Paul found echo in Royce's diagnosis: "I am the divided self. The more I struggle to escape through my moral cultivation, the

more I discern my divided state. Oh, wretched man that I am!"
With such biblical themes that his mother taught him on the California frontier, he matched Sigmund Freud's notions about the primal crime that results from childhood revolt against the father.
The adult American, in Royce's biblical terms, henceforth "wanders in waste places, and, when he returns, finds the lonely house
of his individual life empty, swept, and garnished."

12:24   The philosopher moved more and more toward Christian story.
The prodigal son parable showed how those who had sinned
against their father could rejoin community. He celebrated "aton-
ing deeds, deeds that, through sacrifices, win against the lost
causes of the moral world, not by undoing the irrevocable, nor by
making the old bitterness of defeat as if it never had been, but
by creating new good out of ancient ill." Royce chose St. Paul's
words about salvation and healing to focus on the vocation or
cause to which one could be supremely loyal. This was a search
beyond the modern condition in which Americans would both use
and be free of the machinery of a world in which they might learn
to live with less alienation.

12:25   In the end Royce's salvation seemed too secular to be picked
up in the churches and too transcendental for experimental psychologists. Neighbors pictured him aged, shuffling, a defeated-
looking figure when World War I came. The young philosopher
Horace Kallen remembered the tired sage piecing bits of conversation together, "wholly inhibited by the war, and by its chaos of
sorrows and of crimes" that would destroy the community to
which one was to have been loyal. While Royce was almost forgotten as therapist, his examination of his own ambitious scope
and sometimes hollow inner response was a model for the psycho-
biography through which later Americans walked themselves
seeking restitution to wholeness.

12:26   Of more direct influence on religious development was a contemporary, G. Stanley Hall, who while president of fledgling
Clark University at Worcester, Massachusetts, lured Freud there
in 1909. Hall shared Royce's analysis of overcivilized America
and of the urban onslaught against personal identity and social
location. With James he attacked the turning of work into com-
pulsiveness and measured the psychic damages of political imperialism. If there was any major intellectual who wished he could
repeal modernity with the instruments of modern discovery themselves, it was Hall. He hooked evolutionary theory to the notion

that persons could retrace their steps and relive the whole history
of the human race. His word for the goal, the whole community,
was Mansoul.

12:27   What dividedness did for James and alienation for Royce, fragmentation and its cognates did for Hall. The individual seemed a
"fragment broken off and detached from the great world of soul."
For Hall restitution meant disclosing the "buried tree" or rejoin-
ing the great "cosmos of soul." This meant that one acquired good
habits of conduct by giving expression to the good of the whole
human race and by nurturing harmony with nature. He used language about God that he learned first as a child and later at Union
Theological Seminary and then elaborated on the concept of the
whole human race in a two-volume work that referred to the role
of Jesus.

12:28   Whoever remembers the pathfinder Hall at all knows him as
one engrossed in studies of adolescence, the period that was
key to producing a unified social self. His own boyhood western
Massachusetts town became the ideal image of a place and way
for education. When Hall revisited his boyhood home he could revisit the virtues of early America and reencounter the best in the
history of the race. The enemy was modernity in the form of
machinery, the city, industry, and technology, all of which undercut intimacy and tradition alike. They would harm the individual
along with America. No country was so precociously old, he
thought, as the America which always had to absorb newcomers
without having time or freedom to revisit and enjoy its own adolescence. The psychological result was an increase of dementia
praecox: people were obsessed with their unrelated inward selves.

12:29   Hall first entered pastoral ministry, but soon found himself
caught between traditional Christianity and more vague post-
Christian liberalisms. Henry Ward Beecher arranged for him to
study in Germany, there to embark on a decade-long odyssey that
left him in what Royce would call the restless or unsettled state.
After ministry faded and philosophy came and went, Hall found
his true repose in psychology. He returned to complete a Ph.D. at
Harvard in 1878. After Harvard and Johns Hopkins years he was
named president of Clark University.

12:30   No pluralist in philosophy, Hall could still side with Royce and
Peirce in his search for "the sense of unity and law at the root of
things and pervading every action and corner of space." Progressive evolution, which he sentimentalized into gentility, was his
scientific base, almost his new religion. "Bio-logos," which was

"the spirit of life that had brooded over the universe," gave life to all that existed. Seldom had a more audacious vision of unity, a more integral monism, been devised by an American who had any power to gain a hearing. Hall's concept of soul he defined as "homogeneous and also continuous throughout the animal kingdom." How could one defend the prevailing naturalistic and religious individualisms? People must pursue "the true paradise of a restored intuitive human nature," within community.

12:31   Equipped with such a philosophy, Hall never tired of seeking and presenting data to confirm it. His was a world of charts and graphs, interviews and surveys. Then he used religious language to translate it all. The psychologist who used the gospel of love became the high priest of souls. Given what totalitarianisms have done with concepts like "folk" or "people" or "race," Hall's images may sound ominous. In his time they were harmless, creative attempts to restore Eden, to relive the rhythms of the life of Christ. "All men are born twice, once as individuals and once as representatives of the species," he summarized. Hall thought late adolescence merged the lower "into the higher, social self."

12:32   His terms could be reminiscent of evangelical atmospheres but he had moved far from his childhood church. Hall began to speak of sacrosanct schools and consecrated teachers as bearers of wholeness. Even his half-fulfilled university was a temple, a shrine, a "church of science." He launched a short-lived *The American Journal of Religious Psychology and Education*. Now was to come "a new revival of a kind and degree that the Christian world has not known in recent centuries." Hall moved on to work on an unsatisfying book that came out in 1917 as *Jesus the Christ in the Light of Psychology*. His Jesus would incorporate "all the good tendencies in man," but turned out chiefly to be Hall's late adolescent Superman writ large.

12:33   Hall lived a life of frustration despite his prominence. He seldom saw his revered small-town parents. His first wife died; his second went mad and was institutionalized. Clark hardly survived financial woes. The journal amounted to little. Its editor's personal life was lonely. His Jesus kept Hall far from conventional religion and pushed him too far from conventional science. Colleagues turned critical. He did, however, help found modern psychology in America and forced attention to the religious theme. In April 1924, when he was laid to rest at a church in Worcester, the local parson publicly grumbled over his late parishioner's neglect of the local church. Eden remained beyond range.

12:34   The turn of the century also saw the rise and fall of a psychology of religion movement concurrent with the work of James and Hall. James H. Leuba and Edwin Diller Starbuck led some who wanted scientific views of religion to help address the psychic ills of the modern condition. Armed with a questionnaire, they sampled opinions of thousands of people to discern patterns of life. In 1896 Leuba broke ground with a study of conversion, and in 1899 Starbuck published *The Psychology of Religion*.

12:35   E. L. Schaub, the chronicler of the movement, boasted near its end that "in the psychology of religion American scholars were the pioneers; and they have throughout remained in the vanguard of progress." Their problem was that the procession was too brief. Leuba and Starbuck were too critical to gain churchly support, while their religious subject matter made them suspect among empirical scientists. Schaub spoke of their new approach to the study of religion as being strictly empirical and scientific. That "strictly" was attacked by both sides. Starbuck had been optimistic: "Science has conquered one field after another, until now it is entering the most complex, the most inaccessible and, of all, the most sacred domain—that of religion." That sacred domain bore examination, but Leuba and Starbuck were not as neutral about it as they thought they were. Their view of the empirical came to be seen as naive. Freudian psychoanalysis left little room for religion as it came to make its way after Freud's visit in 1909. In the seminaries and churches psychological insight was used for pastoral care, not further clinical research.

12:36   Rescued from its debris, however, was one longer-lived movement to which George Coe gave shape and which found institutional embodiment. Coe applied Leuba and Starbuck to children, whom he saw less as sinners needing salvation than as beings natively capable of good who need nurture for life in "the democracy of God," no longer the Kingdom of God. When the Religious Education Association that Coe influenced was founded in 1904, its president, Frank Knight Sanders, urged the need "to define religious education in such a way that it shall not mean sectarianism or sentimentalism, but a kind of culture which is indispensable to the normal man." Modernity and science would help promote wholeness, so conferees could show that "religion is as broad as life itself, and that life without religion is impossible."

12:37   One association founder, William Rainey Harper at the University of Chicago, saw a place for the Bible in such education since, he argued, "it was the misinterpretation of the Bible that furnished the occasion of all skepticism." Harper scowled at the reactionaries, who claimed to be the friends of the Bible but who were its worst enemies. Meanwhile, he was sure, "a faith in the Bible constructed upon a scientific basis will be acceptable to everyone who will take the pains to look into it." With such a charter, in 1894 REA founders needed only a view of the human to match such views of religion and scriptures. Psychology of religion provided it, chiefly through Coe himself, who published *The Spiritual Life* in 1900 during his tenure at Northwestern University. For him, if the Bible disagreed with the findings of Leuba and Starbuck, then it was the Bible that needed reinterpretation. It had never been a document for science but, by its own claims, for instruction in righteousness. Nor should it be used to stimulate preconversion crisis. Teachers should introduce religious themes "at just the point where the child's mind has a natural instinct" for them. He believed that women had natural predispositions toward certain kinds of spirituality, for, as he said, "the female mind tends more than male to feeling," being more suggestible. In a sense, then, women read a different Bible than did men.

12:38   A new book by Coe with a chapter titled, significantly, "Salvation by Education," thumbed a nose at the old-style Sunday Schools. American public schools were better because they had won freedom from ecclesiastical control. Since Coe fused the sacred and the secular, he did not fear the secularity of public schools. Jesus, by living a human life, exhibited for all to see what God was. Therefore the Incarnation collapsed the sacred and secular and removed old boundaries. Similarly, as America evolved secularly, the Christian life could be "an incarnation, a realization of divine purpose, presence, and communion" in its everyday occupations. Here was the modernist program applied to the young, with an accent on wholeness: Thus, "the field of the divine life in us is simply our life in its totality."

12:39   Coe's view of God was also typically modernist in its immanental mode. For him, "the immanent God is the deepest fact of man's mind." Sooner or later, he went on, progress in the theory of mental development would "compel recognition of the religious phase as a necessary part of general education." Churches should employ secular pedagogy to advance religious nurture, using "the information that general psychology yields concerning the structure of the mind, the information that biology, physiology, and child study can garner with respect to the laws of child development." Then, to complete the sweep by the Zeitgeist, Coe added, churches should use "all the principles and methods that the history and philosophy of education have stamped with approval." How could the part-time and amateur evangelical Sunday School teachers know and bear such a stamp?

12:40   The new Religious Education Association competed with the International Sunday School Association, seeing it as an old-fashioned instrument. The REA founders scored a coup by attracting John Dewey to address them. Dewey bridged the growing gulf between himself and his childhood faith by returning in his talk to the language of piety that his mother taught him in Vermont. Then Dewey transformed it all by calling for a "return to the idea of Jesus, of the successive stages through which the seed passes into the blade and then into the ripening grain." The REA by using such a developmental approach, said Dewey, "would mark the dawn of a new day in religious education."

12:41   The host council spoke of its moment as "a normal, timely, and vital step in the development of our Christian civilization." Expectations were high. *The Christian Century*'s reporter came down the street to cheer it as one of the greatest and most significant religious conventions of modern times. The 407 participants whose sessions attracted up to 3,000 visitors and who needed 422 pages for their proceedings were, he thought, characterized by a "constructive conservatism," which meant anything but what the Protestant reactionaries would have meant.

12:42   In the association Coe had his best platform. Religion, he said, develops from within, "in the normal unfolding of a child's soul." There was no evil heart, no original sin, to be overcome. He wanted no boundaries, since "the spirit of religion must be infused into the whole educational organism." He seemed at this point to be unaware of the growing pluralism of public schools, which by now were including Lower East Side Jews in New York and West Coast Asians, with many nonreligious in between. Yet the school was somehow an extension of home and church where, he thought, it was "no longer the exception but the rule for children to 'grow up Christians and never to know themselves as being otherwise.'"

12:43   Coe dominated this quiet rival to the old Sunday School, devising for it what amounted to a new Christology of expression. "Jesus, himself, enters scientific theology through the door of experience." Instead of scripture or dogma, experience and relation form Coe's frequently quoted definition of Christian education: "It is the systematic, critical examination and reconstruction of relations between persons, guided by Jesus' assumption that persons are of infinite worth, and by the hypothesis of the existence of God, the Great Valuer of Persons." Schools, culture, and society all converged to promote such a democracy of God.

12:44   Public educators could not easily adapt to these calls even if they heard them in the first place. So the association finally had strongest influence in the church and, eventually, in the synagogue. Its journal kept touting modernity. In this respect, John H. T. Main was as enthusiastic as his colleagues: "Who is modern man. . . . He believes in One God—the God of science, of history, of social progress of religion. He believes that God has put His spirit into all life and into his own heart as well." Chicago Theological Seminary's Graham Taylor found his apocalyptic analogue to the premillennial vision. With religious education, the Social Gospel, a reformed America, and the scientific spirit, he gloried, the "vision of the last of the apostles of the 'City of God coming down out of the heaven from God,' prepared as the earthly bride of the heavenly bridegroom" was imminent.

12:45   The Sunday School of this period should not be pictured as declining, dying, or being intransigent. Much of its leadership shared the buoyancy and hopefulness of the REA modernists. They simply had less faith in a progressivist metaphysic and in a semisecular institution. Their World Sunday School Convention, founded in 1889, was tied to a cosmopolitan outlook, and conferences at London, Jerusalem, Rome, and Zurich from 1898 to 1913 drew hundreds of teachers and leaders, while thousands of Americans hosted foreign visitors to St. Louis and Washington in 1893 and 1910. The world in question was an Anglo-Saxon empire, which was not insignificant in this period.

12:46   As if unaware of the extreme ethnocentrism of its Anglo-American outlook and the makeup of its conferences, speakers kept talking in universal terms for world and church. So the images of restored wholeness took an ecclesiastical guise. The International Lesson Committee chairman, John Potts, knew that it could not bring uniformity, but unity was the desirable object to be attained. The WSSC avoided biblical criticism and other unsettling questions that might disrupt education or evangelism. Unlike the REA, "we can not have scientific study in the Sunday School," said the lesson committee report of 1893. "It would require a search with lighted candles to find either higher or lower critics in our ordinary Sunday school classes." There was also little social or psychological analysis. In the era of progressive reform, social problems went virtually unnoticed in all the proceedings. Finally in the Tokyo meeting of 1920 the influential Herbert Welch showed alertness to concerns like those of the REA. "Anything that will make for human happiness, well-being, goodness, has a relation to the Sunday School." This was the case not only with personal wholeness but also social conditions: "Questions of sanitation, housing, accident, factory conditions, wages . . . all of these are not alien to the purpose of Sunday school."

12:47   Now, at last, self-questioning and ominous notes began to appear. Margaret Slattery told Asians that they must worry about the smoke of their cities, the entrance of their girls into factories. Secretary Frank L. Brown feared the engulfing Bolshevik revolution, which used as its means to propagate in New York a favored institution: the Sunday School! "In these schools a catechism is taught including the teachings of Marx, atheistic in doctrine and subversive of government." The old Sunday School optimism was still there for the revisiting. Competition by the Catholic parochial schools and the successes of public schools increasingly distracted from the old Protestant monopoly in nurture. The Sunday School, instead of bringing the unity and wholeness its propagators sought, was chopped up into competing agencies and was denominationalized. Despite its reach, it settled for a bit of the child's attention as it tried to deal with a part of life in a vulnerable segment of the week. In such fragmentation it even took on the character it sought to transcend. It was modern. If the *restitutio ad integrum* was the goal of therapy and nurture, it seemed undercut at the start, in the world of the child.

13

The Sin of Schism and the Reunion of the Churches

13:1   Turn-of-the-century leaders in America's vast Christian majority knew that church and society needed the same *restitutio* they prescribed for individuals. Indeed, individualism, choice, and competition had gone so far that these leaders must reach all the way back to the time of Christ for models of the *integrum*, the whole Church. Then they knew they had to project into the progressive future the fulfillment of the one Kingdom of God. Between these times of original and final wholeness the church was divided and confusing, its denominations were largely uncooperative and inefficient. In response to this situation, between the early 1890s and around 1920, the modern ecumenical movement was born. Within that period it acquired most of the forms it would keep. Leaders expressed their intentions, and saw some fulfilled and others contradicted in surprising ways.

13:2   Advocates were to call the ecumenical movement the great new fact of the twentieth century. It did change the face and ethos of the Christian world. At the same time, with all its achievements, it presents an ironic aspect. Since denominations were the problem, if not the enemy, one would have expected them to yield as this new movement was born. They were left without much of a theological rationale once the *integrum* of Christ's first and final intention was proposed. Instead, they had to dig in, and did. Almost all of them survived and prospered, while scores of new ones were

269

born. Meanwhile, the ecumenical leaders came to have the theological case and morale on their side. They took the meaning out of denominational competition, but they did not reduce the competition. The denomination and the local church remained the basic forms for the people in the figurative huts. These laypeople, though often tolerant and congenial, found the ecumenical movement to be remote, sometimes a part of the storm of modern change itself.

13:3   The new ambivalence in Protestant intentions and strategy bears watching through the shaping generation, both for its intrinsic interest and its permanent legacy. This ambivalence was to produce a mediating form, the federative or conciliar movement. From the first, this seemed to be advisable if one wished to speak of cooperation at all. Thus in 1893 for a meeting of the Evangelical Alliance at the World's Columbian Exposition Philip Schaff, the greatest scholar-proponent of Christian unity of the day, bestirred himself for a last urgent address. He knew the trip would harm him, and he died soon after. Schaff dared not pass up the chance of the moment.

13:4   In America, he said, "where the sin of schism has abounded the grace of future reunion will much more abound." He defined the new means, which would be a federal or confederate union. This was defined as "a voluntary association of different churches in their official capacity, each retaining its freedom and independence in the management of its internal affairs, but all recognizing one another as sisters with equal rights, and cooperating in general enterprises." These tasks included spreading the gospel, defending the faith, and engaging in charity and moral reform. Ecclesiastical confederation would look and work like the political side of Schaff's childhood Switzerland and his chosen United States. He knew that beauty and strength there came from the "union of the general sovereignty with the intrinsic independence of the several cantons, or states, or kingdoms, and duchies."

13:5   From early charters like this it is clear that federation did not develop only as a compromise. Schaff and other leaders with cosmopolitan habits wanted the independence of denominations in the meantime to serve a good cause. Five years later, Leonard Woolsey Bacon remembered some civil reasons to support the model. This ecumenical historian did complain of the 143 competing churches as listed in the 1890 census. Each was affected by its own corporate interests, sympathies, and antipathies. Without doubt this comminution of the church, as he named it, was frankly accepted in America not only as an inevitable drawback to the blessings of religious freedom, but as a good thing in itself. The prophet of this vision had been founder James Madison. The constitutionalist foresaw a degree of security for citizens in a republic marked by sectarian disunity.

13:6   As a Christian, however, Bacon had to be of two minds. He did not see how a Christian could find schism "a very good condition for the church of Christ." How could one square the business model with its destructive argument that, as "competition is the life of business," so it should be in religion, with St. Paul's biblical word that division represented sin, the "works of the flesh"? That business model, he complained, even led Christians to strange business devices to secure the revenue needs of competitive churches.

13:7   Bacon's pages found him darting back and forth between arguments. He was cheered by signs that Christian church leaders were "coming to discover that the essence of Christian fellowship does not consist in keeping people out." Let them get together. Then he turned and kept his fingers crossed about the possible consolidations of power. If all seventeen Methodist bodies would unite and then confront other Protestant groups that similarly got their own houses in order, might this not raise "intestine conflict" and sectarian animosities to the highest power? Having worked himself into a corner on this level, Bacon joined Schaff in going to the other level. He would begin with the humbler ways of local unity. Maybe God was there grinding up material for what Bacon called a "nobler manifestation of the unity of his people. The sky of the declining century is red with promise." Maybe some "great providential preparations as for some 'divine event' still hidden behind the curtain that is about to rise on the new century" would resolve the confusion. In any case, Bacon could then lapse into the historian's luxury of observation: "Here," he closed this musing, "the story breaks off half told."

13:8   Promoters had no luxury of this sort. They had to propose and act. Mention of actors naturally brings Josiah Strong on stage. He had been an agent of the Evangelical Alliance, the chief anticipator of the new federations and council. By 1901, he also worked with a National Federation of Churches and Christian Workers. There he attacked the denominational zeal which still, he claimed, "blinds many eyes to the real relation of the churches to the Kingdom of God." Their "inherited prejudices and ecclesiastical conditions" stood, he said, in the way of cooperative action.

13:9   Further up their sleeves, Schaff, Bacon, Strong, and other pioneers knew that the coming church and the Kingdom of God demanded more than even denominations effecting cease-fires enough to cooperate could offer. Through the theological literature of the era the organic model of the *integrum* remained for people of conscience who were seeking models to help restore it. This dream was best expressed by Washington Gladden, the Columbus, Ohio, leader. "The principle which underlies the whole matter is the principle which is revolutionizing modern sociology and economics,—The conception of society as an organism." This conception was most vitally true of Christian society. It was to illustrate the relations of members of churches to the churches and the relations of groups of Christians to the Christian community. Pioneer ecumenical bureaucrat Elias B. Sanford underscored this: "It is in this conception of Christian Society as an organism that we find the hope of the future." Sanford admitted that talk of an organism was what he had to call an illustration, a metaphor, a dream. He was also practical. "Organic unity is still a dream of the future. Federation is a present possibility."

13:10   Lay men and women thenceforth were left with a confusion of appeals and demands. Reminded that Christ and Paul pictured the church as one and that practical necessities demanded cooperation, they were told at the same time that the republic prospered from contention between sects and they noticed that competitive denominations prospered. In any case, much ecumenical activity went on at a distance from the local church, so apathy about details and energies was endemic. As early as 1916 Sanford complained on behalf of the small Christian unity bureaucracy. They were disappointed that the laity "to a large extent were not interested in, or rather, perhaps, were indifferent to the cause of Christian unity." Ecumenists looked to them, he thought, like a "part of a procession of beggars" for their causes. He could cite splendid exceptions, but they were only that, exceptions.

13:11   In 1901, Reverend Levi Gilbert was already speaking of church unity in the spirit as an accomplished fact, and credited modernity for it. "The humane sentiments of the age have mitigated theological asperities." Meanwhile, the trend was toward the experimental phases of religion, and here "all true Christians use the same idiom. Dialects disappear."

13:12   Despite this factor, the leaders created a world of achievement in which they spoke in triumphal terms. University of Minnesota president Cyrus Northrup told the 1903 National Federation of Churches and Christian Workers that the Christian army after federation would bring about "Waterloo for the Prince of Darkness, and his empire will dwindle to a lone St. Helena of the sea."

13:13   Reactionaries who opposed the movement had other explanations. To them, dogma was important, and they thought unity was being achieved among churches which no longer cared about Christian teaching. They got some outside support from articles like one that appeared in *Century* magazine for September 1905. "Creed distinctions often of a minor and technical character have kept the churches apart in the past but now that less interest is taken in doctrinal points this barrier becomes unimportant."

13:14   The ecumenical movement for the most part lacked such crowd-pleasing personalities as Dwight L. Moody or Billy Sunday. Instead a new kind of statesman emerged in the mold of John R. Mott, a future Nobel Prize winner. Mott as a young man had attended the World's Parliament of Religions. An Iowa farm boy converted to Christian action while at Cornell University, he set out to convert and organize Christians everywhere. As he traveled around the world Mott came to see that the time had at last arrived when a worldwide union of Christians might be achieved. It would help him fulfill his slogan, "the evangelization of the world in this generation." The campus was Mott's natural milieu and he organized students there for mission and unity tasks in ways that anticipated civil rights causes at colleges almost a century later. In 1895 at Vadstena castle in Sweden he helped form a World's Student Christian Federation.

13:15   For thirty years Nettie Fowler McCormick of Chicago's McCormick reaper family backed him, saying that he was the one man who would specialize in worldwide work. She liked his aggressiveness, symbolized by the sixth word in his book plan of 1897: *Strategic Points in the World's Conquest: The Universities and Colleges as Related to the Progress of Christianity.* Mott cheered her with reports of how educated people in the non-Christian world were being attracted, a fact that made support of the educated in America ever more urgent.

13:16   In 1910 he chaired sessions at the largest symbolic event inaugurating modern worldwide ecumenism, where he won the respect of 1,200 delegates to an International Missionary Conference in Edinburgh, Scotland. An admirer and sometime colleague of evangelist Moody, he soon adopted the style of humanitarians and more liberal church leaders. Mott refused, however, to be drawn into the growing disputes between church conservatives and liberals. In his organic model, he said, "there are not two gos-

pels, one social and one individual. There is but one Christ."
Against his will, however, he came to be typed with the Social
Gospel liberals and helped lead a Conference on Social Needs at
Garden City, New York, in 1914. The conference paper showed
how the liberal ecumenical and Social Gospels were fusing. The
existing social order, it said, was "unchristian and contrary to the
will of Christ" because it supported competition. Americans must
be penitent because they shared in the corporate sins of society
and must work for "a new faith, a new order, a new devotion of
service." On such terms, the leaders began to develop a set of languages that were not always representative of lay life and were
opposed by militants who favored laissez-faire models for economy and denominations.

13:17   In the United States the main energies of united ecumenical
and social forces were poured for some time after 1908 into a Federal Council of Churches. Already back in 1893 Josiah Strong
feared that federation "could never go faster than the slowest denomination entering into the federation," but the emergent council was ready to take that risk. From the first it followed Syracuse
University Law School Dean James Brooks's advice not to quibble
over theology but to emphasize moral issues such as sabbath observance, enactment of city ordinances, state laws, and the like.
The council also wanted to take over the spirit of a predecessor,
the Open and Institutional Church League. The league platform
in 1895 urged that Christ's church be "brought back to the simplicity and comprehensiveness of its primitive life," but simplicity
was precisely what the complex federative form did not permit.

13:18   The denomination was the problem, as any number of speakers
at the organizing meeting at Philadelphia in 1908 and soon after
made clear. An anthology of such expressions includes H. L.
Morehouse's call for "peace with honor" as denominations surrendered, but kept fundamental beliefs. Frederick D. Power wanted
the "surrender of our denominational badges for the sake of
Christ." One delegate called denominations "bird-tracks in pre-
historic mud." Not one denomination ever surrendered autonomy
for council life. The founders seemed to want to paper over this
issue by being busy. Delegate George Elliott captured the mood:
"The cry of the day is for applied Christianity rather than for intellectual and ecclesiastical forms."

13:19   Still, such forms had to be reckoned with somehow. The council shunned and was shunned by Catholics, over-looked the conservative evangelicals, and distanced the Unitarians, to whom an

invitation had been missent. Unitarians had the integrity not to join a council whose charter referred to Jesus as divine Lord and Savior. Much more precise than that creed the pioneers could not get, but delegate Samuel J. Niccolls was among those who insisted on it, since, he said, there must be "some definite centre of unity or the plan will have no cohesion." Niccolls knew that extended doctrinal statement was not desirable, even were it possible. The reference to the divinity of Christ existed not to shut people out or to pass judgment on anyone "because of his intellectual belief" but simply because fidelity to the truth as leaders saw it demanded such reference.

America, where church division was most extensive, provided much impetus for church union. Here John R. Mott, a young ecumenist, presides at the World Missionary Conference at Edinburgh, Scotland, in 1910. (Yale Divinity Library.)

13:20   The Federal Council slapped its own encroaching fingers in advance by declaring that to "draw up a common creed or form of government or of worship or in any way to limit the full autonomy of the Christian bodies adhering to it" was out of line. The council could only counsel and recommend to churches, local councils, and individual Christians, who yielded nothing. That did not mean that the council acquired no power. For one thing, the public press found it more convenient to report on this organized voice than on dispersed denominations. In Chicago the *Interior* called the plan of federation "the morning star of the millennium."

13:21   The gap between the fiscal energies put into the Federal Council by denominations and the language of its promoters was vast. When Charles S. Macfarland came to serve as secretary of its Social Service Commission in 1911 he observed that administratively speaking the institution consisted of little more than a constitution, a small office, and a typewriter. To go with the largest institution embodying the dreams of unity and attracting most press attention, the budget was minuscule. In 1909 the churches came up with only $9,000 while by 1911 the figure had risen to only $12,000. Private individuals added $5,000. Council leaders boasted that they served 18 million Christians but many of these were in larger congregations each of which raised more than the council lived on. When Macfarland approached bankers for loans they told him the council was a charming proposition but not a banking one. In 1912, for all his energies, he could raise only $18,500 from individuals and $15,000 from the denominations, which remained preoccupied with their own financial life.

13:22   Weak as it was on lay interest, theology, and finances, so it remained on evangelism, which came to be a specialty of other wings of Protestantism. At the organizing meeting Methodist Charles L. Goodell sounded defensive when, speaking up for council evangelism, he urged that nothing he would utter should be construed as an attack against those concerted movements of independent evangelists. Not until 1912 did the FCC even start a Commission on Evangelism, and not until 1918 was there a paid executive secretary for the commission cause—Goodell. Gaining new Christians remained the task of entrepreneurial evangelists or local congregations within the competitive denominations.

13:23   Despite these small beginnings, it would be a mistake to underestimate the symbolic value of a council of this sort. Elias B. Sanford remembered after World War I how for years as an agent of the FCC he was "looked upon by those outside the little circle" who stood by him, as a "man with a wild vision trying to earn a salary to keep him alive." The council gained some definition from the attacks by those outside its circle. Specialists at anti-ecumenism arose. Some opposed doctrinal vagueness while others professed to see in the council a desire for a superchurch. The Southern Baptists, as we have seen, vehemently rejected the unity movement entirely. While council leaders often sounded and were anti-Catholic and never expected much amity with Catholicism, they were more nettled by evangelistic and evangelical opposition within the Protestant house.

13:24   Lacking ecclesiastical support, the founders tied their destiny to that of imperial America. At the founding session Bishop Charles Fowler announced that the Republic was itself the "greatest missionary, home and foreign." Dr. William H. Roberts thought it felicitous "that the attitude of our nation is largely a Christian one," and that Washington policies were "prevailingly Christian in their spirit. The essential spirit of our nation is that of Jesus Christ." Methodist Bishop E. R. Hendrix stepped furthest over the bound. The state, he argued "does not exist for the church but church for state. . . . The nation is the last and truest development of the church." Hendrix cited the late Mr. Justice Brewer, who spoke at a meeting of the executive committee in Washington in 1911: America "is a Christian nation despite the fact that we have no established Church."

13:25   The language of prophetic criticism in which the Federal Council and, later, its successor, the National Council of Churches, engaged was rare and muffled in the founding years. World War I gave the FCC a chance to put its patriotic interests to work. The government could not deal with over a hundred separate churches as efficiently as it could with a General War-time Commission of the Churches which the council formed. A postwar rival to the council made a part of its rationale the claim that "every office of the government with a war message to deliver appealed to the ministers first of all," and that the council had reached them best.

13:26   World War I did seem to do more to unite the Protestant churches than had the peacetime activities; in this respect, the process was similar to that which brought dispersed Catholics together into the NCWC. The council was weak at the beginning of the war and quite powerful after it. Council delegates entered the seasons of war in May 1917, at a Washington meeting where highmindedly they hoped that after the war they could join with people of good-will everywhere "to make the kingdoms of the world the Kingdom of the Christ." Individual leaders spoke in the mood of Frederick Lynch, who saw a new epoch in history in Woodrow Wilson's war aims. For the first time a nation went to war for altruistic ends; it was "a religious thing coming straight from the heart of Jesus Christ." Worth M. Tippy saw the churches in the thick of the greatest opportunity that their generation would ever see, because it was disinterested and generous. While council leaders did not join many clergy in promoting hatred of Germany, they never questioned a United States wartime policy. The immanental theology of liberalism muted criticism and led to the act of identifying God's way with Wilsonian democracy. Dr. J. H. Jowett told the Washington conference that American sacrifice actually meant "supplementing the sufferings of Christ."

13:27   The Federal Council did little or nothing to protect conscientious objectors and, if anything, isolated their leaders. When the Civil Liberties Bureau in June of 1917 asked the council to stand ready to give friendly help for support of freedom of conscience, Charles Macfarland responded that the council had to act in a representative capacity and be very careful to consider the psychology of the people it represented. After the war, liberal minister John Haynes Holmes looked back in scorn with a *J'accuse*: "I charge the men at the head of this body with cowardice and hypocrisy. They are guilty of the final indecency—that of doing late and in security, as though of their own accord, what they refused to do at some cost, when the honor and lives of men were hanging in the balance." Macfarland dug up in self-defense a resolution in support of conscience that was dated May 1917, but which he admitted lay unused while the council catered to the psychology of the people it served. It was clear that the council prospered thanks to its function and stance during the war. When modernist theologian William Adams Brown gloried in 1919 in the pages of a council pamphlet, "God has given us a triumph beyond our hopes," he could have applied his language concerning the nation to the smaller triumph of the council itself.

13:28   The God who gave triumph could also allow for problems. Immediately after the war, perhaps thanks to its precedent and first popularity, the Federal Council inspired a rival, this time from within the pragmatic ecumenical camp. In December of 1918 the Interchurch World Movement was born to work the same territory and to appeal to some of the same motives that had belonged to the Federal Council. There were other precedents. A Men and Religion Forward Movement, for example, showed the potential of individual members, claiming to have reached 1,492,646 people in 60 cities through 7,062 meetings and 6,349 personal interviews in the half year after October 1911 alone. Reciting those statistics serves the purpose of reminding how efficient and practical the new IWM would be.

13:29   On December 17, 1918, hardly a month after the Armistice, Robert E. Speer, a noted Presbyterian layman, led a meeting in New York to plan this unified program of Christian service which would "unite the Protestant churches of North America in the performance of their common task." There would be surveys, analyses, studies, campaigns "to redeem the world." An observer noted that they were afraid of nothing. John R. Mott used the language of organism to ready conferees for a World Survey Conference in November of 1919. He promised that a survey would create atmosphere and make vivid "the wholeness and oneness of the task now confronting the Protestant church." Early response suggested to leaders that such an atmosphere was eliciting action from a Protestant church that would be and should be whole and one. Mott inspired conferees at Atlantic City in January 1920. He contended that "the ideal of the whole church facing the whole task appeals to us as scriptural and practicable."

13:30   It was time to talk money, but not like the thousands with which the puny Federal Council began in 1908. The immediate goal was $300 million and a five-year goal was $1.33 billion. No wonder Mott could call this the greatest program undertaken by Christians since the days of the Apostles. Advocates vied with each other in using hyperbole to speak of this greatest revival in history, this crowning movement for the churches of Jesus Christ, the greatest forward movement for evangelical Christianity in history, this new epoch in Christianity. Leaders welcomed military terms for this campaign of "masculine Christianity," and relegated women to the second echelons. They were ready to march.

13:31   Leaders invented a category called "friendly citizens" who must share IWM purposes but who were not church members, only culturally Protestant. They were to be canvassed for financial support in the amount of millions of dollars. The denominations, however, dragged their feet or blocked access to their own well-off members and the friendly citizens proved to be unfriendly, aloof, or nonexistent. Some thought that strength would come if the council and the movement merged, but FCC General Secretary

Charles S. Macfarland was wise enough to be cautious about the upstart. The FCC's endorsement was nominal and soon to be regretted.

13:32   Despite danger signals, the IWM pressed forward. "Christ needs big men for big business," one heard. The bulletins from the Interchurch Headquarters showed obsession with bigness. "Christ

Liberal Protestantism was anything but alienated from sources of wealth and power; Sunday, after church, two John D. Rockefellers, senior and junior, take a walk.

was big, was He not? None ever bigger. Christ was busy, was He not? None ever busier." Headquarters people wanted a building of their own at a cost of $25 million. They said it would pay for itself in thirty years. Then on second thought they retreated, saying that first they should prove themselves. That turned out to be the only wise decision of the organization. Still John D. Rockefeller, Jr., the major backer, encouraged the movement to develop "the maximum of efficiency in doing the Lord's business." Leaders, thus encouraged, budgeted a campaign of $336,777,720 for 1920 and entered the year spending a million a month of uncollected money. Rockefeller, a victim of his own dream, said that "the plans are wisely and conservatively drawn."

13:33   Big business leaders were generally conservative and Protestant social activists were usually progressive, so tensions developed. Both sides could meet to oppose Bolshevism, and the Prohibition cause helped hold the coalition together. Then came the major steel strike of 1919–20. Business naturally backed U.S. Steel. IWM people backed the American Federation of Labor. Subsequently an IWM Commission of Inquiry in an investigation concluded that U.S. Steel was largely the offender. Later observers have praised the report for its scope and fairness, but it roused fierce opposition from those to whom the movement wanted to appeal.

13:34   Late in 1919 and through 1920 the progressives began to get an education in realism. The League of Nations failed to win approval in the United States Congress. The steel strike showed that issues of injustice were not easily overcome. Hard cash was hard to come by. The IWM denominations pledged $200 million, most of which they would have raised anyhow but channeled differently. They sent very little to headquarters and by then only $3 million of the $40 million expected from friendly citizens had been pledged. By then $8 million dollars borrowed against the credit of the denominations were gone. A second fund-drive did worse. The movement's management was exposed as inept and lax, and denomination followed denomination in a scramble to bail out. What followed was, as a staff member put it, shell shock. The *Literary Digest* wrote the epitaph for this "most colossal collapse in the church since the days of Pentecost . . . the greatest blow to Protestantism since the Reformation," and "the greatest tragedy that has occurred in the history of the Christian Church." Hyperbole afflicted the fall, just as it had the rise, of the IWM.

13:35   The denominations survived their participation in the movement, and the Federal Council worked away, chastened and cautious. At Buffalo the Baptists convened in a doleful mood. "We are in an hour of spent enthusiasm. Perhaps the greatest disappointment the world has ever known, the deepest depression, is today upon us." After two years of enthusiasms, "to mention the glowing ideals for which we fought brings a smile to men's faces."

13:36   The original intention of the first generation of ecumenists was to use the language of organic wholeness, a restitution of primitive simplicity and unity or a convergence in the coming Kingdom. They accompanied this with plans that had to settle for and justify full autonomy to denominations. This compromise of the vision denied the promise and fitness of the unity dream. Meanwhile the denominations had given enough of their hearts and heads for council unity to have lost some of their rationale for autonomy and competition. Yet both conciliar and denominational activities survived in uneasy alliance on the leadership level, while the laity through the twentieth century was selective about the ecumenical causes it would support. Whatever is to be said of the limits of vision by the pioneers of Christian unity, however, they did more than others in centuries to turn around the direction of unprincipled competition and to provide a new ideal of some effective patterns of action. They displayed a search for wholeness that showed their intention to go beyond the modern style, with its schisms and divisions.

14

Social Christianity as a Recovered Wholeness

14:1   T o meet the needs of the immigrant-crowded industrial city where individuals seemed powerless, numbers of turn-of-the-century agents used the adjective "social" to describe their goals. Social work as a profession and social settlement houses attracted people of secular or diverse, often Jewish, religious sympathies. The Roman Catholic Bishops' Program of 1919 brought together forces that were long gathering to promote the causes of labor and the urban poor in movements identified as social. Anglican Christian socialism on both sides of the Atlantic left its mark. The Protestant Social Gospel became the best known of all such movements and will shortly receive attention.

14:2   It is important to keep in mind, however, at the outset, that these groups and their ideologies did not have a monopoly on social service. The individualists who made up evangelistic, premillennial, and pentecostal camps were by no means inhumane or uninvolved. Many of them were closer to the victims, more ready to roll up their sleeves and get to work, than were the Social Gospel theorists. They generated no social theology, and even resisted one, but they were not blind to human need even if the coming millennium would be needed to bring an end to it.

14:3   Concentrating on such movements also might lead to the overlooking of numbers of groups with a social agenda but without a social ideology. To provide balance to the Social Gospel, a brief focus on one of them is valid. The Salvation Army was best known both in its time and subsequently. Still a young movement when it arrived in America in 1880, it experienced two schisms, the more important being the splitting off into the Volunteers of America by Ballington Booth, son of the Army's founder, General William Booth. Yet the Salvation Army was most visible, and entered American folklore because of its uniforms, bands, street-corner solicitations, and distributing of cheer and doughnuts to troops in Europe during World War I. Its perfectionist theology was demanding, obscure, and probably irrelevant to most of the public, but its practices came to be admired.

14:4   It may seem curious to locate the Salvation Army as an agent seeking the *restitutio ad integrum* of persons or society. Its theology was too radically aware of human evil and the brokenness of human solutions to be progressive. The fifth of its eleven principal doctrines held that in consequence of the human fall all "have become sinners totally depraved and as such are justly exposed to the wrath of God." Yet the tenth principle also says that "we believe that it is the privilege of all believers to be 'wholly sanctified' and that their 'whole spirit and soul and body' [can be] 'preserved blameless unto the coming of Our Lord Jesus Christ.'" The "wholes" and "whollys" in such declarations showed the extent of Salvationist commitment to perfection tempered by realism about the world.

14:5   The Army leadership always insisted that its fundamental rescue work was spiritual before it was physical, yet the physical relief was what the world observed. Along with other holiness and perfectionist groups, the Army was venturesome in many ways. While the Social Gospel neglected women's themes and was almost entirely a male venture using male imagery, the Army from the beginning heard women preachers and assigned them major roles. Back when she was being courted in England by founder William Booth, Catherine Booth let him know that she and other women were in no way inferior. Women's names appeared at the top level in both the Army and the Volunteers. Frances Willard of the Women's Christian Temperance Union thought the Army was "the nearest approach to primitive Christianity" in the modern era because of such attitudes toward women. No wonder the gospel rescue organizations were more ready than the general religious public to back the woman suffrage movement.

14:6   It was difficult in 1900 as it was later to push the Army into a mold or get it into focus. In 1900 the progressive William T. Stead referred to the late Catherine Booth as a socialist. A friend outside the Army said she was something more, in "complete revolt against the existing order." Here were theological conservatives who were ready for much readjustment in social arrangements. At times the Army's *War Cry* editor had to express concern lest there be "an abnormal amount of sympathy with our inflammatory neighbors the anarchists." The Volunteer's *Gazette* incautiously featured the activities of secular social critics like Jacob Riis and Florence Kelley. The Booths were cautiously prepared for the role of government in helping face social ills and were opposed to more radical schemes of capitalist competition. Some were pro-labor when most Protestants opposed labor organization. Socialist leader Eugene Debs returned compliments. "In its main purposes," he said, the Army "has my unqualified approval and my hearty sympathy." Rescue, to the movements, meant help for hungry bodies, the diseased, the exploited, and not only the saving of souls.

14:7   Sometimes the Church of the Nazarene, the Christian and Missionary Alliance, and the Pentecostal Mission, politically unsophisticated and theologically conservative as they were, used their ideals of perfection to deal with the debris of industrial society. While returning to the Bible, old standards, and old creeds, they addressed social issues. Thus in 1907 the Pentecostal Church of the Nazarene was not merely Prohibitionist, as one might expect. It connected liquor interests with social existence and saw that these must be attacked for having "taken possession of the ruling powers in politics and in the official life of the nation." The trusts and Standard Oil, implicitly stigmatized even in the comparison, were by contrast "angels in comparison to this black demon of hell."

14:8   In east Texas, *Holiness Evangel* writer J. D. Scott claimed that political reform was the greatest need of the American people aside from the cleansing blood of Jesus Christ. Until that reform happened, power purchased with money was in command and politicians would remain corrupt. Such reform did not conflict with Scott's belief in an imminent second coming of Jesus. He and his colleagues in the Peniel Mission could share causes with the progressives and yet have no interest in their philosophy and secular ambitions.

14:9   Though some of these voices were silenced as premillennialism prospered or as they found the social cause to be a distraction from soul-winning, they had set a precedent and achieved some ends. Thus a Pentecostal source in 1907 insisted that the same divine call which had worked to erect the old standards and spiritual landmarks, to restore to the people the apostolic faith, and which attracted people mostly in the lowly walks of life and of very modest means, had led them to see the continent shaken. God, it went on, has "commenced to do it already. The great reforms which have recently taken place in our political and commercial institutions, the wonderful and sweeping advance of prohibition," were signs alongside the spread of the Holy Spirit and holiness movements.

14:10   The "Social Gospel," was probably given its name in 1886 by Dubuque, Iowa, Congregationalist minister Charles O. Brown, in the context of a reference to Henry George's *Progress and Poverty*. Small-town Iowa was awakening. At Iowa College, later Grinnell College, President George A. Gates and radical professor George Herron wished well to several hundred people who between 1895 and 1900 colonized a Christian Commonwealth Colony in Georgia. They gave further publicity to the term "Social Gospel" by their attempts to live communally. This they did until disease, weather, and opposition ended the experiment. One day the phrase was to become common in book titles such as *The Social Gospel* by the University of Chicago's Divinity dean, Shailer Mathews.

14:11   The movement is hard to measure. Vida Scudder, a Christian socialist, is the only woman mentioned as part of it. The leaders were seminary professors or leading Protestant pastors. They produced the Methodist Social Creed, dominated the Federal Council of Churches, and promoted progressive legislation. Socialists and labor leaders usually tended to overlook the leaders, since these represented no voting blocs and were sometimes remote from churchly constituencies. However, because of the ambition of the vision and the clarity of their expression they have exerted influence beyond their numbers. The vision is what matters here, since it shows how one set of people wanted to move beyond the individualism of modern church and society into a transmodern situation, one which stressed the organic character of society to match that of the church ecumenical.

14:12   The theology schools, often those at universities, were in the advance guard. In them specialization and the professional style won their place, but these scholars did not welcome the way life was being segmented and religion was becoming a private affair. Too many church people in the preceding Gilded Age who were moved by the gospel of Social Darwinism settled too easily for a soul-saving church distanced from the centers of political, economic, and social decision. While the new voices often came to be associated with the modernist camps, they were strenuous in their claim of a *restitutio ad integrum* also in this field. Josiah Strong summed it all up in his notice that "there are two types of Christianity, the old and the older. The one is traditional, familiar, and dominant. The other, though as old as the Gospel of Christ, is so rare that it is suspected of being new, or is overlooked altogether." Now it was coming to light.

14:13   Harvard's Francis Peabody in the 1880s ventured a course in Christian sociology called "Peabo's drainage, drunkenness and divorce," by irreverent students. Andover Seminary followed with social economics in 1887 and Hartford the next year required a sociology course. Yale followed in 1892 and in 1893 the University of Chicago encouraged such studies under Albion Small, the religious-minded head of the Department of Sociology. One year earlier Graham Taylor had arrived to introduce the vision of wholeness at Chicago Theological Seminary. In a syllabus for 1900 he saw the Kingdom of God as being essential "to the disclosure of Christ's purpose and a Christian social order." He connected this with biblical study and ethics. Then one could find the "cosmic order of human life as it was made and meant to be in harmony with the creative idea and redemptive purpose and indwelling life of God."

14:14   Peabody, meanwhile, knew that one must convert the students first. In 1903 he wrote that the serious-minded youth in the new century would no longer be torn by the heartbreaking conflict between his spiritual ideals and his scholarly aims. Philosophy, science, and theology were all committed to the problem of unification. The often cynical George Santayana looked at university people in his day and saw among them a shrinkage of theological concerns. "About high questions of politics and religion their minds are open but vague; they seemed not to think them of practical importance; they acquiesced in people having any views they liked on such subjects; the fluent and fervid enthusiasms so common among European students were unknown to them." The symbol of the Kingdom of God, Protestant leaders thought, might change all that.

14:15   It was this that Taylor remembered addressing as early as 1893. For him, the family, neighborly, industrial, civic, cultural, and other groupings and agencies were tributary to the whole endeavor to realize the ideals of religion. This approach reversed the plot of secular folk and conservative religionists who saw religion as a private affair. No, the Kingdom was "the progressive realization in human experience and history of the divine ideal of relationship between man and God and man and man" in the spheres of life. In 1913 Taylor stayed with the theme in a book for which Jane Addams wrote the introduction. Christians must "apply the Gospel's age-long, time-tested, saving truths so much further as to bring the whole of a human life under their sway and the whole world into the Kingdom." It was always *the whole*.

14:16   The acknowledged professorial leader was Walter Rauschenbusch, a German Baptist who kept credentials in a small denomination and won others as a pastor in Hell's Kitchen, New York's crowded West Side. There he saw that individual efforts at charity only confirmed a bad system. He wanted to socialize America and American Christianity. Rauschenbusch was adept at the language of prayer and at home with the old piety of conversion. This he combined with rather sophisticated awareness of the work of Henry George, economist Richard Ely, and others. There were gains. He expected to be hounded for heresies when he published *Christianity and the Social Crisis* in 1907 but instead won followers. When, however, he wrote a synthetic *A Theology for the Social Gospel* in 1917 his and its energies were largely spent, his in grief over the war, and its in the face of changes it could not control or meet. When it reappeared after the war this social movement acquired a less progressive aspect but never forgot the address to the whole of life that its pioneers favored.

14:17   Rauschenbusch and his colleagues organized a Brotherhood of the Kingdom. They grimly pursued the Kingdom motif in order to help overcome the disunities and conflicts of modern life. "Wherever I touched life, there was the Kingdom of God. That was the brilliancy, the splendor of that conception—it touches everything with religion," he remembered. The Brotherhood members, who began to meet in 1893, all thought that the idea of a kingdom of God on earth was the central thought of Jesus and ought to be the great aim of the church. Now it was "not a matter of getting individuals to heaven, but of transforming the life on earth into the harmony of heaven." For Rauschenbusch this meant Christianizing the social order progressively. The economic order must follow the family, political life, educational institutions, and the church toward Christianization.

14:18   The leaders were true-blue Americans. William Newton Clarke in 1911 said "we mean national when we say social hope," and he had plenty of imitators. Now these articulators could criticize the old Social Darwinism which saw the social body in the metaphor of an evolving biological organism. "The nineteenth century,"

Social Gospel pioneer Walter Rauschenbusch (lower left) was but one of ten pastors in the succession at "Hell's Kitchen's" Second German Baptist Church, but there he learned of social problems up close—and thence he set out to address them. (By permission of *Heritage and Ministry of the North American Baptist Conference*, by Frank H. Woyke, published by the North American Baptist Conference, Oakbrook Terrace, Ill.)

wrote Peabody, "had for its subject the social body; the twentieth century has for its subject the social soul."

14:19   All this ran counter to the individualism of the day. From the Episcopalian wing, William Dwight Porter Bliss gave support for this consistent attack. In his *Encyclopedia of Social Reform*, Bliss insisted that a social law must be fulfilled *socially*, not individualistically. Protestantism had made a grievous mistake by misconceiving the incarnation of God in Christ, when God "entered into all life." Businessmen were wrong: "God's way demands a social basis." Rauschenbusch thought the same: "Individualistic theology has not trained the spiritual intelligence of Christian men and women to recognize and observe spiritual entities beyond the individual." He would draw on the writings of St. Paul about the body of Christ, "the first and classical discussion in Christian thought of the nature and functioning of a composite spiritual organism."

14:20   Rauschenbusch was a church historian who reverted to the Hebrew prophets, Jesus and Paul, the Middle Ages, and sometimes colonial America for precedents. Wellesley professor Vida Scudder, a well-read Christian socialist author, was also drawn to a kind of contemplative style: "Friends are justified who tell me laughing that my real home is either in the Middle Ages or in the Utopian future." Eager to overcome the disjunctions of modern life, she was plaintive in 1901: "But where was unity for me?" One of the few Christian leaders to become a member of the Socialist party (in 1911), she failed to convince others to join her in that move and remained a gifted marginal person whose vision had more influence than did her practical effects.

14:21   Given the constancy of language about the whole of life and about the organic connectedness of things, there are surprising blind spots in the social Christianity record. Many remained put off by the industrial city that had to be the milieu for change. Some activists started what were called settlements and institutional churches, to deal with many needs of immigrants and the poor. Vague on program, weak on detail, generally out of touch with laborers, inept at politics, most Social Gospel people were still prophets of a new order. Almost tidily and sanitarily, without violence, this gospel had to alter the whole economic pattern toward one of cooperation.

14:22   Technology elicited another ambiguity. Most observers cite it as a major feature of modernization, so such social theologians might have been expected to promote it. Curiously, it was the conservatives who welcomed the new instruments of communication and transportation as agencies for spreading the Gospel. Liberals accepted technology's gifts but were wary of what these did to the person. Peabody at Harvard feared the damage in his students. "The future for them," he wrote in 1909, "is the kingdom of elevators, telephones, motor cars, and flying machines." The principle of the universe was acceleration. And mindless madness. "We do not know whence we come, or whither we go, and what is more important, we do not care; what we do know is that we are moving faster than any one ever moved before," thus generating only a spiritual void.

14:23   Social Gospel leaders failed to involve themselves with the causes of women that were coming to a head in the battle for woman suffrage. Few were ready to see an enlarged role for women at all and some were almost obsessive about having them remain restricted to homemaking. Some have seen their concern as born of personal circumstances. Gladden, Rauschenbusch, Strong, and Peabody experienced either some separation of their parents or the death of a parent in childhood. Did each lack a secure sense of a protecting father and therefore project the Fatherhood of God to fill a need that had not been filled close to home?

14:24   Thus Rauschenbusch's father, though a pastor in a conservative group, was addicted to alcohol and was cool in his marriage. Mrs. Rauschenbusch took the children to Europe for some time and brought home a son who idealized the Victorian family. He was to praise the thorn bush of procreation as "aflame with a beautiful fire that does not consume," a force "essential for the very existence of human society." Of course, one might say, such an outlook did lead Rauschenbusch to slight the problems of the family and regard it as already Christianized. He opposed socialist notions that encouraged women to enter the work force. Christianity had a "finer sense of the right of a soul to its own body," he thought, than did the feminists who claimed that submissive women were slaves or prostitutes in their own houses. Men should protect the domestic sphere of women in the small nuclear family. The family as an organism even became the model for what society was to be. It would help civilize the world. Few Social Gospel leaders deviated from this line.

14:25   The fusion of energies that produced woman suffrage and Prohibition amendments in 1919 and 1920 revealed the ambiguities of the Social Gospel men. Both movements had long roots and their basic visions were formed before the 1890s, though the successful organizing efforts occurred after 1893. Their detailed stories await a full retrospective accounting in the second volume of this series, when wets versus drys fought over repeal during the Prohibition era, and when social feminism entered a new stage and induced new controversy among both women and men in the churches in the 1920s.

14:26   Woman suffrage had been promoted since 1848 by women, often the restlessly religious but sometimes the necessarily aggressive critics of religion, but in either case women seen as radical. Curiously, for a complex of reasons including conservative impulses by old-stock settlers to hold power against alien kinds of newcomers, Wyoming before this period and Colorado in 1893 and Utah and Idaho in 1896 made pioneering provision for women's votes long before progressive states did. Temperance was a century-long interest of both reactionary and progressive church leadership, but the rise of the Women's Christian Temperance Union and the Anti-Saloon League, its rival after 1893, gained momentum when women such as Frances Willard and Carrie Nation made national headlines. The Social Gospel leaders were unanimously for temperance causes, but uncertain about women's rights if these in any way threatened the conventional family.

14:27   Walter Rauschenbusch typically resisted but one Democratic party platform plank in 1912—the one that had to do with women's rights; he had no use at all for suffrage. Most works on the Social Gospel and Christian socialism have few or no references to the women's cause. Even Vida Scudder, the solitary well-known woman among the theorists, herself a walking embodiment of assertive womanhood, makes no mention of feminist issues in her *On Journey* in this autobiography's references to her prime years. They were precisely the three decades of the climactic suffrage struggle and victory. Yet, all the while, many of the main exemplars of Social Gospel action in slum and settlement were themselves women, and, as mentioned, women were most prominent in the temperance moves, favorites of the Social Gospel.

14:28   Since women evidently were generally more reluctant to promote suffrage than were men, radical feminists, who replaced the older Puritans as heads of the drive for votes and other rights, had to persuade them. Some chose the route of radical faith or, in the case of the exceptional Elizabeth Cady Stanton, rejection of organized religion. In 1895 she saw to the publication of a *Woman's Bible*, an attack on conventional views of scripture because it was seen as inhibiting women's development. Most feminist leadership reacted. Susan B. Anthony refused to have her name on the Bible committee which produced the book. "*You* fight that battle—and leave me to fight the secular—the political fellows. . . ." She was smart enough not to allow a negative aspect to blight the cause.

14:29   Mrs. Stanton did not learn, and her movement did suffer from the vehement reactions to the *Woman's Bible*. In 1896 the National American Woman Suffrage Association repudiated its eighty-one-year-old former president and her colleagues. A new cast, including Anna Howard Shaw and Carrie Chapman Catt, were taking leadership. Like abolitionists before them, they knew how to find latencies for change in the Bible itself, or at least did not want to pick up opponents on the biblical front. They were gaining new allies among moderate women and knew better than to alienate them from the cause.

14:30   Anna Howard Shaw reworked the historic symbols. "The great defect in the religious teaching to and accepted by women is the dogma that self-abnegation, self-effacement, and excessive humility were ideal feminine virtues," she was to say during the war years. From Jesus she would learn and then teach new approaches to the sacredness of life, all life, including women's life. It was also becoming clear that, even without Social Gospel leadership, the clergy far more than any other professionals were coming to support suffrage. In 1902, the NAWSA set up a Committee on Church Work to advance a cause that was becoming more attractive, in part because it offered male clergy allies in the Prohibition cause.

14:31   That fact, the partial disengagement from the temperance battle after 1908 by radical feminists, enabled leaders like Walter Rauschenbusch, Josiah Strong, and others, to put more energies than before into Prohibition as part of the reform needed for Christ's coming Kingdom. While Prohibitionists later came to be seen as cramped and crabby repressors of individual vice, the liberal leadership had been expansive about what abolition of liquor traffic would do for the progressive cause. One can find endless parallels to a typical advocacy by Reverend Charles F. Aked, who wrote in 1908 in *Appleton's Magazine*: "We want to make possible for all a life in the whole, the good and the beautiful. . . . And the common sale of intoxicating liquors renders our work a thousand times more difficult."

14:32   During the war, modernist Shirley Jackson Case at Chicago wrote on *The Millennial Hope*: "This course of history exhibits one long process of evolving struggle by which humanity as a whole rises constantly higher in the scale of civilization and attainment, bettering its condition from time to time through its great skill and industry." It was clear that part of the program by which "the world is found to be growing constantly better" was, for most progressives as it was for conservatives, the prohibition of alcoholic beverages. Another reformer talked about new hope for "the bright morning of the millennium" dawning upon this "sin-cursed and rum-soaked world." The liquor traffic was one of its greatest obstacles. It merited Social Gospel energies.

14:33   Race was an even bigger blind spot. Few pages of the Social Gospel are given over to creativity in respect to native Americans, Orientals, or blacks, in their hour of need and generation of crisis. These leaders shared the Anglo-Saxon outlook about limited Negro potential. Whoever thought about it felt most at home with the adaptive Booker T. Washington. They were generous in support of colleges for blacks in the South, but were satisfied with the new U.S. Supreme Court concept of "separate but equal" approaches to black life. They made no efforts to propose or participate in legislation assuring rights for what they saw as the unready black race.

14:34   Expectably, this left them uncritical of Anglo-Saxon racist claims. In 1902 Walter Rauschenbusch made a commencement day address linking Anglo-Saxons with the "princely stock," the Teutons, who together would properly rule and dominate the world. How, he asked, could the good Germans of Rochester now hold their own while "alien strains" arrived from France, Spain, Slavic lands, Bohemia, Poland, and Russian Jewish zones? Lyman Abbott had supported the Dawes Act in 1887. He joined colleagues in posing barbarianism against civilization in inherited Darwinian terms. "Barbarians have rights which civilized folk are bound to respect; but barbarism has no rights which civilization is bound to respect. In the history of the human race nothing is more certain than that civilization must conquer and barbarism must be subdued."

14:35   The Social Gospel stood apart from socialism, which crested as a political force with 6 percent of the vote in the 1912 election. Social Gospel leaders feared socialism, feminism, and what Peabody called socialism's "unflinching radicalism." He and Rauschenbusch favored cooperativism but felt that private prop-

erty did spur morality and participation in the republic. Only in
his support of Henry George's single tax did Rauschenbusch come
close to the support of a socialist program. Otherwise, socialism
stimulated class conflict and violence while for the Christian, he
believed, love creates fellowship. "In the measure in which love
increases in any social organism, it will hold together without
coercion."

14:36   It may seem amazing that the Social Gospel in its time connoted something radical, given its programmatic timidity and
gentility. W. D. P. Bliss was a rare exception when he led Boston's
Church of the Carpenter into socialist experiment. He explained,
"I was made a Christian by Karl Marx, and a Socialist by Jesus
Christ." As he studied Jesus' cross, he learned that "one must
come out a Socialist." Yet he did little for socialism and almost
went unnoticed by partisans.

14:37   The other strongly socialist advocate was George Herron, but a
marital scandal at Grinnell and his subsequent high life in Florence made him an eccentric liability for the cause. In 1904 at a
socialist convention Herron did prophesy capitalist catastrophe as
an American possibility. "The sun of that Co-operative Commonwealth will rise here on the American continent, and in this republic." He used his preacherly rhetoric to effect: "Now is the
time of Socialist salvation, if we are great enough to respond to
the greatness of our opportunity." There was pathos when he had
to write six months before his death in 1925: "I really believed
. . . that America would . . . become a Messianic nation and
would establish a new world in which war would be forever ended
and in which there would be a new human order that would be at
least an approach to the kingdom of heaven." Instead, he said,
something nearer the kingdom of hell had come. Herron spent his
declining years in Italy and by 1923 even expressed some hope for
Mussolini's Fascism.

14:38   When the Social Gospel people in the Federal Council of
Churches finally made friendly gestures toward labor, American
Federation of Labor vice president, D. A. Hayes, spoke reveal-
ingly about how little connection there had been. "We may as well
speak frankly about it—many working people have felt that the
churches were unsympathetic, if not indifferent" to aspirations of
workers.

14:39   A Presbyterian agitator for labor causes in the Federal Council,
Charles Stelzle, thought change must come at seminaries. Semi-

narians studied luxuriously "*the Israelites, the Jebusites, the Hivites, and the Hittites,*" and all was well. When they addressed the social life of the Chicagoites or the Buffaloites or the Pittsburghites, some good brother would calmly remind each that "*he might better preach the 'simple Gospel.'*" In due course the Federal Council advocated a living wage, the limitation of work hours, the abolition of child labor, regulation of the conditions of toil for women, equal rights and complete justice for all people in all stations of life, and other issues not yet on many denominational agenda.

14:40   This portrait may have left the Social Gospel looking a bit precious. In its moderate forms it attracted large audiences, as evidenced by the multimillion sales of *In His Steps: What Would Jesus Do?* In 1898 Topeka minister Charles M. Sheldon, its author, preached narrative Sunday night sermons designed to propagate practical Christianity. The tinge was utopian. The novel had imitators enough to show that there was some market for books about people who overcame the conflicts and chaos of modern life through reversion to an old Gospel, now applied to a new scene.

14:41   The turn-of-the-century needs of the industrial city also saw the rise of Jewish social service that drew on ancient prophetic impulses and modern secularity. The Catholic Bishops' Program relied on papal teaching, including that of the encyclical by Leo XIII issued in 1891. It could be used by conservatives and progressives alike. In any case, the Catholic approach has always been characterized by pragmatic realism. Conservative Protestants individually and collectively moved to address human need, even if they had despaired of the world and thought it would soon end. It was the Protestant Social Gospel, however, which is remembered as the most daring engagement with the situation. In it the Kingdom of God was used toward progressive ends as a symbol of a new heaven on earth, a cooperative and partly collective replacement of the competitive individualist order that now prevailed.

14:42   This Social Gospel was to be undercut by the realities of World War I and by opposition from within the Protestant camp. Laypeople often resisted its socializing program, or lost interest when its organizations grew grandiose. Chastened, it would live on as a permanent expression of liberal Protestantism. Without question, it drew on very traditional prophetic, evangelical, medieval, and other historic models in order to criticize the differentiations by which modernity assigned religion a little private corner of life.

This criticism was designed to move American Christianity beyond such a settlement into what we have called a transmodern scheme. Yet tradition was not so easily recoverable or recognizable. Ironically, the creative movement that was to have restored wholeness to a broken church and world came to be seen as one more novelty, one more contending party, tied to a theological modernism that was soon to be called into question.

15

The Nation:
Beyond Divisions,
One Cause

15:1   The language of restitution and of progress toward wholeness
called believers beyond private interest toward cosmic concerns.
Such calls demanded institutions larger than the separated
churches for its embodiments. A true cosmopolitanism should
have spoken in terms of the whole world, yet in America the leaders stopped short. The human race, as well as the nation, in its
expansive and imperial awakening, was pressed into service.
Meanwhile, the language of conservatives who repudiated such
progressivism was no less nationalist in religious senses. Suspect
in their ethnic enclaves or suspicious of earthly programs, they
were no less loyal to America. They grafted religious symbols
onto the imperial mission. They overlooked many of their divisions when a small war in 1898 and a great one in 1917 provoked
obsessive passions. They let wars serve as the major ecumenical
and interfaith instruments, while the nation itself became a transcendent religious symbol.

15:2   Could a nation, even America, while it was undergoing an
awakening toward international assertiveness serve such divine
purposes? The gap between ideals as expressed by leaders and the
reality of means used or ends achieved was never so wide in the
years before or, possibly, since. Indeed, the ironic theological interpretations of American religion were first and best applied to
this period. The promise and fitness of things, according to the

agents' descriptions of what they intended, were to come to contradictory outcomes, in part because of their own doings, whose limits they did not foresee. In any case, across the spectrum, the America they all had come to love attracted energies that they would apply to causes larger than private life, and in their own ways greater than their separate religious causes. The public or civil religion of the society was to be transformed in this time.

15:3   Students of such a public religion usually turned to Abraham Lincoln. He was the prophet of the union as religious mysticism, the theological interpreter of the union. For decades after the War Between the States, however, the South ritualized its lost cause over against Lincolnian symbols. North and South therefore generated separate civic pieties at least until the war in 1898. Each Confederate memorial planted in a courthouse square in the South further enhanced the ideology that claimed a separate righteousness, and each statue of a Union soldier on northern courthouse lawns was a sign of separatism as well, to southern eyes. So strong were these two parallel civic faiths that even during and after these wars they evoked their own languages. Thus Mrs. M. D. Farris in Texas drew on a common store of meanings when she asked the United Daughters of the Confederacy to guard its sacred archives "even as the children of Israel did the Ark of the Covenant."

15:4   This southern division of nationalist faith found distinct Christian symbols more congenial. Ritual gatherings usually ended with prayers that would conclude "in the name and for the sake of Christ our dear Redeemer." A man called "The Fighting Parson" of the lost cause, J. William Jones, won crowds as late as 1908 with a militancy that called for prayer at veterans' gatherings to the "God of Israel, God of the centuries, God of our forefathers, God of Jefferson Davis and Sidney Johnston and Robert E. Lee, and Stonewall Jackson, God of the Southern Confederacy." An acclaimed novel, *White Blood*, in 1906 depicted a parson connecting the southern cause with the crucifixion in a typical linking. The South near the Civil War's end was like "the blessed Savior who passed from gloomy Gethsemane to the judgment hall, through the fearful ordeal of being forsaken by his friends, and then on to the bloody Cross." Prominent cleric Randolph McKim in Washington consistently touted Robert E. Lee not as commander, but as Father to his troops in a sacred cause. The southern people had pressed sorely upon Lee a true crown of thorns. It was, he said, "borne silently and uncomplainingly."

15:5   Analysts of such rhetoric have compiled virtual sourcebooks of pulpit talk all the way to World War I concerning how the heathen, in this case, the North, led God's chosen people into captivity. But "that fact did not prove the heathen to be right in the cause nor that the Israelites were upholding a bad cause," preached Nashville Presbyterian James H. McNeilly. He recalled his days as a Confederate chaplain, when troops poured blood like festal wine in a losing but not wrong cause. He reminded hearers that questions of right and wrong before God were not settled by success or defeat of arms.

15:6   When southerners did envision reunited spiritualities, these had to be on southern terms. The North was corrupted by foreign immigrants and industrialization. The potent Southern Baptist leader James Gambrell feared that northern materialism would corrupt even the South, which had yet to play a great part in saving American institutions from "the foreignizing deluge in the north." Some day, he thought, the Southern Baptists must send a multitude of evangelists north to contend with these immigrants.

15:7   The Spanish-American War in 1898 first allowed southern clerics to resume national roles. Baptist, Methodist, and Presbyterian churches did not reunite, but the southern wings felt ready to speak for the nation. Thus Methodist A. N. Jackson had to answer the question as to how southerners could now honor the Union that their fathers combated. The answer: "Here is the South's holy of holies. The veil is not rent, and only they can know what is within whose own have been to the sacrifice. And they are legion." Southern sons were again ready to "go bravely up to new baptisms of blood." The *Christian Advocate*, which published Jackson, thought that this war was the destroyer of the lingering remnants of sectional prejudice in every part of the land.

15:8   There were grumblers, however, typified by resentful James McNeilly, who thought it was showing defensiveness to boast about the high level of southern enlistments in 1898. This was to be no compensation for past dishonor, "accompanied by the usual flood of gush about the blue and the gray marching shoulder to shoulder and keeping step to the music of the Union." The different drummers of the South still deserved to be heard.

15:9   Attention to the South's racial and religious purity over against northern alien blood led men like Thomas Frank Gailor, Episcopal bishop and leader at the University of the South in Tennessee, to learn the language of progress and apply it to the South. The War Between the States, he said, had been "an epoch in the process of the evolution of the nation," and he welcomed the results. Over against the McNeillys of the South, he preached the message of wholeness, for "the nation is greater than any section, than any class, than any generation." Such language, however, had to wait the time and needs of the World War I era. Not all southern preaching and editorializing was that generous to the North. Some southerners blamed the war itself on rationalist German philosophy, which had left its mark in the often infidel North.

15:10   On the positive side, President Woodrow Wilson's southern religious heritage made it easy for clerics from the South to legitimate the war as a crusade. Five days before that war was declared, on April 6, 1917, Randolph McKim used his Washington pulpit on Palm Sunday to preach on "America Summoned to a Holy War." He left no doubt: "Let me say then, as plainly and as strongly as I can, speaking as a minister of Christ, speaking as a messenger of God, speaking with a solemn sense of the obligations of my sacred office, speaking in the sanctuary of Christ,"— one draws up ready to hear more—"that it is the high and sacred duty of the American people" to crush Germany "if the world is to be made safe for Democracy." Therefore, "this conflict is indeed a Crusade. The greatest in history—the holiest. It is in the profoundest and truest sense a Holy War" in the tradition, he said, of the Bible and Robert E. Lee. The South was only the largest of the elements that saw in the imperial and military moments the occasions to join and even lead in bringing religious meanings to national life. Others also deserve notice.

15:11   The best illustration of the way in which rejected or marginal groups used the occasion to gain credentials is that of the Latter-day Saints, safely describable as the most despised large group as of 1893. While the Mormons did not win acceptability, they convinced themselves that they truly belonged in America and had a right to leadership in its mainstream even as they retained the base of their kingdom in Utah.

15:12   On the eve of the period Daniel Dorchester spoke in characteristic language of the way Mormonism had become "an ecclesiastical despotism of immense strength." The stigma of Mormon polygamy still afflicted the church but, and he quoted a student of Mormonism: "Eradicate polygamy and leave Mormonism," and you have the system with the disease " 'struck in,' " in other words, still latent. Dorchester was stunned by the reported power of a church which had 28,838 officials, one for every five persons in its 138,000 membership, with all the threads of authority gathered

At the beginning of the period, as Mormons pressed for statehood in Utah, they brought
memories of scenes like this one from the 1880s, when polygamists were jailed at Utah State
Prison. (Utah State Historical Society.)

into the hands of its president. Here was a church and a state that
claimed infallibility "unequaled by the Pope of Rome." Dorchester
quoted from 1882 a word of Mormon Bishop Lunt: "This is our
year of jubilee. We look forward with perfect confidence to the day
when we will hold the reins of the United States Government."

15:13   Henry K. Carroll was a man of more equanimity who tried to
do justice to the Latter-day Saints. When he wrote in 1893 he could
cite the great change that came when in 1890 the seer, revelator,
and first president of the church, Wilford Woodruff, announced a
revelation prohibiting the contracting of further polygamous marriages. He stuck to reporting when he mentioned that for Mormons "Zion is to be built on this continent." He lost nothing of his
dispassion as he reported on the nonpolygamous Mormons, the
21,773 members of the Reorganized Church of Jesus Christ of
Latter Day Saints in Iowa and Missouri.

15:14   On the other hand, ecumenically benign historian Leonard
Woolsey Bacon lost his composure and poured vitriol on the
single page devoted to the church. "In its origin Mormonism is

distinctly American," he wrote, but "it is only incidentally that
the strange story of the Mormons . . . is connected with the history of American Christianity." It did please Bacon to be able to
point out that Europe, not America, was the best Mormon recruit-
ing ground. It was not the number of 150,000 members that made
this a body of fanatics formidable to the Republic. Rather he
blamed "the solidity with which they are compacted into a political, economical, religious, and, at need, military community,
handled at will by unscrupulous chiefs." Bacon spoke for the high
and cosmopolitan culture as he dismissed it as a "system of gross,
palpable imposture contrived by a disreputable adventurer." Its
history was pitiable, dramatic, and tragic.

15:15   As for the insiders of the kingdom, the Saints saw the period
from 1887 to 1896 as a turning point. In 1887 the Edmunds-
Tucker Act was designed to demolish the public and political aspects of the Mormon church. It dissolved the legal corporation of
the Church of Jesus Christ of Latter-day Saints. The federal government arrested church leaders in the late 1880s over the polygamy issue, but the arrests produced heroes and martyrs to the
cause. Not until the Woodruff declaration, called the Manifesto,
abolished plural marriage, were Utah lobbyists free to make their
patriotic case in Washington. The continued appeal to Mormon
millennialism now was less offensive because, unlike polygamy,
this millennialism was not unique; it could be stated vaguely that
this church, too, only expected some sort of Kingdom of God on
earth. On January 4, 1896, Utah became a state.

15:16   A church built on progressive revelation had no trouble with
the Zeitgeist, so on New Year's Day, 1901, President Lorenzo
Snow greeted the century in language that matched modernist
Protestantism's. "The lessons of the past century should have prepared us for the duties and glories of the opening era. It ought to
be the age of peace, of greater progress, of the universal adoption
of the golden rule." Now the barbarism of the past should be buried and "the welfare of humanity should be studied instead of the
enrichment of a race or the extension of an empire." No more than
mainstream Protestantism with its Jesus-centered universalism
was this a merely general language. It still spoke for a cognitive
minority, people who partook of the diffuse national life with a
different interpretation for every act of that life.

15:17   Mormons escaped the worst of the modernist traumas. Since
the church did not pin everything on an inerrant, closed canon,
biblical criticism was not as threatening there as it was in the or-

thodox bodies. Evolution was an issue decided on tactical, not theological grounds. When President George H. Brimhall lured professors from Chicago, Cornell, Harvard, and California to Brigham Young University, before 1910, they openly taught organic evolution. Yet it violated some of the sensibility that Mormon converts brought West with them, and in 1911 President Joseph F. Smith, without resort to dogma, reined them in: "In reaching the conclusion that evolution would best be left out of discussion in our Church schools, we are deciding a question of propriety and not undertaking to say how much of evolution is true or how much false." He did not want to see the rise of what he called a "theological scholastic aristocracy in the Church." Brimhall advised against too much speculation about the creation of the world. Manners and democracy determined an agenda where dogmatic decrees could not avail.

15:18   The public energies of Mormonism were designed to reassure the Saints that they really belonged in America and to assure onlookers of the same fact. The rite of passage which best demonstrated this was the Pioneer Jubilee of July 20–24, 1897. Typically it combined Latter-day Saint and American historical themes in a patriotic blend that was henceforth to characterize Mormon Fourth of July celebrations. Who more than the Mormons had a claim on the overland coaches, pony express souvenirs, pioneer cabins featured at the jubilee? There was by now even room and time for some eclecticism including a "wild east" show in the wild west, a show featuring Sie Hassan Ben Ali and his Bedouin Arab gymnasts. The Mormons enjoyed Indian war dances, balloon ascensions, parachute jumps, baseball, fireworks, and the requisite "Pageant of Progress." Here was a more-than-American America as portrayed by what had once been a kingdom half-poised against America.

15:19   The Mormons were now at home with an America that remained ill at ease with less cause against these patriots. It was hard to make a case against the Saints who as newcomers to the Union at least reluctantly supported the Spanish-American War. The Council of the Twelve member Brigham Young, Jr., was even told to cease and desist from opposing that war by the First Presidency of the Church, and a Mormon recruitment drive helped furnish troops.

15:20   When Elder Reed Smoot was elected to the United States Senate in 1903, Utah Gentiles linked with others to bring back all the Mormon anti-American charges. Smoot was accused of condoning plural marriages, among other charges that preoccupied the first three years of his three decades in the Senate. By then, however, some Gentiles were beginning to moderate their criticism of Mormons and turn some on themselves. Thus one notable said during the Smoot hearings that he "preferred a polygamist that didn't polyg," like Smoot, "to a monogamist that didn't monog."

15:21   In April of 1907, the First Presidency was ready with a widely publicized *An Address: The Church of Jesus Christ of Latter-day Saints to the World*. It affirmed true Americanism and patriotic loyalty while it renounced all quasi-political notions of a kingdom. So far as the Saints in their house were concerned, the transition was complete. *Cosmopolitan* and *McClure's* in 1910 and 1911 built circulation by attacking Mormonism for a dream of attempting to take over America. Yet President and Mrs. William Howard Taft invited the Mormon Tabernacle Choir to the White House. The Saints had taken one more step toward national acceptability. Then in April, 1911, Theodore Roosevelt wrote a seal of approval in the form of a letter to *Collier's* defending the church. When the World War came it should have surprised no one that Utah church members went over the top in selling and buying Liberty Bonds and oversubscribed enlistment quotas. They had in two decades become superAmericans.

15:22   Other suspect groups also supported the public religion and the patriotic civic faith in crucial moments and thus moved further toward the American mainstream. The Spanish-American War, seen in retrospect as America's least plausible military encounter was accompanied by the most ambitious efforts to gain plausibility. It is thus in its own way a better test case or illustration than the more credible World War resistance. Because the enemy in the brief and small war of 1898 was Catholic, the course American Catholicism would take was closely observed. In a supplement to the Catholic historian John Gilmary Shea's *The Cross and the Flag*, John L. MacDonald pointed out that more than half of the men who went down with the battleship *Maine* in Cuba—an act which hastened the onset of war—were Catholics. One-fourth to one-third of the military forces were Catholic, said MacDonald. "When we reflect that this war was one waged against a Catholic country . . . surely our non-Catholic brethren will not allow prejudice to prevent them from rising to a full appreciation of how grandly their Catholic fellow citizens have again given conclusive evidence that our country can always rely upon them."

15:23   Archbishop John Ireland saw the war as unnecessary, which

Catholicism, long excluded from power, came into its own with leaders like James Cardinal Gibbons. Here he joins President McKinley and Admiral George Dewey in prayer at the Capitol in Washington after the Spanish-American War. (Courtesy of the Library of Congress.)

meant that it did not pass all the historic criteria for a just war. He should as a Catholic have opposed it. Yet Ireland greeted the war in a sermon in which he claimed to see God assigning at that moment "to this republic the mission of putting before the world the ideal of popular liberty, the ideal of the high elevation of all humanity." When the war came, James Cardinal Gibbons offered at once that Catholics in the United States have but one sentiment. Aware that "the eyes of the world are upon us," and that he belonged to a nation "too brave, too strong, too powerful, and too just to engage in an unrighteous or precipitate war," he justified this one. "Whatever may have been their opinions as to the expediency of the war, now that it is on," the Catholics, he said, "are united in upholding the government."

15:24   Immigrant Catholicism used the same kind of chance that the Confederacy had had to show that it led in patriotism. Maine state deputy John F. Crowley of the Knights of Columbus acknowledged that there had been differing attitudes, but at the declaration of war all personal opinions as to the wisdom of a course were forgotten. Catholics, in the spirit of Holy Church, showed themselves to be "always ready to sacrifice everything for our Faith and Country." Their participation, he pointed out, refuted cheap agitators whose only principle was hatred of Catholics and who, although professing ardent love for America and American institutions, flew to the woods whenever danger threatened the flag they professed to love so much.

15:25   It was true that after four hundred years some Protestants still nurtured the Black Legend of Spanish cruelty and corruption and looked for a chance to wage war against Spain. Thus the *Advance* linked the tensions of the year 1898 to cosmic history itself. "The Fatherhood of God which broods over the great nations, nurturing and cherishing all good hope and progress, also broods over the islands of the sea." This Providence "which has worked to weaken this relentless power will work until its cruel grasp upon its last victim has been unloosed." *The Christian and Missionary Alliance* was one of scores of journals whose editors kept up the anti-Catholic theme. "God is stronger than either the Romish Church or the Catholic powers of Europe," but soon Cuba and far eastern isles, the Philippines, would be the scenes of Gospel triumphs and the salvation of countless souls.

15:26   The Spanish-American War, then, came to be linked by Protestants with their missionary venture to civilize and convert the world. The Presbyterian *Interior* in 1898 looked beyond the

Philippines and foresaw change in China as a supreme missionary opportunity. There could be heard "the ringing of the bell of Divine Providence calling upon those who have the gospel of the world's salvation to see and to seize this new, this august opportunity for preaching it in a world-empire that has so long been waiting for it." That year the World's Parliament of Religions leader, John H. Barrows, at Union Theological Seminary in New York, lectured on how God had placed America like Israel of old in the center of nations. With Asia ready to wake out of sleep, he continued, "wherever on pagan shores the voice of the American missionary and teacher is heard, there is fulfilled the manifest destiny of the Christian Republic."

15:27   To such Protestants victory over Catholic Spain meant an obligation to evangelize, to bring the Gospel as if for the first time. The Baptist *Union* projected the little war onto a big screen: "In the divine administration the election and separation of a people to peculiar privilege has always been with a view to the wider diffusion of blessing." Even the Baptist *Standard*, a more reluctant participant in expansion, began to publish writers on the "imperialism of righteousness." Some Methodist periodicals did remain anti-imperial, but all supported the new missions. And the Presbyterian Church in the United States supported a periodical that hooked the ventures to progress: "The Great Ruler of the nations is able to use this conflict for the furtherance of his purposes, so that the ultimate issue may be the progress of his kingdom."

15:28   America should keep the blood-bought Philippines as a duty in the interest of human freedom and Christian progress, said the Presbyterian *Interior* in a language that most of the Protestant press supported. Its editors saw no way that America could become an oppressor. It was only an agent of providential emancipation. In respect to the Philippines, the Congregationalist *Advance* urged that "morally and religiously, we should not shun an opportunity to lift up a barbarous people." It asked, "Who knows but that this is a plan of Providence to bring the land favored of God and flowing with religious speech into touch with a land in need of the Gospel?" The Episcopal Board of Missions credited Providence for the move into the Pacific islands of "American civilization and American ideals and institutions, with American power to uphold and extend them." Soon "we shall have no more talk of *foreign* missions, for every Christian man, in every land, will realize that humanity is one, as Christ is one."

15:29   Such a holistic approach was treated with suspicion by some

Catholics who wanted to remind their neighbors that many of these subjects of future mission were already Christian. The *Ave Maria* was sardonic as it recalled how Protestants had by invading Hawaii robbed a widow woman of her domain. "The unfortunate people of Manila will remember Dewey's bombardment as a restful holiday compared with the times that will come if the preachers ever invade the Philippines, bringing divorce and sundry other things with them." The *Catholic World* was finally reassured: "Spanish America may be wicked and irreligious, but it will never be Protestant." So Catholics should be sent to reform it.

15:30   While Methodists and others were of two minds about the war of 1898 in the imperial scheme, only Quakers and Unitarians presented voices of peace and criticism of missionary expansion. The Unitarians' *Christian Register* stressed commercialism. There was a smokescreen. Millions of dollars would be wasted on showy missionary ventures when it was all really being prosecuted "for the benefit of our manufactures and our commerce." Self-control was both needed and lacking. The editor wrote: "As Washington refused to be king, so must America refuse to join the partnership of the giants, who are dividing among themselves the spoils of the half-civilized world." Such voices from small denominations stood little chance of being heard.

15:31   America's public religion draws on but has never been confined to churchly support, and, indeed, is a form of faith that lives alongside churchly expression. While advocates of civil religion like to point to its prophets named Franklin and Washington, Jefferson and Madison, Melville and Emerson, and, supremely, Lincoln, there is a priestly advocacy with which to reckon as well. Never has that been clearer than when presidents of both parties, McKinley and Roosevelt and Wilson most of all, spoke up in imperial terms. President William McKinley, whose policies had helped bring on the Spanish-American War, anticipated Wilsonian language. McKinley told how he paced White House halls toward midnight until God answered his prayers. There was "nothing left for us to do," he said, but to take up the cause, and then "to educate the Filipinos, and uplift and civilize and Christianize them, and by God's grace do the very best we could by them as our fellow-men for whom Christ also died."

15:32   The literary, political, and academic communities also came through with religious language to promote the general civic faith. While there were critics, many brought Anglo-Saxon racism and old-fashioned Social Darwinism to bear on the cause. Editor

Whitelaw Reid in the *New York Herald Tribune* argued that "the American people is in lawful possession of the Philippines, with the assent of all Christendom." Senator W. A. Peffer said of the war that "God must have intended that savage life and customs should yield to higher standards of living, or he would have made the earth many times larger." Best known was Senator Albert J. Beveridge, who thought that the opportunity for new territory was part of a law of history not to be denied. "The American Republic is a part of the movement of a race,—the most masterful race of history,—and race movements are not to be stayed by the hand of man. They are mighty answers to Divine commands. Their leaders are not only statesmen of peoples—they are prophets of God." One welcomes glimpses of humor from those who pricked pride— literary artists, or, on occasion, members of the Anti-Imperialist League. In the *Arena*, for instance, after he had been sent to help quell the rebels who were with Aguinaldo, a Negro soldier was quoted: "Dis shyar white man's burden ain't all its cracked up to be."

15:33   Since race and religion were fused, the Spaniards of Cuba and the Philippines had to be rediscovered as "browns." As yet there was no common sense of opposing white imperialism. Blacks could be ambivalent as Americans, Christians, and minorities. Bishop W. J. Gaines of the African Methodist Episcopal Church was ready to doff his cassock, don a uniform, and fight, because victory would enlarge work among Filipinos who are, "like us a colored people." Meanwhile the language of racism was still transmittable. Methodist chaplain George W. Prioleau, himself a black, urged readers of *The Colored American* to be prowar and for conquest. Americans, he said, must not allow "their indolence and laziness to retard American progress."

15:34   McKinley and Roosevelt joined the parade of priests in public religion, but when the Great War came, Woodrow Wilson most profoundly invoked its rhetoric. The son of a southern Presbyterian pastor, Wilson valued the cozier small-town values, but by the turn of the century he had already favored expansion and imperialism. "We are a sort of pure air blowing in world politics, destroying illusions and cleaning places of morbid miasmatic gases." Not to see American illusion while announcing the need to destroy illusion set Wilson up as a subject for all students of irony in American history. "The Anglo-Saxon people have undertaken to reconstruct the affairs of the world, and it would be a shame upon them to withdraw their hand." He could sound like historian Frederick Jackson Turner in praise of the frontier. "It was not an accident that we annexed the Philippines. We had to have a frontier; we got into the habit, and needed one. The characteristic American is an exploiter." Yet he tried to reach for a transcendent note in early twentieth-century speeches. America was great "not because of what she held in her hand but because of what she held in her heart, because of the visions she has seen." Here was the *restitutio ad integrum* in national terms: America would lose her greatness "if in her too sophisticated majority she forgets the visions of her youth." Wilson dedicated himself to his version of them. In a 1906 baccalaureate address at Princeton University, which he headed, Wilson asked individuals to help do what the country must, and then spoke of the "renewal of your minds," "refreshment," of a moral climate and landscape "purified," "undefiled," "pure," and "untainted."

15:35   Wilson reflexively and for political reasons kept specifically churchly and Christian themes in the center of philosophy and politics. In 1909 he balanced soul-saving and the social works of the church. "Christianity came into the world to save the world as well as to save individual men, and individual men can afford in conscience to be saved only as part of the process by which the world itself is regenerated," said the future president. When he became president of the nation he remained particular in his witness, as was his right: "If I were not a Christian, I think I should go mad." He was aware of a stern Covenanter tradition behind him in Presbyterianism; it impelled him morally, as he admitted, with "many an echo down the years." From this tradition he drew a passion for ordering and organizing life and took great pleasure, he said, in writing constitutions. Wilson combined that organicist sense with an often uncritical view of his own rectitude. In that interest of peace and the hope of order he led America to a fateful war for democracy.

15:36   His sometime rival, sometime supporter, and, for a time, peace-minded secretary of state, William Jennings Bryan, through his career reveals how one need not be president to contribute to American public religion. A religious conservative, between 1896 and 1920 Bryan was best known as a perennial presidential candidate, and then as a stemwinding moralistic speaker for interests of farmers and westerners who felt left out by eastern urban sophisticates. In the imperial age he wanted to separate the Gospel from warfare: " 'Go ye into all the world and preach the gospel to every creature,' has no gatling gun attachment." Bryan took into the

Racism was not subtle at a time when William Jennings Bryan, opposing expansionism in 1900, was pictured by *Judge* alongside an Asian and an African.

public order a personal piety formed at his parents' knees and called it "applied Christianity." Such application could be missionary, for, he asked, "if truth must, according to eternal law, triumph," how could it triumph over lower ideals unless it is brought into contact with them? If the Christian ideal was worthy to be followed in America, it was worthy to be presented in every land.

15:37   Though Bryan first opposed the war against Spain in 1898, he was ready to take up arms as soon as the fighting started. Between wars, however, Theodore Roosevelt disdained him for attracting what Roosevelt called "professional pacifists, the flubdubs and the mollycoddles." He accepted from Wilson the secretary of state post and found himself in an impossible situation as Wilson moved from neutrality to Allied support, and he had to resign. When war came he again immediately if regretfully fell into line and tried also to turn the trauma into crusade. "Gladly would I have given my life to save my country from war, but now that my country has gone to war, gladly will I give my life to aid it." When peace came again, he worked strenuously for international peace even while he helped divide American Protestantism as the best-known lay figure in the new decade's modernist-fundamentalist war. Meanwhile, however, Bryan's turns show how war was the great ecumenical force that helped diminish conflict between farm and city, West or South and East, conservative and liberal.

15:38   Sometimes an outsider, who was neither a Jew nor a believing Christian, might be expected to bring a critical voice, but seekers

William Jennings Bryan, briefly serving in Wilson's cabinet, came as close as a secretary of state would or could to being a pacifist in 1914–15. William Henry Walker made fun of it all in *Life*, November 11, 1915. Bryan is singing "I didn't raise my boy to be a soldier." (William Henry Walker Archive, Princeton University Library.)

of peace like Andrew Carnegie, the tycoon who saw himself as an agnostic, also saw his peace efforts collapse into wartime ideology. While organizing a Church Peace Union that he helped fund, Carnegie challenged: "If Christians were all one, in one Church, of one mind, and all the power now used in rivalry with each other unitedly [were] directed against the evils of the world, intemperance, war, poverty, ignorance, superstition and disease—they could all soon be banished." He wanted to include Catholics and Jews in his proposed Church Peace Union. The Federal Council of Churches, however, dominated trustee posts and the two priests, one rabbi, the Universalist and the Unitarian, along with a lay Catholic and a Jew played little part in it. On August 1, 1914, the CPU held a largely Protestant International Peace Conference of Churches at Constance, Germany. A week later there was to have been a clerical follow-up in Liege, Belgium. The World War, on Belgian soil, intervened. Three years later the CPU became an instrument of United States war propaganda.

15:39   More radical questioning came from the Fellowship of Reconciliation, organized on a Quaker base in 1915. It tried to get along without a complex bureaucracy or large conferences. Henry T. Hodgkin, a founder, went against the spirit of the times as he warned that "big visions are very dangerous, unless we start at once to work them out in little things." Yet Rufus Jones and other pacific leaders had big visions, because war, Jones said, was not "the only form of evil which is inconsistent with the spirit of the kingdom." While war was then the most vivid horror, the ministry of reconciliation had to apply the remedial force of love to every feature of the social life of fellow humans everywhere. As war came, the pioneers warned that social progress would be arrested for years to come. Harry F. Ward and Norman Thomas, extreme theological liberals, helped start *The New World* to chide their fellow-citizens. "It is not . . . Anti-Christ in Europe which concerns the sober American half so much as Anti-Christ in his own country and his own city." This kind of language was too strong for the mainstream clergy, most of whom had dropped out of pacifist causes by 1918.

15:40   Wilson, reelected in 1916 because he kept America out of war, knew that it was "a fearful thing to lead this peaceful people into war, into the most terrible and disastrous of all wars," but lead it he must and did. The churches fell into line. The Catholic archbishops on April 18, 1917, twelve days into the war, said that their people, as ever, would rise as one person to serve the nation. This despite the fact that among the American Irish there were anti-British impulses and among the Germans in American Catholicism there was original reluctance to fight Germany. Both national groups fell into line, just as the Germans did in the Lutheran constituency in America. When the war ended, Gibbons made his contribution to the rhetoric of public religion. "We have conquered because we have fought for the eternal principles of truth and because we realize that our hope and our dependence, our trust and our success, repose in Him who is alike the God of battles and of justice." Only four of 3,989 registered conscientious objectors during the war had been listed as Catholic, and not a single priest was visible in pacifist ranks.

15:41   To see how unsafe criticism of the war was, the case of the International Bible Students' Association, later called Jehovah's Witnesses, is instructive. The Russellites, as they were called, had always chosen to stand completely outside the civil and religious consensus. Still a small group in 1917, they were rendered suspect by those who did not understand their apocalyptic message. Charles Taze Russell made the mistake of publishing an idiosyncratic *The Finished Mystery*, which looked subversive. It argued that patriotism was never licensed by the New Testament, that killing in every form, including military killing, was simply forbidden. Yet, it went on, "under the guise of patriotism civil governments of the earth demand of peace-loving men the sacrifice of themselves and their loved ones and the butchery of their fellows, and hail it as a duty demanded by the laws of heaven." Three years earlier any cleric could have said this. Now the clergy turned against the Russellites and cheered to hear that twenty-year sentences were to be imposed upon convicted Jehovah's Witnesses leaders. When they were freed after the war, there were no cheers by the orthodox church members. The Russellites stood alone for having violated consensus to the point that they antagonized the federal government over their religion.

15:42   Prowar statements by religious leaders, especially in Protestantism, kept up the missionary themes. The Congregational church's American Board set out a fund appeal that had parallels in most denominations, so far as language was concerned. "Our soldiers and sailors are preparing 'The Way of the Lord.' They are 'making straight in the desert the highway for our God.' . . . *We Must Win the War to Win the World.*" Popular novelist Harold Bell Wright interrupted his fiction writing to tell *American Magazine* readers that a "thirty-centimeter gun may voice the edict of God as truly as the notes of a cooing dove." This Disciples of Christ minister added that "the sword of America is the sword of Jesus." University of Chicago New Testament professor Ernest De Witt Burton, urging that the Germans would profit from the defeat of their armies, saw the Allied effort as obedience to the Golden Rule. Henry B. Wright of Yale Divinity School coauthored a YMCA tract which argued that the American nation was attempting to "Christianize every phase of a righteous war waged to save the very life of democracy."

15:43   America was losing its innocence in an effort to reclaim the purity and innocence that came with its founding. Such at least was the war aim as argued by religious leaders who paradoxically wanted to use the most deadly, divisive instrument—war—hoping or claiming to bring wholeness to a world. What missionaries would not accomplish, war might, in the effort to overcome the disruptions of barbarism and the conflict of nations. The Anglo-Saxon race and nations with their churches had a vision of the whole that was not yet to be denied. Modernity had brought corrupting influences and materialist selfishness. War was a purifier, and the sacrifice of blood in a national cause was both ennobling, healing, and uniting. The world would be safe for democracy, peace would come, and religious America would take its place at last as the conscience and example and unifier of the world.

Conclusion:
On Ironic
Interpretation

Historical narrative takes life from its interpretative aspects, be these conscious or not, explicit or not. An ironic interpretation informs this story of late nineteenth- and early twentieth-century American religion. At this turn toward the proposed second volume, which will address the next three decades, the author quite naturally is moved to review the perspective and plot. In a bold question addressed to the self, this comes down to: "Am I ready to 'go' with this ironic vision?"

To exclude interpretation as much as possible would leave the author and readers lost amid hundreds of religious groups and thousands of events and movements. To interpret without awareness would be a sign of the author's confusion or lack of reflection and would leave readers busy guessing. To overinterpret would mean forcing complex events into distorting molds. Thus to suggest that all things religious enacted by all citizens at all times lead to ironic outcomes would risk trivializing their endeavors and the concept of irony alike.

What, one asks, are the alternatives? American religion in this period includes comic, pathetic, and tragic dimensions, but the ironic understanding best addresses the varieties of intentions and outcomes. An author is free to discern or impose any number of themes or plots, but this one emerged persistently during research and out of the particulars of the cases. That it was *congruent with the author's general outlook on history is a fact that would surprise no one who knows how history gets written. Awareness of this also served to restrain me from over-interpreting.*

One can assume a transcendent viewpoint and say that all human endeavor is subject to irony in retrospect, because hindsight reveals that no outcomes ever quite match intentions, that all events make some sort of mockery of the promise and fitness of things. Such an approach may be theologically valid, but it would allow for no scaling of human expression and achievement. Similarly, one can say that all periods of American history, from the discovery by an unwitting Columbus through the projections of witting Puritans, down to the present are open to such interpretation. The theistic and deistic outlooks that informed the nation's prime agents contribute to this possibility. Yet the particular intentions of leaders in the imperial and progressive age stand out in this respect.

Other nations also live with ironies, even if their religions are not theistic or deistic; one thinks, for example, of Japan. The claim here is not that this nation, this period, and this religious complex are in all ways unique but that they are distinctive and that the distinctiveness bears exposure to view.

Conflict replaces irony as the major theme in the next three decades, yet ironic legacies from this earlier period will color the stories that will follow. While I have resisted the impulse to follow consquences beyond about 1920, it is possible now to look ahead and say that as a result of these "early modern" activities there have been legacies and continuities. In respect to the five parts of this book, thus, subsequently:

Whenever religious modernists confused their plausible and humane endeavors with facile expectations that their progressivism would prevail, they have found themselves almost instantly dated, dismissed as prematurely obsolete.

Whenever academic, literary, intellectual, and other culturally active moderns have set out to repudiate tradition, sacrality, transcendence, and ecclesial forms, their critics and legatees have found surprising revisitations of what the moderns thought they were leaving behind.

Whenever ethnicity has been bonded with religion to screen people from the amalgamating and assimilating processes of modernity, these antimoderns have been finally frustrated by the pervasive changes "Americanism" worked with its own lures. At the same time, such bonded people have clung to their separate sets of ways more than the amalgamators or assimilators expected they would or could.

Whenever religious conservatives, the countermoderns, *reacted to modernity and its changes, their responses have turned out not to be merely conservative but innovatively reactive. They have been seen as inventors of new, particular, competitive "old-time religions." At the same time, they have frustrated modernizers who expected more uniform adaptations by all to the presumed trend and spirit of the time.*

Whenever holistic-minded agents have sought to be of service by going transmodern, *restoring and retrieving models of wholeness from the individual and social past, they have been perceived as being merely modern innovators. Far from being integrators of much of life, as they hoped they might be, they came to be contributors to the very fragmented and differentiated life they abhorred.*

The five "whenever's," however, are too bald, too rigid or deterministic, too fateful. Replace each with "ordinarily, when . . ." because the ironic, as opposed to the tragic, interpretation, has to be seen as other than simply fated. Otherwise, ironically, they would end the possibility of ironic interpretation, which depends upon some measures of human possibility and enterprise. Irony, especially in the religious sphere, depends upon some measure of freedom and permits meaningful activity in response to the sacred, the divine, the gods, or God. Thus its perspective allows for not only human folly but also for enhancement of the humane; in this case, the humane in respect to modern American religion.

Notes

Chapter One

1:1. Richard McKeon, ed., *The Basic Works of Aristotle* (New York: Random House, 1941), 8.

1:2. Paul Tillich, *Systematic Theology*, 3 vols. (Chicago: University of Chicago Press, 1951–63), 1:193.

1:3. On mapping, see Arthur H. Robinson and Barbara Bartz Petchenik, *The Nature of Maps: Essays toward Understanding Maps and Mapping* (Chicago: University of Chicago Press, 1976), 4. On space, see Tillich, *Systematic Theology*, 1:194–95.

1:4. A widely noted anthropological definition of religion appears in Clifford Geertz, *The Interpretation of Cultures: Selected Essays by Clifford Geertz* (New York: Basic Books, 1973), 87–125, especially 90. On substance, see Tillich, *Systematic Theology*, 1: 197–98.

1:5. For a summary of theories about religious decline and evidences from Europe, see S. S. Acquaviva, *The Decline of the Sacred in Industrial Society*, trans. Patricia Lipscomb (New York: Harper and Row, 1979).

1:6. Ernest Gellner, "Mohammed and Modernity," a review of Daniel Pipes, *In the Path of God: Islam and Political Power* (New York: Basic Books, 1983), which asserts the conventional wisdom; in *The New Republic* (5 December 1983): 22–23.

1:7. McKeon, *Basic Works of Aristotle*, 23, 27.

1:8. *Oxford English Dictionary*, s.v. "irony." On literary irony, see Wayne C. Booth, *The Rhetoric of Irony* (Chicago: University of Chicago Press, 1974); Douglas C. Muecke, *The Compass of Irony* (London: Methuen, 1969); Norman Knox, *The Word Irony and Its Context, 1500–1755* (Durham, N.C.: Duke University Press, 1961).

1:9. *Oxford English Dictionary*, s.v. "irony"; Gene Wise, *American Historical Explanations* (Homewood, Ill.: Dorsey Press, 1973), 300.

1:10. See Hayden White, *Metahistory: The Historical Imagination in Nineteenth-Century Europe* (Baltimore: Johns Hopkins University Press, 1973); Richard Reinitz, *Irony and*

Consciousness: American Historiography and Reinhold Niebuhr's Vision (Lewisburg, Pa.: Bucknell University Press, 1980); Reinhold Niebuhr, *The Irony of American History* (New York: Charles Scribner's Sons, 1952).

1:11. On understanding and pre-understanding, *Verständnis* and *Vorverständnis*, as understood by the major proponents of these concepts as they relate to history, see Michael Ermarth, *Wilhelm Dilthey: The Critique of Historical Reason* (Chicago: University of Chicago Press, 1978), 241–322, and Theodore Plantinga, *Historical Understanding in the Thought of Wilhelm Dilthey* (Toronto: University of Toronto Press, 1980), 98–121, especially 113–14.

1:12. Reinitz, *Irony and Consciousness*, 178, summarizes these four major categories of illusion in American life; he also calls attention to Perry Miller, 88. See further, David Noble, *Historians Against History: The Frontier Thesis and the National Covenant in American Historical Writing Since 1830* (Minneapolis: University of Minnesota Press, 1965).

1:13. On Parkman, Adams, and Hofstadter, see Reinitz, *Irony and Consciousness*, 70–71, 85–86, 74–75, 131–47.

1:14. Muecke, *The Compass of Irony*, 14; Samuel Hynes, *The Pattern of Hardy's Poetry* (Chapel Hill, N.C.: University of North Carolina Press, 1969), 41–42; on Burckhardt, see White, *Metahistory*, 230–64.

1:15. White, *Metahistory*, 433.

1:16. Ibid., xii, 38.

1:17. Reinitz, *Irony and Consciousness*, 19, 23, 28–29, 37.

1:18. Niebuhr, *The Irony of American History*, 155; on "atheists for Niebuhr," see June Bingham, *Courage to Change: An Introduction to the Life and Thought of Reinhold Niebuhr* (New York: Charles Scribner's Sons, 1960), 360.

1:19. Niebuhr, *The Irony of American History*, 153, viii.

1:20. Frederick A. Olafson, *The Dialectic of Action: A Philosophical Interpretation of History and the Humanities* (Chicago: University of Chicago Press, 1979), 36–37, 165; see also D. C. Muecke, *Irony and the Ironic* (London: Methuen, 1970), 52.

1:21. John Murray Cuddihy, *The Ordeal of Civility: Freud, Marx, Lévi-Strauss, and the Jewish Struggle with Modernity* (New York: Basic Books, 1974), 9.

1:22. On hurricane-measuring devices, see Marc Stern, "New Sky Spies for Killer Hurricanes," *Popular Mechanics* 158 (August 1982): 65–66, 102–3.

1:23. On the fourth aspect, the scholar's personal involvement, see the eloquent passage beginning, "I am an impure thinker . . . ," Eugen Rosenstock-Huessy, *I Am An Impure Thinker* (Norwich, Vt.: Argo Books, 1970), 2.

1:24. Jacob Burckhardt, *Force and Freedom: An Interpretation of History*, ed. James Hastings Nichols (New York: Meridian Books, 1955), 72; Robert F. Berkhofer, Jr., *A Behavioral Approach to Historical Analysis* (New York: The Free Press, 1969), 271–72, 277–78, 317–20, helpfully discusses complexity of narrative sequences and styles. Wayne A. Meeks, *The First Urban Christians: The Social World of the Apostle Paul* (New Haven: Yale University Press, 1983), ix, suggests the validity of synthesis based on monographs.

1:25. On the problems of dealing with the more recent past, see H. Stuart Hughes, "Is Contemporary History Real History?" in his *History as Art and as Science: Twin Vistas on the Past* (New York: Harper and Row, 1964), 89–90, 93, 95. See also Martin E. Marty, *A Nation of Behavers* (Chicago: University of Chicago Press, 1976), 1–17.

1:26. Ernest Gellner, *Thought and Change* (Chicago: University of Chicago Press, 1964), 123.

1:27. E. J. Hobsbawm, *The Age of Revolution, 1789–1848* (Cleveland: World Publishing, 1962), 29.

1:28. Further illustration of the appropriateness of beginning with 1893 in reference to the parliament, Turner, Strong, and Carroll will appear in the next chapter.

1:29. *Oxford English Dictionary*, s.v. "modern"; see Christopher Lasch, "Experiment and Resistance," *Times Literary Supplement* (25 May 1984): 574.

1:30. Lasch was reviewing Peter Conn, *The Divided Mind: Ideology and Imagination in America, 1898–1917* (Cambridge: Cambridge University Press, 1983).

1:31. A searching criticism of assumptions behind uses of modernization theory in religious studies, one which this book takes into account, is Mary Douglas, "The Effects of Modernization on Religious Change," in Mary Douglas and Steven Tipton, eds., *Religion and America: Spiritual Life in a Secular Age* (Boston: Beacon Press, 1983), 25–43.

1:32. An influential discussion of social history in respect to intellectual and narrative history appears in Lawrence Stone, *The Past and the Present* (Boston: Routledge and Kegan Paul, 1981); see especially 3–44 and 74–96.

1:33. A history of rhetoric differs from but is influenced by "rhetorical criticism," which is usefully summarized by George A. Kennedy, *New Testament Interpretation Through Rhetorical Criticism* (Chapel Hill, N.C.: University of North Carolina Press, 1984), especially 3–38.

1:34. Paul Crawford, "The Farmer Assesses His Role in Society," in Paul H. Boase, ed., *The Rhetoric of Protest and Reform, 1878–1898* (Athens, Ohio: Ohio University Press, 1980), especially 102–3. Crawford cites and I have employed insights from, among others, Lloyd F. Bitzer, "The Rhetorical Situation," *Philosophy and Rhetoric* 1 (January 1968): 1–14; Leland M. Griffin, "The Rhetoric of Historical Movements," *Quarterly Journal of Speech* 38 (April 1952): 184–88; and Herbert Simons, "Requirements, Problems, and Strategies: A Theory of Persuasion for Social Movements," *Quarterly Journal of Speech* 56 (February 1970): 1–11.

1:35. On forensic versus empirical quotations, see David Hackett Fischer, *Historians' Fallacies: Toward a Logic of Historical Thought* (New York: Harper and Row, 1970), 286–87.

1:36. Gellner, *Thought and Change*, 124.

1:37. On "moderns" and "modern consciousness," see the typical subtitle of John Carlos Rowe, *Henry Adams and Henry James: The Emergence of a Modern Consciousness* (Ithaca, N.Y.: Cornell University Press, 1976). See also E. J. Hobsbawm, *Primitive Rebels: Studies in Archaic Forms of Social Movement in the 19th and 20th Centuries* (New York: Praeger, 1959), 108.

1:38. This concept of bonding to withstand modernity is influenced by the chapter on religion and, indeed, by the whole argument in Harold R. Isaacs, *Idols of the Tribe: Group Identity and Political Change* (New York: Harper and Row, 1975), 144–70. See also the discussion of religion as compartmentalization in Robert H. Wiebe, *The Segmented Society: An Introduction to the Meaning of America* (New York: Oxford University Press, 1975), 30–33, 42–46.

1:39. Cuddihy, *The Ordeal of Civility*, 10, discusses more radical versions of this phenomenon as "antimodernism," "demodernization," and "dedifferentiation," in response to what Peter Gay has called "The Hunger for Wholeness: Trials of Modernity"; see Peter Gay, *Weimar Culture: The Outsider as Insider* (New York: Harper and Row, 1968), 70–101. Gay reuses this concept in "Weimar Culture: The Outsider as Insider," in Donald Fleming and Bernard Bailyn, eds., *The Intellectual Migration: Europe and America, 1930–1960* (Cambridge, Mass.: Belknap Press, 1969), 49–54.

Chapter Two

2:1. George A. Gordon, *The Christ of To-Day* (Boston: Houghton Mifflin, 1895), 20, 28–29.

2:2. David F. Burg, *Chicago's White City of 1893* (Lexington, Ky.: University of Kentucky Press, 1976), 100–108 accounts for opening day and includes remarks by Davis. For contexts, see also Reid Badger, *The Great American Fair: The World's Columbian Exposition and American Culture* (Chicago: Nelson-Hall, 1979), and Jeanne Madeline Weimann, *The Fair Women* (Chicago: Academy Chicago, 1981).

2:3. George Dana Boardman, *The Parliament of Religions: An Address before the Philadelphia Conference of Baptist Ministers, October 23, 1893* (Philadelphia: National Baptist Printing Agency, 1893), 5.

2:4. Rev. Mr. Wendte of Oakland, California, reported on the personnel and garb; see John Henry Barrows, ed., *The World's Parliament of Religions: An Illustrated and Popular Story of the World's First Parliament of Religions, Held in Chicago in Connection with the Columbian Exposition of 1893*, 2 vols. (Chicago: Parliament Publishing Company, 1893), 1:62, 64.

2:5. William R. Alger, "How to Achieve Religious Unity," in Barrows, *The World's Parliament of Religions*, 2:1313.

2:6. Paul Carus, "Science a Religious Revelation," in Barrows, *The World's Parliament of Religions*, 2:980–81; see also Paul Carus, "The Dawn of a New Religious Era," *Forum* 16 (November 1893): 388–96.

2:7. Charles Carroll Bonney's addresses appear in Barrows, *The World's Parliament of Religions*, 2:1488; 1:67, 72. Müller is quoted by Burg, *Chicago's White City*, 285.

2:8. Mary Eleanor Barrows, *John Henry Barrows: A Memoir* (Chicago: Fleming H. Revell, 1904), 162.

2:9. Barrows, *The World's Parliament of Religions*, 2:1579, 1568, 1572.

2:10. Billy Sunday is quoted in Jacob Henry Dorn, *Washington Gladden* (Columbus: Ohio State University Press, 1966), 388. Kenten Druyvesteyn, "The World's Parliament of Religions" (Ph.D. diss., University of Chicago, 1976), 124–29, 132, cites *Minutes* of the General Assembly of the Presbyterian Church and various writings of Arthur Tappan Pierson against the parliament.

2:11. Reports on the denominational congresses make up part 4 of Barrows, *The World's Parliament of Religions*, 2:1383–1544.

2:12. Josiah Strong, "The Evangelical Alliance Congress," in Barrows, *The World's Parliament of Religions*, 2:1442–43, 1448.

2:13. Josiah Strong, *The New Era or the Coming Kingdom* (New York: Baker and Taylor, 1893), 35–36, 54–80, on the Anglo-Saxon race's comparative achievements; especially 74 for the five "greatest's" cited here.

2:14. Strong, *The New Era*, 79, 348, 354.

Chapter Three

3:1. On modernism, see William R. Hutchison, *The Modernist Impulse in American Protestantism* (Cambridge: Harvard University Press, 1976).

3:2. Two works on liberalism also discuss the modernist element: Lloyd J. Averill, *American Theology in the Liberal Tradition* (Philadelphia: Westminister Press, 1967), and Kenneth Cauthen, *The Impact of American Religious Liberalism* (New York: Harper and Row, 1962). Averill divides between "evangelical liberals" and "empirical modernists," and restricts the term "modernist" to postwar figures; Cauthen includes "modernistic liberalism" alongside "evangelical liberalism" under the category of "liberalism," while Hutchison includes some liberals in the rubric of "modernism." For our purposes, the term "modernist" is generic, and includes both kinds of adapters.

3:3. George Harris, "The Rational and Spiritual Verification of Christian Doctrine," *Christian Union* 27 (June 14, 1883): 471; quoted in Hutchison, *The Modernist Impulse*, 102.

3:4. Gerald Birney Smith, ed., *A Guide to the Study of the Christian Religion* (Chicago: University of Chicago Press, 1916), 570.

3:5. William Adams Brown, *The Essence of Christianity: A Study in the History of Definition* (New York: Charles Scribner's Sons, 1902), 6–7, 11.

3:6. Frank Hugh Foster, *The Modern Movement in American Theology: Sketches in the History of American Protestant Thought from the Civil War to the World War* (New York: Fleming H. Revell, 1939), 144–45, 161, 185.

3:7. *Minister's Monthly* 2 (September 1923): 5–6; (October 1923), 3–5; cited by Hutchison, *The Modernist Impulse*, 3–4.

3:8. James Russell Parsons, Jr., *Professional Education*, from *Monographs on Education in the United States*, ed. Nicholas Murray Butler (St. Louis: Division of Exhibits, Department of Education, Universal Exposition, 1904), 2, 6–7, lists professional schools in 1899; the originally large theology school sector now grew more slowly compared to schools for law, medicine, dentistry, pharmacy, and veterinary science.

3:9. Washington Gladden, *How Much Is Left of the Old Doctrines? A Book for the People* (Boston: Houghton Mifflin, 1899), 1; Herbert Alden Youtz, *Democratizing Theology* (Boston: The Pilgrim Press, 1919), 13.

3:10. Josiah Strong, *The New Era or the Coming Kingdom* (New York: Baker and Taylor, 1893), 18, 20, 21–22.

3:11. Ibid., 130, 131.

3:12. Ibid., 6, 10.

3:13. Ibid., 234–36.

3:14. Ibid., 222.

3:15. Ibid., 81–113; see especially 113.

Chapter Four

4:1. Willett is quoted from a clipping of around 1905 in a scrapbook at the Disciples of Christ Historical Society in Nashville, Tennessee, in Ferenc Morton Szasz, *The Divided Mind of Protestant America, 1880–1930* (University, Ala.: University of Alabama Press, 1982), 26. Szasz's book is a helpful discussion of the themes of this chapter.

4:2. On Lamarckian evolution, see James R. Moore, *The Post-Darwinian Controversies: A Study of the Protestant Struggle to Come to Terms with Darwin in Great Britain and America, 1870–1900* (Cambridge: Cambridge University Press, 1979), 140–52. Moore's work is an important revisionist approach.

4:3. On the Lamarckian-Darwinian controversy in philosophical circles, see Elizabeth Flower and Murray G. Murphey, *A History of Philosophy in America*, 2 vols. (New York: G. P. Putnam's Sons, 1977), 2:524–38.

4:4. On Social Darwinism, which ought to be related more to Herbert Spencer than to Charles Darwin, see Richard Hofstadter, *Social Darwinism in American Thought* (Philadelphia: University of Pennsylvania Press, 1944), 24–30.

4:5. John Bascom, *Evolution and Religion; or, Faith as a Part of a Complete Cosmic System* (New York: G. P. Putnam's Sons, 1897), 10–16; for earlier citations from Bascom, see Moore, *The Post-Darwinian Controversies*, 223–24.

4:6. Joseph LeConte, *Evolution: Its Nature, Its Evidences, and Its Relation to Religious Thought*, rev. ed. (New York: D. Appleton, 1891), 8, 9–29, 258ff., 301, cited by Moore, *The Post-Darwinian Controversies*, 225.

4:7. Joseph LeConte, *The Autobiography of Joseph LeConte*, ed. William Dallam Armes (New York: D. Appleton, 1903), 17.

4:8. The trend in scholarship has been progressively to downplay the element of crisis; Moore wants to minimize the very notion of "the military metaphor" or consistent conflict between science and theology; see *The Post-Darwinian Controversy*, 19–122.

4:9. On the Woodrow incident and the *New York Times* dismissal of its significance in the north, see Szasz, *The Divided Mind*, 5–6. See also Ernest T. Thompson, *Presbyterians in the South*, 3 vols. (Richmond: John Knox, 1973), 2:457–90.

4:10. Moore, *The Post-Darwinian Controversies*, 226–27, cites Lyman Abbott, *The Evolution of Christianity* (Boston: Houghton Mifflin, 1892), 1, 3, 8–9, 246–47; *The Theology of an Evolutionist* (Boston: Houghton Mifflin, 1897), 10–15, 96, 176; and *Reminiscences* (Boston: Houghton Mifflin, 1915), 449–50, 458.

4:11. Newell Dwight Hillis, *The Influence of Christ in Modern Life, Being a Study of the New Problems of the Church in American Society* (New York: Macmillan, 1900), 211.

4:12. George Frederick Wright, "The Passing of Evolution," is in the series *The Fundamentals: A Testimony to the Truth*, 12 vols. (Chicago: Testimony Publishing, 1910–15), 7:9.

4:13. George M. Marsden, *Fundamentalism and American Culture: The Shaping of Twentieth-Century Evangelicalism, 1870–1925* (New York: Oxford University Press, 1980), 264–65, cites these from *The Fundamentals*, 9:23 and 8:67.

4:14. On eugenics, see Hamilton Cravens, *The Triumph of Evolution: American Scientists and the Heredity-Environment Controversy, 1900–1941* (Philadelphia: University of Pennsylvania Press, 1978), 46–53.

4:15. Szasz, *The Divided Mind*, 35, cites Crawford from Protestant Episcopal Church, *Papers and Speeches of the Church Congress* (New York, 1897), 104.

4:16. This item from *Public Opinion* 14 (1893): 333, is also cited by Szasz, *The Divided Mind*, 29.

4:17. William R. Hutchison, *The Modernist Impulse in American Protestantism* (New York: Oxford University Press, 1976), recounts the Briggs case, 91–94, and cites these references from Briggs's inaugural address of 1891 and from Charles A. Briggs, *Whither? A Theological Question for the Times* (New York: Charles Scribner's Sons, 1889); see ix–x, 6–22, and especially 21.

4:18. George Harris, *A Century's Change in Religion* (Boston: Houghton Mifflin, 1914), 65, 76–78, 84.

4:19. William Newton Clarke, *Sixty Years with the Bible: A Record of Experience* (New York: Charles Scribner's Sons, 1910), 199, 253–54; *An Outline of Christian Theology*, 12th ed. (New York: Charles Scribner's Sons, 1903), 22; William Adams Brown, *Modern Theology and the Preaching of the Gospel* (New York: Charles Scribner's Sons, 1914), 76ff.

4:20. George A. Gordon, *The New Epoch for Faith* (Boston: Houghton Mifflin, 1901), 171–73.

4:21. Henry Churchill King, *Reconstruction in Theology* (New York: Macmillan, 1901), 116, 118ff.

4:22. James P. Wind, "The Bible and the University: The Messianic Vision of William Rainey Harper" (Ph.D. diss., University of Chicago, 1983), 111–12.

4:23. William Rainey Harper, "Editorial," *The Biblical World* 2 (August 1893): 81; "The Rational and the Rationalistic Higher Criticism," *Chautauqua Assembly Herald* 17 (August 4, 1892): 2–3, 6–7; see Wind, "The Bible and the University," 114–17.

4:24. Wind, "The Bible and the University," 126, 128, 142, 145–47, cites various Harper writings from *The Biblical World* and *The Old and New Testament Student* between 1891 to 1909. The quote is from a letter to the Rev. G. D. Edwards dated February 11, 1905.

4:25. Wind, "The Bible and the University," 152, 174–75, 178–80, gathers these citations from editorial work of Harper through the years.

4:26. Upton Sinclair, *The Goose-Step: A Study of American Education*, rev. ed. (Los Angeles: Upton Sinclair, 1922), 240–41, 246–47, includes sarcastic references to Harper.

4:27. George F. Parker, *Recollections of Grover Cleveland* (New York: The Century Company, 1911), 382.

4:28. Hutchison, *The Modernist Impulse*, 257–87, discusses "The Odd Couple: Fundamentalism and Humanism in the Twenties"; I found a similar dismissal of modernism by secular intellectuals in the first two decades of the century.

4:29. Harold Bolce, "Christianity in the Crucible," *Cosmopolitan* 47 (1909): 315, 317.

4:30. John Horsch, *Modern Religious Liberalism: The Destructiveness and Irrationality of the New Theology* (Scottdale, Pa.: Fundamental Truth Depot, 1921), 249, 276–77.

4:31. Ibid., 289.

4:32. Ibid., 303.

4:33. Ibid., 317–18.

4:34. Ibid., 289–90.

Chapter Five

5:1. Martin E. Marty, *The Modern Schism: Three Paths to the Secular* (New York: Harper and Row, 1969), contrasts American patterns of change ("Controlled Secularity") with Continental and British styles of "Utter Secularity" and "Mere Secularity." This chapter reflects that tracing.

5:2. Typical of numerous works which show survivals and transformations of religious themes among "secular" intellectuals is R. Jackson Wilson, *In Quest of Community: Social Philosophy in the United States, 1860–1920* (New York: Oxford University Press, 1968), which includes reviews of religion in the career of all its major subjects, including Charles Sanders Peirce, James Mark Baldwin, Edward Alsworth Ross, Granville Stanley Hall, and Josiah Royce.

5:3. E. J. Hobsbawm, *Primitive Rebels: Studies in Archaic Forms of Social Movement in the 19th and 20th Centuries* (New York: Praeger, 1959), 108.

5:4. Carl L. Becker, *The Heavenly City of the Eighteenth-Century Philosophers* (New Haven: Yale University Press, 1932), 18–19.

5:5. John Higham, ed., *History* (Englewood Cliffs, N.J.: Prentice-Hall, 1965), for instance, treats Brooks Adams, Charles Francis Adams, Charles Kendall Adams, Ephraim D. Adams, George Burton Adams, Herbert Baxter Adams, and James Truslow Adams in addition to Henry Adams.

5:6. Edward Eggleston, "Books That Have Helped Me," *Forum* 3 (August 1887): 584–86.

5:7. On Turner's childhood faith and Wilson's chagrin, see Ray Allen Billington, *Frederick Jackson Turner: Historian, Scholar, Teacher* (New York: Oxford University Press, 1973), 424–25; "chagrin" quote from p. 152.

5:8. On the rejection of his childhood Calvinism, see the introduction by Harvey Wish to the paperback reprint of James Harvey Robinson, *The New History: Essays Illustrating the Modern Historical Outlook* (New York: Macmillan, 1912; reprint, The Free Press, 1965), vii.

5:9. Charles A. Beard, *The Industrial Revolution* (London: S. Sonnenschein, 1901), 86; see also 42, 54.

5:10. Biographical details are in Burleigh Taylor Wilkins, *Carl Becker: A Biographical Study in American Intellectual History* (Cambridge: MIT Press, 1961), 1–18.

5:11. The comment on Iowa Methodism is cited by Wilkins, *Carl Becker*, 13.

5:12. Eggleston, "Books That Have Helped Me," 586.

5:13. Edward Eggleston, *The Beginners of a Nation*, 4th ed. (New York: D. Appleton, 1899), vii–viii, 300–301, 176; *The Transit of Civilization: From England to America in the Seventeenth Century* (New York: D. Appleton, 1900), 2, 3. See the treatment of Eggleston by Robert Allen Skotheim, *American Intellectual Histories and Historians* (Princeton, N.J.: Princeton University Press, 1966), 48–65.

5:14. Frederick Jackson Turner, "Contributions of the West to American Democracy," reprinted in his *The Frontier in American History* (New York: Henry Holt, 1920), 267; Frederick Jackson Turner, *The Early Writings of Frederick Jackson Turner* (Madison: University of Wisconsin Press, 1938), 49–52. On the pathos of Turner's outlook, see David W. Noble, *Historians against History: The Frontier Thesis and the National Covenant in American Historical Writing since 1830* (Minneapolis: University of Minnesota Press, 1965), 37–55.

5:15. Robinson, *The New History*, 75–76, 24, 23.

5:16. Ibid., 22–23, 247, 263–65; see also the same author's *The Mind in the Making* (New York: Harper, 1921), 41–44, 125–26.

5:17. Charles A. and Mary A. Beard, *The Rise of American Civilization*, 2 vols. (New York: Macmillan, 1927), 1:151; Beard, *The Industrial Revolution*, 91.

5:18. Notebook references by Becker from March 5, 1894; quoted by Wilkins, *Carl Becker*, 24–25.

5–19. Carl L. Becker, "Some Aspects of the Influence of Social Problems and Ideas upon the Study and Writing of History," *American Journal of Sociology* 18 (March 1913): 641–42, 663–64.

5:20. Eggleston, *The Transit of Civilization*, 193–94.

5:21. Turner, *The Frontier in American History*, 311.

5:22. James Harvey Robinson, "Religion," in Charles A. Beard ed., *Whither Mankind: A Panorama of Modern Civilization* (New York: Longmans, Green, 1928), 264.

5:23. James Harvey Robinson and Charles A. Beard, *The Development of Modern Europe*, 2 vols. (Boston: Ginn, 1907), 1:167.

5:24. These references are from letters Beard wrote late in life, before and after World War II, quoted in Cushing Strout, *The Pragmatic Revolt in American History: Carl Becker and Charles Beard* (New Haven: Yale University Press, 1958), 87, 111.

5:25. Carl L. Becker, *Everyman His Own Historian: Essays on History and Politics* (New York: Appleton-Century-Crofts, 1935), 28; Carl L. Becker, "Some Aspects of the Influence of Social Problems," 675; the letter to Dodd is quoted in Wilkins, *Carl Becker*, 132–33.

5:26. Carl L. Becker, *The Declaration of Independence* (New York: Harcourt, Brace, 1922), 39, 278–79.

5:27. Carl L. Becker, *The Heavenly City of the Eighteenth-Century Philosophers*, 7; "The New History," *Dial* 53 (1912): 20; W. Stull Holt commented on sacrilege; for that and the Robinson poem, see Strout, *The Pragmatic Revolt*, 49, 48.

5:28. The comment on progress is quoted by T. J. Jackson Lears, *No Place of Grace: Antimodernism and the Transformation of American Culture, 1880–1920* (New York: Pantheon, 1981), 265. Lears's approach parallels the theme of this chapter and makes unnecessary a full-dress literary analysis of the period. Henry Adams, *Esther: A Novel* (New York: Henry Holt, 1884), illustrates the early changes in Adams.

5:29. Lears, *No Place of Grace*, 275, 277, quotes Adams on Jews and hell in correspondence from 1897, 1893, and 1900.

5:30. Henry Adams, *The Education of Henry Adams* (Boston: Houghton Mifflin, 1973; reprint of the 1918 version), 225–26, 301.

5:31. Adams, *The Education of Henry Adams*, 26; Worthington C. Ford, ed., *Letters of Henry Adams*, 2 vols. (Boston: Houghton Mifflin, 1938), 2:80.

5:32. Henry Adams, *Mont-Saint-Michel and Chartres* (Boston: Houghton Mifflin, 1904), 197, 363, 380–81.

5:33. Ibid., 332; *The Education of Henry Adams*, 34, 12.

5:34. For examples of such churches see G. E. Kidder Smith, *A Pictorial History of Architecture in America*, 2 vols. (New York: American Heritage, 1976): 2:770–71, 482–83; Roger G. Kennedy, *American Churches* (New York: Crossroad, 1982), 34–37.

5:35. Cram's work is treated in Calder Loth and Julius Trousdale Sadler, Jr., *The Only Proper Style: Gothic Architecture in America* (Boston: New York Graphic Society, 1975), 147–53.

5:36. Lears, *No Place of Grace*, 205, cites Ralph Adams Cram, "On the Restoration of Idealism," *The Knight Errant* 1 (1893). On individualism, see Ralph Adams Cram, *The Substance of Gothic: Six Lectures on the Development of Architecture from Charlemagne to Henry VIII* (Boston: Marshall Jones, 1917), 34.

5:37. Cram, *The Substance of Gothic*, 183–84.

5:38. Ibid., 194–95.

5:39. Ibid., 198–200.

5:40. For examples of "history set in stone," see Paul Venable Turner, *Campus: An American Planning Tradition* (Cambridge: MIT Press, 1984), 215–48, which shows how regularly the major modern secular schools reverted to monastic medieval styles.

Chapter Six

6:1. Orvin Larson, *American Infidel: Robert G. Ingersoll* (New York: The Citadel Press, 1962), tells the story of Ingersoll's efforts. General works of interest on the religious theme in philosophy are John E. Smith, *The Spirit of American Philosophy* (New York: Oxford University Press, 1963), and Robert J. Roth, S. J., *American Religious Philosophy* (New York: Harcourt, Brace and World, 1967). Both treat Peirce, James, Royce, and Dewey, as we do, and both neglect Santayana, who belongs in this chapter; they include Whitehead, whose achievement occurs at a later date.

6:2. Michael A. Weinstein, *The Wilderness and the City: American Classical Philosophy as a Moral Quest* (Amherst, Mass.: University of Massachusetts Press, 1982), 1, poses this theme and the whole book sustains it. Benjamin K. Rand, *Modern Classical Philosophers* (Boston: Houghton Mifflin, 1908), v, gives the classic name to this modern group.

6:3. On James and religion, see Julius Seelye Bixler, *Religion in the Philosophy of William James* (Boston: Marshall Jones, 1926); Robert J. Vanden Burgt, *The Religious Philosophy of William James* (Chicago: Nelson-Hall, 1981); Henry S. Levinson, *Science, Metaphysics, and the Chance of Salvation: An Interpretation of the Thought of William James* (Missoula, Mont.: Scholars Press, 1978).

6:4. From a letter of April 12, 1900, quoted in Ralph Barton Perry, *The Thought and Character of William James* (briefer version) (Cambridge: Harvard University Press, 1948), 257.

6:5. William James, *Pragmatism: A New Name for Some Old Ways of Thinking*

(Cambridge: Harvard University Press, 1975), 14–15; *The Varieties of Religious Experience* (New York: Longmans, Green, 1902), 519.

6:6. For samples, note several authors in H. Newton Malony, ed., *Current Perspectives in the Psychology of Religion* (Grand Rapids, Mich.: William B. Eerdmans, 1977), for their view of James's *Varieties of Religious Experience*. Benjamin Beit-Hallahmi calls it "epoch-making" (17); Orlo Strunk, Jr., sees it as the launcher of a discipline (27); Paul W. Pruyser calls it "the most important single psychological work on religion" (54); David A. Flakoll's word is "landmark" (78).

6:7. James, *The Will to Believe and Other Essays in Popular Philosophy*, ed. Frederick H. Burkhart, Fredson Bowers, Ignas K. Skrupskelis (Cambridge: Harvard University Press, 1979), 17–18, 13.

6:8. Perry, *The Thought and Character of William James*, 214–15, cites L. T. Hobhouse, "Faith and the Will to Believe," *Proceedings of the Aristotelian Society* 4 (1904): 91; James's reply was in a letter of August 12, 1904.

6:9. James, *The Will to Believe*, 50.

6:10. William James, *Pragmatism: A New Name for Some Old Ways of Thinking* (New York: Longmans, Green, 1943; enlarged edition of the 1907 work), 20.

6:11. James, *The Will to Believe*, 14, 20.

6:12. James, *Varieties of Religious Experience*, 254, 31–32, 42, 427.

6:13. James, *The Will to Believe*, 48, 50.

6:14. Perry, *The Thought and Character of William James*, 266, cites a note to students from 1896–97 and a letter to James H. Leuba, April 17, 1904.

6:15. James, *Varieties of Religious Experience*, 91.

6:16. William James, *Essays in Radical Empiricism* (New York: Longmans, Green, 1912), 39; *Pragmatism*, 106–7.

6:17. Charles Hartshorne and Paul Weiss, eds., *Collected Papers of Charles Sanders Peirce*, 8 vols. (Cambridge: Harvard University Press, 1931–55, 1958), 5:311; 8:16, 38, cited in Bruce Kuklick, *The Rise of American Philosophy: Cambridge, Massachusetts, 1860–1930* (New Haven: Yale University Press, 1977), 116.

6:18. Hartshorne and Weiss, *Collected Papers of Charles Sanders Peirce*, 6:465, 487.

6:19. Ibid., 6:437, 447.

6:20. On the later Peirce's religious practices and outlook, see the summary in Paul K. Conkin, *Puritans and Pragmatists: Eight Eminent American Thinkers* (Bloomington: Indiana University Press, 1976), 253–65.

6:21. See Kuklick, *The Rise of an American Philosophy*, 259–64, for a discussion of the absolute and the individual.

6:22. Josiah Royce, *The Philosophy of Loyalty* (New York: Macmillan, 1908), 121–23; *The Problem of Christianity*, 2 vols. (New York: Macmillan, 1913); 2:247–49; 2:37.

6:23. Josiah Royce, *The Sources of Religious Insight* (New York: Charles Scribner's Sons, 1912), 8; *The Problem of Christianity*, Lecture II, 1:47–106.

6:24. Royce, *The Problem of Christianity*, 1:16–21.

6:25. Ibid., 1:385–87, 387–90, 390–97.

6:26. Ibid., 1:398–400, 403–6, 409–17.

6:27. George Santayana, "A Brief History of My Opinions," a retrospect written for a book published in 1930, reprinted in Richard Colton Lyon, ed., *Santayana on America* (New York: Harcourt, Brace and World, 1968), 7–8.

6:28. George Santayana, *Character and Opinion in the United States* (Garden City, N.Y.: Doubleday, 1956, paperback ed.; first published in 1920), 29–30.

6:29. Reprinted in Lyon, *Santayana on America*, 37–38, from Santayana, *Winds of Doctrine: Studies in Contemporary Opinion* (New York: Charles Scribner's Sons, 1913).

6:30. Santayana, *Character and Opinion in the United States*, 130, 132.

6:31. The judgment on Dewey is from a later period; see George Santayana, *Obiter Scripta* (New York: Charles Scribner's Sons, 1936), 216–18, reprinted in Lyon, *Santayana on America*, 111–12.

6:32. Santayana, *Character and Opinion in the United States*, 19–20, 23, 27, 38.

6:33. Ibid., 117.

6:34. Ibid., 118.

Chapter Seven

7:1. These and other social philosophers sit for group portraits in books like Jean B. Quandt, *From the Small Town to the Great Community: The Social Thought of Progressive Intellectuals* (New Brunswick, N.J.: Rutgers University Press, 1970), and Roscoe C. Hinkle, *Founding Theory of American Sociology, 1881–1915* (Boston: Routledge and Kegan Paul, 1980). These works also include other candidates for a chapter like this: Franklin Giddings, Edward Ross, and Lester F. Ward. Albion Small was an exception for his more positive relations to the institutional church.

7:2. Charles H. Cooley, *Social Process* (New York: Charles Scribner's Sons, 1918), 417–18.

7:3. Charles H. Cooley, *Life and the Student* (New York: Alfred A. Knopf, 1927), 200–201.

7:4. Charles H. Cooley, *Social Organization* (New York: Charles Scribner's Sons, 1909), 116, 193, 244, 180.

7:5. Ibid., 203–5.

7:6. Ibid., 381, 379; 372–80. The journal entry of 1914 is quoted in Quandt, *From the Small Town to the Great Community*, 74, 192.

7:7. For biographical details, see David L. Miller, *George Herbert Mead: Self, Language and the World* (Austin: University of Texas Press, 1973), xi–xiii.

7:8. Quoted in ibid., xvii.

7:9. George Herbert Mead, *The Philosophy of the Act*, ed. Charles W. Morris (Chicago: University of Chicago Press, 1938), 625.

7:10. George Herbert Mead, *Mind, Self, and Society from the Standpoint of a Social Behaviorist*, ed. Charles W. Morris (Chicago: University of Chicago Press, 1934), 258.

7:11. Ibid., 295–96.

7:12. Ibid., 271–72, 275–76, 286–87.

7:13. Darnell Rucker, *The Chicago Pragmatists* (Minneapolis: University of Minnesota Press, 1969), 120–23, expounds these undated papers from the University of Chicago archives.

7:14. Cited in ibid., 123–25.

7:15. On the subject of professions open to women, see Burton J. Bledstein, *The Culture of Professionalism: The Middle Class and the Development of Higher Education in America* (New York: W. W. Norton, 1976), 118–20.

7:16. From a letter of January 29, 1889, to Ellen Gates Starr, in the Smith College, Northampton, Mass., library; quoted by Ann Firor Scott, "Jane Addams," in *Making the Invisible Woman Visible* (Urbana, Ill.: University of Illinois Press, 1984), 110.

7:17. On the bullfight and Tolstoy, see ibid., 112–14.

7:18. Jane Addams, *Democracy and Social Ethics* (New York: Macmillan, 1902), 210, 206.

7:19. Jane Addams, "A Function of the Social Settlement," *Annals of the American Academy of Political and Social Science* 13 (May 1899): 339–40; *Democracy and Social Ethics*, 214, 209, on the Arts and Crafts movement; see the brief bibliography presented by Jean B. Quandt, *From the Small Town to the Great Community*, 200–201.

7:20. See the section, "The Satire of His Presence," in John P. Diggins, *The Bard of Savagery: Thorstein Veblen and Modern Social Theory* (New York: Seabury Press, 1978), 34–39.

7:21. See the assessment in Diggins, *The Bard of Savagery*, 210–26.

7:22. The interest in a republic of engineers was outlined in raw form in two chapters of Thorstein Veblen, *The Theory of Business Enterprise* (New York: Macmillan, 1904).

7:23. Thorstein Veblen, *An Inquiry into the Nature of Peace and the Terms of Its Perpetuation* (New York: Macmillan, 1917), 33.

7:24. Veblen shared some romantic and nostalgic notions about the Christendom of medieval times, in respect to the guild and craft tradition; see *The Instinct for Workmanship* (New York: Macmillan, 1914), 256–57.

7:25. Thorstein Veblen, "Christian Morals and the Competitive System," *Essays in Our Changing Order* (New York: The Viking Press, 1943), 200–218. Veblen wrote this essay in 1910.

7:26. For a critique of Veblen's naiveté in respect to the republic of engineers and shortcomings in his Christian analysis, see Diggins, *The Bard of Savagery*, 135–38.

7:27. George Dykhuizen, *The Life and Mind of John Dewey* (Carbondale, Ill.: Southern Illinois University Press, 1973), 6; 329 n. 25, tells how Dykhuizen earlier had written that Dewey himself wrote the note; later studies suggest that his mother did.

7:28. John Dewey, "From Absolutism to Experimentalism," in George P. Adams and William P. Montague, eds., *Contemporary American Philosophy*, 2 vols. (New York: Macmillan, 1930), 2:19; see Max Eastman, "John Dewey," *Atlantic* 168 (1941): 672–73.

7:29. On developing religious attitudes at Ann Arbor, see Neil Coughlan, *Young John Dewey: An Essay in American Intellectual History* (Chicago: University of Chicago Press, 1975), 88–90; John Dewey, "Christianity and Democracy," in (no author or editor given), *Religious Thought at the University of Michigan* (Ann Arbor, Mich.: Register Publishing Co., Inland Press, 1883), 60–69.

7:30. John Dewey, "Christianity and Democracy," 67; cited in Dykhuizen, *The Life and Mind of John Dewey*, 73.

7:31. From an early essay, quoted in ibid., 73.

7:32. John Dewey, *Reconstruction in Philosophy* (Henry Holt, 1920), 211; *Experience and Nature* (New York: W. W. Norton, 1929), 202, 205.

7:33. Dykhuizen, *The Life and Mind of John Dewey*, 71, 73, quotes these references to Renan and the future of science; see John Dewey, *The Early Works of John Dewey, 1882–1898*, ed. Jo Ann Boydston (Carbondale, Ill.: Southern Illinois University Press, 1967), 4:17–18; John Dewey, *Philosophy and Civilization* (New York: Minton, Balch, 1931), 330.

7:34. Douglas Clyde Macintosh, "Pragmatism and Mysticism," *American Journal of Theology* 15 (January 1911): 142–43.

7:35. John Dewey, *Human Nature and Conduct: An Introduction to Social Psychology* (New York: Henry Holt, 1922), 330–32; *A Common Faith* (New Haven: Yale University Press, 1934), 51, 25, 59–62, 83–86.

7:36. Dewey, *A Common Faith*, 9, 31f., 19.

7:37. Ibid., 87.

7:38. As an example, see John W. Whitehead and John Conlan, "The Establishment of the Religion of Secular Humanism and Its First Amendment Implications," in *Texas Tech Law Review* 10 (1978): 1–66; see especially 56–57. This essay has been widely quoted by conservative Protestant movements seeking to introduce Christianity as a formal alternative in public schools.

7:39. See Seymour Martin Lipset, *The First New Nation: The United States in Historical and Comparative Perspective* (New York: Basic Books, 1963), 140–69. There Lipset argues that the mix of all-pervasiveness and secularity is continuous throughout American history.

Chapter Eight

8:1. Modernity as science, technology, and industry did not represent the basic spiritual threats in respect to the question of peoplehood. The "chopping up" of sectors of life or differentiation, as we shall see, more accurately describes what they reacted against. The review of this approach to modernization is in John Murray Cuddihy, *The Ordeal of Civility: Freud, Marx, Lévi-Strauss, and the Jewish Struggle with Modernity* (New York: Basic Books, 1974), 3–14.

8:2. The reference to the hurricane metaphor draws from Cuddihy, *The Ordeal of Civility*, 9; see my argument in 1:15 to 1:17 above.

8:3. On the subject of ethnicity, peoplehood, and immigration, see the bibliographical essay in Leonard Dinnerstein and David M. Reimers, *Ethnic Americans: A History of Immigration and Assimilation* (New York: New York University Press, 1977), 157–60.

8:4. *Oxford English Dictionary*, s.v. "cocoon."

8:5. A subtle essay on assimilation and resistance, chiefly in this period, is Arthur Mann, *The One and the Many: Reflections on the American Identity* (Chicago: University of Chicago Press, 1979).

8:6. Such attitudes were rooted in the experience of immigration, a subject introduced with sensitivity in a collection of essays by John Higham, *Send These to Me: Jews and Other Immigrants in Urban America* (New York: Atheneum, 1975), esp. 3–28.

8:7. The indispensable reference on the subject of ethnicity is Stephen Thernstrom, ed., *Harvard Encyclopedia of American Ethnic Groups* (Cambridge: Harvard University Press, 1980).

8:8. Henry K. Carroll, *The Religious Forces of the United States* (New York: The Christian Literature Company, 1893), xxix. A summary of the Christian missionary relation to native Americans is Henry Warner Bowden, *American Indians and Christian Missions: Studies in Cultural Conflict* (Chicago: University of Chicago Press, 1981), with valuable "Suggestions for Further Reading," 234–44.

8:9. On the Dawes bill, see Francis Paul Prucha, *American Indian Policy in Crisis: Christian Reformers and the Indian, 1865–1900* (Norman: University of Oklahoma Press, 1976), 176–84.

8:10. The anonymous agent is quoted by D'Arcy McNickle, *Native American Tribalism: Indian Survivals and Renewals* (New York: Oxford University Press, 1973), 81.

8:11. Pratt's words appear in *Senate Executive Document* 17, 50th Cong., 2d sess., serial 2610, 23, 29–30, quoted by Prucha, *American Indian Policy*, 183–84. On the segregating process, see Elaine Goodale Eastman, *Pratt: The Red Man's Moses* (Norman: University of Oklahoma Press, 1935), 77. Pratt compared Indians to immigrants in Richard Henry Pratt, *How to Deal with the Indians: The Potency of Environment* (Carlisle, Pa.: Hamilton Library Association, 1908), 3. Eastman, *Pratt*, also quotes her subject in respect to ethnologists, 112, 194–95.

8:12. Morgan, on philanthropy, is quoted from some 1889 *Proceedings of the Lake Mohonk Conference*, in Robert M. Kvasnicka and Herman J. Viola, eds., *The Commissioners of Indian Affairs, 1824–1977* (Lincoln: University of Nebraska Press, 1979), 194–95. On pedagogy, Thomas Jefferson Morgan, *Studies in Pedagogy* (Boston: Silver, Burdett, 1889), 327–28, 348–50. Quoted by Prucha, *American Indian Policy*, 296. His comments on "true religion" from the Lake Mohonk Conference are quoted by Kvasnicka and Viola, *The Commissioners*, 196–97, and the reference to "one God" is in Morgan, *Studies in Pedagogy*, 327–38, 348–50. On tribal provincialism and on Luther, see Prucha, *American Indian Policy*, 301 and 308 (quoting an address by Morgan to the National Educational Association in 1888).

8:13. Kvasnicka and Viola, *The Commissioners*, 213, quotes Jones from his annual report of 1903; McNickle, *Native American Tribalism*, 81–82, quotes Teller.

8:14. Theodore Roosevelt, *The Winning of the West*, 4 vols. (New York: G. P. Putnam's Sons, 1889–96), 1: 333–35. For Roosevelt's quote about Indians, see Herman Hagedorn, *Roosevelt in the Bad Lands* (Boston: Houghton Mifflin, 1921), 355.

8:15. A general history of white and black Christian relations in this period is David M. Reimers, *White Protestantism and the Negro* (New York: Oxford University Press, 1965), which tells how the South "won" Reconstruction and saw its segregating policies prevail in the North.

8:16. Indispensable for understanding the black church in this time is its background under slavery; see Albert J. Raboteau, *Slave Religion: The "Invisible Institution" in the Antebellum South* (New York: Oxford University Press, 1978), and Eugene D. Genovese, *Roll, Jordan, Roll: The World the Slaves Made* (New York: Pantheon, 1974).

8:17. A standard history written soon after this period speaks of it as "The New Century Epoch." "There were no exciting events, no clashes of loyalties; and as a result the history of this period is comparatively dull," in state as in church, judged Benjamin Elijah Mays and Joseph William Nicholson, *The Negro's Church* (New York: Institute of Social and Religious Research, 1933), 32–33.

8:18. Lyman Abbott, *Reminiscences* (Boston: Houghton Mifflin, 1915), 270; Washington Gladden, *Recollections* (Boston: Houghton Mifflin, 1909), 371–72.

8:19. James McGurrin, *Bourke Cockran: A Free Lance in American Politics* (New York: Charles Scribner's Sons, 1948), 213–18, reproduces the Murphy letter to Cockran.

8:20. Rufus Spain, *At Ease in Zion: Social History of Southern Baptists, 1865–1900* (Nashville, Tenn.: Vanderbilt University Press, 1967), 112, quotes the *Christian Index*; on white clergy who took risks, see Ernest Trice Thompson, *Presbyterians in the South*, 3 vols. (Richmond: John Knox Press, 1973), 3:255. For reference to the Presbyterian General Assembly, see Andrew E. Murray, *Presbyterians and the Negro—A History* (Philadelphia: Presbyterian Historical Society, 1966), 235.

8:21. Carroll's position is summarized in a book useful for understanding racial attitudes not only in religion but also in the academy, I. A. Newby, *Jim Crow's Defense: Anti-Negro Thought in America, 1900–1930* (Baton Rouge: Louisiana State University Press, 1965), 93–97. H. Paul Douglass, *Christian Reconstruction in the South* (Boston: The Pilgrim's Press, 1909), 114, comments on Carroll. Reimers, *White Protestantism and the Negro*, 28, reports on the Texas Baptist resolution.

8:22. Thomas Dixon, Jr., *The Clansman: An Historical Romance of the Ku Klux Klan* (New York: Doubleday Page, 1905); *The Leopard's Spots: A Romance of the White Man's Burden 1865–1900* (New York: Doubleday Page, 1902; reprint ed., Ridgewood, N.J.: The Gregg Press, 1967), 200–201, 446.

8:23. Spain, *At Ease in Zion*, 107, cites the *Christian Index* of August 22, 1889, and, 109, the May 26, 1892, issue.

8:24. Spain, *At Ease in Zion*, 126 and 64, quotes *Alabama Baptist*, April 26, 1900, and the Southern Baptist Convention *Annual* of 1901.

8:25. Emory Stevens Bucke, ed., *The History of American Methodism*, 3 vols. (Nashville: Abingdon, 1964), 3:363, cites Lovinggood in the New York *Christian Advocate*, April 5, 1900, and, 3:364, the Nashville *Christian Advocate*, July 5, 1906. Reimers, *White Protestantism and the Negro*, 32, quotes the Methodist bishops in the journal of the *General Conference of the Methodist Episcopal Church, South*, 1898, 22.

8:26. *The Daily Christian Advocate*, The Methodist Episcopal Church, May 26, 1900, 339. Cited in Bucke, *The History of American Methodism*, 3:361.

8:27. Charles Reagan Wilson, *Baptized in Blood: The Religion of the Lost Cause, 1865–1920* (Athens: University of Georgia Press, 1980), 109, cites Galloway's "Oration at the Dedication of the New Capitol of Mississippi." Andrew Sledd, "The Negro: Another View," *Atlantic Monthly* 90 (July 1902): 66–67, was answered by Mrs. Felton in the *Atlanta Constitution*, August 3, 1902. See H. Shelton Smith, *In His Image, But . . .: Racism in Southern Religion, 1780–1910* (Durham, N.C.: Duke University Press, 1972), 283–84.

8:28. Thompson, *Presbyterians in the South*, 3:25, quotes *Central Presbyterian*, May 30, 1900; Murray, *Presbyterians and the Negro*, 196, cites Hon. E. E. Beard on Cumberland negotiations and, 197, the *Africo-American Presbyterian*.

8:29. Murray, *Presbyterians and the Negro*, 201, reports on the voting; 198–99 alludes to the Dakota Indian Presbytery and the committee report as well as the six-commissioner dissent, first recorded in *Presbyterian Church in the U.S.A., General Assembly*, Minutes for 1904.

8:30. George Bragg, in *Church Advocate* 16 (May 1907): 2; cited in Reimers, *White Protestantism and the Negro*, 68.

8:31. Newby, *Jim Crow's Defense*, 87–88, reports on Brown's career, while Smith, *In His Image, But . . .*, 285–88, deals with Murphy. See Edgar Gardner Murphy, *The Basis of Ascendancy* (New York: Longmans, Green, 1909), xvi–xvii.

8:32. Booker T. Washington, *Up from Slavery: An Autobiography* (New York: Doubleday, 1909), 218–25, reprints the Atlanta address. See also W. E. Burghardt Du Bois, *The Souls of Black Folk* (Chicago: McClurg, 1903), 41–59.

8:33. Henry McNeal Turner is the main subject of chapters 2 and 8 and appears in the context of the early back-to-Africa movements of Edwin S. Redkey, *Black Exodus: Black Nationalist and Back-to-Africa Movements, 1890–1910* (New Haven: Yale University Press, 1969), 24–46 and 170–94.

8:34. Reimers, *White Protestantism and the Negro*, 54, discusses the Federal Council of Churches; see also the *Northwestern Christian Advocate* 62 (April 23, 1913), 4–5; cited in Reimers, ibid., 82.

8:35. *The Ku Klux Klan* 67th Cong., 1st sess., 1921, 67–68, quoted by Arnold S. Rice, *The Ku Klux Klan in American Politics* (Washington, D.C.: Public Affairs Press, 1962), 2. William Peirce Randel, *The Ku Klux Klan: A Century of Infamy* (New York: Chilton, 1965), 182–216, tells of the Simmons era.

8:36. Mary R. Coolidge, *Chinese Immigration* (New York: Henry Holt, 1909), dates from this period and is still considered a classic survey of the early decades; nothing comparable exists on the Japanese, but see Harry H. L. Kitano, *Japanese Americans: The Evolution of a Subculture* (Englewood Cliffs, N.J.: Prentice-Hall, 1969). Japanese statistics are in Robert A. Wilson and Bill Hosokawa, *East to America: A History of the Japanese in the United States* (New York: William Morrow, 1980), 44–46.

8:37. Carroll, *The Religious Forces*, 86–88.

8:38. "Chinatowns" as a social form are discussed in Betty Lee Sung, *The Story of the Chinese in America* (New York: Collier Books, 1971), 130–50.

8:39. Tien-Lu Li, *Congressional Policy of Chinese Immigration* (New York: Arno Press and New York Times, 1979; reprint of 1916 ed.), 38.

8:40. Carroll, *The Religious Forces*, 86–88.

8:41. Sung, *The Story of the Chinese in America*, 130, 132, discusses the stereotypes of Chinese Buddhist worship in America against the reality.

8:42. The Soyen Shaku visit is described in Bernard Phillips, ed., *The Essentials of Zen Buddhism: Selected from the Writings of Daisetz T. Suzuki* (New York: E. P. Dutton, 1962), xxxvi. See Soyen Shaku, *Sermons of a Buddhist Abbot: Addresses on Religious Subjects*, trans. Daisetz Teitaro Suzuki (LaSalle, Ill.: Open Court, 1906).

8:43. Wilson and Hosokawa, *East to America*, 60, describes the Christian organizations.

8:44. Tetsuden Kashima, *Buddhism in America: The Social Organization of an Ethnic Religious Institution* (Westport, Conn.: Greenwood Press, 1977), 1–8, accounts for Buddhist beginnings in America, and 12–15 continues with the Honda encounter.

8:45. Ryo Munekata, ed., *Buddhist Churches of America: Vol. 1, 75 Year History* (Chicago: Nobart, 1974), 46. Quoted in Kashima, *Buddhism in America*, 15.

8:46. Kashima, *Buddhism in America*, 20–21, describes Akira Hata's response to a questionnaire in 1972 about the Placer community of 1902, and the Guadalupe incident, based on an interview with the Reverend Hiroshi Futaba of Guadalupe Buddhist Church on October 16, 1972.

8:47. Ibid., 24–25 and 29–30, enlarges upon Buddhist organization and increasing immigration.

8:48. John S. Chambers, "The Japanese Invasion," *Annals of the American Academy of Political and Social Science* 93 (January 1921): 26–27.

8:49. The Phelan testimony is in Kiichi Kanzaki, *California and the Japanese* (San Francisco: Japanese Association of America, 1929), 24; see also V. S. McClatchy, "Japanese in the Melting Pot," *Annals of the American Academy of Political and Social Science* 93 (January 1921): 30. For Koya Uchida's testimony, see K. K. Kawakami, *The Real Japanese Question* (New York: Macmillan, 1921), 154.

8:50. James Mencarelli and Steve Severin, *Protest 3: Red, Black, Brown Experience in America* (Grand Rapids, Mich.: William B. Eerdmans, 1975), 73–128, trace the prehistory of the Mexican moves from 1536 to 1910, seen as the first of three waves of migration.

8:51. On segregation, see Albert Camarillo, *Chicanos in a Changing Society: From Mexican Pueblos to American Barrios in Santa Barbara and Southern California, 1848–1930* (Cambridge: Harvard University Press, 1979), 58–65 and 189–90.

8:52. Camarillo, *Chicanos in a Changing Society*, interviewed Walter Cordero and Federico López, 188–90. See also Carey McWilliams, *North from Mexico: The Spanish-speaking People of the United States* (Philadelphia: J. B. Lippincott, 1949), 209–10.

8:53. For the El Paso story, see Mario T. García, *Desert Immigrants: The Mexicans of El Paso, 1880–1920* (New Haven: Yale University Press, 1981), especially 131–35 on church locations.

8:54. García, *Desert Immigrants*, 186, 6, 9, 191, relates "nigger" episodes; 212–19 discuss the churches' roles.

8:55. S. Earl Taylor and Halford E. Luccock, *The Christian Crusade for World Democracy* (New York: The Methodist Book Concern, 1918), 53, 59.

8:56. Ward's speech was reported in the *El Paso Times*, February 24, 1906, and Escobar spoke up in the *El Paso Herald*, April 13, 1916. Cited in García, *Desert Immigrants*, 220–21.

8:57. Alfredo Mirandé and Evangelina Enríquez, *La Chicana: The Mexican-American Woman* (Chicago: University of Chicago Press, 1979), 79–86, condenses the Teresa

Urrea story; see also Richard Rodríguez and Gloria L. Rodríguez, "Teresa Urrea: Her Life as It Affected the Mexican-U.S. Frontier," *El Grito: A Journal of Contemporary Mexican American Thought* 5 (Summer 1972): 48–68.

8:58. That Teresa Urrea was herself concerned about her media image was clear from a statement in the *El Paso Herald*, September 11, 1896, reported in Frank Bishop Putnam, "Teresa Urrea, the Saint of Cabora," *Southern California Quarterly* 45 (September 1963): 245–64.

8:59. *Harvard Encyclopedia of American Ethnic Groups*, s.v. "Mexicans," by Carlos E. Cortés, presents the statistics from 1900 to 1975.

8:60. *A Supplement to the Oxford English Dictionary*, s.v. "ghetto," for the first time has a "transferred" and "figurative" use for the term to include any thickly populated slum area inhabited by a minority group; before World War I the term referred still only to Jewish sectors.

8:61. The statistics are from Charles Herbert Stember et al., *Jews in the Mind of America* (New York: Basic Books, 1966), 354, 364.

8:62. Moses Rischin, *The Promised City: New York's Jews 1870–1914* (New York: Corinth Books, 1964), 241, discusses defense leagues; 265 contains the quote from the *American Citizen*.

8:63. Some scholars have considered the Associated Press account as it ran in the *New York Sun*, July 23, 1896, to be exaggerated; on Populist anti-Semitism, see Edward Flower, "Anti-Semitism in the Free Silver and Populist Movements and the Election of 1896" (M.A. thesis, Columbia University, 1952), especially 27. Bryan's disavowal of anti-Semitism is in William J. Bryan, *The First Battle: A Story of the Campaign of 1896* (Chicago: W. B. Conkey, 1896), 581. Donnelley's editorials are quoted in Louis Harap, *The Image of the Jew in American Literature: From Early Republic to Mass Immigration* (Philadelphia: The Jewish Publication Society of America, 1974), 430–32.

8:64. Gustavus Myers, *History of Bigotry in the United States* (New York: Capricorn, 1960), 203, 205–6, discusses Watson's case, quoting *Watson's Magazine* (January 1915).

8:65. Quoted by Harap, *The Image of the Jew*, 362, 375–76.

8:66. Kingsley novels are also discussed in ibid., 181–82.

8:67. *The American Hebrew* (April 4, 1890), 167–92, includes these and other responses; see also *Harper's Weekly* 49 (February 4, 1905): 150.

8:68. Joseph Hoffman Cohn, *I Have Fought a Good Fight* (New York: American Board of Missions to the Jews, 1953), 42; Charles Meeker, "Evangelization of the American Jews," *Christian Workers Magazine* 19 (August 1919): 868. See Timothy P. Weber, *Living in the Shadow of the Second Coming: American Premillennialism, 1875–1925* (New York: Oxford University Press, 1979), 144–46.

8:69. Samuel Freuder, *A Missionary's Return to Judaism* (New York: Sinai Publishing, 1915), 164–66, 36–59, 7–20. Weber, *Living in the Shadow*, 150–51, elaborates on these accounts.

8:70. Such incidents are reported in John Higham, *Send These to Me*, 135–36; see especially 116–246 for many helpful comments on anti-Semitism.

8:71. James G. Heller, *Isaac M. Wise: His Life, Work and Thought* (New York: Union of American Hebrew Congregations, 1965), 584–86, reproduces comments from *The American Israelite* from 1894 and 1887.

8:72. John Henry Barrows, ed., *The World's Parliament of Religions*, 2 vols. (Chicago: Parliament Publishing Company, 1893), 1:367, 372–73, reprints Kohler's address.

8:73. Silverman's speech is also in ibid., 2:1121–22.

8:74. See ibid., 1:705–6, Lazarus speech.

8:75. Ibid., 1:711–12, 714.

8:76. Gabriel Davidson, *Our Jewish Farmers and the Story of the Jewish Agriculture Society* (New York: Fischer, 1943), 33–35. Israel Friedlaender, *The Jews of Russia and Poland* (New York: G. P. Putnam's Sons, 1915), 208–9; quoted by Moshe Davis, *The Emergence of Conservative Judaism* (New York: The Burning Bush Press, 1963), 262.

8:77. The comment appeared on September 7, 1896, and is quoted in Rudolf Glanz, "Jewish Social Conditions as Seen by the Muckrakers," *YIVO Annual of Jewish Social Science* 9 (1954): 326.

8:78. Irving Howe, *World of Our Fathers* (New York: Harcourt Brace Jovanovich, 1976), 193, quotes the newspaper of April 11, 1895; 242–44 tell Feigenbaum stories, based on *Jewish Daily Forward* accounts. See also Rischin, *The Promised City*, 153–54, 164.

8:79. See Abraham J. Karp, "New York Chooses a Chief Rabbi," *Publications of the American Jewish Historical Society* 44 (March 1955): 129–98.

8:80. Evocations of ghetto Orthodoxy appear in Gerard R. Wolfe, *The Synagogues of New York's Lower East Side* (New York: New York University Press, 1978); 27–33 discuss this era, but the photographs of the now often abandoned synagogues are the chief value of the book.

8:81. Discussions of the rise of Conservative Judaism and Zionism appear later in this book.

8:82. Daniel Dorchester, *Christianity in the United States from the First Settlement down to the Present Time* (New York: Hunt and Eaton, 1890), 668; Henry K. Carroll, *The Religious Forces*, 80–82; Leonard Woolsey Bacon, *A History of American Christianity* (New York: Charles Scribner's Sons, 1898), has no reference.

8:83. Constance J. Tarasar and John H. Erickson, eds., *Orthodox America, 1794–1976* (Syosset, N.Y.: The Orthodox Church in America, Department of History and Archives, 1975), 73. Bishop Nicholas was quoted in the *Washington Post*, November 5, 1897.

8:84. In Barrows, *The World's Parliament*, 1:353.

8:85. See Barbara S. Smith, *Russian Orthodoxy in Alaska: A History, Inventory, and Analysis of the Church Archives in Alaska with an Annotated Bibliography* (Alaska Historical Commission, 1980); Nedzelnitsky is quoted in Tarasar and Erickson, *Orthodox America*, 91; see ibid., 32, 34–35, on West Coast tensions.

8:86. Tarasar and Erickson, *Orthodox America*, 127–29.

8:87. Ibid., 175–76.

8:88. George Papaioannou, *From Mars Hill to Manhattan* (Minneapolis: Light and Life Publishing Company, 1976), 26–33, reports on beginnings. Some have faulted Theodore Saloutos, *The Greeks in the United States* (Cambridge: Harvard University Press, 1964), for overstressing chaos and then strong centralism in his chapter on "The Greek Orthodox Church: The Beginnings," 118–37, but it remains a helpful introduction. Lacking access to the languages of modern Orthodoxy, I am dependent on works like those of Saloutos or Tarasar and Erickson for data for these paragraphs.

8:89. Saloutos, *The Greeks in the United States*, 118, on *kinotitos*; p. 72, on schools, quoting *Hellinikos Astir* (March 15, 1907); p. 74, on "Goodbye to Hellenism," in *Saloniki* (October 10, 1914; August 21 and September 18, 1915).

8:90. Saloutos, *The Greeks in the United States*, 123–25.

8:91. Ibid., 132.

8:92. Ibid., 133.

8:93. Tarasar and Erickson, *Orthodox America*, 144.

8:94. Ibid., 147.

8:95. Gerald J. Bobango, *The Romanian Orthodox Episcopate of America: The First Half Century, 1929–1979* (Jackson, Mich.: Romanian-American Heritage Center, 1979), 18–39, "A House Built on Sand, 1904–24," tells of the early days.

8:96. Tarasar and Erickson, *Orthodox America*, 43–48; for the Uniate side of the Orthodox struggles, see Walter C. Warzeski, *Byzantine Rite Rusins in Carpatho-Ruthenia and America* (Pittsburgh: Byzantine Seminary Press, 1971), "The Rusin Emigration to the United States and Its Consequences (1870–1910)," 95–111, and "The Rusin Church in America, 1902–1925: National Dissention, Religious Defection, Consolidation," 112–28.

8:97. For theoretical background to these pages, see Martin E. Marty, "The Catholic Ghetto and All the Other Ghettos," *The Catholic Historical Review* 68 (April 1982): 185–205.

8:98. The standard history is Donald L. Kinzer, *An Episode in Anti-Catholicism: The American Protective Association* (Seattle: The University of Washington Press, 1964).

8:99. Ibid., 33–57. See also Seymour Martin Lipset and Earl Raab, *The Politics of Unreason: Right-Wing Extremism in America, 1790–1977*, 2d ed. (Chicago: University of Chicago Press, 1978); 82 lists organizations; see Humphrey J. Desmond, *The A.P.A. Movement* (Washington: New Century Press, 1912), 9–10, for earlier assessments of its focus and membership. Kinzer, ibid., 45–46, 49, 92, prints the principles and oaths.

8:100. The false encyclical is discussed in "The Anti-Catholic Crusade," *The Century Magazine* 47 (March 1894), 790–91; cited in Kinzer, *An Episode in Anti-Catholicism*, 49. Lipset and Raab, *The Politics of Unreason*, 80, discuss Huntington's work. See also John Higham, *Strangers in the Land: Patterns of American Nativism, 1860–1925* (New Brunswick: Rutgers University Press, 1963), 85.

8:101. Kinzer, *An Episode in Anti-Catholicism*, 98–99; Lipset and Raab, *The Politics of Unreason*, 80; and Higham, *Strangers in the Land*, 84, discuss violence. *The American Patriot* (October 19, 1895) published the sexual charges; see Gustavus Myers, *History of Bigotry*, 183.

8:102. Thomas J. Morgan, "Renaissance of Patriotism," *Baptist Home Mission Monthly* 16 (June 1894): 185–87; Lawrence B. Davis, *Immigrants, Baptists, and the Protestant Mind in America* (Urbana, Ill.: University of Illnois Press, 1973), 69–80, discusses the Baptist response; see also Dwight Spencer, "Divine Adjustments," *Baptist Home Mission Monthly* 17 (September 1895): 334–36.

8:103. Kinzer, *An Episode in Anti-Catholicism*, 84, refers to *The Catholic Record*, April 27 and June 1, 1893; for Ireland, see James H. Moynihan, *The Life of Archbishop John Ireland* (New York: Harper and Brothers, 1953). On the limits of APA power and the McQuaid incident as well as Elliott's comment, see Robert D. Cross, *The Emergence of Liberal Catholicism in America* (Cambridge: Harvard University Press, 1958), 52–53, 103–4.

8:104. "Anti-American, Anti-Christian, Anti-Baptist," *Examiner* 72 (May 3, 1894):4. On Gladden, see Kinzer, *An Episode in Anti-Catholicism*, 84.

8:105. Richard Jensen, *The Winning of the Midwest: Social and Political Conflict, 1888–1896* (Chicago: University of Chicago Press, 1971), 222, 225–26.

8:106. See Higham, *Strangers in the Land*, 180, 57–58, and 173–74, for reference to vestigial anti-Catholicism in the period.

8:107. Christopher J. Kauffman, *Faith and Fraternalism: The History of the Knights of Columbus, 1882–1982* (New York: Harper and Row, 1982), 81, the standard history, quotes "New Haven Celebration, Elm City in the Hands of the Knights of Columbus," *Connecticut Catholic* 17 (October 15, 1892):1.

8:108. Kauffman, *Faith and Fraternalism*, 139–40, cites handwritten archive copies of these rites.

8:109. Ibid., 88–89, quotes Thomas H. Cummings, "Gentlemen in Fraternity," *Donahoe's Magazine* 33 (November 1895): 1240–42.

8:110. Kauffman, *Faith and Fraternalism*, 153–59.

8:111. The bogus oath is in ibid., 169–71; see 169–89 for the whole episode.

8:112. Harold A. Buetow, *Of Singular Benefit: The Story of Catholic Education in the United States* (New York: Macmillan, 1970), 179, compiled statistics from various sources; see George D. Wolff, "Our Parochial School System—The Progress It Has Made and Is Making," *American Catholic Quarterly Review* 17 (October 1892):866–72.

8:113. Louis S. Walsh, "Unity, Efficiency, and Public Recognition of Catholic Elementary Schools," *American Ecclesiastical Review* 25 (December 1901):486–87; Buetow, *Of Singular Benefit*, 203, quotes Gibbons from *The Catholic Standard and Times*, December 21, 1907.

8:114. George H. Martin, *The Evolution of the Massachusetts Public School System* (New York: D. Appleton, 1894), 233.

8:115. This story has been told by Paul R. Messbarger, *Fiction with a Parochial Purpose: Social Uses of American Catholic Literature, 1884–1900* (Boston: Boston University Press, 1971), 57–62; Katherine Conway, "Catholic Summer School and the Reading Circles," in *World's Catholic Columbian Conference* (Chicago: T. S. Hyland, 1893), 110; on the Guild, see *Publishers' Weekly* 53 (1898):63.

8:116. *The Nation* 53 (1891):472, reviewed Egan's *Introduction to English Literature*; Messbarger, *Fiction with a Parochial Purpose*, 81–87.

8:117. Messbarger, *Fiction with a Parochial Purpose*, 87–88; see Lelia Hardin Bugg, ed., *The People of Our Parish* (Boston: Marlier, Callanan, 1900), and *The Prodigal's Daughter* (New York: Benziger Brothers, 1898).

8:118. Messbarger, *Fiction with a Parochial Purpose*, 128–31; see Mary Agnes Tincker, *San Salvador* (Boston: Houghton Mifflin, 1892).

8:119. With Polish sources linguistically inaccessible, I shall follow Anthony J. Kuzniewski, *Faith and Fatherland: The Polish Church War in Wisconsin, 1896–1918* (Notre Dame: University of Notre Dame Press, 1980); p. 93 is the Luther reference; see also *Handbook for Catholic Parishioners of the Archdiocese of Milwaukee* (Milwaukee: Catholic Archdiocese, 1907), 23–27; Cited in Kuzniewski, *Faith and Fatherland*, 8.

8:120. William I. Thomas and Florian Znaniecki, *The Polish Peasant in Europe and America*, 5 vols. (Boston: The Gorham Press, 1920), 5:41–42. Charles Shanabruch, *Chicago's Catholics: The Evolution of an American Identity* (Notre Dame: University of Notre Dame Press, 1981), 247 n. 76, has citations on internal rivalries and calls for unity.

8:121. Shanabruch, *Chicago's Catholics*, 45–46, quotes a letter in *Dziennik Chicagoski*, November 28, 1893.

8:122. Kuzniewski, *Faith and Fatherland*, 22, 41, tells of parishes like St. Josaphat.

8:123. Ibid., 5–6, 7–12, 81–82, 125.

8:124. Ibid., 50, 83.

8:125. Ibid., 61, 67–68, 43–44, 64–65.

8:126. Ibid., 117–18, 59.

8:127. Ibid., 54, 57.

8:128. Ibid., 82, 91–96, 75–76, 107, 103–5.

8:129. Ibid., 100, 120, 114.

8:130. Edith Abbott and Sophonisba P. Breckinridge, *The Delinquent Child and the Home* (New York: Survey Associates, 1916), 55; W. H. Agnew, S. J., "Pastoral Care of Italian Children in America: Some Plain Facts about the Condition of Our Italian Children," *American Ecclesiastical Review* 48 (March 1913):258.

8:131. An important bibliography is Silvano M. Tomasi and Edward C. Stibili, *Italian-Americans and Religion: An Annotated Bibliography* (New York: Center for Migration Studies, 1978). Luciano J. Iorizzo and Salvatore Mondello, *The Italian-Americans* (New York:

Twayne, 1971), 179–92, details church life; on festivals, see Jacob A. Riis, "Feast-Days in Little Italy," *The Century Magazine* 58 (August 1899):491–99.

8:132. Iorizzo and Mondello, *The Italian-Americans*, 180–82.

8:133. On the Denver incident, see ibid., 184–86, and Rudolph J. Vecoli, "Prelates and Peasants," *Journal of Social History* 2 (Spring 1969):225.

8:134. Stefano L. Testa, "Strangers from Rome in Greater New York," *The Missionary Review of the World* 31 (March 1918):217; Frederick H. Wright, "How to Reach Italians in America," *The Missionary Review of the World*, 40 (August 1917):589–94; A. Di Domenica, "The Sons of Italy in America," *The Missionary Review of the World* 41 (March 1918):191; J. C. Monaghan, "Immigration Problems," *The Catholic World* 79 (June 1904): 287; See Iorizzo and Mondello, *The Italian-Americans*, 186–92.

8:135. Emily Green Balch, *Our Slavic Fellow-Citizens* (New York: Charities Publication Committee, 1910), 8, 379, 381–84.

8:136. Ibid., 384–88.

8:137. Ibid., 390–93.

8:138. Ibid., 419, 424–25.

8:139. Thomas Čapek, *The Čechs (Bohemians) in America: A Study of Their National, Cultural, Political, Social, Economic, and Religious Life* (Boston: Houghton Mifflin, 1920), 119–20.

8:140. Edward A. Steiner, *On the Trail of the Immigrant* (New York: Fleming H. Revell, 1906), 230; see Čapek, *The Čechs*, 121–36, especially 122–23, 132–34, 136.

8:141. Bruce M. Garver, "Czech-American Freethinkers on the Great Plains," in Frederick C. Luebke, ed., *Ethnicity on the Great Plains* (Lincoln: University of Nebraska Press, 1980), 152, 157, 160, 163 (quoting Vojan).

8:142. Kenneth D. Miller, *The Czecho-Slovaks in America* (New York: George H. Doran, 1922), 119–22, 124–36.

8:143. Miller, *The Czecho-Slovaks in America*, 126–34, 146–47, 156–57, 186.

8:144. See Čapek, *The Čechs*, 246, 248, 254, on other agencies and on European battles in America.

8:145. Compare the cosmopolitan model, as outlined in chapter 2 above.

8:146. On the role of leadership in monitoring adaptation, see the essays on leadership in general and on Jews, Japanese, Germans, Afro-Americans, native Americans, eastern and southern Europeans, and Irish, in John Higham, ed., *Ethnic Leadership in America* (Baltimore: Johns Hopkins University Press, 1978).

Chapter Nine

9:1. A review of ethnic white Protestant outcomes throws light on questions of this period; see Charles H. Anderson, *White Protestant Americans: From National Origins to Religious Group* (Englewood Cliffs, N.J.: Prentice-Hall, 1970).

9:2. On these subjects see the essays collected in Russell E. Richey, ed., *Denominationalism* (Nashville: Abingdon, 1977), especially Sidney E. Mead, "Denominationalism: The Shape of Protestantism in America," 70–105, and Martin E. Marty, "Ethnicity: The Skeleton of Religion in America," 251–72.

9:3. S. S. Acquaviva, *The Decline of the Sacred in Industrial Society*, trans. Patricia Lipscomb (New York: Harper and Row, 1979), 136.

9:4. Josiah Strong, *The New Era or the Coming Kingdom* (New York: Baker and Taylor, 1893), 201, 216–20.

9:5. Edwin Scott Gaustad, *Historical Atlas of Religion in America*, rev. ed. (New

York: Harper and Row, 1976), 52, charts denominational growth in the 1890s. Catholics, Methodists, Baptists, Presbyterians, Lutherans, Disciples of Christ, Episcopalians, Congregationalists, and Mormons, in that order, topped the list; during that decade Episcopalians overtook Congregationalists for the first time. All others held relative position.

9:6. Kevin J. Christiano, "Religious Diversity and Social Change in Turn-of-the-Century American Cities" (Ph.D. diss. Princeton, 1983), 26–78, discusses criticisms of religious censuses.

9:7. Daniel Dorchester, *Christianity in the United States* (New York: Hunt and Eaton, 1890), 781–84; Henry K. Carroll, *The Religious Forces of the United States* (New York: The Christian Literature Co., 1893), 378ff.

9:8. Carroll, *The Religious Forces of the United States*, xxx–xxxvi.

9:9. Gaustad, *Historical Atlas*, 53, continues the chart of growth from 1900 to 1920; at the end of this period the Baptists overtook Methodists for second place; all denominations grew. (For comparison, see note 9:5 above.) Gaustad, 48–51, gives state-by-state graphs in 1906 reckonings.

9:10. Christiano, "Religious Diversity and Social Change," tables 1.1, p. 197, and 1.7, p. 203.

9:11. Carroll, *The Religious Forces*, xiv, xv, xvii, xviii.

9:12. Ibid., xx, xxiv, xxvii.

9:13. Leonard Woolsey Bacon, *A History of American Christianity* (New York: Charles Scribner's Sons, 1898), 411–19.

9:14. William Adams Brown, *The Church in America: A Study of the Present Condition and Future Prospects of American Protestantism* (New York: Macmillan, 1922), 73.

9:15. Howard B. Grose, *Aliens or Americans?* (New York: Young People's Missionary Movement, 1906), 196–97; Howard B. Grose, *The Incoming Millions* (New York: Fleming H. Revell, 1906), 99.

9:16. Ozra S. Davis, "The Church and the Immigrant," in Elias B. Sanford, *Origin and History of the Federal Council of the Churches of Christ in America* (Hartford, Conn.: The S. S. Scranton Company, 1916), 254–62.

9:17. Max Weber, "The Protestant Sects and the Spirit of Capitalism," in H. H. Gerth and C. Wright Mills, *From Max Weber: Essays in Sociology* (New York: Oxford University Press, 1946), 307. For more recent sociology, see Bryan R. Wilson, *Religion in Secular Society* (Baltimore: Penguin, 1966), 40–56.

9:18. On historic rivalry among these three groups, see Walter Brownlow Posey, *Religious Strife on the Southern Frontier* (Baton Rouge: Louisiana State University Press, 1965).

9:19. Orvin Larson, *American Infidel: Robert G. Ingersoll* (New York: Citadel, 1962), 255, includes the McCabe incident; see the New York *Journal*, April 12, 1897. On decline in the growth rate, see *The Independent* 52 (January 4, 1900):20–57.

9:20. See Frederick E. Maser, "The Story of Unification, 1874–1939," 3: 407–78 in Emory Stevens Bucke, ed., *The History of American Methodism*, 3 vols. (Nashville: Abingdon Press, 1964).

9:21. John C. Kilgo, "A Plea for the Union of Methodism in America," *The South Atlantic Quarterly* 5 (July 1906):209; quoted in Bucke, *The History of American Methodism*, 3:441–42.

9:22. *Joint Commission on Unification of the Methodist Episcopal Church, South, and the Methodist Episcopal Church* (Nashville: Publishing House of the Methodist Episcopal Church, South; New York: The Methodist Book Concern, 1918), 2:24, 137–39; see also 143, 162, 253. Cited in Bucke, *The History of American Methodism*, 3:429–31.

9:23. John Monroe Moore, *The Long Road to Methodist Union* (Nashville: Abingdon-Cokesbury Press, 1943), 179. See Maser's chapter in Bucke, *The History of American Methodism*, 3:434–38.

9:24. Earl Cranston, *A Working Conference on the Union of American Methodism, Northwestern University, Evanston, Illinois* (New York: The Methodist Book Concern, 1916), 77. Cited in Bucke, *The History of American Methodism*, 3:415.

9:25. Samuel S. Hill, Jr., and Robert G. Torbet, *Baptists North and South* (Valley Forge, Pa.: Judson Press, 1964), 137–39, offer helpful annotated reading lists on Baptists after updating explanations of Southern Baptist differences.

9:26. Thomas Treadwell Eaton, in an editorial in *Western Recorder* 69 (November 15, 1894):4; See James Leo Garrett, ed., *Baptist Relations with Other Christians* (Valley Forge, Pa.: Judson Press, 1974), 67–70.

9:27. *Annual, Southern Baptist Convention* (1912), 73, 14; James B. Gambrell, *Baptists and Their Business* (Nashville: Sunday School Board, Southern Baptist Convention, 1919), 140. Cited in Garrett, *Baptist Relations*, 70–72.

9:28. *Annual, Southern Baptist Convention* (1914), 73–76; 77–78. Cited in Garrett, *Baptist Relations*, 72.

9:29. James B. Gambrell, "The Union Movement and Baptist Fundamentals," *Southwestern Journal of Theology* 3 [Old Series], (January 1919):39, 43. Cited in Garrett, *Baptist Relations*, 74–75.

9:30. J. S. Rogers et al., "A Symposium by Southern State Secretaries on the Union Movement," *Southwestern Journal of Theology* 3 [Old Series], (January 1919):23. Garrett, *Baptist Relations*, 70–79, recounts the whole episode.

9:31. Garrett, *Baptist Relations*, 76–77; *Annual* (1919):19–23; James B. Gambrell, *Baptists and Their Business*, 95–96; *Annual* (1919):111–13.

9:32. Garrett, *Baptist Relations*, includes a chapter by Raymond O. Ryland, on Southern Baptist nonecumenical stances, 67–82.

9:33. Carroll, *The Religious Forces*, 91–93 and 125–28.

9:34. For these and other approaches to Disciples of Christ social issues, see David Edwin Harrell, Jr., *The Social Sources of Division in the Disciples of Christ, 1865–1900: a Social History of the Disciples of Christ*, 2 vols. (Atlanta and Athens, Ga.: Publishing Systems, 1973), 2:23–24; "The Standard Bearers of Protestantism," *Christian Standard* 34 (April 16, 1898):483; "God and Our Native Land," *Christian Standard* 35 (January 28, 1899):101; "The King of Nations," *Christian Oracle* 15 (May 12, 1898):290.

9:35. See Harrell, *The Social Sources of Division*, 2:24–25; "The White Man's Burden," *Christian Standard* 35 (March 4, 1899):274; "The Divine Law of Expansion," *Christian Oracle* 16 (January 18, 1899):2; "This and That," *Christian Oracle* 16 (April 27, 1899):6.

9:36. Harrell, *The Social Sources of Division*, 2:1–32, offers an invaluable introduction to the cultural stance of the Disciples of Christ as it approached the turn of the century.

9:37. *Census of Religious Bodies*, 2 vols. (Washington, D.C.: U.S. Bureau of the Census, 1906), 2:236, 243. Lipscomb is quoted by Alfred T. DeGroot, *The Grounds of Division among the Disciples of Christ* (Chicago: Privately printed, 1940), 130, and Earl West, *The Life and Times of David Lipscomb* (Henderson, Tenn.: Religious Book Service, 1954), 258.

9:38. "Burnett's Budget," *Gospel Advocate* (May 9, 1895): 291, quoted in William E. Tucker, *J. H. Garrison and Disciples of Christ* (St. Louis: Bethany Press, 1964), 199.

9:39. Edward Scribner Ames, "Christian Union," *The Quarterly Bulletin of the Campbell Institue* (April 1, 1904): 1; Edgar F. Daugherty, " 'Forward'—Not 'Backward'—'Realization'—Not 'Restoration,'" *Christian-Evangelist* (April 6, 1922):432; see Tucker, *J. H. Garrison*, 158–61.

9:40. "The Jubilee Conventions," *The Christian Oracle* 16 (October 26, 1899):4.

9:41. Harrell, *The Social Sources of Division*, 2:83–84; "Pathfinder," *Christian Oracle* 9 (October 11, 1894):596; editorial, *Octagraphic Review* 40 (October 13, 1887):4; "Signs of the Times," *Octagraphic Review* 40 (October 5, 1897):1.

9:42. Harrell, *The Social Sources of Division*, 2:324–29; *Census of Religious Bodies* (1906), 2:240, 243; "From the Papers," *Gospel Advocate* 33 (March 25, 1891):177.

9:43. Harrell, *The Social Sources of Division*, 2:336–44; James Small, "A Visit in Iowa," *Christian Standard* 33 (October 23, 1897):1356; H. C. Alleman, "Better Church Buildings," *Business in Christianity* 4 (January–March, 1897):14; an editorial in *Christian Standard* 35 (February 18, 1899):209.

9:44. Louis Cochran and Bess White Cochran, *Captives of the Word* (Garden City, N.Y.: Doubleday, 1969), 210–11.

9:45. William J. Lhamon, letter to the editor, *Christian-Evangelist* (January 31, 1907):158, quoted by Tucker, *J. H. Garrison*, 207.

9:46. The practice spread slowly beyond the circle of radicals who advocated open membership; see Tucker, *J. H. Garrison*, 63–66.

9:47. *Christian Standard* (August 7, 1909):1377. Cited in Tucker, *J. H. Garrison*, 93.

9:48. Tucker, *J. H. Garrison*, 101–4; on student support, "Think on These Things," *Christian Standard* (March 31, 1917):764–65.

9:49. Benjamin C. Deweese, "The Disciples' Divinity House," *Christian-Evangelist* (August 2, 1894):487; for McGarvey's writings in this period, see Tucker, *J. H. Garrison*, 106, and *Christian Standard* (September 14, 1907):1521; the reference to isolation is in J. H. Garrison, "Bible School at Ann Arbor," *Christian-Evangelist* (October 13, 1892):644; cited by Tucker, *J. H. Garrison*, 107.

9:50. Cochran and Cochran, *Captives of the Word*, 219–20.

9:51. James Garrison, "Editor's Easy Chair," *Christian-Evangelist* (December 3, 1908):1542; see Tucker, *J. H. Garrison*, 96–101, for the convention story.

9:52. Cochran and Cochran, *Captives of the Word*, 224–28.

9:53. For the Garrison letter, see Tucker, *J. H. Garrison*, 179.

9:54. For a general account of the Lutherans, see E. Clifford Nelson, ed., *The Lutherans in North America* (Philadelphia, Pa.: Fortress, 1975).

9:55. For a chart of Lutheran divisions as of 1914, see E. Clifford Nelson, *Lutheranism in North America, 1914–1970* (Minneapolis: Augsburg, 1972), end papers.

9:56. George H. Gerberding, *Problems and Possibilities* (Columbia, S.C.: Lutheran Board of Publication, 1914), 171. Cited in Nelson, *Lutheranism in North America*, 8.

9:57. For statistics, see Richard Jensen, *The Winning of the Midwest: Social and Political Conflict, 1888–1896* (Chicago: University of Chicago Press, 1971), 87; Gaustad, *Historical Atlas*, 48–51; Carroll, *The Religious Forces of the United States*, 175–205. See also *Harvard Encyclopedia of American Ethnic Groups*, s.v. "Germans," 412.

9:58. Eugene L. Fevold, "Merger Developments—Americanization," in Nelson, *The Lutherans*, 339–40.

9:59. Lars Ljungmark, *Swedish Exodus*, trans. Kermit B. Westerberg (Carbondale, Ill.: Southern Illinois University Press, 1979), is a popular account of migration and Americanization: 115–20 discuss church life.

9:60. See Paul C. Nyholm, *The Americanization of the Danish Lutheran*

Churches in America (Minneapolis: Augsburg, 1963), and John M. Jensen, *The United Evangelical Lutheran Church: An Interpretation* (Minneapolis: Augsburg, 1964).

9:61. Blom is quoted by Nyholm, *The Americanization of the Danish Lutheran Churches*, 136; P. S. Vig, "Annual Report from Trinity Seminary," *Yearbook* (1918):81–83, which Nyholm translated in *The Americanization of the Danish Lutheran Churches*, 176, and "Annual Report from Trinity Seminary," *Yearbook* (1913):105–7, quoted by Nyholm, ibid., 174.

9:62. Arthur Edwin Puotinen, *Finnish Radicals and Religion in Midwestern Mining Towns, 1865–1914* (New York: Arno Press, 1979), 163–66.

9:63. Puotinen, *Finnish Radicals*, 181–82; the *Worker* incident, ibid., 189, 197–98.

9:64. Ibid., 271–77.

9:65. Ibid., 277–88.

9:66. On relations between the Missouri Synod and the General Council, see Nelson, *The Lutherans in North America*, 234–38.

9:67. Ibid., 377–81.

9:68. For Schwann, see Everette Meier and Herbert T. Mayer, "The Process of Americanization," in Carl S. Meyer, ed., *Moving Frontiers: Readings in the History of the Lutheran Church—Missouri Synod* (St. Louis: Concordia, 1964), 356.

9:69. Wefel is quoted in Martin A. Haendschke, *The Sunday School Story: The History of the Sunday School in the Lutheran Church—Missouri Synod* (River Forest, Ill.: Lutheran Education Association, 1963), 26; Pieper attacked the Sunday School in *Der Lutheraner* 55 (June 13, 1899):107, quoted by August C. Stellhorn, *Schools of the Lutheran Church—Missouri Synod* (St. Louis: Concordia, 1963), 303.

9:70. Jensen, *The Winning of the Midwest*, 123–46, writes on the Bennett law and, 125, quotes the president of the Missouri Synod from *The Lutheran Witness* 8 (September 7, 1889):53–54. Nelson, *The Lutherans*, 396, quotes *Der Lutheraner*, the Missouri president's comment (February 15, 1916):63; Lodge is in Nelson, *The Lutherans*, 396 n. 16.

9:71. Stellhorn, *Schools of the Lutheran Church*, 314–15, reproduces such stories.

9:72. Ray H. Abrams, *Preachers Present Arms* (Scottdale, Pa.: Herald Press, 1933), 212, quotes Miller from the *New York Times*, April 25, 1918.

9:73. Carl S. Meyer, *Log Cabin to Luther Tower* (St. Louis: Concordia, 1965), 127–31, discusses boisterousness and cites Theodore Graebner from *Alma Mater* 19 (December 1, 1928):85.

9:74. See Nelson, *The Lutherans*, 377, for Wisconsin's praise, in *Theological Monthly* 19 (August–September 1922):263; see also Franz Pieper, *Missouri Synod Synodalbericht* (1905):17. Nelson, *The Lutherans*, 378, cites Friedrich Bente, *Lehre und Wehre* 50 (1904):1–20.

9:75. For the *Fundamentals* comment, see *Theological Quarterly* 15 (January 1911):50–53, cited by Milton L. Rudnick, *Fundamentalism and the Missouri Synod: A Historical Study of Their Interaction and Mutual Influence* (St. Louis: Concordia, 1966), 75–76; see 87–88 for Graebner on "false prophets"; see Graebner, "Higher Criticism in the Pulpit," *Theological Quarterly* 7 (April 1903):114.

9:76. On Missouri's staying out of the National Lutheran Council in 1917, see Nelson, *The Lutherans*, 403–4.

9:77. James Hennesey, S. J., *American Catholics: A History of the Roman Catholic Community in the United States* (New York: Oxford University Press, 1981), 184–220, extends the story of Catholicism in this period.

9:78. On the transit in question, see Thomas T. McAvoy, "The Formation of the Catholic Minority," in Philip Gleason, ed., *Catholicism in America* (New York: Harper and Row, 1970), 10–27.

9:79. For an exceptional progressive in labor disputes, see the case of John Lancaster Spalding and the coal strike of 1902; David Francis Sweeney, *The Life of John Lancaster Spalding, First Bishop of Peoria, 1840–1916* (New York: Herder and Herder, 1965), 316–23.

9:80. See Henry J. Browne, *The Catholic Church and the Knights of Labor* (Washington: Catholic University of America Press, 1949).

9:81. Elizabeth McKeown, "War and Welfare: a Study of American Catholic Leadership" (Ph.D. diss., University of Chicago, 1972), 54ff., provides a profile of Catholicism in 1916; see the U.S. Department of Commerce, Bureau of the Census, *Survey of Religious Bodies: 1916*, 2 vols. (Washington, D.C.: Government Printing Office, 1919), for statistics.

9:82. Ireland is cited in Aaron I. Abell, "Origins of Catholic Social Reform in the United States: Ideological Aspects," *Review of Politics* 11 (July 1949): 304–6; see Merwin-Marie Snell, "The Ethical Kinship between Protestant Radicalism and Catholic Conservatism," *Christian Register* (July 27, 1893); "Pen-Pictures of the American Hierarchy," *Independent* (April 27, 1893); cited by Aaron I. Abell, *American Catholicism and Social Action* (Notre Dame: University of Notre Dame Press, 1963), 97–98.

9:83. On ways in which Nativism did help shape Catholic identity and lead to retention of ethnic diversity, see Charles H. Shanabruch, "The Catholic Church's Role in the Americanization of Chicago's Immigrants, 1833–1928," (Ph.D. diss., 2 vols., University of Chicago, 1975), 1:202–4.

9:84. Abell, *American Catholicism*, 111–12, quoting *Church Progress* (September 16, 1893), and *Independent* (September 21, 1893). The offending phrase about national welfare was from William J. Onahan, "Columbian Catholic Congress at Chicago," *Catholic World* 57 (August–September 1893): 607–8.

9:85. For Satolli's comment, see J. S. Hyland and Co., compilers, *Progress of the Catholic Church in America and the Great Columbian Catholic Congress of 1893*, 4th ed. (Chicago, 1897), 46; for Pallen's comment, see *Church Progress* (September 16, 1893).

9:86. See Abell, *American Catholicism*, 118; Gibbons is quoted in F. Tennyson Neely, *History of the Parliament of Religions and Religious Congresses at the World's Columbian Exposition* (Chicago: F. T. Neely, 1893), 45–46, 185–91; Pallen reacted in "A Religious Midway Plaisance," *Church Progress* (September 23, 1893).

9:87. William J. Kerby, "Reinforcement of the Bonds of Faith," *Catholic World* 84 (January 1907): 511, 515.

9:88. McKeown, "War and Welfare," 103, cites Burke, "War Problems and American Catholics," an address at the National Catholic War Conference, August 11–12, 1917, and 105, 112, other Burke addresses of 1920.

9:89. McKeown, "War and Welfare," 24, quotes a letter from Burke to Kerby, November 7, 1906; see also Leo XIII, *"Longinqua oceani,"* *Catholic University Bulletin* (April, 1895): 243.

9:90. John A. Ryan, "Some Effects of Rerum Novarum," *America* 45 (April–October 1931): 59.

9:91. Leo XIII, "The Condition of Labor," in Leon Stein and Philip Taft, eds., *Wages, Hours and Strikes: Labor Panaceas in the Twentieth Century* (New York: Arno Press, 1969), 137.

9:92. Abell, *American Catholicism*, 78; John J. Keane, "The Catholic Church and Economics," *Quarterly Journal of Economics* 6 (October 1891): 25–46.

9:93. For Ireland, see Aaron I. Abell, "American Catholic Reaction to Industrial

Conflict: The Arbitral Process: 1885–1900," *Catholic Historical Review* 41 (January 1956): 405; William Stang, *Socialism and Christianity* (New York: Benziger Brothers, 1905), 33, 63.

9:94. Abell, *American Catholicism*, 137–88, details the story of socialism and Catholicism.

9:95. Roderick A. McEachen, "The Immigrant Problem—Its Solution," *Extension Magazine* 2 (August 1907):11. Cited in Abell, *American Catholicism*, 161.

9:96. See Robert D. Cross, *The Emergence of Liberal Catholicism in America* (Cambridge: Harvard University Press, 1958), 34–35; J. G. Pyle, *The Life of James J. Hill*, 2 vols. (New York: 1917), 1:64–65; Editorial Notes, *Catholic World* 65 (September 1897): 851; Henry F. Pringle, *The Life and Times of William Howard Taft*, 2 vols. (New York: Farrar and Rinehart, 1939), 2:834.

9:97. On "anti-democratic," see Shanabruch, "The Church's Role," 1:317–18; Kerby is quoted by Donald P. Gavin, *The National Conference of Catholic Charities, 1910–1960* (Milwaukee: Bruce, 1962), 14.

9:98. For the relation of Ryan to the Catholic bishops' program, see Joseph Michael McShane, S.J., "The Bishops' Program of Social Reconstruction of 1919: A Study in American Catholic Progressivism" (Ph.D. diss., University of Chicago, 1981).

9:99. McShane, "The Bishops' Program," 97–100, recounts Ryan's encounter with the encylical; see also John A. Ryan, *Social Doctrine in Action: A Personal History* (New York: Harper and Brothers, 1941), 43–44; *Declining Liberty and Other Papers* (New York: Macmillan, 1927), 180–81; the reference to the Middle Ages is in unpublished papers, cited by McShane, "The Bishops' Program," 98.

9:100. See Francis L. Broderick, *Right Reverend New Dealer: John A. Ryan* (New York: Macmillan, 1963), 152–53; John A. Ryan and Francis J. Boland, *Catholic Principles of Politics* (New York: Macmillan, 1940), 1; John A. Ryan, "Assaults Upon Our Civil Liberties," *Catholic Charities Review* 7 (January 1923):17; McShane points to Ryan's strategic poise in "The Bishops' Program," 115.

9:101. John A. Ryan, *Declining Liberties and Other Papers*, 194–95; "The Need of Legal Standards of Protection for Labor," *American Labor Legislation Review* 11 (1921):221–26; *The Church and Socialism and Other Essays* (Washington, D.C.: Catholic University Press, 1919), 17–19; the final citation dates from 1939, cited by McShane, "The Bishops' Program," 128–29.

9:102. Dietz and the *True Voice* are cited in McShane, "The Bishops' Program," 134.

9:103. John Ireland, *The Church and Modern Society* (St. Paul, Minn.: Pioneer Press, 1905), 73, 138–39, 58.

9:104. John Lancaster Spalding, *Opportunity and Other Essays and Addresses* (Chicago: McClurg, 1900), 193–94, 215, 221.

9:105. John Gilmary Shea, *The Cross and the Flag: Our Church and Country* (New York: Catholic Historical League of America, 1900), 85. This speech is quoted in an addendum written by John L. MacDonald, Shea having died prior to the outbreak of the Spanish-American war.

9:106. Michael Williams, "Great Episcopal Bishop Flays Organized Greed and American Militarists," *Reconstruction* (March 1919), 70. Cited by McShane, "The Bishops' Program," 146–47.

9:107. The Gibbons letter of June 18, 1918, is cited by McShane, "The Bishops' Program," 150; see also *National Catholic War Council Handbook* (Washington, D.C.: NCWC, 1918), 1.

9:108. McKeown, "War and Welfare," 81–82 quotes Cusack's speeches to a Catholic Boys Brigade and Catholic Women in October and June of 1918.

9:109. Michael Williams, *American Catholics in the War: National Catholic War Council 1917–21* (New York: Macmillan, 1921), 113. On the irony of late credentialing, see Abell, *American Catholicism*, 194; McShane, "The Bishops' Program," details the public relations program, 171–77.

9:110. "With Our Readers," *Catholic World* (February, 1919): 716.

9:111. McShane, "The Bishops' Program," 194, discusses Reconstruction fever; see Glenn Frank, *The Politics of Industry: A Foot-Note to the Social Unrest* (New York: Century Company, 1919), 26. See also John A. Ryan, *Social Reconstruction* (New York: Macmillan, 1920), 16. McShane, "The Bishops' Program," 287–88 quotes Ryan on government and the industrial system.

9:112. McShane, "The Bishops' Program," 311, 331, discusses passage of the program and socialist fears; the O'Connell letter dates from November 2, 1924.

9:113. Ryan, *Social Reconstruction*, 18 cites Hard's "The Catholic Church Accepts the Challenge," *Metropolitan Magazine* (January 1920): 27; McShane, "The Bishops' Program," 359, quotes John Fitzpatrick, "The Bishops' Labor Programme," *NCWC Bulletin* 1 (July 1919): 9.

Chapter Ten

10:1. Most treatments of cultural and political conservatism connect it with the two decades before 1890, in the Gilded Age, during the prevalence of Social Darwinism, when laissez-faire economics went unchallenged, and pick up the strand again in the 1920s, seeing only one or two lonely conservatives during the progressive, liberal, modernist decades. Thus, Robert M. Crunden, ed. *The Superfluous Men: Conservative Critics of American Culture, 1900–1945* (Austin: University of Texas Press, 1977) anthologizes only Santayana and Cram from this turn-of-the-century period; most others had a later prime. See also Clinton Rossiter, *Conservatism in America: The Thankless Persuasion*, 2d. ed., rev. (New York: Alfred A. Knopf, 1962), 128–62.

10:2. On the cultural shift toward the end of this period, see Henry F. May, *The End of American Innocence: A Study of the First Years of Our Own Time, 1912–1917* (New York: Oxford University Press, 1959), especially 20–29 and 219–48.

10:3. To anticipate one subject, biblical inerrancy, note the strenuousness with which those must state their case who argue for simple continuity between "classic Protestantism" and modern reactive evangelicalism in this matter; for example, John D. Woodbridge, *Biblical Authority: A Critique of the Rogers/McKim Proposal* (Grand Rapids, Mich.: Zondervan, 1982). To speak of the strenuousness is not to suggest that the effort is beside the point or wholly unsuccessful.

10:4. A modern militant anti-assimilationist accounts for native American Indian resistance to Christian "civilizing" and progressivism in Vine Deloria, Jr., *God Is Red* (New York: Grosset and Dunlap, 1973); for a close-up of a resistance religion, see Joseph G. Jorgenson, *The Sun Dance Religion: Power for the Powerless* (Chicago: University of Chicago Press, 1972).

10:5. E. Franklin Frazier, *The Negro Church in America* (New York: Schocken, 1963), in sections on "The Church as an Agency of Social Control," and "A Refuge in a Hostile White World," 37–40, 50–51, shows how the church in the era of Booker T. Washington was anything but a progressive or radical agency.

10:6. While there are a number of books like Robert D. Cross, *The Emergence of Liberal Catholicism in America* (Cambridge: Harvard University Press, 1958), we lack books on the same period that describe "the emergence of conservative Catholicism in America."

10:7. The Propaganda is quoted from Vatican archival documents in Gerald P. Fogarty, *The Vatican and the American Hierarchy from 1870 to 1965* (Stuttgart: Anton Hiersemann, 1982), 129.

10:8. Francesco Satolli, *Loyalty to Church and State*, John R. Slattery, ed. (Baltimore: John Murphy, 1895), 150. Fogarty, *The Vatican and the American Hierarchy*, 131, quotes Gibbons to Cardinal Rampolla on October 27, 1893.

10:9. Fogarty, *The Vatican and the American Hierarchy*, 137, quotes the apostolic letter.

10:10. James F. Cleary, "Catholic Participation in the World's Parliament of Religions, Chicago 1893," *Catholic Historical Review* 55 (January 1970):605-7.

10:11. O'Connell is quoted by Fogarty, *The Vatican and the American Hierarchy*, 148.

10:12. Thomas T. McAvoy, *The Americanist Heresy in Roman Catholicism, 1895-1900* (Notre Dame: University of Notre Dame Press, 1963), 102-3, quotes Ireland's speech from the New York *Freeman's Journal*, April 3, 1897.

10:13. Fogarty, *The Vatican and the American Hierarchy*, 152-53, quotes O'Connell's letter to Ireland (August 12, 1897); the gloating is quoted on 159.

10:14. Ibid., 159, quotes O'Connell to Ireland, December 2, 1897, and, 163, May 24, 1898; McAvoy, *The Americanist Heresy*, 162-66, makes the whole letter available.

10:15. Thomas T. McAvoy, *The Great Crisis in American Catholic History, 1895-1900* (Chicago: Henry Regnery, 1957) 275-79; the direct citation is quoted from a reprint of *Testem Benevolentiae*, ibid., 382.

10:16. See Ralph E. Weber, *Notre Dame's John Zahm: American Catholic Apologist and Educator* (Notre Dame: University of Notre Dame Press, 1961); J. A. Zahm, *Evolution and Dogma* (New York: Arno Press, 1978; reprint of 1896 edition).

10:17. Arthur J. Scanlon, *St. Joseph's Seminary, Dunwoodie, New York, 1896-1920* (New York: United States Catholic Historical Society, 1922), 109, has Klein's views.

10:18. James F. Driscoll, "Recent Views on Biblical Inspiration, 1," *The New York Review* 1 (June-July 1905):81-95; Francis E. Gigot, "The Higher Criticism of the Bible: The Name and the Thing," *The New York Review* 1 (May-June 1906):723; Francis E. Gigot, "The Higher Criticism of the Bible: Its General Principles," *The New York Review* 2 (September-October 1906):158-62; Francis E. Gigot, "The Higher Criticism of the Bible: Its Constructive Aspect," *The New York Review* 2 (November-December 1906):302-5; Francis E. Gigot, "The Higher Criticism of the Bible: Its Relation to Tradition," *The New York Review* 2 (January-February 1907):442-43.

10:19. William L. Sullivan, "Catholicity and Some Elements in Our National Life," *The New York Review* 1 (October-November 1905):239; see also 3 (November-December 1907):342-49.

10:20. A brief narrative of the modernist theme is in Fogarty, *The Vatican and the American Hierarchy*, 190-94.

10:21. Quoted in ibid., 194.

10:22. There are only two extensive writings on Catholic Modernism in America; one is a Ph.D. dissertation at the University of Chicago (1985) by R. Scott Appleby, the other is Michael V. Gannon, "Before and after Modernism: The Intellectual Isolation of the American Priest," in John Tracy Ellis, ed., *The Catholic Priest in the U.S.: Historical Investigations* (Collegeville, Minn.: St. John's University Press, 1971), 293-383. See also R. Scott Appleby, "American Catholic Modernism: Dunwoodie and the *New York Review*, 1895-1910," *American Catholic Studies Working Paper Series* (Charles and Margaret Hall Cushwa Center, Notre Dame, Ind., 1983):no. 3.

10:23. The standard account of this movement is Moshe Davis, *The Emergence of Conservative Judaism* (New York: The Burning Bush Press, 1963).

10:24. See "The Years of Indecision," chap. 2, in Herbert Parzen, *Architects of Conservative Judaism* (New York: Jonathan David, 1964), 12–17.

10:25. On relations between Orthodoxy and the Jewish Theological Seminary and the Historical School, see Davis, *The Emergence of Conservative Judaism*, 311–26.

10:26. Solomon Schechter discusses "order and decorum" in *The Report of the United Synagogue* (1913):17, quoted by Parzen, *Architects of Conservative Judaism*, 63. The reference to "Catholic Israel" is in Solomon Schechter, *Studies in Judaism*, 3 vols. (Philadelphia: Jewish Publication Society of America, 1911), 1:xviii.

10:27. On the meeting with Schiff, Guggenheims, and Sulzberger, see Davis, *The Emergence of Conservative Judaism*, 322.

10:28. A portrait of Schechter is in Parzen, *Architects of Conservative Judaism*, 26–78.

10:29. On the half-way house problem of Conservatism, see Solomon Schechter, *Seminary Addresses and Other Papers* (New York: The Burning Bush Press, 1959), 25.

10:30. Schechter, *Studies in Judaism*, 3:82–83; 1:xvii–xix; 2:41.

10:31. Schechter, *Studies in Judaism*, 2:185–86; *Seminary Addresses*, 25.

10:32. Schechter, *Seminary Addresses*, 19–20.

10:33. Ibid., 10, 88–89.

10:34. Cited by Parzen, *Architects of Conservative Judaism*, 71.

10:35. Schechter, *Seminary Addresses*, 48–49.

10:36. Ibid., 231–32.

10:37. The story of American Zionism is best told in Melvin I. Urofsky, *American Zionism from Herzl to the Holocaust* (Garden City, N.Y.: Doubleday Anchor, 1975).

10:38. James G. Heller, *Isaac M. Wise: His Life, Work and Thought* (New York: The Union of American Hebrew Congregations, 1965), 506, 586, 595, 603, 605, 608, quotes *New York Jewish Times* 5 (July 25, 1873) and *The American Israelite* 33 (January 28, 1887):4; 40 (February 22, 1894); 43 (July 2, 1896):4; 44 (September 9, 1897):4; 45 (October 13, 1898):4.

10:39. David Polish, *Renew Our Days: The Zionist Issue in Reform Judaism* (Jerusalem: The World Zionist Organization, 1976), 50, quotes the Pittsburgh Platform.

10:40. David Polish is the source for reference to these three addresses; see *The Central Conference of American Rabbis Yearbook* 9 (1899):174–78; 16 (1906):209–13; 18 (1908):145–47.

10:41. Ibid., 30 (1920):163, 169.

10:42. On the absence of conflict at the time of his appointment, see Urofsky, *American Zionism*, 121, a letter from Brandeis to Jacob H. Kaplan, February 10, 1916; see ibid., 118, for a comment on dual loyalties, from a speech in 1905; the italicized quotation is from the *Baltimore American*, September 16, 1914; on national suicide, see "A Call to the Educated Jew," *Menorah Journal* 1 (January 1915):13–19. Cited in Urofsky, *American Zionism*, 120.

10:43. Davis, *The Emergence of Conservative Judaism*, 274, 273; H. P. Mendes, *Ruach Hayim (The Spirit of Life), or Jewish Daily Life Ethically Presented* (New York: 1917), 185–88.

Chapter Eleven

11:1. Psychologist Robert Jay Lifton, in *Boundaries: Psychological Man in Revolution* (New York: Random House Vintage, 1970), discerns a "constrictive" psychological type which resists the "protean" type responsive to the appeals of pluralism and modernity, p. 51; he refers "to the closing off of identity, the constriction of self-process, to a straight-and-narrow specialization in psychological as well as in intellectual life, and to reluctance to let in any extraneous influence."

11:2. Thus, for one sample, James Barr in *Fundamentalism* (Philadelphia: Westminster Press, 1978), 195, appraising "dispensationalism," about which more later, sees it as anything but the mere conservatism its fashioners claimed it to be. It was "a remarkable achievement of the mythopoeic fantasy," a "feat of the imagination [that] might well compare with the apocalyptic poems of Blake." It "has originality and creativity. . . . It offers something new. Its most fervent devotee can hardly boast that dispensationalism is the faith which all the saints through all the ages have professed."

11:3. On this progressive revivalist theme, consult William G. McLoughlin, *Revivals, Awakenings, and Reform: An Essay on Religion and Social Change in America, 1607–1977* (Chicago: University of Chicago Press, 1978); Donald W. Dayton, *Discovering an Evangelical Heritage* (New York: Harper and Row, 1976); Timothy L. Smith, *Revivalism and Social Reform: In Mid-Nineteenth Century America* (Nashville: Abingdon Press, 1957).

11:4. James F. Findlay, Jr., *Dwight L. Moody: American Evangelist, 1837–1899* (Chicago: University of Chicago Press, 1969), is the standard biography. Stanley N. Gundry, *Love Them In: The Proclamation Theology of D. L. Moody* (Chicago: Moody Press, 1976), an insider's view, takes issue with Findlay on some theological points.

11:5. Timothy Weber, *Living in the Shadow of the Second Coming: American Premillennialism, 1875–1925* (New York: Oxford University Press, 1979), 32, 34, 36, 44, 52–54, traces Moody's career as a premillennialist of moderate outlook; Findlay, *Dwight L. Moody*, 127, points to disagreements between Moody and other premillennialists.

11:6. Weber, *Living in the Shadow*, 33.

11:7. Henry L. Drummond, *Dwight L. Moody: Impressions and Facts* (New York: McClure, Phillips, 1900), 25–30; Howard Pope in "How I Became a Premillennialist," in James M. Gray, ed., *The Coming and Kingdom of Christ* (Chicago: Bible Institute Colportage Association, 1914), 75–77. Cited in Weber, *Living in the Shadow*, 36, 41.

11:8. Reuben A. Torrey, *The Return of the Lord Jesus* (Los Angeles: Bible Institute of Los Angeles, 1913), 7–8. Quoted in Weber, *Living in the Shadow*, 101–2.

11:9. Paul D. Moody, "Moody Becoming 'a Veiled Figure,'" *The Christian Century* (August 2, 1923):979; George Adam Smith, "Dwight L. Moody: A Personal Tribute," *The Outlook* (January 20, 1900):163. Quoted in Gundry, *Love Them In*, 199.

11:10. Dwight L. Moody, *Pleasure and Profit in Bible Study* (Chicago: Bible Institute Colportage Association, 1895), 25–26; "Mr. Moody's Meeting," *Montreal Daily Star*, November 29, 1894. Quoted in Gundry, *Love Them In*, 203.

11:11. Quoted by Gundry, *Love Them In*, 209–13; "Moody Comes to Exhort," *Chicago Tribune*, September 30, 1899; the call to separatism was in a typed manuscript of August 16, 1898; see also Dwight L. Moody, *Thou Fool: And Eleven Other Sermons Never Before Published* (New York: Christian Herald, 1911), 150; the Smith reference is in his introduction to Drummond, *Dwight L. Moody*, 25–30.

11:12. William G. McLoughlin, Jr., *Modern Revivalism: Charles Grandison Finney to Billy Graham* (New York: Ronald Press, 1959), 282–329, is the most extensive account of Jones's activities; see especially 300 and 310. Laura M. Jones, assisted by Walt Holcomb, *The Life and Sayings of Sam P. Jones* (Atlanta, 1906), quotes the anti-intellectual comment, while the "hog" item is from an undated clipping in a Jones scrapbook; see McLoughlin, *Modern Revivalism*, 288.

11:13. McLoughlin, *Modern Revivalism*, 321–22, 324–25; the "shotgun" reference is in Brand Whitlock, *Forty Years of It* (New York: D. Appleton, 1914), 114.

11:14. For an account of the encounter between Gladden and supporters of Sunday, see Jacob Henry Dorn, *Washington Gladden* (Columbus: Ohio State University Press, 1966), 395–401.

11:15. Amzi C. Dixon, *Evangelism Old and New* (New York: American Tract Society, 1905), 43ff. See McLoughlin, *Modern Revivalism*, 352–53.

11:16. On Dixon and *The Fundamentals*, see Ernest Sandeen, *The Roots of Fundamentalism: British and American Millenarianism, 1800–1930* (Chicago: University of Chicago Press, 1970), 194–206.

11:17. Reuben A. Torrey, *Soul Winning Sermons* (New York: Fleming H. Revell, 1925), 290; the *Philadelphia North American*, February 8, 1906; see McLoughlin, *Modern Revivalism*, 373.

11:18. McLoughlin, *Modern Revivalism*, 329–45, tells the story of Mills; see also B. Fay Mills, *God's World* (New York, 1894), 229–30, 279; Henry Stauffer, ed., *The Great Awakening in Columbus, Ohio, Under the Labors of Rev. B. Fay Mills and His Associates* (Columbus, Ohio, 1895), 44, 61–62; 59; *The Congregationalist* (September 9, 1897):350.

11:19. B. Fay Mills, "My Practical Evolution," *The Advance* 67 (June 24, 1915):1251–52; see McLoughlin, *Modern Revivalism*, 345.

11:20. Ford C. Ottman, *J. Wilbur Chapman: A Biography* (New York: Doubleday Page, 1920), 203, 274; see McLoughlin, *Modern Revivalism*, 377–88.

11:21. The standard work is William G. McLoughlin, Jr., *Billy Sunday Was His Real Name* (Chicago: University of Chicago Press, 1955), 17, 24; the sources are the *Audubon* [Iowa] *Republican*, January 23, 1902, and the *Keokuk* [Iowa] *Daily Gate City*, October 1, 1904.

11:22. McLoughlin, *Billy Sunday*, 36, 39, 58, 115, 47, 121, 123, 132.

11:23. Ibid., 140, 224, 256, 258; on Roosevelt's appearance, see *Providence News*, October 18, 1918, 10.

11:24. On the later period, see McLoughlin, *Billy Sunday*, 270–72.

11:25. For a latter-day comment on outcomes, see David O. Moberg, *The Great Reversal: Evangelism versus Social Concern* (Philadelphia: Lippincott, 1972), 20–22.

11:26. That this specialization instead left evangelicals committed unreflectively to political conservatism as opposed to privatism or neutrality is a frequent charge; see for example Richard V. Pierard, *The Unequal Yoke: Evangelical Christianity and Political Conservatism* (Philadelphia: Lippincott, 1970).

11:27. Arthur C. Danto, *Analytical Philosophy of History* (Cambridge: Cambridge University Press, 1965), 11; see chap. 1, "Substantive and Analytical Philosophy of History."

11:28. Works on philosophy of history regularly include critical or eschatological Christian views, including those of Reinhold Niebuhr, but even anthologizers of evangelical conservative bent have rarely seen premillennialism as the complex alternative and competitive philosophy of history that it is. Thus, C. T. McIntire, ed., *God, History, and Historians: An Anthology of Modern Christian Views of History* (New York: Oxford University Press, 1977), includes none among his twenty-two Christian authors.

11:29. Weber, *Living in the Shadow*, 6, 8–12, recognizes the "insider/outsider" distinction and begins to introduce the arcane terminology of the movements.

11:30. C. I. Scofield, *Scofield Reference Bible* (New York: Oxford University Press), editions after 1917.

11:31. *Scofield Reference Bible*, 5 n. 4, thus defines dispensationalism; see also

C. I. Scofield, *Rightly Dividing the Word of Truth* (Oakland: Western Book and Tract Company, n.d.), 18. Cited by Weber, *Living in the Shadow*, 17.

11:32. C. I. Scofield, "God's Purpose in This Age," *Our Hope* 8 (March 1902): 465–66. Cited in C. Norman Kraus, *Dispensationalism in America: Its Rise and Development* (Richmond, Va.: John Knox Press, 1958), 112.

11:33. The reference to absence of orginality is from the preface to the *Scofield Reference Bible*; for the Seventh dispensation, see 1227, 1250.

11:34. C. I. Scofield, *Scofield Bible Correspondence Course* (Chicago: Moody Bible Institute, 1907), 45–46. Quoted in Clarence B. Bass, *Backgrounds to Dispensationalism: Its Historical Genesis and Ecclesiastical Implications* (Grand Rapids: Mich.: Eerdmans, 1960; reprinted, Grand Rapids, Mich.: Baker, 1977), 150.

11:35. Arthur T. Pierson, "The Coming of the Lord: The Doctrinal Center of the Bible," *Addresses on the Second Coming of the Lord: Delivered at the Prophetic Conference, Allegheny, Pa., December 3–6, 1895* (Pittsburgh: W. W. Waters, 1895), 82.

11:36. Nathaniel West, *The Thousand Years: Studies in Eschatology in Both Testaments* (Fincastle, Va.: n.d.), 339, 343–44; the best treatment of religious Baconianism is Theodore Dwight Bozeman, *Protestants in an Age of Science: The Baconian Ideal and Antebellum American Religious Thought* (Chapel Hill: University of North Carolina Press, 1977).

11:37. *Scofield Reference Bible*, Introduction, iii.

11:38. On dispensationalism see David MacPherson, *The Incredible Cover-Up: The True Story on the Pre-Trib Rapture* (Plainfield, N.J.: Logos International, 1975); Bass, *Backgrounds to Dispensationalism;* Kraus, *Dispensationalism in America*, 45–56; Sandeen, *The Roots of Fundamentalism*.

11:39. Barr, *Fundamentalism*, 191–95, is another condensation of the dispensationalist scheme.

11:40. On Moody, see Gundry, *Love Them In*, 175–93; the lifeboat quotation is from Dwight L. Moody, *New Sermons, Addresses and Prayers* (St. Louis: N. D. Thompson, 1877), 535.

11:41. On millennial ambivalence about the end and planning for the future, see Weber, *Living in the Shadow*, 43–46.

11:42. On the ethos and morals of premillennialists, see ibid., 56–64.

11:43. A chart summarizing this scheme is in the best book on its subject, George Marsden, *Fundamentalism and American Culture: The Shaping of Twentieth Century Evangelicalism, 1870–1925* (New York: Oxford University Press, 1980), 53.

11:44. C. H. Mackintosh, *Papers on the Lord's Coming* (Chicago: Bible Institute Colportage Association, n.d.), 101–5; *Scofield Bible Correspondence Course*, 23–25. Quoted in Bass, *Backgrounds to Dispensationalism*, 28.

11:45. Reuben A. Torrey, "That Blessed Hope," in Arno C. Gaebelein, ed., *Christ and Glory: Addresses Delivered at the New York Prophetic Conference, Carnegie Hall, November 25–28, 1918* (New York: Publication Office of *Our Hope*, 1919), 33–34; Cortland Myers, "War on German Theology," *Light on Prophecy: A Coordinated Constructive Teaching, Being the Proceedings and Addresses at the Philadelphia Prophetic Conference, May 28–30, 1918* (New York: The Christian Herald, 1918), 176.

11:46. Shailer Mathews, *Will Christ Come Again?* (Chicago: American Institute of Sacred Literature, 1919); Shirley Jackson Case, *The Millennial Hope; A Phase of War Time Thinking* (Chicago: University of Chicago Press, 1918), v–vi; see Marsden, *Fundamentalism and American Culture*, 147, on governmental investigation; the quotation is from the *Chicago Daily News*, January 21, 1918, and *The King's Business* 9 (April 1918):276.

11:47. James M. Gray, "Practical and Perplexing Questions," *Christian Workers' Magazine* 16 (October 1915):97–98. Quoted in Weber, *Living in the Shadow*, 122.

11:48. Arno Gaebelein, *Our Hope* 19 (July 1912):49–50; Charles Reihl, "Solution to Prohibition," *The Truth* 15 (1889):370–75. Quoted in Weber, *Living in the Shadow*, 94–96.

11:49. James M. Gray, *Prophecy and the Lord's Return* (New York: Fleming H. Revell, 1917), 109. Quoted in Weber, *Living in the Shadow*, 98.

11:50. Gundry, *Love Them In*, 189–90; Dwight L. Moody, "When Jesus Comes Again," *The Christian Herald* (December 21, 1910):1208–9.

11:51. Robert Cameron, "Prophetic Teachers," *The Watchword* 18 (October 1896):258–59, quoted in Kraus, *Dispensationalism in America*, 48; James H. Brookes, in *Watchword and Truth* 24 (1902):302; Nathaniel West, *The Apostle Paul and the "Any Moment" Theory* (Philadelphia, 1893), 34. The Cameron-Brookes conversation is in *Watchword and Truth* 24 (1902):302. Quoted in Sandeen, *The Roots of Fundamentalism*, 209–12.

11:52. *Watchword and Truth* 24 (1902):238.

11:53. Sandeen, *The Roots of Fundamentalism*, 213–24, and especially 222 on the origin of the Scofield Bible; also *Moody Monthly* 43 (1943): 278.

11:54. A revised edition of Timothy Weber, *Living in the Shadow of the Second Coming* (Grand Rapids: Zondervan, 1983), adds two chapters and a conclusion offering an update on Protestant Zionism to 1982.

11:55. Weber, *Living in the Shadow*, 138, 140, describes the later memorial; see Reuben Fink, ed., *America and Palestine* (New York: American Zionist Emergency Council, 1944), 21, concerning the earlier efforts; on the Bible base, see Beth M. Lindberg, *A God-Filled Life: The Story of William E. Blackstone* (Chicago: American Messianic Fellowship, n.d.), 14.

11:56. Lindberg, *A God-Filled Life*, 14–16. Quoted in Weber, *Living in the Shadow*, 140–41.

11:57. Weber, *Living in the Shadow*, 128–57, enlarges on the Zionist theme; see also David A. Rausch, *Zionism within Early American Fundamentalism, 1878–1918: A Convergence of Two Traditions* (New York: Edwin Mellen Press, 1979); also E. F. Stroeter, "The Second Coming of Christ in Relation to Israel," in *Addresses on the Second Coming of the Lord Delivered at The Prophetic Conference, Allegheny, Pa., December 3–6, 1895* (Pittsburgh, W. W. Waters, n.d.), 151–56. Quoted in Rausch, *Zionism*, 98–99.

11:58. William G. Moorehead, "The Conversion of Israel and the Conversion of the World," *Addresses of the International Prophetic Conference Held December 10–15, 1901 in the Clarendon Street Baptist Church, Boston, Mass.* (Boston, Watchword and Truth, n.d.), 39–43; W. B. Riley, "The Significant Signs of the Times," *The Coming and Kingdom of Christ: A Stenographic Report of the Prophetic Bible Conference Held at the Moody Bible Institute of Chicago, February 24–27, 1914* (Chicago: The Bible Institute Colportage Association, 1914), 103. Quoted in Rausch, *Zionism*, 102, 107.

11:59. Robert McWatty Russell, "The Kingdom View of the Gospel as Related to the Missionary Program of Christ," *The Coming and Kingdom of Christ: A Stenographic Report*, 20. Quoted in Rausch, *Zionism*, 108.

11:60. Arno C. Gaebelein, "The Capture of Jerusalem and the Great Future of the City," in Gaebelein, *Christ and Glory*, 146–47, 156–57; W. B. Riley, "The Last Days; the Last War and the Last King," in ibid., 175. Quoted in Rausch, *Zionism*, 113–15.

11:61. *The Christian Workers' Magazine* 16 (September 1915):37, 17 (August 1917):933–34; C. I. Scofield, *Prophecy Made Plain* (London: Pickering and Inglis, n.d.), 74–77. Quoted in Rausch, *Zionism*, 75–76, 182, 192–93.

11:62. Arno C. Gaebelein, "The Hope of Israel Mission to the Jews," *Our Hope* 1 (July 1894):21.

11:63. A summary of four kinds of conservative Protestant views of millennium are in Robert G. Clouse, ed., *The Meaning of the Millennium: Four Views* (Downers Grove, Ill.: InterVarsity Press, 1977). The wide disagreement suggests how little consensus there is among conservatives about the continuity and tradition.

11:64. Woodbridge, *Biblical Authority*, is a searching historical defense of inerrancy over against charges that it was a novel construct.

11:65. Ibid., 122–28, reviews some non-Princetonian approaches.

11:66. On the early years, see John O. Nelson, "The Rise of the Princeton Theology: A Genetic Study of American Presbyterianism until 1850" (Ph.D. diss., Yale, 1935).

11:67. John C. Vander Stelt, *Philosophy and Scripture: A Study in Old Princeton and Westminster Theology* (Marlton, N.J.: Mack Publishing Company, 1978), addresses this subject; see especially "Common Sense Philosophy," 57–64.

11:68. Charles Hodge, *Systematic Theology*, 3 vols. (New York: Scribner, Armstrong, 1871–75), 1:18.

11:69. Hodge wrote early against the priority of experience, in "Inspiration," *Princeton Review* 29 (October 1857):692. Quoted in Marsden, *Fundamentalism and American Culture*, 112.

11:70. Archibald A. Hodge and Benjamin B. Warfield, "Inspiration," *The Presbyterian Review* 2 (April 1881):237; concerning "facts," see Charles Hodge, *Systematic Theology*, 1:10. Quoted in Marsden, *Fundamentalism and American Culture*, 113.

11:71. See Warfield's introduction to Francis R. Beattie, *Apologetics: Or the Rational Vindication of Christianity* (Richmond, Va., 1903). Quoted in Marsden, *Fundamentalism and American Culture*, 115.

11:72. For a latter-day example, see Harold Lindsell, *The Battle for the Bible* (Grand Rapids, Mich.: Zondervan, 1976), which uses inerrancy as the divider between true and false movements and churches.

11:73. Francis Landey Patton, in *The Centennial Celebration of the Theological Seminary* (Princeton: Princeton Theological Seminary, 1912), 349–50. Quoted in Mark A. Noll, ed., *The Princeton Theology, 1812–1921* (Grand Rapids, Mich.: Baker, 1983), 39.

11:74. Hodge, *Systematic Theology*, 1:170.

11:75. For Warfield's defense, see a later edition of his work, B. B. Warfield, *The Inspiration and Authority of the Bible*, ed. Samuel G. Craig (Philadelphia: Presbyterian and Reformed Publishing Company, 1964), 220–21.

11:76. Cortland Myers, "War on German Theology," *Light on Prophecy*, 178, 181–82.

11:77. For discussion of such creeds, see Sandeen, *The Roots of Fundamentalism*, 273ff. Some critics fault Sandeen for overstressing the role of Warfield and Hodge in patenting modern inerrancy, but he does present a systematic overview of developments.

11:78. See the *Watchman-Examiner* 8 (May 20, 1920):652 and 10 (June 15, 1922):745. Cited by Marsden, *Fundamentalism and American Culture*, 159, 274.

11:79. Some sense of the Pentecostal scope can come from Charles Edwin Jones, *A Guide to the Study of the Pentecostal Movement*, 2 vols. (Metuchen, N.J.: Scarecrow Press, 1983). It includes 9,883 bibliographical items.

11:80. A convenient introduction to the movement is Robert Mapes Anderson, *Vision of the Disinherited: The Making of American Pentecostalism* (New York: Oxford University Press, 1979).

11:81. See ibid., 214–25; *Pentecostal Evangel* (March 6, 1920):8–9; (October 12, 1929):6; (September 19, 1925):3; (November 26, 1927):1.

11:82. C. I. Scofield, *Plain Papers on the Doctrine of the Holy Spirit* (New York: Fleming H. Revell, 1899), 9–11; and Reuben A. Torrey, *The Baptism with the Holy Spirit* (New York: Fleming H. Revell, 1895), 18.

11:83. Anderson, *Vision of the Disinherited*, 52, quotes Ozman from a letter dated February 28, 1922, long after the event had taken on a canonical character in the movement; she may have stylized it by then.

11:84. Sarah Thistlethwaite Parham, compiler, *The Life of Charles F. Parham: Founder of the Apostolic Faith Movement* (Joplin, Mo.: Tri-State Printing, 1930), 52, recalls Parham's coaching; see also Anderson, *Vision of the Disinherited*, 52–53, for a setting of this stage.

11:85. Anderson, *Vision of the Disinherited*, 53, quotes A. N. O. LaBerge from a letter of February 28, 1922, citing Ozman's experiences; also Howard D. Stanley to J. Roswell Flower, February 18, 1949, and May 17, 1954; on "Sweedish," see Parham, *The Life of Charles F. Parham*, 53–54.

11:86. Anderson, *Vision of the Disinherited*, 54–57, raises critical questions about the approved story.

11:87. Vinson Synan, *The Holiness-Pentecostal Movement in the United States* (Grand Rapids, Mich.: William B. Eerdmans, 1971), 99–102, discusses "tongues" and quotes newspaper accounts of Parham; for the burning of the mansion, see Parham, *The Life of Charles F. Parham*, 81.

11:88. Timothy L. Smith, *Called Unto Holiness: The Story of the Nazarenes: The Formative Years* (Kansas City, Mo.: Nazarene Publishing House, 1962), effectively traces one body that moved beyond Methodism but did not become Pentecostal, the Nazarenes.

11:89. *Journal, General Conference of the Methodist Episcopal Church, South* (Nashville: Southern Methodist Publishing House, 1894), 25–26. Quoted in Synan, *The Holiness-Pentecostal Movement*, 50.

11:90. Synan, *The Holiness-Pentecostal Movement*, 52–54, describes the toll Holiness took from Methodism; Vinson Synan, *The Old-Time Power* (Franklin Springs, Ga.: Advocate Press, 1973), 52, lists the denominations.

11:91. George Taylor, "Our Church History," *The Pentecostal Holiness Advocate* (January 20, 1921):9; (February 3, 1921):8–9, on extravagances; Synan, *The Old-Time Power*, 61–63, quotes Crumpler's vituperations from *The Holiness Advocate* (February 15, 1903):4; (October 15, 1903):7.

11:92. Synan, *The Old-Time Power*, 116–17, quotes Crumpler and on 106–21 treats the Crumpler-Cashwell incident.

11:93. Ibid., 82–94, recounts Irwin's career. Taylor's "fire" is in *The Pentecostal Holiness Advocate* (May 22, 1930):8.

11:94. For "Fire-Baptized" ways of life, see *Constitution and General Rules of the Fire-Baptized Holiness Church* (Royston, Ga., 1905), 2–7. A. M. Hills quotes with disapproval the "Dynamite" woman in "Fanaticism Among Holiness People," *The Holiness Advocate* (April 1, 1903):5. On the transition from Irwin to King, see J. H. King and Blanche L. King, *Yet Speaketh: Memoirs of the Late Bishop Joseph H. King* (Franklin Springs, Ga.: Publishing House of the Pentecostal Holiness Church, 1949), 101–3. See Synan, *The Old-Time Power*, 89–97.

11:95. James Gordon Lindsay, *The Life of John Alexander Dowie* (Shreveport, La.: Voice of Healing Publishing Company, 1951), 4, 117, 137–45, 203–5; Synan, *The Holiness-Pentecostal Movement*, 100–101.

11:96. Mary B. Woodworth-Etter, *Signs and Wonders God Wrought in the Ministry for Forty Years* (Chicago: published by the author, 1916), 44–45, 118, 103–4, 108–19; and Anderson, *Vision of the Disinherited*, 34–36.

11:97. Anderson, *Vision of the Disinherited*, 60–61, 65–66, details Seymour's career; see also Alma White, *Demons and Tongues* (Zeraphath, N.J.: The Pillar of Fire, 1949), 68–69. Cited in Synan, *The Holiness-Pentecostal Movement*, 105.

11:98. A modern reprint of Frank Bartleman, *Azusa Street* (Plainfield, N.J.: Logos International, 1980), and Synan, *The Holiness-Pentecostal Movement*, 105–14, are sources on Seymour; see also the *Los Angeles Times*, April 18 and April 19, 1906.

11:99. Frank J. Ewart, *The Phenomenon of Pentecost: A History of the Latter Rain* (St. Louis: Pentecostal Publishing House, 1947), 40–49, provides details; see also Frank Bartleman, *How Pentecost Came to Los Angeles* (Los Angeles, 1925), 63.

11:100. Harwood's comments are in White, *Demons and Tongues*, 71–73, while Parham's comments are strung through Parham, *The Life of Charles H. Parham*, 164–202.

11:101. Synan, *The Holiness-Pentecostal Movement*, 116, discusses "relics." See Frank Bartleman, *From Plow to Pulpit* (Los Angeles: published by the author, 1924), 22–23. Quoted in Anderson, *Vision of the Disinherited*, 78.

11:102. Synan, *The Pentecostal-Holiness Movement*, 79–80, refers to Mason's work.

11:103. Ibid., 83–90; see also A. J. Tomlinson, *Answering the Call of God* (Cleveland, Tenn.: White Wing Publishing House, n.d.), 1–15; and the "dark ages" reference in Synan, ibid., 84–85. Anderson, *Vision of the Disinherited*, 205–6, comments on submission.

11:104. Charles Fox Parham, *The Everlasting Gospel* (Baxter Springs, Kan.: published by the author, 1942), 28–30. Quoted in Anderson, *Vision of the Disinherited*, 209.

11:105. John Thomas Nichol, *Pentecostalism* (New York: Harper and Row, 1966), 79, reproduces the Richardson hymn. Nichol discusses Pentecostal denominations, 94–157. See the *Christian Evangel* (October 10, 1914): 2, for anti-Catholic reference.

11:106. A balanced summary is in Anderson, *Vision of the Disinherited*, 223–40.

Chapter Twelve

12:1. To anticipate a discussion of "becoming post-modern," one might profitably consult Alex Inkeles and David H. Smith, *Becoming Modern: Individual Change in Six Developing Countries* (Cambridge: Harvard University Press, 1974), especially chap. 21. This presents a summary of empirically-based findings concerning the impact of modernization in diverse cultures.

12:2. Here, as before, a useful condensation of the theme is John Murray Cuddihy, *The Ordeal of Civility: Freud, Marx, Lévi-Strauss, and the Jewish Struggle with Modernity* (New York: Basic Books, 1974), 3–14, and especially, p. 10. See also Peter L. Berger, Brigitte Berger, Hansfried Kellner, *The Homeless Mind: Modernization and Consciousness* (New York: Random House, 1973), 189–230, on "demodernization." The authors say that "componentiality" and "multirelationality" produce "a nostalgia for wholeness, unity and comprehensibility," and "simplification" (206).

12:3. Despite the references to more recent sociological literature in note 12:2, the effort here will be to listen to the rhetoric of people in the period from 1893 to 1919 and have their terms and forms dominate the narrative.

12:4. William James, *The Varieties of Religious Experience* (New York: Longmans, Green, 1902), 112, 156. *Oxford English Dictionary*, s.v. "integrum."

12:5. William James, *Talks to Teachers on Psychology and to Students on Some of Life's Ideals* (Cambridge: Harvard University Press, 1983), 122–24, 129–31.

12:6. James, *The Varieties of Religious Experience*, 91, 94, 100, 105, 113.

12:7. Robert Peel, *Mary Baker Eddy: The Years of Authority* (New York: Holt, Rinehart and Winston, 1977), 99, quotes James. Peel is the authority from within Christian Science on the life of Eddy and this volume best covers her years in the period under discussion.

12:8. Stephen Gottschalk, *The Emergence of Christian Science in American Religious Life* (Berkeley: University of California Press, 1973), 211, quotes Green and Gordon; 215 quotes Mrs. Eddy.

12:9. These movements are introduced in Gail Thain Parker, *Mind Cure in New England From the Civil War to World War I* (Hanover, N.H.: University Press of New England, 1973) and Donald Meyer, *The Positive Thinkers: Religion as Pop Psychology From Mary Baker Eddy to Oral Roberts* (New York: Pantheon, 1965). Margaret Connolly, *The Life Story of Orison Swett Marden* (New York: Thomas Y. Crowell, 1925), 60–61, quotes Marden on homelessness. Cited in Parker, *Mind Cure*, 35; Meyer, *The Positive Thinkers*, 40–44, discusses Unity.

12:10. William James, *The Will to Believe and Other Essays in Popular Philosophy* (Cambridge: Harvard University Press, 1979), 7; James was referring to the Salvation Army and the need for science.

12:11. Daniel Dorchester, *Christianity in the United States from the First Settlement down to the Present Time* (New York: Hunt and Eaton, 1889), 520; Henry K. Carroll, *The Religious Forces of the United States* (New York: The Christian Literature Co., 1893), 8–11.

12:12. Leonard Woolsey Bacon, *A History of American Christianity* (New York: Charles Scribner's Sons, 1898), 336–37.

12:13. Ronald L. Numbers, *Prophetess of Health: A Study of Ellen G. White* (New York: Harper and Row, 1976), 81–83; Lay's conversation is reported by W. C. White, "The Origin of the Light on Health Reform among Seventh-Day Adventists," *Medical Evangelist* 20 (December 28, 1933):2. Numbers is the best introduction to White.

12:14. Numbers, *Prophetess of Health*, 172–75.

12:15. Ibid., 200.

12:16. E. Brooks Holifield, *A History of Pastoral Care in America: From Salvation to Self-Realization* (Nashville: Abingdon Press, 1983), 156, 164, introduces these themes and is the best treatment of the subject. See Washington Gladden, *Ruling Ideas of the Present Age* (Boston: Houghton Mifflin, 1895), 294; H. M. Sydenstricker, "The Science of Conversion," in *The Fundamentals*, 12 vols. (Chicago: Testimony Publishing Co., 1910):8:64–65, 70–72.

12:17. For these trends, see Holifield, *A History of Pastoral Care*, 176–77, 189–90, 195.

12:18. Jeffrey P. Hantover, "Sex Role, Sexuality, and Social Status: The Early Years of the Boy Scouts of America" (Ph.D. diss., University of Chicago, 1976), chap. 4, "Forces of Feminization," and an Appendix, with its list of male or mixed youth organizations, numbering more than eighty between 1893 and 1919; more than half had "religious" as their main purpose. See also Holifield, *A History of Pastoral Care*, 168–75.

12:19. William Newton Clarke, *An Outline of Christian Theology* (New York: Charles Scribner's Sons, 1899), 19; for Emmanuel, see Holifield, *A History of Pastoral Care*, 201–9; see Holifield's references, pp. 386–87, for bibliography.

12:20. See Richard Cabot, "Whose Business is Psychotherapy?" in John Gardner Greene, "The Emmanuel Movement, 1906–29," *New England Quarterly* 7 (September 1934):516. Quoted in Holifield, *A History of Pastoral Care*, 206.

12:21. Josiah Royce, "The Modern Psychotherapeutic Movement in America," *Psychotherapy* (1909); 3:4:20, 33. Quoted in Holifield, *A History of Pastoral Care*, 209. Some of this Roycean analysis follows John Owen King III, *The Iron of Melancholy: Structures of Spiritual Conversion in America from the Puritan Conscience to Victorian Neurosis* (Middletown, Conn.: Wesleyan University Press, 1983), 198–253. Royce wrote James on May 21, 1888; see Josiah Royce, *The Letters of Josiah Royce*, ed. John Clendenning (Chicago: University of Chicago Press, 1970), 216.

12:22. King, *The Iron of Melancholy*, 232, 240, 245–46.

12:23. Ibid., 247–49; see also Josiah Royce, *The Problem of Christianity: Lectures Delivered at the Lowell Institute in Boston, and at Manchester College, Oxford* (Chicago: University of Chicago Press, 1968), 115–16, 131.

12:24. See King, *The Iron of Melancholy*, 250–51, for a collation of such themes from *The Problem of Christianity*.

12:25. Horace M. Kallen, "Remarks on Royce's Philosophy," *The Journal of Philosophy* 53 (February 2, 1956): 132–37; King, *The Iron of Melancholy*, 251–53, sees Royce at the time of his decline as an almost pathetic figure.

12:26. The standard life is Dorothy Ross, *G. Stanley Hall: The Psychologist as Prophet* (Chicago: University of Chicago Press, 1972). G. Stanley Hall, *Jesus the Christ in the Light of Psychology*, 2 vols. (New York: Doubleday, Page, 1917); 2:368 discusses Mansoul.

12:27. G. Stanley Hall, *Adolescence: Its Psychology and Its Relations to Physiology, Anthropology, Sociology, Sex, Crime, Religion and Education*, 2 vols. (New York: D. Appleton, 1904), 2:66, 69. See also, Hall, *Jesus the Christ*, 2:368.

12:28. Hall's theory of the recapitulation of the race is in Hall, *Adolescence*, 1:viii–ix, xv. See comment on this strand in R. Jackson Wilson, *In Quest of Community: Social Philosophy in the United States, 1860–1920* (New York: John Wiley and Sons, 1968), 114–43.

12:29. Ross, *G. Stanley Hall*, 34–35, 60–79, 134–47, 179–85.

12:30. See Wilson, *In Quest of Community*, 130–32, for citations on this subject.

12:31. Hall, *Adolescence* 2:304; and Wilson, *In Quest of Community*, 133–36.

12:32. Wilson, *In Quest of Community*, 136–38, cites scores of "sacral" references. On the journal and Jesus, see Ross, *G. Stanley Hall*, 417–18.

12:33. Ross, *G. Stanley Hall*, 417, 436.

12:34. James H. Leuba, "A Study in the Psychology of Religious Phenomena," *American Journal of Psychology* 7 (April 1896): 309–85; Edwin Diller Starbuck, *The Psychology of Religion* (New York: Scribner's, 1899). See Benjamin Beit-Hallahmi, "Psychology of Religion, 1880–1930: The Rise and Fall of a Psychological Movement," in H. Newton Malony, *Current Perspectives in the Psychology of Religion* (Grand Rapids, Mich.: William B. Eerdmans, 1977), 17–25.

12:35. Edward L. Schaub, "The Psychology of Religion in America during the Past Quarter Century," *Journal of Religion* 6 (March 1926): 113–34; Starbuck, *The Psychology of Religion*, 1.

12:36. Stephen A. Schmidt, *A History of the Religious Education Association* (Birmingham, Ala.: Religious Education Press, 1983), introduces the subject of the REA. See Frank Knight Sanders' address in *Official Bulletin* 3 of the Religious Education Assocation (May 1904), quoted by Schmidt as epigraph to his book (5).

12:37. William Rainey Harper, Editorial, *The Biblical World* 3 (1894): 3; quoted in Schmidt, *A History of the Religious Education Assocation*, 11; George A. Coe, *The Spiritual Life* (New York: Eaton and Mains, 1900), 12–15, 61, 236–43.

12:38. George A. Coe, *The Religion of a Mature Mind* (New York: Fleming H. Revell, 1902), 47ff., 299–302.

12:39. Ibid., 298–304.

12:40. John Dewey, "Religious Education as Conditioned by Modern Psychology and Pedagogy," in *Proceedings of the First Annual Convention, The Religious Education Association* (Chicago: REA Office, 1903), 62, 66.

12:41. *The Biblical World* (February 1903):10, reprinted this document for the convention; quoted by Schmidt, *A History of the Religious Education Association*, 34–35.

12:42. George Albert Coe, "Religious Education as a Part of General Education," in *Proceedings of the First Annual Convention*, 48–52.

12:43. George A. Coe, *Religious Experience and the Scientific Movement* (n.p., 1897), 6; *What Is Christian Education?* (New York: Charles Scribner's Sons, 1929), 296; *A Social Theory of Religious Education* (New York: Charles Scribner's Sons, 1917), 15, 54, 67, 225.

12:44. Schmidt, *A History of the Religious Education Association*, 44, selects these samples from John H. T. Main, "The Modern Man and Religious Education," *Religious Education* 4 (December 1909):478–79, and Graham Taylor, "Church and Civic Education: Community Activities as a Means of Education in Civic Righteousness," *Religious Education* 5 (October 1910):385–90.

12:45. Gerald E. Knoff, *The World Sunday School Movement: The Story of a Broadening Mission* (New York: Seabury, 1979), 6ff., describes the ethos.

12:46. Robert W. Lynn and Elliott Wright, *The Big Little School: Sunday Child of American Protestantism* (New York: Harper and Row, 1971), 72–73, reports on the 1893 committee; Welch is in *The Sunday School and World Progress Report, the Eighth World Convention* (Tokyo, 1920) of the USSC, 321–22; see Knoff, *The World Sunday School Movement*, 70–71.

12:47. *Eighth World Convention*, 279; Frank L. Brown, *Report to the Executive Committee, American Section* (1919), 17; quoted by Knoff, *The World Sunday School Movement*, 71–72.

Chapter Thirteen

13:1. The standard sourcebook and bibliography of the movement in these years is Ruth Rouse and Stephen Charles Neill, eds., *A History of the Ecumenical Movement, 1517–1948* (Philadelphia: Westminster Press, 1967).

13:2. Works like Russell E. Richey, ed., *Denominationalism* (Nashville: Abingdon Press, 1977), suggest that the denomination is more the subject of historical and sociological inquiry and a practical instrument than a topic which evokes theological rationales.

13:3. Schaff told Parliament people he was warned that it would kill him if he came to Chicago. "Well, let it kill me." He gathered strength for one last witness to Christian Union. John Henry Barrows, *The World's Parliament of Religions*, 2 vols. (Chicago: The Parliament Publishing Company, 1893), 1:138.

13:4. Elias B. Sanford, *Origin and History of the Federal Council of the Churches of Christ in America* (Hartford, Conn.: The S. S. Scranton Company, 1916), 96–97, quotes Schaff, placing him in the continuity of the conciliar movement.

13:5. Leonard Woolsey Bacon, *A History of American Christianity* (New York: Charles Scribner's Sons, 1898), 400–401.

13:6. Ibid., 402–3.

13:7. Ibid., 410, 416–17, 419.

13:8. Josiah Strong was quoted in an issue of *The Federation Chronicle*, by John A. Hutchison, *We Are Not Divided: A Critical and Historical Study of the Federal Council of the Churches of Christ in America* (New York: Round Table Press, 1941), 28.

13:9. Sanford, *Origin and History*, 79–80.

13:10. Ibid., 303.

13:11. Hutchison, *We Are Not Divided*, 32, quotes these words from *The Federation Chronicle*, January 1902.

13:12. Ibid., 31, quotes Northrup in *The Federation Chronicle*, January 1903.

13:13. Ibid., 29, quotes the *Century* item from a National Federation citation.

13:14. C. Howard Hopkins, *John R. Mott, 1865–1955* (Grand Rapids, Mich.: William B. Eerdmans, 1979), 710 n. 89, discusses Mott at the Parliament. See also 129.

13:15. Ibid., 205–6, discusses Mrs. McCormick.

13:16. Ibid., 418–19.

13:17. Josiah Strong, *The New Era or the Coming Kingdom* (New York: Baker and Taylor, 1893), 314; Hutchison, *We Are Not Divided*, 29, quotes Brooks from a pamphlet, *Church Federation: What It Is and What It Is Not* (New York: n.p., 1903). Sanford, *Origin and History*, 38–39, quoted the Open and Institutional Church League program on simplicity.

13:18. Hutchison, *We Are Not Divided*, 42, quotes comments on antidenominationalism.

13:19. Elias B. Sanford, *Church Federation: Inter-Church Conference on Federation, New York. November 15–21, 1905* (New York: Fleming H. Revell, 1906), 84–85, quotes Niccolls.

13:20. Ibid., 34–35 and 20; for *The Interior*, p. 678.

13:21. See Samuel McCrea Cavert, *The American Churches in the Ecumenical Movement, 1900–1968* (New York: Association Press, 1968), 65ff.

13:22. For Goodell on evangelism, see Samuel McCrea Cavert, *Church Cooperation and Unity in America: A Historical Review: 1900–1970* (New York: Association Press, 1970), 140.

13:23. Cavert, *The American Churches*, 42 n. 21, cites a letter by Sanford dated August 16, 1922.

13:24. Hutchison, *We Are Not Divided*, 49–50, quotes imperialists; see Elias B. Sanford, *Origin and History*, 291–95, for Brewer comment in context.

13:25. The rival was an Interchurch World Movement, whose advertisement of March 1920, was an epigraph in Ray H. Abrams, *Preachers Present Arms* (New York: Round Table Press, 1933), 144.

13:26. Charles S. Macfarland edited "The Churches of Christ in Time of War," which was reprinted in his *Christian Unity in Practice and Prophecy* (New York: Macmillan, 1933), 63–65; the other comments are cited in Hutchison, *We Are Not Divided*, 178–83.

13:27. Abrams, *Preachers Present Arms*, 147–48, reprints a letter from Norman Thomas to Roger Baldwin, June 20, 1917; the Holmes-Macfarland exchange, mentioned by Abrams, ibid., 151–52, appeared in *New Republic* 18 (March 15, 1919):217–18; (April 12, 1919):351. Hutchison, *We Are Not Divided*, quotes Brown, 191–92.

13:28. The story of the IWM is well told in Eldon G. Ernst, *Moment of Truth for Protestant America: Interchurch Campaigns Following World War One* (Missoula, Montana: Scholar's Press, 1972); 18–23 discuss antecedent movements.

13:29. Ibid., 52–58, quotes a "Report of the Committee of Twenty," while the unified program was discussed by Lyman P. Powell, "Real Cooperation of the Churches," *The American Review of Reviews* 59 (June 1919):633; and *World Call* 1 (June 1919):51; portions of Mott's speech are recorded in *I.W.M. Documents*, 5:38–40; the "whole church" matter is in *Federal Council Bulletin* 3 (February 1920):25; and *World Call* 2 (February 1920):15.

13:30. A catena of hyperbolic sayings is in Ernst, *Moment of Truth*, 58–63; masculine Christianity is discussed on 67 n. 32.

13:31. Ibid., 73–84, tells of organizational rivalry and friendly citizens; see *Saturday Evening Post* (April 24, 1920):122–23; *New York Times* (April 8, 1920):32; Macfarland's resistance is recalled in his *Christianity Unity*, 69.

13:32. Ernst, *Moment of Truth*, 89–109, tells the business story, most of whose documentation is in the National Council of Churches Research Library in New York. See also Edward Earl Purinton, "Big Ideas from Big Business," *The Independent* (April 16, 1921):395; and "Efficiency in the Lord's Business," *New Era Magazine* 2 (June 1920):418–19. For Rockefeller's opinion of the plans, see *I.W.M. Documents*, 3:115.

13:33. Ernst, *Moment of Truth*, 122–34, on the steel strike.

13:34. Ibid., 137–51, treats the demise of the IWM. See *The Literary Digest* 65 (June 12, 1920):42–43.

13:35. Arthur C. Archibald, "Evangelism Fundamental in Social Reconstruction," *The Baptist* 1 (September 25, 1920):1199.

13:36. See Epilogue, by Stephen Charles Neill, in Rouse and Neill, *A History of the Ecumenical Movement*, 725–31.

Chapter Fourteen

14:1. On the modern preoccupation with the social, see Martin E. Marty, "Religious Development in Historical, Social, and Cultural Context," in Merton P. Strommen, ed., *Research on Religious Development: A Comprehensive Handbook* (New York: Hawthorn, 1971), 42–77.

14:2. The best telling of this story is Norris Magnuson, *Salvation in the Slums: Evangelical Social Work, 1865–1920* (Metuchen, N.J.: The Scarecrow Press, 1977).

14:3. Ibid., 153–64, concentrates on the Army in World War I.

14:4. Principles quoted by Arthur Carl Piepkorn, *Profiles in Belief: The Religious Bodies of the United States and Canada*, 4 vols. (New York: Harper and Row, 1977–79), 3:76–77.

14:5. Magnuson, *Salvation in the Slums*, 112–17, especially p. 115, citing a letter from Willard to *The War Cry* (May 5, 1894):928.

14:6. Magnuson, *Salvation in the Slums*, 165–78; William T. Stead, *Life of Mrs. Booth, The Founder of the Salvation Army* (New York: Fleming H. Revell, 1900), 195; *The War Cry* (November 7, 1891):527; Magnuson, ibid., 168, lists featured thinkers and activists; *The War Cry* (September 4, 1897):6, 14, refers to Debs.

14:7. Pentecostal Church of the Nazarene, First General Assembly, *Proceedings* (1907):57, quoted by Timothy L. Smith, *Called Unto Holiness: The Story of the Nazarenes: The Formative Years* (Kansas City, Mo.: Nazarene Publishing House, 1962), 201.

14:8. Smith, *Called Unto Holiness*, 201–2; see J. D. Scott, "God's Standard," *Holiness Evangel* (January 15, 1907):1.

14:9. Smith, *Called Unto Holiness*, 203; Pentecostal Church of the Nazarene, First General Assembly, *Proceedings* (1907):43.

14:10. See Ronald C. White, Jr., and C. Howard Hopkins, *The Social Gospel: Religion and Reform in Changing America* (Philadelphia: Temple University Press, 1976), 167 n. 13, on the naming; on the Georgia colony, see James Dombrowski, *The Early Days of Christian Socialism in America* (New York: Columbia University Press, 1936), 132–70. See Shailer Mathews, *The Social Gospel* (Philadelphia: The Griffith and Rowland Press, 1910).

14:11. A judicious assessment of impact is in Robert T. Handy, ed., *The Social Gospel in America, 1870–1920: Gladden-Ely-Rauschenbusch* (New York: Oxford University Press, 1966), 3–16.

14:12. Josiah Strong, *The Next Great Awakening*, 10th ed. (New York: Baker and Taylor, 1913), iii.

14:13. Arthur Cushman McGiffert, Jr., *No Ivory Tower: The Story of Chicago Theological Seminary* (Chicago: Chicago Theological Seminary, 1965), 94–95, cites Graham Taylor, *Syllabus in Biblical Sociology, Printed for Use in the Class-Room, 1900*.

14:14. Francis G. Peabody, *The Religion of an Educated Man* (New York: Macmillan, 1903), 4–5; George Santayana, *Character and Opinion in the United States* (New York: Charles Scribner's Sons, 1921), 49.

14:15. Graham Taylor, *Pioneering on Social Frontiers* (Chicago: University of Chicago Press, 1930), 398; *Syllabus in Biblical Theology*, 23, 26–27; *Religion in Social Action* (New York: Dodd, Mead, 1913), 99; see also Louise C. Wade, *Graham Taylor: Pioneer for Social Justice, 1851–1938* (Chicago: University of Chicago Press, 1964), 83–116.

14:16. While literature on Rauschenbusch is extensive, there is no critical biography. Dores R. Sharpe, *Walter Rauschenbusch* (New York: Macmillan, 1942), was by both a friend and admirer.

14:17. Ibid., 62–63, cites Rauschenbusch's words to the Cleveland Young Men's Christian Association in 1913; on the aim of the church, see "The Kingdom of God," *Brotherhood Leaflets* 4 (1894): 2, 4–5, 7–8; in the Baptist Historical Collection, quoted by Peter J. Frederick, *Knights of the Golden Rule: The Intellectual as Christian Social Reformer in the 1890s* (Lexington, Ky.: University of Kentucky Press, 1976), 151; see also Walter Rauschenbusch, *Christianity and the Social Crisis* (New York: Macmillan, 1907), 65.

14:18. William Newton Clarke, *The Ideal of Jesus* (New York: Charles Scribner's Sons, 1912), 64; Francis G. Peabody, *Jesus Christ and the Christian Character* (New York: Macmillan, 1905), 76.

14:19. William Dwight Porter Bliss, *The New Encyclopedia of Social Reform* (New York: Funk and Wagnalls, 1908), 204; Walter Rauschenbusch, *A Theology for the Social Gospel* (New York: Macmillan, 1917), 69–70.

14:20. Frederick, *Knights of the Golden Rule*, 119; see Vida D. Scudder, "Socialism and Sacrifice," *Atlantic Monthly* 105 (June 1910):839.

14:21. These generalizations are best checked out by reading of sources, as in Handy, *The Social Gospel in America*.

14:22. Francis Greenwood Peabody, *The Approach to the Social Question* (New York: Macmillan, 1909), 6.

14:23. For an imaginative address to this issue, see Janet Forsythe Fishburn, *The Fatherhood of God and the Victorian Family: The Social Gospel in America* (Philadelphia: Fortress Press, 1981).

14:24. Ibid., 8–10; see also Benson Y. Landis, ed., *A Rauschenbusch Reader* (New York: Harper and Brothers, 1957), 79; Rauschenbusch, *Christianity and the Social Crisis*, 135.

14:25. Fishburn, *The Fatherhood of God*, 124, is the single reference to woman suffrage in the context of the Social Gospel in a work which is seeking to make such reference; the connection (between Rauschenbusch and feminists) is negative. A review of literature on women and religion, especially in respect to social causes, could begin with Janet Wilson James, ed., *Women in American Religion* (Philadelphia: University of Pennsylvania Press, 1980); and Rosemary Radford Ruether and Rosemary Skinner Keller, eds., *Women and Religion in America*, Volume 1: *The Nineteenth Century* (New York: Harper and Row, 1981). Volume 2 in my four-volume history will take advantage of the impressive if tardy beginnings of research in this field in recent years.

14:26. See Alan P. Grimes, *The Puritan Ethic and Woman Suffrage* (New York: Oxford University Press, 1967), especially 102–4.

14:27. See Fishburn, *The Fatherhood of God*, 124. On Scudder and feminism, see Frederick, *Knights of the Golden Rule*, 124–26. On the connection between women's movements and temperance, see Ruth Bordin, *Woman and Temperance: The Quest for Power and Liberty, 1873–1900* (Philadelphia: Temple University Press, 1981).

14:28. On the "Woman's Bible" controversy, see Aileen S. Kraditor, *The Ideas of the Woman Suffrage Movement, 1890–1920* (New York: Columbia University Press, 1965), 78–86; Susan Anthony wrote Mrs. Stanton on July 24, 1895.

14:29. On Shaw and Catt and the Bible, see Kraditor, *The Ideas of the Woman Suffrage Movement*, 87–93.

14:30. Wilmer Albert Linkugel, "The Speeches of Anna Howard Shaw" (Ph.D. diss., Wisconsin, 1960), 2:83–84, quotes "The Women Who Publish the Tidings Are a Great Host." Cited by Kraditor, *The Ideas of the Woman Suffrage Movement*, 92.

14:31. Charles Aked, "Man and His Neighbor," *Appleton's Magazine* 12 (July 1908):9. See James H. Timberlake, *Prohibition and the Progressive Movement 1900–1920* (Cambridge: Harvard University Press, 1966), 4–38.

14:32. Shirley Jackson Case, *The Millennial Hope: A Phase of War-Time Thinking* (Chicago: The University of Chicago Press, 1918), 238.

14:33. Comments on race include Washington Gladden, *Recollections* (Boston: Houghton Mifflin, 1909), 371–72; Lyman Abbott, *Reminiscences* (Boston: Houghton Mifflin, 1915), 270; Ira V. Brown, *Lyman Abbott: Christian Evolutionist* (Cambridge: Harvard University Press, 1953), 31, 46, 63, 95ff.

14:34. Rauschenbusch is quoted by John R. Aiken, "Walter Rauschenbusch and Education for Reform," *Church History* 36 (December 1967):459–60; Lyman Abbott, *The Rights of Man* (Boston: Houghton Mifflin, 1901), 219.

14:35. Francis G. Peabody, *Jesus Christ and the Social Question* (New York: Grosset and Dunlap, 1900), 7, 149; Walter Rauschenbusch, *Christianity and the Social Crisis*, 67–68.

14:36. Bliss is quoted by Frederick, *Knights of the Golden Rule*, 86–87.

14:37. See *Proceedings, Socialist National Convention of 1904* (Chicago: 1904), 219; "The Curtain is Rung Up," *The Challenge* (February 6, 1901); the final quotation is from Herron papers, cited by Frederick, *Knights of the Golden Rule*, 182.

14:38. Elias B. Sanford, *Federal Council of the Churches of Christ in America: Report of the First Meeting* (New York: Fleming H. Revell, 1909), 444.

14:39. Charles Stelzle, "Jebusites versus Chicagoites," *The Outlook* 92 (May 1909):76.

14:40. Charles M. Sheldon, *In His Steps: What Would Jesus Do*? (New York: Grosset and Dunlap, n.d.; 1st ed., 1898).

14:41. For a summing up that concentrates on the Protestant dimension and its aftermath, see "The Social Gospel Today," in White and Hopkins, *The Social Gospel*, 285–95.

14:42. On the fate of the Social Gospel, see Paul A. Carter, *The Decline and Revival of the Social Gospel: Social and Political Liberalism in American Protestant Churches, 1920–1940* (Hamden, Conn.: Archon Books of Shoestring Press, 1971; 1st ed., 1956).

Chapter Fifteen

15:1. For a discussion of public or civil religion, see Russell E. Richey and Donald G. Jones, eds., *American Civil Religion* (New York: Harper and Row, 1974), especially 14–18, where the editors offer a useful typology including "religious nationalism," evident in this period.

15:2. Reinhold Niebuhr, *The Irony of American History* (New York: Charles Scribner's Sons, 1962), for example, 36–38, 71–72.

15:3. Charles Reagan Wilson, *Baptized in Blood: The Religion of the Lost Cause, 1865–1920* (Athens, Ga.: University of Georgia Press, 1980), is the best source on the South; see 33.

15:4. Wilson, *Baptized in Blood*, 33, 43, 45, 117, 49; Henry M. Wharton, *White Blood: A Story of the South* (New York: Neale Publishing, 1906), 117; see Randolph H. McKim, *The Soul of Lee* (New York: Longmans, Green, 1918), for extended reference.

15:5. Wilson, *Baptized in Blood*, 71, quotes McNeilly references from 1894 and 1916.

15:6. James B. Gambrell, "The Southern Outlook," *Baptist Standard* (March 28, 1895):1; "A Call to the Universal Conquest of the World," *Baptist Standard* (May 26, 1892):3; see Wilson, *Baptized in Blood*, 91.

15:7. A. N. Jackson, "Southern Loyalty," *Christian Advocate* (October 13, 1898):3; see Wilson, *Baptized in Blood*, 159–82, for this episode; and "The Good Effects of the War," *Christian Advocate* (July 21, 1898):2.

15:8. James H. McNeilly, "The Failure of the Confederacy—Was It a Blessing?" *Confederate Veteran* 24 (February, 1916):65–68.

15:9. Wilson, *Baptized in Blood*, 168–70, features Gailor, "National Self-Consciousness and National Responsibility," *Confederate Veteran* 11(May 1903):210–12.

15:10. Randolph McKim, *For God and Country: or, The Christian Pulpit in War-Time* (New York: E. P. Dutton, 1918), 81–83, 90–92, 102f., 116, are all samples of his wartime rhetoric; see Wilson, *Baptized in Blood*, 171–72.

15:11. An introduction to Mormon themes is Marvin S. Hill and James B. Allen, eds., *Mormonism and American Culture* (New York: Harper and Row, 1972).

15:12. Daniel Dorchester, *Christianity in the United States from the First Settlement down to the Present Time* (New York: Hunt and Eaton, 1890), 646–48.

15:13. Henry K. Carroll, *The Religious Forces of the United States* (New York: Christian Literature Society, 1893), 167, 172.

15:14. Leonard Woolsey Bacon, *A History of American Christianity* (New York: Charles Scribner's Sons, 1898), 335.

15:15. For a Mormon accounting, see James B. Allen and Glen M. Leonard, *The Story of the Latter-day Saints* (Salt Lake City, Utah: Deseret, 1976), 401–19.

15:16. Ibid., 431, cites Snow from the Deseret Evening News, January 1, 1901.

15:17. Joseph F. Smith is quoted from the *Instructor* 46 (April 1911):209, from Allen and Leonard, *The Story of the Latter-Day Saints*, 484–85.

15:18. Horace Whitney, "A Jubilee Review," *Improvement Era* 1 (December 1897):65–76. See Howard R. Lamar, "Statehood for Utah: A Different Path," in Hill and Allen, eds., *Mormonism in American Culture*, 140–41.

15:19. Allen and Leonard, *The Story of the Latter-day Saints*, 436–47, discusses wartime relations.

15:20. The "notable" was quoted by Jan Shipps from a paper she read in 1973, cited by Klaus J. Hansen, *Mormonism and the American Experience* (Chicago: University of Chicago Press, 1981), 173.

15:21. Allen and Leonard, *The Story of the Latter-day Saints*, 436–47, 472–75, 491.

15:22. John Gilmary Shea, *The Cross and the Flag: Our Church and Our Country* (New York: Catholic Historical League of America, 1900), 80, 85–86.

15:23. Quoted by John Tracy Ellis, *The Life of James Cardinal Gibbons*, 2 vols. (Milwaukee: Bruce, 1952); 2:86–90.

15:24. From the "State Deputy's Report, Fourth Annual Convention, Maine State Council," quoted by Christopher J. Kauffman, *Faith and Fraternalism: The History of the Knights of Columbus, 1882–1982* (New York: Harper and Row, 1982), 141.

15:25. *Advance* 35 (April 7, 1898):453; *Christian and Missionary Alliance* 2 (April 27, 1898):393. Cited by Julius W. Pratt, *Expansionists of 1898: the Acquisition of Hawaii and the Spanish Islands* (Baltimore: The Johns Hopkins University Press, 1936), 285, 287.

15:26. Pratt's *Expansionists of 1898* is a dated but valuable introduction to this theme; see 279–316, especially 281. *Interior* 29 (March 17, 1898):323–24; and John Henry Barrows, *The Christian Conquest of Asia* (New York: Charles Scribner's Sons, 1899), 237–39, 248–49.

15:27. *Baptist Union* 8 (1898):338, is quoted by Pratt, *Expansionists of 1898*, 291; see also Alexander Blackburn, "The Imperialism of Righteousness," *Standard* 45 (August 6, 1898):913. The Presbyterian magazine was *Church at Home and Abroad* 23 (June, 1898): 471. Cited by Pratt, *Expansionists of 1898*, 293 n. 53; 296 n. 65.

15:28. Pratt, *Expansionists of 1898*, 297–305; see *Interior* 29 (June 23, 1898): 779; (May 19, 1898):616; *Advance* 35 (May 19, 1898):658; *Church Standard* 75 (October 29, 1898):792.

15:29. *Ave Maria* 47 (July 2, 1898):23; *Catholic World* 67 (September, 1898): 854. Cited by Pratt, *Expansionists of 1898*, 309 n. 108.

15:30. *Christian Register* 78 (March 23, 1899):312; 77 (May 12, 1898): 514–15. Cited by Pratt, *Expansionists of 1898*, 313 nn. 119, 120.

15:31. Charles S. Olcott, *The Life of William McKinley*, 2 vols. (Boston: Houghton Mifflin, 1916), 2:109–11.

15:32. An anthology of racist rhetoric is Thomas F. Gossett, *Race: The History of an Idea in America* (Dallas: Southern Methodist University Press, 1963), especially 310–38; Whitelaw Reid, *Our New Duties* (New York: printed for the University of Miami, 1899), 5–6; W. A. Peffer, "A Republic in the Phillippines," *North American Review* 168 (1899):319; Albert J. Beveridge, *For the Greater Republic, Not for Imperialism. An Address Delivered at the Union League of Philadelphia February 15, 1899* (Philadelphia: 1899), 4–6; Peter MacQueen, "When Will the War Cease?" *Arena* 22 (December 1899):702.

15:33. Gaines and Prioleau are cited in Richard E. Welch, Jr., *Response to Imperialism: The United States and the Philippine-American War, 1899–1902* (Chapel Hill: University of North Carolina Press, 1979), especially pp. 109–10. Prioleau appeared in print, July 13, 1901.

15:34. See John M. Mulder, *Woodrow Wilson: The Years of Preparation* (Princeton: Princeton University Press, 1978), 229–68; Mulder, 231–32, 237, and 241, quotes Wilson's speeches from 1903–5 and his Princeton Baccalaureate Address of June 9, 1907.

15:35. Mulder, *Woodrow Wilson*, 255–56, quotes "The Present Task of the Ministry," from May 26, 1909; he referred to the Covenanter tradition in a speech in London, December 28, 1918; other references are from diaries and papers.

15:36. William Jennings Bryan, *The Memoirs of William Jennings Bryan* (Chicago: John C. Winston, 1925) 501; ibid., 34; Kenrick A. Clements, *William Jennings Bryan: Missionary Isolationist* (Knoxville: University of Tennessee Press, 1982), 3–22.

15:37. Roosevelt is quoted by Lawrence W. Levine, *Defender of the Faith: William Jennings Bryan: The Last Decade, 1915–25* (New York: Oxford University Press, 1965), 92, 12; see also *The New York Times*, April 7, 1917.

15:38. See C. Roland Marchand, *The American Peace Movement and Social Re-*

form, 1898–1918 (Princeton, N.J.: Princeton University Press, 1972), 351 especially, and 351–70 in general.

15:39. Marchand, *The American Peace Movement*, 373–75, 277; Hodgkin wrote in a memoir to FOR members, November 19, 1915; Jones wrote Edward Evans, August 3, 1916; see *The Survey* 37 (March 3, 1917):636–37; *The New World* 1 (Janaury 1918):2, 14–16.

15:40. Allen Sinclair Will, *Life of Cardinal Gibbons*, 2 vols. (New York: Dutton, 1922), 2:829; on objectors, see Patricia McNeal, "Catholic Conscientious Objection during World War II," *Catholic Historical Review* 61 (April 1975):232.

15:41. Quoted by Ray H. Abrams, *Preachers Present Arms* (Scottdale, Pa.: Herald Press, 1933), 183.

15:42. The American Board appeal was in *The Congregationalist* 103 (April 4, 1918):418; Harold Bell Wright, *The American Magazine* 85 (February, 1918):56–57; Burton wrote in *The Biblical World* 51 (March, 1918):137–38; see also George Stewart, Jr., and Henry B. Wright, *The Practice of Friendship* (New York: Association Press, 1918), 13.

15:43. On the war and the limiting of innocence, see Henry F. May, *The End of American Innocence: A Study of the First Years of Our Own Time, 1912–1917* (New York: Oxford University Press, 1959), 355–98.

Index

Note: In a book on modern American religion the words "modern," "American," and "religion" appear too frequently to be indexed; so do terms for some major clusterings such as "Christian," "Catholic," and "Protestant."

369